PRAISE FOR THIS B

"This book is a must for anyone who has looked across a lectern at a sea of panicked expressions on the first day of a Program Evaluation class. It will calm everyone's nerves and create a bit of excitement at the prospect of learning how to evaluate programs and activities."

—Terry Anderson, Troy University

"This is a great book that provides the details you need to teach and study program evaluation. The author has tremendous skill and ability to present the materials in an interesting and understandable fashion."

—Michael J. Scicchitano, University of Florida

"This text will be a great addition to a research methods course providing the history as well as the various types of evaluations for the appropriate type of programs."

—Bret D. Cormier, Southeast Missouri State University

"An excellent addition to books on program evaluation. This book's practicality and focus on techniques of embedding evaluations in program design and development is invaluable. Multiple audiences, including graduate students, researchers, practitioners and policymakers, would find the text useful."

—Margaret Lombe, Boston College

"This unique book relates contemporary realities of program evaluation with a particular focus on 'how to' with relevant real-world examples. It provides insights on the rudiments of evaluation from beginning to the end and serves as an invaluable resource to faculty, students, policymakers, and key administrators across various levels of government/public affairs. The author candidly narrates the benefits and challenges of evaluation in ways that anyone involved in evaluation at any level can relate to. The book's uniqueness makes it a key addition to the existing literature on evaluation in theory, policy, and praxis terms."

—James Agbodzakey, University of North Texas at Dallas

"This book serves as an excellent 'how to' manual for conducting program evaluations. The presentation is both interesting and concise."

—Sandra Schrouder, Barry University

Program Evaluation

Program Evaluation

Embedding Evaluation Into Program Design and Development

Susan P. Giancola

University of Delaware

Los Angeles | London | New Delhi
Singapore | Washington DC | Melbourne

FOR INFORMATION:

SAGE Publications, Inc.
2455 Teller Road
Thousand Oaks, California 91320
E-mail: order@sagepub.com

SAGE Publications Ltd.
1 Oliver's Yard
55 City Road
London, EC1Y 1SP
United Kingdom

SAGE Publications India Pvt. Ltd.
B 1/I 1 Mohan Cooperative Industrial Area
Mathura Road, New Delhi 110 044
India

SAGE Publications Asia-Pacific Pte. Ltd.
18 Cross Street #10-10/11/12
China Square Central
Singapore 048423

Library of Congress Cataloging-in-Publication Data

Names: Giancola, Susan P., author.

Title: Program evaluation : embedding evaluation into program design and development / Susan P. Giancola.

Description: First edition. | Los Angeles : SAGE, [2021] | Includes bibliographical references. | Summary: "An Introduction to Program Evaluation: Embedding Evaluation into Program Design and Development provides an overview of fundamental concepts in evaluation theory and practice, with an emphasis on an embedded approach, where evaluation is an explicit part of a program, leading to the refinement of the program. Students will learn how to conduct effective evaluations that foster continual improvement and enable data-based decision making. Rigorous yet practical, this book provides students with both the theoretical understanding and the practical tools to conduct effective evaluations. Sue Giancola's clear language and presentation style make the book's concepts accessible to students, and opportunities in each chapter for self-review and application offer ample practice"— Provided by publisher.

Identifiers: LCCN 2019045624 | ISBN 9781506357447 (paperback) | ISBN 9781506357461 (epub) | ISBN 9781506357454 (epub) | ISBN 9781506357430 (ebook)

Subjects: LCSH: Evaluation—Textbooks. | Evaluation—Methodology—Textbooks.

Classification: LCC AZ191 .G53 2021 | DDC 001.4—dc23

LC record available at https://lccn.loc.gov/2019045624

This book is printed on acid-free paper.

Acquisitions Editor: Helen Salmon
Content Development Editor: Chelsea Neve
Editorial Assistant: Megan O'Hefferman
Marketing Manager: Shari Countrymen
Production Editor: Karen Wiley
Copy Editor: Taryn Bigelow
Typesetter: Hurix Digital
Proofreader: Sarah J. Duffy
Indexer: Michael Ferriera
Cover Designer: Dally Verghese

20 21 22 23 24 10 9 8 7 6 5 4 3 2 1

BRIEF CONTENTS

DETAILED CONTENTS

ACKNOWLEDGMENTS

Writing acknowledgments for this book is the easiest part. So many people helped me get to this point (i.e., finished!), and this is my chance to recognize and thank them. First of all, I would like to thank Helen Salmon from SAGE for finding a previous guide I wrote and giving me the opportunity to share my views and experiences with evaluation more widely. That brings me to my next thank you: Nancy Loy, who is now retired from the U.S. Department of Education. She worked tirelessly to review drafts and support me in my writing of the original *Evaluation Matters* for the grantees with whom she worked. For making an arduous process fun and for always putting a smile on my face, thank you to the best copy editor ever, Taryn Bigelow. I would also like to thank Chelsea Neve and Megan O'Heffernan, my developmental editor and editorial assistant, respectively, from SAGE. Without them, we could not have received the invaluable feedback from the many reviewers, who undoubtedly made this text much better.

Thanks to the following reviewers for their feedback:

James Agbodzakey, University of North Texas at Dallas

Terry Anderson, Troy University

Ronald Black, Southern New Hampshire University

Bret D. Cormier, Southeast Missouri State University

Susan Douglas, Vanderbilt University

Sebastian Galindo, University of Florida

Susan Hall, Texas State University

Margaret Lombe, Boston College

Christopher Niileksela, University of Kansas

Sandra Schrouder, Barry University

Michael J. Scicchitano, University of Florida

Gary W. Reinbold, University of Illinois at Springfield

I would also like to thank several colleagues who made special contributions. Alyssa Shapiro, an undergraduate research assistant at the University of Delaware, assisted with the background research for Chapter 2; D. Layne Humphrey, MSEd, assisted with Chapter 3; Danielle Riser, MS, and Katherine Tilley, both doctoral candidates in the College of Education and Human Development at the University of Delaware, assisted with Chapter 4; Katrina Morrison, EdD, coauthored Chapters 9 and 10; Akisha Osei Sarfo, PhD, coauthored Chapter 11; and Allison Karpyn, PhD, coauthored Chapter 12. I also truly appreciate the efforts of Haley Meyer, Lydia Pebly, and Julianne Matthias, undergraduate research assistants with the Center for Research in Education and Social Policy (CRESP), who worked with me on editing and preparing the manuscript for publication.

I would also like to thank the Mom Squad: Rachel Brunke, Bethany Chapman, Sue Magasiny, Vickie Petersen, and Kathy Salameda. You are my support system and I look forward to many more years of friendship.

Most important, I would like to thank my family. My husband, Tom, and my two girls, Mia and Emma, were very patient throughout this process. They encouraged me to take writing retreats at the shore and supported my long days and weekends of writing. I appreciate you more than you know.

PREFACE

Evaluation matters. It really does. It has implications for just about everything we encounter in our daily lives. The toothpaste we use to brush our teeth each morning: Is it safe? Hopefully someone has carefully evaluated its safety and effectiveness before putting it on the shelves for purchase. The training program for the driver of the bus we might ride to work or school: Was it effective in adequately training the driver? We hope so, because we are putting our lives in the bus driver's hands. The commercials on TV: Could they adversely impact young, impressionable minds? We imagine the purpose is to influence, but whom and to what extent? The government unemployment program, should we find ourselves without a job: Is it effective as a short-term measure while individuals actively seek new employment? This is the same program that part of your income goes toward every pay period. Is it a good use of your money? Is there a more effective way to facilitate employment? More than anything, this textbook is about thinking critically. It provides approaches and methods to systematically examine interventions, programs, and policies in order to make decisions about effectiveness, develop ideas for improvement, and assess impact.

Thus, the mission of this textbook is to increase the use of evaluation. I realize this statement has a double meaning, and that is intentional. In whatever path you choose, I hope this text provides you with the tools to be an evaluator. Further, I hope this text encourages you to use findings from evaluation to make decisions. So, while the mission is to increase the use of evaluation, the goal is to build capacity across multiple fields to prioritize evaluation, by increasing knowledge about evaluation and improving skills to conduct evaluations.

I have been working with practitioners most of my career to evaluate programs. I saw sophisticated evaluations funded and conducted. And I saw no evaluation processes left behind when the funding was gone. I saw expectations at the local, state, and federal levels for data-based decision making, without the accompanying capacity building to use data and conduct evaluation. I worked with programs that saw evaluation as purely compliance, in order to check the box that they did what they were supposed to, missing an opportunity for program improvement based on data. I saw millions of dollars spent on untested programs. And I saw uneasiness and dread when practitioners spoke of evaluation. For these reasons, among others, I changed my approach to evaluation from one of expert to one of partner. When working with clients, I focused on the opportunity of evaluation, rather than the requirement of evaluation. I worked to build evaluation processes that were not dependent upon me, but that built capacity among program staff to continue those processes once I was no longer there. I came to understand that evaluation should not be superimposed upon a program, but rather integrated into a program. And I came to believe that evaluation is an obligation to the people that a program or policy is supposed to benefit, and for that reason alone, it was necessary that the tools of evaluation be *not only* in the hands of the professional evaluator.

As described above, I also changed my view of what it means to be a professional evaluator. There are times an evaluator might look only at a program's impact, with no need or intention to provide information or processes for improvement. However, more often than not, an evaluator has the opportunity to do more. In such cases, I believe a professional evaluator can be a facilitator of a continuous improvement mind-set, an architect of processes to support the data collection necessary for informed decision making, and a capacity builder of skills to use information for continuous improvement.

This textbook is intended for use by students studying to become evaluators, as well as students who intend to develop or manage programs and policies as part of whatever career they pursue. Perhaps this textbook will even persuade students who may not have thought of evaluation as a viable career to pursue becoming an evaluator. The chapters provide the necessary information for those who have no idea what evaluation is, who have never had a course in evaluation, and for those who have evaluation knowledge and experience, but would like to enrich their understanding. It is meant to be a comprehensive text in evaluation. It is not meant to be a comprehensive text in research methods or statistics. While research methods are reviewed, if the reader would like further study, resources are provided for more in-depth examination.

This textbook uses an embedded evaluation approach, in which evaluation is integrated into the program's theory. The embedded approach uses logic modeling and an evaluation matrix to structure the evaluation within the program. The approach is systematic and focused on continuous improvement. The textbook is divided into four sections. The first section includes an introduction to evaluation, a discussion of the history of evaluation, ethical considerations in research and evaluation, and an overview of evaluation approaches. The second section takes the reader through a systematic process of understanding the program, delineating the program's theory, and using logic modeling to build evaluation into the program's theory; creating an evaluation matrix to detail indicators, data sources, and analysis methods; and choosing a research design for the evaluation. The third section discusses data collection, data analysis, interpretation, and reporting. Finally, the fourth section includes three case studies of embedding evaluation into a program's theory. The first case study is a program intended to improve the quality of life for children with neurodevelopmental disabilities and their families, by increasing the number of highly trained professionals in the field. The second case study is a program that intends to improve health by improving the quality of clinical and translational research. The third case study is of a fictitious youth abstinence-plus program used throughout the text for illustrative purposes.

This textbook includes objectives at the start of each chapter. Within each chapter, readers are provided with "In the Real World" examples, "Quick Check" questions, and, at the end of each chapter, items for "Reflection and Application." References are also included at the end of the text, in case the reader would like additional information. A glossary of key terms, defined throughout the chapters, is included at the end of the text.

DIGITAL RESOURCES

study.sagepub.com/giancola1e

The **SAGE Instructor Companion Site**, a password-protected resource, supports teaching by making the classroom a learning-rich environment for students. The following assets are available on the teaching site:

- **Editable, chapter-specific Microsoft® PowerPoint®** slides offer you complete flexibility in easily creating a multimedia presentation for your course.

- **Lecture notes**, including Outline and Objectives, may be used for lecture and/or student handouts.

- A **sample syllabus** provides a suggested course model for using the book.

- **Assignments and a semester-long course project** are available for download, along with grading rubrics.

- **Full-text case studies and journal articles from the Appendix** are accompanied by critical thinking and discussion questions.

- **Tables and figures** from the book are available in an easily-downloadable format for use in papers, hand-outs, and presentations.

ABOUT THE AUTHOR

Susan P. Giancola, PhD, has over 20 years of experience as an evaluator in both academia and private business. Prior to becoming an evaluator, she worked in corporate and higher education settings on process improvement initiatives. Dr. Giancola is a graduate of the University of Pennsylvania's Policy Research, Evaluation, and Measurement Program. She also has a bachelor's degree from the University of Virginia in systems engineering and a master's degree in management from Pennsylvania State University. She is currently senior associate director of the Center for Research in Education and Social Policy at the University of Delaware. Her work focuses on research and evaluation of programs to improve human services, primarily in the areas of education and health. She evaluates many local, state, and federal initiatives, including projects funded through the National Institutes of Health, the National Science Foundation, the U.S. Department of Health and Human Services, and the U.S. Department of Education. Dr. Giancola is a member of the American Evaluation Association and the American Educational Research Association. She lives in Kennett Square, Pennsylvania, with her husband and two daughters.

ABOUT THE CONTRIBUTORS

Allison Karpyn, PhD, is a graduate of the University of Pennsylvania's Policy Research and Evaluation doctoral program and has practiced in the field of evaluation for 16 years. She currently serves as associate professor and senior associate director of the University of Delaware's Center for Research in Education and Social Policy. She is an active evaluator and researcher and her work spans issues of community health and education. She lives in Pennsylvania with her husband, two daughters, and two stepchildren.

Katrina K. Morrison, EdD, is a research associate III at the University of Delaware's Center for Research in Education and Social Policy. She has conducted research and evaluation in education, health, and policy for over 10 years. She is a Partnership for Public Education fellow, conducting research on restorative practices. Katrina holds an EdD in teaching, learning, and teacher education from the University of Pennsylvania, an MA in criminal justice from Temple University, and a BA in political science and educational studies from Swarthmore College.

Akisha Osei Sarfo, PhD, is chief performance officer at Guilford County Schools. She has over 10 years of experience conducting research and evaluation in public and non-profit sectors of education, including two years as a Harvard Strategic Data Project fellow. Prior to earning her PhD in education, specializing in evaluation, measurement, and statistics, from the University of Delaware, Dr. Sarfo earned a bachelor's degree in political science with a minor in African diaspora and a master's degree in educational research methods from the University of Michigan.

EVALUATION MATTERS

One of the great mistakes is to judge policies and programs
by their intentions rather than their results.

—Milton Friedman

Upon completion of this chapter, you should be able to

- Define evaluation.
- Identify programs and policies that might be evaluated.
- Describe the purpose of evaluation and its relationship to research.
- Distinguish between formative and summative evaluation.
- Compare and contrast internal and external evaluation.
- Discuss the embedded evaluation model.
- Explain the first step in embedded evaluation.

1.1 WHAT IS EVALUATION?

Welcome to the field of evaluation! Whether you are new to the field and this is your first course in evaluation or you are a seasoned evaluator looking to explore new approaches, we are thrilled to walk with you on this journey and hope that you find the material in this text helpful to you. So, a good place to start . . . what is evaluation? Merriam-Webster online defines evaluation as the "determination of the value, nature, character, or quality of something." We all do that on a daily basis:

- We estimate if a product is worth buying (are the upgraded features on this new iPhone version worth the additional $100?).

- We judge whether spending extra time on a homework assignment is worth a higher grade and if a lower grade will impact our overall course average.

- We rate our professors (yes, professors really do look at these ratings from time to time).

- We appraise the work ethic and quality of one of our coworkers or fellow students.

- We assess the extent to which we will use a textbook in the future and determine whether it is more advantageous for us to rent the book for the semester or purchase a copy.

- We make decisions about whether we can afford to rent an apartment on our own or if we have to get a roommate.

If you have contemplated any of the above, you are already an evaluator of sorts. While we will not spend class time debating the merits of the new iPhone, we will provide you with strategies to systematically make evaluative decisions.

I am sure you have noticed the "valu" embedded in the word evaluation. Like many words, "value" has multiple dimensions. The Etymology Dictionary online asserts that the term "value" is derived from the Latin word *valere*, meaning to be well, strong, and of worth. Well and strong relate to merit and have to do with inherent value, while worth is typically interpreted within a certain context. Thus, what is being evaluated, the evaluand (Scriven, 1979), may have an inherent value that is free of any context. On the other hand, the evaluand may only be of value to a particular group or in a specific context. In their analysis of the two aspects of value—merit and worth—Lincoln and Guba (1980) use the example of gold. They explain that gold can be judged on its merit or its worth. Judged on its merit, gold has inherent beauty. Judged on its worth, gold has a variable value according to the gold trading markets. Likewise, an SAT or GRE prep course may be judged on its merits based on its coverage of material and clarity of instruction. However, judgments based on worth to you will likely relate to how well you performed on the SAT or GRE. While Lincoln and Guba recognize that both the merit and worth of an evaluand can change over time, they emphasize the importance of deliberately considering context, and perhaps even multiple contexts, when making evaluative judgments. So, whether you are evaluating a new purchase or a course you are taking, consider both its intrinsic value and its value to you at this time in your life.

Evaluation: a method used to determine the value of something.

As described above, **evaluation** is a method of determining value and the evaluand is the subject of the evaluation. While we all evaluate as part of our human nature, this textbook focuses on **program evaluation**. That is, the evaluand is the program and the focus is on determining the merit or worth of that program. For the purposes of this textbook, a **program** will be defined broadly to include

- A group of activities;

- Small, focused interventions;

- Organization-wide projects;

- Statewide initiatives;

- National reforms and policies; and

- International programs.

Program evaluation: evaluation used to determine the merit or worth of a program.

Program: defined broadly in this text to include a group of activities ranging from a small intervention to a national or international policy.

The tools explored in this text will be applicable to evaluating a set of activities or small interventions, as well as larger initiatives and multifaceted policies. Examples of programs include focused interventions such as the Olweus Bulling Prevention Program (Olweus & Limber, 2007) as well as national reforms such as Head Start (2019). See the "In the Real World" box for several additional examples of programs.

IN THE REAL WORLD . . .

First Year Experience (FYE) Courses are required courses for freshman at over half of four-year institutions. FYE courses intend to aid students both academically and socially. The What Works Clearinghouse (2006b) examined several quasi-experimental evaluations of FYE programs and found potentially positive effects for credit accumulation, degree attainment, and general academic achievement.

The Too Good for Drugs (TGFD) program is designed to help students develop the skills to resist negative peer influences and the use of drugs, alcohol, and tobacco. The What Works Clearinghouse (2006a) examined two evaluations of TGFD programs using randomized controlled designs and found a potentially positive impact on behavior. No discernable effects were found for values or knowledge of and attitudes toward drugs and alcohol.

Financial Incentives for Teen Parents to Stay in School is a strategy used by state welfare programs to promote school attendance and graduation. The belief is that by supporting graduation from high school, the teens will be less likely to depend on welfare in the future. The What Works Clearinghouse (2016) examined two evaluations of such programs. While it found potentially positive effects for teens staying in school, it found no discernable effects for students progressing to the next grade level or graduating from high school.

Source: What Works Clearinghouse (http://ies.ed.gov/ncee/wwc).

1.1.1 What Is the Purpose of Evaluation?

Evaluation intends to determine merit and worth. Yet, as discussed in the previous section, evaluation is also contextual. Determining the merit and worth of a program and focusing on its value for a group of people, under a certain set of circumstances, and in a specific context, is no easy task. This is especially true when the consequences of your evaluation might have human and financial implications. Thus, the way we go about evaluating a program is critical to making evaluative determinations. We trust that medical schools effectively evaluate their students to ensure that the cardiothoracic surgeon operating on a loved one has the skill to do so. We often have no choice but to trust that the auto mechanic evaluating why our car broke down is competent at repairing engines and ethical in quoting prices. As a medical school has procedures to evaluate its students and mechanics have protocols to assess car problems, program evaluators have methods, processes, standards, and tools to guide their evaluation.

The evaluative methods I have adopted over the course of my career have been heavily influenced by two factors. The first is my undergraduate training as an engineer. As an engineer, I learned how to think systematically. Engineering is a process and a way of thinking, as well as a discipline. The approach I learned in this context is one that starts with problem identification and description and ends with a set of solutions or recommendations—after which, the process starts again. The second influence on my thinking regarding evaluation is a well-known evaluator named Carol Weiss. Unfortunately, I never met her, but her seminal book titled *Evaluation* (Weiss, 1998) has been a trustworthy companion for decades. Of all who have attempted to define evaluation, Weiss's definition strikes me as the most comprehensive (pp. 4–5):

> Evaluation is a systematic assessment of the operations and/or the outcomes of a program or policy, compared to a set of explicit or implicit standards, as a means of contributing to the improvement of program or policy.

The primary tenets of Weiss's definition are as follows:

- Evaluation is systematic.

- Evaluation focuses on operations.

- Evaluation focuses on outcomes.

- Evaluation evidence is compared to a standard.

- Evaluation is about improving programs and policies.

Systematic: logical and organized; undertaken according to a plan.

Evaluation is a systematic examination of a program. It uses the scientific method. Remember that from grade school?! The scientific method has been around since the

1600s, at least, and involves asking a question, researching the question, making and testing a hypothesis, analyzing data, and documenting results. It is what engineers, psychologists, biologists, and social scientists use in their work. It is the basic science that underlies evaluation. Evaluation is a formal, logical, and organized endeavor undertaken according to a plan.

Evaluation examines the **operations** of a program. The operations of a program include both what is implemented as part of the program and how it is implemented; operations are the processes involved with implementing the activities of a program. Operations are important for two main reasons—interpretation and improvement. Understanding the state of operations allows us to document how a program is operating. Understanding how a program operates, in turn, allows us to determine whether the operations are in fact in accordance with what was intended. This is important for interpreting any results. For instance, if depressive symptoms decrease after a new medication is dispensed, one might be led to believe the medication is effective in treating depression. However, examination of operations might show that over 50% of patients did not take their medication. Without examining how a program operates in actuality, versus how it might have been planned, one can draw inaccurate conclusions. The second reason to examine operations is similar to the first, but involves using the information gathered when looking at operations to make improvements to a program while in operation. So, if it is noticed two months in that patients are not taking their medication, new interventions could be put in place to improve compliance.

Evaluation also examines the **outcomes** of a program. Outcomes are the results that occur during and after implementation of a program. Examining the outcomes of a program allows you to make determinations about the effectiveness of a program. If, for instance, we are examining the instructional program at your college or university, the operations might be the quality of teaching and the rigor of assignments, but the outcome would likely be student learning. Knowing the extent to which students are learning can help (or hurt) a college with recruitment, fund-raising campaigns with alumni, and partnerships with organizations that may be interested in hiring graduates. By measuring outcomes, we can make determinations about whether the program worked, to what extent, in what ways, and for whom.

Evaluation evidence is compared to a **standard**. A standard is a target or yardstick that informs us of the ideal state. Standards are what we use, implicitly or explicitly, to judge the merit or worth of a program. The standard directs us in making this judgment. In our examples at the start of the chapter, we mentioned purchasing a new cell phone. How much greater would it need to be than the former model for you to purchase it? Likewise, the conflict of how much time to put in on an assignment versus the value of that assignment was introduced. Do you have an implicit standard, one you may not have written down or expressed, that drives whether spending an hour on a 5-point extra credit assignment is worth it to you? People who operate programs and those who evaluate those

Operations: processes involved with implementing the activities of a program.

Outcomes: results that occur during and after implementing a program.

Standard: target that we use, implicitly or explicitly, to judge the merit or worth of a program.

programs wrestle with similar decisions. If a medication helps 50% of the people who take it, is that enough to continue dispensing the medication? Probably. What if it helps 25%? Or what if it helps 50%, but makes the symptoms of 25% of the people worse? There are no easy answers when it comes to standards, though we will explore this thinking further in Chapter 7 in the section on program indicators and targets.

Finally, evaluation is not performed in a vacuum and it is not simply an exercise in curiosity. Evaluation is focused on how well a program works, under what conditions, and for what people. Evaluation is intended to provide information aimed at **improving programs and policies**. Ideally, the information obtained through an evaluation will be used to create more effective and efficient programs and policies. And, I imagine for most using this textbook, the programs and policies you might examine are intended to help people. For evaluators, that is the end result. It is the reason we do what we do—to inform programs and policies that will ultimately improve the lives of people. A secondary reason we evaluate programs and policies is to contribute to the field through informing theory and practice.

1.1.2 How Is Evaluation Different From Research?

Like evaluation, **research** is a systematic investigation in a field of study. In many ways, evaluation is a form of research. In fact, some refer to evaluation as evaluation research. Evaluation and research use the same methods and designs. The underlying science is the same. However, unlike evaluation, pure research is primarily focused on contributing to the greater body of knowledge in a certain area. This is in contrast to the primary purpose of program evaluation, which is to improve and make decisions about programs and policies.

Evaluation is more practice oriented than research. Evaluation findings are intended for use within a program or policy to effect change. In addition, while researchers often develop their own research hypotheses, evaluators typically work with program staff to develop questions to shape and focus the evaluation. In addition, as stated in the discussion of standards, evaluation intends to compare the evaluation results with what should be. That is, it is judgmental in nature and the eventual intention is to make a decision about whether a program should be continued, expanded, scaled down, or discontinued. Moreover, because evaluators are working in action settings where programs are being implemented in real time, we often face obstacles that might not be encountered in a lab or controlled research setting. For instance, in an evaluation relying on state test scores to examine the impact of curricular changes over a five-year period, policymakers discontinued use of the test and instead adopted an assessment that hindered comparisons to previous scores. Finally, evaluators depend upon people for data collection. As such, interpersonal skills, such as strong communication and listening skills, as well as flexibility and even a positive attitude, can be determinants of whether an evaluation is efficacious or unsuccessful.

Improving programs and policies: the purpose of evaluation; to create more effective and efficient programs and policies.

Research: a systematic investigation in a field of study; evaluation is a type of research.

FIGURE 1.1 ◆ Research and Evaluation

RESEARCH

EVALUATION

Seek to generate new knowledge

Seek to provide information for decision making

Researcher focused

Stakeholder focused

Research hypotheses

Evaluation questions

METHODS & DESIGNS

Make recommendations based on research hypotheses

Make recommendations based on evaluation questions

Publish results

Report to stakeholders

Source: Adapted from LaVelle (2010).

However, there are some elements that evaluation and research share. As stated above, program evaluation and research use the same methods and designs to frame and conduct their studies. Additionally, like researchers, evaluators have an obligation to disseminate their research. Sometimes this may be publication in peer-reviewed journals, as is common for researchers. However, for both researchers and evaluators, findings should also be shared with individuals or organizations that may benefit from understanding or adopting recommendations, as well as policymakers who are responsible for making policy that may be impacted and improved by the findings. Finally, both evaluators and researchers have ethical obligations and a code of conduct that guide how, why, from whom, and under what conditions data are collected. See Figure 1.1, adapted from a post by Lavelle (2010) on AEA365, a daily blog sponsored by the American Evaluation Association (AEA), for an illustration of some of the differences and intersections between evaluation and research.

1.2 WHY EVALUATE?

A pioneer in the field of research for effective marketing, Arthur C. Nielson based his work on the philosophy that "the price of light is less than the cost of darkness." I know this is deep. Perhaps too deep for the hour in which you have to read this text. But it is definitely worth the time to think about the implications of his statement. If we are honest with ourselves, it is why we further our education. We go to school, we read, we study because in the long run we believe it will make a difference in our quality of life that is worth the price we pay for our education.

In fact, it would be difficult to find an example where knowledge and truth do not matter. Yet so much *light* is ignored because of the immediate and short-term cost, resulting in a great long-term cost of managing the *darkness*. There is no place this is truer than in policy making. For instance, it is well documented that drug treatment is a more effective as well as cost-efficient solution than minimum mandatory sentences for and incarceration of drug offenders (McVay, Schiraldi, & Ziedenberg, 2004). Yet policymakers often reject the up-front costs of effective drug treatment programs, which result in a much heavier burden on society in the long run due to incarceration, recidivism, reduced productivity, and decreased safety. Similarly, the cost to treat mentally ill individuals is much less than the cost of incarceration after a crime has been committed. The deinstitutionalization of mental health treatment in the 1960s and 1970s, by the shuttering of state mental hospitals, resulted in a large increase of severely mentally ill individuals in the U.S. prison system (Collier, 2014). While state mental hospitals may not have been a humane solution, an alternative, community-based treatment for the mentally ill was not developed. Thus, prisons became the new asylum for the mentally ill. Treatment of the mentally ill in the community focusing on medication compliance, counseling, housing support, and job opportunities is a much less expensive alternative to unsafe communities and incarcerating mentally ill individuals. The National Alliance on Mental Illness (Giliberti, 2015) estimates an annual cost of $31,000 to incarcerate an individual with mental illness, while community-based mental health care costs about $10,000 annually.

The previous example is well documented in the literature. Another well-documented example is the Scared Straight program. See "In the Real World" for information on the program and related evaluations.

Unfortunately, not all policies and programs are as well researched as investments in community-based mental health treatment and the Scared Straight program, reinforcing the need to have data regarding policy and program effectiveness. In addition, even for programs that have been well researched, such as Scared Straight, policymakers and practitioners may still decide to use them. Both of these issues, a lack of informative research as well as an underuse of available research in decision making, are of relevance to evaluators and we hope by the end of the text, you will have the knowledge and tools to

- Design rigorous and informative evaluations;
- Collect evaluative information on programs and policies;
- Interpret evaluation data to inform policies and programs; and
- Effectively present and disseminate data to increase opportunities for use.

IN THE REAL WORLD ...

Scared Straight was introduced in the 1970s as a program to prevent juvenile delinquency. Participants were youth at risk of becoming delinquent; the program introduced them to prisons and hardened criminals in order to deter them from continued criminal activity.

Multiple randomized trials in the United States showed the program did not work, and in fact was harmful to many youth (Aos, Phillips, Barnoski, & Lieb, 2001; Lilienfeld, 2005; Petrosino, Turpin-Petrosino, Hollis-Peel, & Lavenberg, 2012). Youth who went through the program had a higher rate of reoffending than similar youth who did not participate in the program.

Why did policymakers continue to use the program? Because it cost less than $100 per child. It seemed like a low-risk program; if it didn't work, little money would be lost. Think again. Evaluations showed that in the long run, taxpayers and crime victims paid much more than the program costs because of the additional criminal activity of those who participated. In fact, a comprehensive cost-benefit study found that for every $100 spent on Scared Straight, taxpayers and victims paid an additional $10,000 in costs due to increased contact with the criminal justice system after participating in the program (Washington State Institute for Public Policy, 2007, 2018).

Source: Petrosino et al. (2012); Washington State Institute for Public Policy (2018).

1.2.1 Evaluation Is an Ethical Obligation

When presented with information regarding the costs of ineffective programs, it is not a leap to conclude that it is an ethical obligation of those who implement programs and policies to also have those programs and policies evaluated. Yet program planning in general is often one of those areas where many opt to forgo evaluation, due to the up-front costs, in favor of spending those funds on program services. While serving more people may seem noble, it is not at all noble if the program is ineffective at best, and harmful at worst. While perhaps an unpopular view, my view nonetheless is that claiming ignorance to a program or policy being ineffective or even harmful, due to a lack of available data to make a judgment or due to an unwillingness to listen to available data, is an unacceptable and unethical assertion. What is your viewpoint? There is no right or wrong answer, but certainly it is an interesting question to consider.

Some readers of this text may think it is understandable that program leaders want to maximize program funds used to deliver services. I tend to agree with you. It is a dilemma . . . spend money on program services (and serve more people) or spend money on evaluation (and serve fewer people). If you have donated money to a charity to provide a new after-school mentoring program for middle-school students, you may want the charity to put all donated funds into the mentoring. However, what if the mentoring is ineffective and a waste of your donated dollars? Would you be willing to let the charity allocate a portion of the donation to evaluate the effectiveness of the mentoring program? Using policy and program resources to collect the necessary data to evaluate effectiveness is the only way, as Nielson might say, to live in the *light*. That is, using funds now to determine if the outcomes of a program warrant continued funding of the program in the future is a long-game mindset.

1.2.2 Evaluation Fosters Quality

It is the very nature of evaluation to increase knowledge and this knowledge can be used to improve programs. Thus, evaluation fosters quality. It provides the necessary information to improve a program continuously, allocate resources in ways that can maximize effectiveness, and refine program strategies for greater impact. A student's improvement can be facilitated with constructive teacher feedback. An employee's performance is supported when provided with ways to improve. An organization's productivity is enhanced when there is a culture of process improvement. And the quality of a program is fostered when program components are examined and sound evaluative information is made available. Thus, the premise holds for people, organizations, and programs: When good information is provided, better decisions can be made.

Have you ever heard anyone say, the more you know, the less you know? This is directly tied to one of my favorite statements: Ignorance is bliss. While it might be blissful to the ignorant, to those who have to deal with the consequences of ignorance, it can be aggravating, troubling, and costly. Yet the more we learn, the more we understand all that we do not know. This journey of learning empowers us to make better, more informed decisions. And it also inspires us to search for greater understanding. Thus, evaluation produces knowledge that informs decisions, which in turn creates the need for more knowledge. This cycle of knowledge generation and use is a continuous improvement process that fosters informed decision making and, in turn, promotes quality in programs and policies.

1.2.3 Evaluation Is a Viable Career

If evaluation as an ethical obligation as well as something that fosters quality in programs and policies has not convinced you to learn all you can about evaluation, perhaps knowing that evaluation is a growing field with many job opportunities will spark your interest. A decade ago, Russ-Eft and Preskill (2009) included in their list of reasons to pursue a career in evaluation the increasing respect for evaluation experience as a skill that is highly marketable. Indeed, there is a need for trained evaluators with nonprofit organizations, corporations, and research centers. There are many opportunities for evaluators internationally. In this era of data-driven decision making, thankfully organizations are recognizing the value that data can provide to their operations. It is also a time of accountability, with many programs being required to show evidence of impact to receive continued funding.

1.3 VALUES AND STANDARDS IN EVALUATION

For evaluators, the creation of knowledge is based upon data. But how do we decide what data to collect? How do we decide what questions to ask? And once knowledge is generated, how are the data used? In evaluation, the people who use evaluation findings are called stakeholders. In fact, a **stakeholder** is anyone who has an interest in or is involved with the operation or success of a program. Key stakeholder groups often include program staff, program participants, community members, and policymakers. In what ways do different stakeholder groups use evaluation findings? How do stakeholders weigh evaluation data in making decisions? Evaluation is the activity of examining programs and collecting information, as well as the process of determining how that information will be used. Both aspects, how we collect data and how we use data, are influenced by factors related to evaluator skills and preferences, as well as stakeholder values and the context within which the program operates.

Thus, the *valuing* that is part of evaluation is influenced by context, including our own values, the values of stakeholders, as well as politics, resources, and even history. As evaluators, it is important that we are clear about the values and standards upon which our evaluative judgments are based.

An important tenet of Weiss's definition of evaluation involves the comparing of evaluation evidence to a standard, in order to make a judgment about a program or policy. Thus, the standard holds power. For instance, in your classes, you must achieve a certain grade to pass a course. That grade requirement is the standard. Likewise, states set cut scores for state achievement testing that are used to determine course placement and even graduation. The cut score is a standard that has the power to affect a student's future. How was that cut score set? The standard was likely set by a group of administrators based upon something. That *something* likely includes data, professional judgment, research, and experience—all of which are influenced by values.

Valuing is the process of estimating the importance of something. A **value** is a principle or quality that we use to estimate that importance. Value is also the estimate of importance. That is, we use values to assign value. A teacher might value effort over performance, and thus assign grades based largely on effort. A manager might value quantity of work over quality of work, and use standards based on these values for employee performance appraisals.

Earlier we mentioned that evaluation, or the process of valuing, has two components: merit and worth. The merit of an evaluation may be determined by the methods used and the rigor of the design. But what influences methods and design? An evaluator's own values often guide the choice of design and methods. What does the evaluator value? Hearing stories from participants detailing personal experiences with the program? Studying quantitative indicators of program impact? Involving stakeholders in all aspects of the evaluation? Being the expert and using that expertise to design and implement the evaluation? Ensuring all possible

Stakeholder: anyone who has an interest in or is involved with the operation or success of a program. Key stakeholder groups often include program staff, program participants, community members, and policymakers.

Value: a principle or quality used to estimate importance; an estimate of importance.

participants receive the program being evaluated? Using the most rigorous evaluation design, even if that means some potential participants do not receive the program or are delayed in receiving it? There are no right answers to these questions; all are debated among evaluators.

The worth of an evaluation is dependent upon context and who is making the judgment of worth. Worth to an evaluator may raise the same questions described earlier relating to merit. Worth to stakeholders is influenced by their own values. In order to design an evaluation that is useful to stakeholders, it is important for an evaluator to understand stakeholder values. These values will likely vary across stakeholder groups, and thus the design of the evaluation will have multiple components to address issues that allow for judgments of worth to be made.

If at this point you are ready to throw your hands up in frustration at the subjectivity inherent in valuing, instead marvel at the complexity of human thought. Okay—enough marveling. There are tools to guide evaluators in understanding not just our own values, but more important, those of our stakeholders. There are also guidelines and principles evaluators can use to conduct evaluations with objectivity.

1.3.1 Guiding Principles for Evaluators

The American Evaluation Association (AEA) provides guiding principles for evaluators. The **AEA Guiding Principles for Evaluators** (AEA, 2018) is a set of five principles that embody the values of the American Evaluation Association, an international professional association of evaluators. And yes, the guiding principles are based on values. However, these are values accepted by evaluators across disciplines and have been ratified by a membership of over 7,000 evaluators. So, they have merit in their interdisciplinary nature and worth in their widespread acceptance. The guiding principles are intended to promote the ethical behavior of evaluators, and address ideals that reach across disciplinary boundaries, such as an evaluator's obligation to be professionally and culturally competent. They include guidance in the following domains:

AEA Guiding Principles for Evaluators: a set of five principles intended to guide the ethical behavior of evaluators; the guiding principles are systematic inquiry, competence, integrity, respect for people, and common good and equity.

- systematic inquiry

- competence

- integrity

- respect for people

- common good and equity

Each of these five guiding principles for evaluators will be described more fully in Chapter 3. The full text of the *American Evaluation Association Guiding Principles for Evaluators* appears, with permission from the AEA, at the end of this chapter (see Figure 1.4).

1.3.2 Program Evaluation Standards

Another important resource for evaluators is a set of standards issued by the Joint Committee on Standards for Educational Evaluation. The Joint Committee is a group of representatives from multiple professional organizations, including the American Evaluation Association, that have an interest in improving evaluation quality. The **Joint Committee's Program Evaluation Standards** (Yarbrough, Shulha, Hopson, & Caruthers, 2011) is a set of 30 standards to guide evaluators in designing and implementing quality evaluations. The standards address five areas:

- utility

- feasibility

- propriety

- accuracy

- evaluation accountability

These standards provide practical guidance on how to conduct effective and equitable evaluations that produce accurate findings and promote usability. See Figure 1.2 for a list and description of the 30 program evaluation standards.

In addition to the AEA Guiding Principles and the Joint Committee's Program Evaluation Standards, experienced evaluators have also provided resources to guide evaluators in the appropriate consideration of values and standards in their evaluation work. Stufflebeam (2001) offers a checklist of values and criteria for evaluators to consider when designing and conducting evaluations. This checklist includes societal values, such as equity, effectiveness, and excellence. Also included are institutional values, such as the organization's mission, goals, and priorities. House and Howe (1999) provide a detailed look at values in evaluation in their book *Values in Evaluation and Social Research*. Should the topic of values in evaluation spark your interest, the House and Howe text is an excellent resource through which to continue your exploration.

In summary, our own values affect all aspects of evaluation, from the research design and methods we choose to how we interact with stakeholders and the way we interpret our findings. Stakeholder values and the political context in which a program operates also affect how an evaluation is conducted and how data are used. However, knowledge is power. Understanding stakeholder values and the political context can aid you in designing an evaluation that meets stakeholder needs and is more likely to be used to influence decision making. Understanding our own values can help us to examine how they might impact our evaluations, as well as increase awareness of ways to improve our practice. Understanding and adhering to professional guidelines and standards can only serve to strengthen the

Joint Committee's Program Evaluation Standards: a set of 30 standards intended to guide evaluators in the areas of utility, feasibility, propriety, accuracy, and evaluation accountability.

FIGURE 1.2 ● Joint Committee's Program Evaluation Standards

Program Evaluation Standards

Infographic created with permission
from the Joint Committee on Standards
for Educational Evaluation
(Yarbrough, Shulha, Hopson,
Caruthers, 2011)

Utility Standards

The utility standards are intended to increase the extent to which program stakeholders find evaluation processes and products valuable in meeting their needs.

U1-Evaluator Credibility: Evaluations should be conducted by qualified people who establish and maintain credibility in the evaluation context.

U2-Attention to Stakeholders: Evaluations should devote attention to the full range of individuals and groups invested in the program and affected by its evaluation.

U3- Negotiated Purposes: Evaluation purposes should be identified and continually negotiated based on the needs of stakeholders.

U4-Explicit Values: Evaluations should clarify and specify the individual and cultural values underpinning purposes, processes, and judgments.

U5-Relevant Information: Evaluation information should serve the identified and emergent needs of stakeholders.

U6-Meaningful Processes and Products: Evaluations should construct activities, descriptions, and judgments in ways that encourage participants to rediscover, reinterpret, or revise their understandings and behaviors.

U7-Timely and Appropriate Communicating and Reporting: Evaluations should attend to the continuing information needs of their multiple audiences.

U8-Concern for Consequences and Influence: Evaluations should promote responsible and adaptive use while guarding against unintended negative consequences and misuse.

Feasibility Standards

The feasibility standards are intended to increase evaluation effectiveness and efficiency.

F1-Project Management: Evaluations should use effective project management strategies.

F2-Practical Procedures: Evaluation procedures should be practical and responsive to the way the program operates.

F3-Contextual Viability: Evaluations should recognize, monitor, and balance the cultural and political interests and needs of individuals and groups.

F4-Resource Use: Evaluations should use resources effectively and efficiently.

Evaluation Accountability Standards

The evaluation accountability standards encourage adequate documentation of evaluations and a metaevaluative perspective focused on improvement and accountability for evaluation processes and products.

E1-Evaluation Documentation: Evaluations should fully document their negotiated purposes and implemented designs, procedures, data, and outcomes.

E2-Internal Metaevaluation: Evaluators should use these and other applicable standards to examine the accountability of the evaluation design, procedures employed, information collected, and outcomes.

E3-External Metaevaluation: Program evaluation sponsors, clients, evaluators, and other stakeholders should encourage the conduct of external metaevaluations using these and other applicable standards.

Accuracy Standards

The accuracy standards are intended to increase the dependability and truthfulness of evaluation representations, propositions, and findings, especially those that support interpretations and judgments about quality.

A1-Justified Conclusions and Decisions: Evaluation conclusions and decisions should be explicitly justified in the cultures and contexts where they have consequences.

A2-Valid Information: Evaluation information should serve the intended purposes and support valid interpretations.

A3-Reliable Information: Evaluation procedures should yield sufficiently dependable and consistent information for the intended uses.

A4-Explicit Program and Context Descriptions: Evaluations should document programs and their contexts with appropriate detail and scope for the evaluation purposes.

A5-Information Management: Evaluations should employ systematic information collection, review, verification, and storage methods.

A6-Sound Designs and Analyses: Evaluations should employ technically adequate designs and analyses that are appropriate for the evaluation purposes.

A7-Explicit Evaluation Reasoning: Evaluation reasoning leading from information and analyses to findings, interpretations, conclusions, and judgments should be clearly and completely documented.

A8-Communication and Reporting: Evaluation communications should have adequate scope and guard against misconceptions, biases, distortions, and errors.

Propriety Standards

The propriety standards support what is proper, fair, legal, right, and just in evaluations.

P1-Responsive and Inclusive Orientation: Evaluations should be responsive to stakeholders and their communities.

P2-Formal Agreements: Evaluation agreements should be negotiated to make obligations explicit and take into account the needs, expectations, and cultural contexts of clients and other stakeholders.

P3-Human Rights and Respect: Evaluations should be designed and conducted to protect human and legal rights and maintain the dignity of participants and other stakeholders.

P4-Clarity and Fairness: Evaluations should be understandable and fair in addressing stakeholder needs and purposes.

P5-Transparency and Disclosure: Evaluations should provide complete descriptions of findings, limitations, and conclusions to all stakeholders, unless doing so would violate legal and propriety obligations.

P6-Conflicts of Interests: Evaluations should openly and honestly identify and address real or perceived conflicts of interests that may compromise the evaluation.

P7-Fiscal Responsibility: Evaluations should account for all expended resources and comply with sound fiscal procedures and processes.

work that we do as evaluators. These same professional guidelines and standards can aid stakeholders and evaluators in assessing the merit and worth of evaluation findings.

1.4 TYPES OF EVALUATION

The terms evaluation, program, research, and embedded evaluation were explained in the previous section. There are several additional important evaluation terms that will be explained in this section. The terminology introduced in this section is often used in evaluation solicitations and requests for proposals. A **request for proposal** (RFP) is an announcement that an agency has funds available for specified work and an invitation for organizations to prepare a description of how they would complete that work. Some RFPs ask specifically for evaluation services and some may ask for program development or implementation, with a stipulation that an evaluation plan must be included in the proposal. RFPs will often use language indicating that formative and summative evaluation is required, or an external evaluator is preferred.

An RFP is only one method through which you might hear about the need for an evaluation. While some of the evaluations I have conducted originated with an RFP, most of my evaluation work comes when an individual or organization directly contacts our evaluation center. Sometimes we are asked to evaluate a program that is being planned or already in operation. Other times we are asked to write an evaluation plan for a project being proposed and submitted for funding, with the understanding that should the project be funded, we will conduct the evaluation. Evaluators might also be hired to be part of an organization; some larger organizations have evaluators on staff to conduct routine evaluations of their programs and policies. Regardless of whether an evaluation comes about due to an RFP, direct contact, in-house planning, or some other means, the terms presented in this section are commonly used when requesting evaluation assistance.

The framework presented in this section to introduce evaluation terminology is adapted from Trochim's (2001) *The Research Methods Knowledge Base.* He categorizes common types of evaluation within the formative and summative domains. **Formative evaluation** is evaluation aimed at providing information to program staff so they can improve the program while it is in operation; formative evaluation methods include

Request for proposal (RFP): a solicitation for organizations to submit a proposal indicating how they would complete a specified project.

Formative evaluation: evaluation aimed at providing information to improve a program while it is in operation.

process evaluation, implementation assessment, needs assessment, and evaluability assessment. **Summative evaluation** is evaluation aimed at providing information to program staff regarding effectiveness so they can make decisions about whether to continue or discontinue a program; summative evaluation methods include outcome evaluation, impact evaluation, cost-effectiveness/cost-benefit analysis, and meta-analysis. Many evaluations have both formative and summative components, with the formative component geared toward improving the impact measured by the summative evaluation.

1.4.1 Formative Evaluation

An important purpose of evaluation is to collect information that enables program staff to improve a program while it is in operation. Formative decisions are those that are intended to form, shape, and improve a program while being implemented. Thus, formative evaluation is performed to provide ongoing data to program staff for continuous improvement. Formative evaluation examines the implementation process, as well as outcomes measured throughout program implementation, to make decisions about mid-course adjustments, technical assistance, or professional development that may be needed, as well as to document the program's implementation so that others can learn from the program's operation.

Evaluators use **process evaluation** to make mid-course adjustments to shape a program. When evaluators conduct a process evaluation, they examine the output of the process of implementing a program's operations. A process evaluation might focus on the number of people trained, types of services delivered, methods of training used, and so forth.

Another form of formative evaluation is **implementation assessment**, that is, determining the degree to which a program is implemented as planned. Implementation assessment examines the fidelity with which a program's strategies or activities have been implemented. In order to assess fidelity of implementation, one must have a model of how a program would "look" if it was implemented as envisioned. Likewise, having a sense of how a program implementation is not optimal can help to establish the degree of fidelity. For instance, think about how your teachers might use a rubric to grade a written assignment. Let's suppose your rubric scores range from 0 to 10 on ten components of the paper, for example, identification of thesis, organization, and grammar. The rubric would tell you what it means to get a 10 on organization versus a 5 or 0. That way, you would know what the teacher sees as an "ideal" paper versus an average or below average paper. Similarly, implementation assessment can help evaluators understand how various activities within a program are implemented and the degree to which implementation matches the intentions of the program developers.

Prior to implementing a new program or restructuring an existing program, **needs assessment** can be used to shape a program by examining the needs of proposed participants, needs of stakeholders, and how to meet the needs of both. Needs assessment is a systematic examination of what program services are needed, who needs these services, and in what ways they need the services.

Summative evaluation: evaluation aimed at providing information about effectiveness in order to make decisions about whether to continue or discontinue a program.

Process evaluation: formative evaluation aimed at understanding the operations of a program.

Implementation assessment: formative evaluation that examines the degree to which a program is implemented with fidelity (according to plan).

Needs assessment: formative evaluation that focuses on what services are needed and who needs them.

Finally, **evaluability assessment** helps determine whether it is feasible to conduct an evaluation of a particular program (Trevisan, 2007; Wholey, 1979, 2002). It addresses whether a program or policy has clearly defined outcomes of interest; if it is feasible to attribute outcomes to the program or policy; whether data are available, reliable, and valid; whether stakeholders are identifiable and accessible; if the necessary resources are available to conduct the evaluation; and the likelihood that findings will be used appropriately. Evaluability assessment also examines how stakeholders might be used within the evaluation to shape the program and its attendant evaluation in a way that best meets the determined needs. An excellent resource on how to conduct evaluability assessments is *Evaluability Assessment: Improving Evaluation Quality and Use* by Trevisan and Walser (2014).

1.4.2 Summative Evaluation

A primary purpose of evaluation is to make summative decisions. Summative decisions are made by looking at all of the information. At the root of the word "summative" is *sum*. A "sum" is a total or a result. Thus, summative evaluation is performed to make final, outcome-related decisions about program funding. Summative decisions include whether to continue, expand, or discontinue a program based on evaluation findings.

Summative evaluation speaks to decisions about a program's future. As such, **outcome evaluation** is summative evaluation focused on how well a program met its specified long-term goals. If a program proposes to improve learning, outcome evaluation would focus on changes in knowledge. If a program proposes to change practices related to healthy eating or medication compliance, outcome evaluation would focus on behavior change.

Impact evaluation also measures the outcomes of programs. However, **impact evaluation** is broader than outcome evaluation, as it measures all impacts of a program, both those intended as specified by a program's goals and those unintended. For example, an impact evaluation of No Child Left Behind (NCLB) showed that principals and teachers made better use of test data after NCLB was passed and that scores on state tests had increased (Center on Education Policy, 2006). However, the study also showed that the curriculum had narrowed to focus on tested material, student creativity had declined, and flexibility within the law might account for more students being classified as proficient (Center on Education Policy, 2006). Other studies have shown that NCLB decreased the average quality of principals at disadvantaged schools due to principals seeking employment at schools less likely to experience NCLB sanctions (Li, 2010), reduced educational programming for gifted students (Beisser, 2008), and raised new challenges specific to using accommodations in high-stakes testing (Cawthon, 2007).

Many program funders request information on the efficiency of a program. That is, they want to know the value of a program, either in terms of dollars saved or benefits to participants or society. Hence, **cost-benefit/cost-effectiveness analysis** is summative evaluation that focuses on estimating the efficiency of a program in terms of dollar costs saved

Evaluability assessment: formative evaluation used to determine if an evaluation is feasible and the role stakeholders might take in shaping the evaluation design.

Outcome evaluation: summative evaluation aimed at measuring how well a program met its stated goals.

Impact evaluation: summative evaluation that measures both the intended and unintended outcomes of a program.

Cost-benefit/ cost-effectiveness analysis: summative evaluation that focuses on estimating the efficiency of a program in terms of dollar costs saved (cost-benefit) or outcomes measured (cost-effectiveness).

(cost-benefit) or outcomes observed (cost-effectiveness). The amount saved by a program might differ depending on the time frame used for the analysis. For instance, recall the example about mental health treatment at the start of the chapter. Estimating the amount saved one year out would not give a full picture of the benefits of the program; the cost savings for some programs are not realized until years or decades after the program ends. The allure of funded preschool programs is not simply preparing a child for kindergarten, but rather, proponents argue, the long-term benefits of preschool programs include increased high school graduation rates, which in turn lead to increased employability and improved quality of life. Estimating the cost-benefit of a program intended to have long-term cost savings is difficult, but can be done (see "In the Real World" on the Scared Straight program). An alternative to measuring program success in terms of cost savings is calculating the benefits of a program in terms of nonmonetary outcomes. While cost-benefit is a ratio of the costs of the program to the costs saved by the program, cost-effectiveness is calculated by using a ratio of the total costs associated with program delivery to the impact of the program on a chosen outcome. For instance, a behavioral intervention program might measure cost-effectiveness as the change in behavioral outcomes for every $1 spent on the program. A program targeting healthy eating might estimate the change in fast food consumption per dollar spent on the program or weight loss associated with each dollar invested in the program. For more information, see Cellini and Kee's (2015) chapter on cost-effectiveness and cost-benefit analysis in the *Handbook of Practical Program Evaluation* (Newcomer, Hatry, & Wholey, 2015).

Meta-analysis is a form of summative evaluation that integrates the findings of multiple studies to estimate the overall effect of a type of program. Meta-analysis is a statistical approach that merges results across a body of research. Such analyses are also referred to as systematic reviews because the methodology is highly structured and involves defining inclusion and exclusion criteria for prospective studies, combining measures across studies, and calculating new estimates of effectiveness based on the pooled data. See the What Works Clearinghouse (https://ies.ed.gov/ncee/wwc/) for more information on systematic reviews of evidence.

Finally, a **meta-evaluation** is an evaluation of an evaluation (Scriven, 1969, 2009; Stufflebeam, 1978). Formative meta-evaluations provide feedback to improve an evaluation. Summative meta-evaluations assess the quality and merits of an evaluation. The Joint Committee's Program Evaluation Standards, discussed earlier, can be used to conduct meta-evaluations.

This text will focus primarily on the process evaluation and implementation assessment components of formative evaluation and the outcome and impact evaluation components of summative evaluation. However, resources will be provided in subsequent chapters for additional information on needs assessment, evaluability assessment, cost-benefit/cost-effectiveness analysis, meta-analysis, and meta-evaluation.

Meta-analysis: summative evaluation that integrates the findings of multiple studies to estimate the overall effect of a type of program.

Meta-evaluation: an evaluation of an evaluation.

1.5 INTERNAL AND EXTERNAL EVALUATION

Because internal and external evaluation are terms commonly used by those within and outside of the evaluation field, I include them under types of evaluation. However, it should be noted that they are not types of evaluation like formative and summative evaluation, but rather a way of describing the relationship of the evaluator to the program itself.

An evaluation can be conducted by someone inside the organization within which a program operates or by someone outside of the organization. However, the optimal arrangement is often a partnership between the two, that is, forming an evaluation team that includes both internal and external evaluators.

An **internal evaluator** may be someone at the organization who is knowledgeable about the program. For evaluations that focus on program improvement and effectiveness, having an internal evaluator on the evaluation team can foster a deeper understanding of the context in which the program operates. Involving people inside the organization also helps to build capacity within the organization to conduct evaluation. However, an internal evaluator should be someone who is in a position to be objective regarding program strengths and weaknesses. For this reason, choosing an internal evaluator who is *responsible* for the program's success is not recommended and may compromise the evaluation. Likewise, any time an internal evaluator is very close to the program being evaluated, objectivity or perceived objectivity may suffer. In order to maintain objectivity, an internal evaluator should be outside of the program. However, while staff from within the program should not be part of the core evaluation team, they should certainly partner with the evaluation team to ensure that the evaluation informs the program during every phase of implementation.

An **external evaluator** is an evaluator who is employed from outside of the organization that operates the program or policy to be evaluated. It is good practice to have an external evaluator be part of your evaluation team. Using an external evaluator as a "critical friend" provides you with an extra set of eyes and a fresh perspective from which to review your design and results. Professional evaluators are trained in the design of evaluations to improve usability of the findings, and they are skilled in data collection techniques such as designing surveys, facilitating focus groups, conducting interviews, choosing quality assessments, and performing observations. An experienced evaluator can also help you analyze and interpret your data, as well as guide you in the use of your results.

Partnering with an external evaluator can improve the **credibility** of the findings, as some may question whether an evaluator from within an organization can have the **objectivity** to recognize areas for improvement and to report results that might be unfavorable to the program. This is not to imply that credibility or objectivity problems are usual or even common with internal evaluations. External as well as internal evaluations can suffer from a lack of credibility or objectivity. But issues of credibility and objectivity in internal

Internal evaluator: an evaluator employed by the organization that operates a program (but preferably not responsible for the program itself).

External evaluator: an evaluator who is employed outside of the organization in which the program operates.

Credibility: in evaluation, the degree of trust someone has that findings are reported accurately and should be believed.

Objectivity: in evaluation, the degree to which an evaluator can put aside any bias and impartially interpret and report findings.

evaluations come up because of the perceived threat to the findings. For that reason, it is important for evaluators to disclose, in a straightforward manner, any conflicts of interest or connections to the program under evaluation when reporting evaluation findings.

The choice of who conducts your evaluation should depend upon the anticipated use of the results and the intended audience, as well as your available resources. If evaluation results are to be used with current or potential funding agencies to foster support and assistance, contracting with an external evaluator would be your most prudent choice. If the evaluation is primarily intended for use by your organization to improve programs and understand impact, an evaluation team composed of an internal and an external evaluator may be preferable. Connecting with someone outside your organization to assist with the evaluation and results interpretation will likely enhance the usability of your evaluation and the credibility of your evaluation findings. Evaluation as a partnership between an internal evaluator and an external evaluator is the ideal arrangement to ensure the utility of the evaluation and its results.

An external evaluator may be a researcher or professor from your local university, a professional evaluator from a private evaluation firm, or an independent evaluation consultant. For programs where an external evaluator might be preferred, funding an outside evaluator may not be feasible. In such cases, partnering with an evaluator within your organization, yet outside your program, might work well. For instance, when evaluating education programs, staff from a curriculum and instruction office implementing a program might partner with staff from another office within the school district, such as an assessment or evaluation office, to conduct the evaluation.

If resources are not available for an external evaluator and there is no office or department in your organization that is not affected by your program, you may want to consider other potentially affordable evaluation options. You could put out a call to individuals with evaluation experience within your community who might be willing to donate time to your program; contact a local university or community college regarding faculty or staff with evaluation experience who might work with you at a reduced rate; ask your

---

✔ QUICK CHECK

1. What is formative evaluation? How does formative evaluation differ from summative evaluation?

2. How can implementation assessment be used to make formative and summative evaluation decisions?

3. Why might someone be skeptical of an evaluation conducted by an internal evaluator? What can be done to strengthen the perceived objectivity when an internal evaluator is used?

local university if there is a doctoral student in evaluation who is looking for a research opportunity or dissertation project; or explore grant opportunities that fund evaluation activities. Overall, it is important to remember that both internal and external evaluations have their benefits and drawbacks. In determining the structure of who conducts an evaluation, weigh the extent to which *perceived* objectivity is a threat to evaluation credibility, as well as the ways in which different stakeholder groups might use the findings.

1.6 EMBEDDING EVALUATION INTO PROGRAMS

The resource tug-of-war between program services and program evaluation is real and has real implications. It is this dilemma that has shaped the way in which I work with my clients, so that evaluation is useful in not only determining the outcomes of their programs but also in helping to improve their programs on an ongoing basis. Embedded evaluation is an evaluation approach that can be built into programs and processes, so that it is part of everyday practice. This method recognizes the preciousness of resources and time, the need for information, and the tension between the two. The embedded approach to evaluation is not an additional step to be superimposed upon a program and the strategies it employs, but rather a way to weave evaluation into the design, development, and implementation of policies, programs, and projects.

1.6.1 Grounded in Continuous Improvement

Embedded evaluation incorporates the underlying philosophies of both total quality management (TQM) and quality improvement (QI) initiatives, in that the purpose of embedding evaluation into your programs is to create continuous improvement processes. Thus, **embedded evaluation** is a method of continuous improvement in which processes and practices are examined and refined to improve outcomes.

If you are not familiar with TQM or QI, TQM is a philosophy and an approach used to improve processes within organizations. See the American Society for Quality website for more information on TQM (asq.org). TQM is based on quality improvement principles. QI is concerned with improving performance in a systematic and continuous manner. Its processes are also referred to as continuous improvement (CI). The U.S. Department of Health and Human Services (Health Resources and Services Administration, 2011) has made available a resource on the principles and processes of QI. This report, titled *Quality Improvement*, explains QI and provides practical guidance in creating and implementing QI programs.

1.6.2 Theory Based and Utilization Focused

The embedded evaluation approach presented in this textbook is one of many approaches that can be used when conducting an evaluation (note that Chapter 4 provides a comprehensive review of evaluation approaches). Embedded evaluation combines elements

Embedded evaluation: an evaluation approach based on continuous improvement, in which program processes and practices are examined and refined to improve outcomes.

from several common evaluation approaches, including theory-based evaluation, logic modeling, stakeholder evaluation, participatory evaluation, and utilization-focused evaluation. Theory-based evaluation, in particular, focuses on indicators related to the logic underlying a program to guide evaluation. Utilization-focused evaluation is based on the premise that an evaluation's worth rests in how useful it is to the program's stakeholders. Both theory-based and utilization-focused evaluation approaches, as well as stakeholder and participatory evaluation, will be described in detail in Chapter 4.

1.6.3 Dynamic and Cyclical

Earlier I mentioned that evaluation is a lot like the scientific method: You define a problem, investigate the problem, document results, refine the problem based on lessons learned from the results, investigate again, and so on. So, while the steps of embedded evaluation presented in this text may appear as if they are linear rungs on a ladder culminating with the final step, they are not rigid steps. Rather, embedded evaluation steps build on each other and depend upon decisions made in prior steps, and information learned in one step may lead to refinement of another step. So, like the scientific method, embedded evaluation is cyclical. The steps of embedded evaluation are components of the evaluation process that impact and influence each other. What you learn or decide in one step may prompt you to return to a previous step for modification and improvement. Just as programs are ongoing, evaluation is dynamic.

The dynamic nature of evaluation and the interconnectedness of an embedded evaluation with the program itself may seem amiss to researchers who prefer to study a phenomenon over time and wait until a predefined time to analyze and report findings. And inarguably, having a program stay its course without mid-course refinements and improvements would make cross-site comparisons and replication easier. However, as stated previously, embedded evaluation is built upon the principle of continuous program improvement. With embedded evaluation, as information is gathered and lessons are learned, the program is improved. However, embedded evaluation goes beyond simply program monitoring. It is a way to build evaluation into a program, as well as to monitor implementation and assess effectiveness.

The focus of embedded evaluation is to enable program staff to build and implement high-quality programs that are continuously improving, as well as to determine when programs are not working and need to be discontinued. The overall purpose of designing a rigorous, embedded evaluation is to aid program staff in providing effective services to their clients.

1.6.4 Program Specific

Just as the first step in solving a problem is to understand the problem, the first step in conducting an evaluation is to *understand what you want to evaluate*. For the purposes of this textbook, what you want to evaluate is referred to as the "program." As noted earlier, the term "program" is used broadly throughout this textbook to represent small interventions, groups of activities, community-based services, agency-wide projects, and statewide initiatives, as well as national or international policy.

You can use the evaluation process that is presented in this textbook to define and evaluate a small project, as well as to understand and evaluate the inner workings of large programs and initiatives. Regardless of the size or type of program, understanding the program is not only the first step in evaluation; it is the most important step. Defining why a program should work and making the theory that underlies a program explicit lay the foundation upon which you can foster program improvement and measure program effectiveness. Further, understanding the program enables you to develop evaluation questions and define metrics, in collaboration with stakeholders, that are meaningful and useful to stakeholders. Understanding how the program operates can also aid you in integrating processes for the collection and use of these indicators into everyday program operation.

1.6.5 A Framework for Evaluation

Embedded evaluation is a framework grounded in continuous improvement, based on a program's theory, focused on utilizing results, dynamic and cyclical in its operation, and built into a specific program's operations to foster data-driven decision making. Chapters 5–12 will guide you through designing and conducting an evaluation using this framework. You will be led step-by-step from documenting how and why a program works to using evaluation results. The embedded evaluation framework is presented graphically in Figure 1.3. The framework is based on the following five steps:

Step 1. DEFINE: What is the program? (Chapters 5–6)

Step 2. PLAN: How do I plan the evaluation? (Chapters 7–8)

Step 3. IMPLEMENT: How do I evaluate the program? (Chapters 9–10)

Step 4. INTERPRET: How do I interpret the results? (Chapter 11)

Step 5. (a) INFORM and (b) REFINE: How do I use the results? (Chapter 12)

Prior to embarking upon the embedded evaluation process, Chapters 2–4 will provide a necessary foundation for future evaluators. This foundation includes a contextual understanding of the history of evaluation and its development over time; an awareness of the ethical obligations of an evaluator and the history of ethical abuses that make this awareness necessary; and a conceptual understanding of different approaches to evaluation.

Whether the program is a new program or one that has been in operation for many years, the process of embedding evaluation into your program is the same. Explicitly defining the program is a critical first step toward responsible program management, as well as program improvement. Program staff and program evaluators should have a clear understanding of the program and its intended goals, as well as how and why the strategies that the program employs relate to the program's goals.

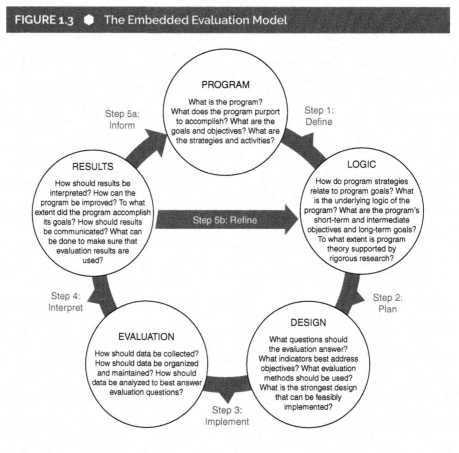

FIGURE 1.3 ● The Embedded Evaluation Model

1.6.5.1 Embedding Evaluation Into Program Development

For a new program, embedding evaluation into the program development process allows data to be built into all future decision making for the program. It provides the opportunity for information to be the foundation of the program's operation from day one. Embedding evaluation during program development also provides the most flexibility with evaluation design, often allowing a more rigorous evaluation than may be feasible with an existing program. When evaluators are involved from the very beginning of a program's development, it provides an opportunity for the evaluator to work collaboratively with program staff to integrate evaluation into the program's operation and to build capacity within the program itself to use and rely upon data for decision making.

1.6.5.2 Embedding Evaluation Into Existing Programs

Existing programs with good documentation and established data management systems may find embedding evaluation into the program a relatively straightforward and educational process. Existing programs with poor documentation and little data supporting their operation may find the process similar to that of embedding evaluation into a new program.

Taking the time to document the logic of an existing program can not only clarify all aspects of a program's implementation, but also provide a good opportunity to examine existing strategies and their relation to the program's goals. The process of embedding evaluation into existing programs can also aid in developing a common understanding of program goals and help to foster buy-in among stakeholders. While examining the program's logic, you will likely uncover data needs that must be adopted by the program. Fostering broad stakeholder involvement during the embedded evaluation process often makes any additional data collection needs easier to implement. However, even if changing data collection methods is cumbersome, remember, it is the responsibility of an evaluator to provide program staff with the information necessary to ensure the program is working for program participants. Just as any organization must periodically reexamine and reaffirm its mission, all programs should routinely examine the logic underlying a program and refine that logic as necessary as lessons are learned and results are measured.

1.7 TEXTBOOK ORGANIZATION

This textbook will provide you with the tools to embed evaluation into programs to foster continuous improvement, by making information and data the basis upon which the program operates. The textbook is divided into four sections:

- **Section 1** includes general evaluation background, including information on key terms, the history of evaluation (Chapter 2), ethical considerations in evaluation (Chapter 3), and evaluation approaches (Chapter 4).

 QUICK CHECK

1. Embedded evaluation is
   a. An evaluation approach used to continuously improve the program.
   b. An evaluation approach that focuses solely on the program's staff.
   c. A linear approach to evaluation.

2. The first step in evaluation is to
   a. Collect data about the program.
   b. Decide on the methods to be used.
   c. Understand the program.

3. What common method is the embedded evaluation approach similar to? In what ways is it similar to this method?

Answers: 1-a; 2-c; 3-scientific method

FIGURE 1.4   ◆   AEA Guiding Principles for Evaluators

Glossary

Common Good — the shared benefit for all or most members of society including equitable opportunities and outcomes that are achieved through citizenship and collective action. The common good includes cultural, social, economic, and political resources as well as natural resources involving shared materials such as air, water, and a habitable earth.

Contextual Factors — geographic location and conditions; political, technological, environmental, and social climate; cultures; economic and historical conditions; language, customs, local norms, and practices; timing; and other factors that may influence an evaluation process or its findings.

Culturally Competent Evaluator — "[an evaluator who] draws upon a wide range of evaluation theories and methods to design and carry out an evaluation that is optimally matched to the context. In constructing a model or theory of how the evaluand operates, the evaluator reflects the diverse values and perspectives of key stakeholder groups."[1]

Environment — the surroundings or conditions in which a being lives or operates; the setting or conditions in which a particular activity occurs.

Equity — the condition of fair and just opportunities for all people to participate and thrive in society regardless of individual or group identity or difference. Striving to achieve equity includes mitigating historic disadvantage and existing structural inequalities.

Guiding Principles vs. Evaluation Standards — the Guiding Principles pertain to the ethical conduct of the evaluator whereas the Evaluation Standards pertain to the quality of the evaluation.

People or Groups — those who may be affected by an evaluation including, but not limited to, those defined by race, ethnicity, religion, gender, income, status, health, ability, power, underrepresentation, and/or disenfranchisement.

Professional Judgment — decisions or conclusions based on ethical principles and professional standards for evidence and argumentation in the conduct of an evaluation.

Stakeholders — individuals, groups, or organizations served by, or with a legitimate interest in, an evaluation, including those who might be affected by an evaluation.

[1] The quotation is from the "Public Statement on Cultural Competence in Evaluation," by the American Evaluation Association, 2011, Washington DC: Author. p. 3.

Purpose of the Guiding Principles: The Guiding Principles reflect the core values of the American Evaluation Association (AEA) and are intended as a guide to the professional ethical conduct of evaluators.

Focus and Interconnection of the Principles: The five Principles address systematic inquiry, competence, integrity, respect for people, and common good and equity. The Principles are interdependent and interconnected. At times, they may even conflict with one another. Therefore, evaluators should carefully examine how they justify professional actions.

Use of Principles: The Principles govern the behavior of evaluators in all stages of the evaluation from the initial discussion of focus and purpose, through design, implementation, reporting, and ultimately the use of the evaluation.

Communication of Principles: It is primarily the evaluator's responsibility to initiate discussion and clarification of ethical matters with relevant parties to the evaluation. The Principles can be used to communicate to clients and other stakeholders what they can expect in terms of the professional ethical behavior of an evaluator.

Professional Development about Principles: Evaluators are responsible for undertaking professional development to learn to engage in sound ethical reasoning. Evaluators are also encouraged to consult with colleagues on how best to identify and address ethical issues.

Structure of the Principles: Each Principle is accompanied by several sub-statements to amplify the meaning of the overarching principle and to provide guidance for its application. These sub-statements do not include all possible applications of that principle, nor are they rules that provide the basis for sanctioning violators. The Principles are distinct from Evaluation Standards and evaluator competencies.

Evolution of Principles: The Principles are part of an evolving process of self-examination by the profession in the context of a rapidly changing world. They have been periodically revised since their first adoption in 1994. Once adopted by the membership, they become the official position of AEA on these matters and supersede previous versions. It is the policy of AEA to review the Principles at least every five years, engaging members in the process. These Principles are not intended to replace principles supported by other disciplines or associations in which evaluators participate.

A: Systematic Inquiry: Evaluators conduct data-based inquiries that are thorough, methodical, and contextually relevant.

A1. Adhere to the highest technical standards appropriate to the methods being used while attending to the evaluation's scale and available resources.

A2. Explore with primary stakeholders the limitations and strengths of the core evaluation questions and the approaches that might be used for answering those questions.

A3. Communicate methods and approaches accurately, and in sufficient detail, to allow others to understand, interpret, and critique the work.

A4. Make clear the limitations of the evaluation and its results.

A5. Discuss in contextually appropriate ways the values, assumptions, theories, methods, results, and analyses that significantly affect the evaluator's interpretation of the findings.

A6. Carefully consider the ethical implications of the use of emerging technologies in evaluation practice.

B: Competence: Evaluators provide skilled professional services to stakeholders.

B1. Ensure that the evaluation team possesses the education, abilities, skills, and experiences required to complete the evaluation competently.

B2. When the most ethical option is to proceed with a commission or request outside the boundaries of the evaluation team's professional preparation and competence, clearly communicate any significant limitations to the evaluation that might result. Make every effort to supplement missing or weak competencies directly or through the assistance of others.

B3. Ensure that the evaluation team collectively possesses or seeks out the competencies necessary to work in the cultural context of the evaluation.

B4. Continually undertake relevant education, training, or supervised practice to learn new concepts, techniques, skills, and services necessary for competent evaluation practice. Ongoing professional development might include formal coursework and workshops, self-study, self- or externally-commissioned evaluations of one's own practice, and working with other evaluators to learn and refine evaluative skills and expertise.

C: Integrity: Evaluators behave with honesty and transparency in order to ensure the integrity of the evaluation.

C1. Communicate truthfully and openly with clients and relevant stakeholders concerning all aspects of the evaluation, including its limitations.

C2. Disclose any conflicts of interest (or appearance of a conflict) prior to accepting an evaluation assignment and manage or mitigate any conflicts during the evaluation.

C3. Record and promptly communicate any changes to the originally negotiated evaluation plans, the rationale for those changes, and the potential impacts on the evaluation's scope and results.

C4. Assess and make explicit the stakeholders', clients', and evaluators' values, perspectives, and interests concerning the conduct and outcome of the evaluation.

C5. Accurately and transparently represent evaluation procedures, data, and findings.

C6. Clearly communicate, justify, and address concerns related to procedures or activities that are likely to produce misleading evaluative information or conclusions. Consult colleagues for suggestions on proper ways to proceed if concerns cannot be resolved, and decline the evaluation when necessary.

C7. Disclose all sources of financial support for an evaluation, and the source of the request for the evaluation.

(Continued)

FIGURE 1.4 ⬣ (Continued)

D: Respect for People: Evaluators honor the dignity, well-being, and self-worth of individuals and acknowledge the influence of culture within and across groups.

D1. Strive to gain an understanding of, and treat fairly, the range of perspectives and interests that individuals and groups bring to the evaluation, including those that are not usually included or are oppositional.

D2. Abide by current professional ethics, standards, and regulations (including informed consent, confidentiality, and prevention of harm) pertaining to evaluation participants.

D3. Strive to maximize the benefits and reduce unnecessary risks or harms for groups and individuals associated with the evaluation.

D4. Ensure that those who contribute data and incur risks do so willingly, and that they have knowledge of and opportunity to obtain benefits of the evaluation.

E: Common Good and Equity: Evaluators strive to contribute to the common good and advancement of an equitable and just society.

E1. Recognize and balance the interests of the client, other stakeholders, and the common good while also protecting the integrity of the evaluation.

E2. Identify and make efforts to address the evaluation's potential threats to the common good especially when specific stakeholder interests conflict with the goals of a democratic, equitable, and just society.

E3. Identify and make efforts to address the evaluation's potential risks of exacerbating historic disadvantage or inequity.

E4. Promote transparency and active sharing of data and findings with the goal of equitable access to information in forms that respect people and honor promises of confidentiality.

E5. Mitigate the bias and potential power imbalances that can occur as a result of the evaluation's context. Selfassess one's own privilege and positioning within that context.

AMERICAN
EVALUATION
ASSOCIATION

2025 M St. NW, Ste. 800, Washington, DC 20036 • eval.org • P: 202.367.1166 • E: info@eval.org •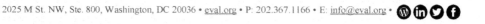

- **Section 2** includes a step-by-step approach to designing an embedded evaluation. It is not intended to be simply a "how to" lesson but rather a comprehensive approach to support you in planning and understanding programs, with a rigorous evaluation included as an integral part of the program's design. The section includes understanding the program (Chapter 5), modeling the program (Chapter 6), planning the evaluation (Chapter 7), and designing the evaluation (Chapter 8).

- **Section 3** focuses on the post-design phases of evaluation, including conducting the evaluation (Chapter 9), analyzing data (Chapter 10), interpreting results (Chapter 11), and using evaluation findings (Chapter 12).

- **Section 4** provides several case studies.

1.8 CHAPTER SUMMARY

Evaluation is a method used to determine the value or worth of something. In our case, that "something" is a program. A **program** is defined broadly in this text to include a group of activities ranging from a small intervention to a national or international policy. **Program evaluation** is evaluation used to determine the merit or worth of a program.

Evaluation has the following attributes, components, and purposes:

- **Systematic**: logical and organized; undertaken according to a plan

- **Operations**: processes involved with implementing the activities of a program

- **Outcomes**: results that occur during and after implementing a program

- **Standard**: the target used, implicitly or explicitly, to judge the merit or worth of a program

- **Improving programs and policies**: the purpose of evaluation; to create more effective and efficient programs and policies

Evaluation is a type of **research**, a systematic investigation in a field of study. **Embedded evaluation**, in particular, is an evaluation approach based on continuous improvement, in which program processes and practices are examined and refined to improve outcomes. A **stakeholder** is anyone who has an interest in or is involved with the operation or success of a program. Key stakeholder groups often include program staff, program participants, community members, and policymakers.

A **request for proposal** (RFP) is a solicitation for organizations to submit a proposal on how they would complete a specified project. Evaluation RFPs often ask for formative and summative evaluation. **Formative evaluation** is evaluation aimed at providing information to improve a program while it is in operation. Formative evaluation techniques include

- **Process evaluation**: formative evaluation aimed at understanding the operations of a program,

- **Implementation assessment**: formative evaluation that examines the degree to which a program is implemented with fidelity (according to plan),

- **Needs assessment**: formative evaluation that focuses on what services are needed and who needs them, and

- **Evaluability assessment**: formative evaluation used to determine if an evaluation is feasible and the role stakeholders might take in shaping the evaluation design.

Summative evaluation is evaluation aimed at providing information about effectiveness, to make decisions about whether to continue or discontinue a program. Summative evaluation techniques include

- **Outcome evaluation**: summative evaluation aimed at measuring how well a program met its stated goals,

- **Impact evaluation**: summative evaluation that measures both the intended and unintended outcomes of a program,

- **Cost-benefit/cost-effectiveness analysis**: summative evaluation that focuses on estimating the efficiency of a program in terms of dollar costs saved (cost-benefit) or outcomes measured (cost-effectiveness),

- **Meta-analysis**: summative evaluation that integrates the effects of multiple studies to estimate the overall effect of a program, and

- **Meta-evaluation**: an evaluation of an evaluation.

Finally, an internal evaluator is an evaluator employed by the organization that operates a program (but preferably not responsible for the program itself). An external evaluator refers to an evaluator who is employed from outside of the organization in which the program operates.

Reflection and Application

1. Research the Drug Abuse Resistance Education (DARE) program. What have past evaluations found regarding the effectiveness of DARE?

2. Why do you think policymakers continue to support programs even after evidence suggests they are ineffective?

3. Explain why it might be considered unethical to not evaluate a program or policy.

4. Find a program or policy where data showed it was not working as intended or had unintended consequences. Was the program continued?

5. Describe embedded evaluation and how it is used.

6. Identify the steps of embedded evaluation.

HISTORY OF EVALUATION

If you don't know history, then you don't know anything. You are a leaf that doesn't know it is part of a tree.

—Michael Crichton

Upon completion of this chapter, you should be able to

- Discuss the historical context of evaluation.
- Describe how the discipline of evaluation has evolved over the last 200 years.
- Identify important contributors to the development of the field of evaluation.
- Explain the history of research and evaluation with respect to ethics.
- Identify current issues in evaluation.

2.1 THE EVOLUTION OF EVALUATION

While evaluation as a profession is new, evaluation activity began long ago, perhaps as early as Adam and Eve. As defined in Chapter 1, evaluation is a method used to determine the value or worth of something. It is a process humans use to make decisions. It is also an imperfect process. As humans, we evaluate with the information available to us, which is often incomplete and nearly always without a clear picture of implication and consequence. Eve made the decision to eat from the forbidden tree, evaluating the information that she had and obviously weighting one source more than another. Her information was conflicting and she did not foresee the consequences of her decision, but it was evaluative nonetheless. Some researchers look back further and place the roots of evaluation with evolutionary biology (Shadish, Cook, & Leviton, 1990). It is reasonable to consider that evaluation is at play when species mutate to adopt new characteristics as a survival adaptation, as with evolutionary developmental biology (Evo-Devo). Evo-Devo, no relation to the 1970s rock band Devo, is the study of when, how, and to what extent genes are turned on to maximize survivability through natural selection (Public Broadcasting Service, 2009). However, evaluation as an activity to improve processes, programs, and policies has more modest roots.

2.1.1 Before and During the 1800s

Beyond the evaluation associated with gene expression and the choices of Adam and Eve, evidence of evaluation has been documented as far back as 2200 BCE with the emperor of China's efforts to evaluate his staff every three years (Shadish et al., 1990; Wainer, 1987). About one thousand years later in 1115 BCE, the Chan dynasty began testing staff before they were hired; and over two thousand years after that, in the late 1700s and early 1800s, France and then Britain adopted a similar assessment system for selecting civil servants (Wainer, 1987).

Also in Britain, in 1792, William Farish of Cambridge University is credited with creating the first system of grades (Hartmann, 2000; Soh, 2011). During the time, some universities in Britain had begun to base professor pay on the number of students they taught. An early entrepreneur of sorts, Farish developed a method to teach as many students as possible with the least amount of work, and thus make more money. His method was to assign quantitative grades to students. While some American universities, such as Yale, assigned categorical grades to students, it was not until the early 1800s that quantitative grading schemes became popular in the United States (Schinske & Tanner, 2014).

In the early to mid-1800s, France and Britain began to look beyond evaluating people and toward evaluating programs and policies. One of the earliest examples of the evaluation of a social policy was in the 1830s by the French researcher André-Michel Guerry. Guerry studied how education relates to crime and concluded that education does not reduce crime (Cullen, 1975). This finding has been argued by statisticians both methodologically and with evidence (Weiss, 1998). Guerry also examined relationships between weather and mortality, as well as crime and suicide (Friendly, 2007). Further, in the 1840s, another French researcher, Jules Depuit, evaluated the usefulness of public works in France from an economic standpoint of supply and demand (Toulemonde & Rochaix, 1994). Also in the 1840s, Great Britain created commissions to focus on social problems. For instance, the Health of Towns Commission was formed to examine and improve conditions in order to decrease death rates in urban areas across England (British Broadcasting Corporation, 2014).

While there is evidence of the United States adopting systematic hiring practices in the late 1800s and group assessment to evaluate the intelligence of military recruits several decades later (Wainer, 1987), perhaps the first large-scale effort at evaluation in the United States was launched by Horace Mann in Boston. Mann was dissatisfied with the Massachusetts education system (Cremin, 2018) and sought to create a free public school system that educated all citizens, regardless of race, religion, or income level (Gale Group, 2002). During the 1830s and 1840s, Mann advocated for education reform and pushed for objective assessment of student learning as a way to examine the effectiveness of Boston schools. The practice introduced by Mann of using student test scores to evaluate educational programs remains in use today (Hogan, 2007). Due to the quantitative nature of evaluative systems through the mid-1800s, many educators and lawmakers equated assessment and measurement to evaluation. That is, evaluation was narrowly seen as the quantitative assessment of outcomes.

2.1.2 Early to Middle 20th Century

Frederick Taylor, an inventor and engineer from Philadelphia, is known as the "Father of Scientific Management." His scientific management movement of the early 1900s was based on objective analysis of tasks and measurement of work outcomes to improve efficiency. Regardless of the many criticisms of scientific management (Locke, 1982), for example, that it did not recognize the more human side of management and employee performance, Taylor's methods of using data to foster change expanded the role of evaluation from mere description of assessment data to the use of those descriptive data for process improvement.

One of the earliest evaluations in social science is the Cambridge-Somerville Youth Study conducted in the 1930s. This study examined the effectiveness of welfare-type interventions, such as medical assistance, counseling, academic assistance, and community-based support, in preventing or reducing delinquency in at-risk boys. See "In the Real World" on the next page for more information on the Cambridge-Somerville Youth Study (Cabot, 1940; McCord, 1978, 2002, 2003; McCord & McCord, 1959).

The first comprehensive, long-term evaluation in the field of education was conducted in Chicago between 1932 and 1940. The Eight-Year Study, spearheaded by Ralph Tyler, was an experiment across 30 secondary schools intended to test the effectiveness of different curricula (Alkin & King, 2016; Pinar, 2010). Tyler's work led to the exploration of national assessments in the United States, which resulted in the National Assessment of Educational Progress (NAEP).

The development of the NAEP began in 1964, despite opposition from the American Association of School Administrators and the National Council of English Teachers,

IN THE REAL WORLD . . .

The Cambridge-Somerville Youth Study (CSYS) is one of the earliest evaluations funded by a private foundation, the Ella Lyman Cabot Foundation. The design of CSYS began in 1935 and took four years to complete. The purpose of CSYS was both to prevent juvenile delinquency among boys and to study the effectiveness of juvenile delinquency interventions.

Participants in the CSYS study were 650 school-aged boys. Boys were matched based on data from a 160-item code sheet including variables such as age, grade, physical health, intelligence, home life, and mental health. One boy in each of the 325 matched pairs was placed into either the Treatment (T) or Control (C) group; the matched boy was placed in the other group (i.e., if a boy was placed in T, his matched pair was placed in C or if a boy was placed in C, his matched pair was placed in T). Boys in the T group were assigned counselors and received specialized services from agencies in the Boston area. While there was some attrition, due to relocation or death, when possible, CSYS arranged for services to continue if a boy changed schools. The study was planned to last ten years, with two- to three-year follow-ups during that time.

Data collected included variables related to personality development, community relationships, school progress, emotional maturity, medical problems, mental health, delinquency, and incarceration.

The theory behind CSYS was that interventions focused on character development, emotional security, social development, and related matters would decrease the likelihood of delinquency in boys during childhood and be preventive of later criminal activity.

Source: Cabot (1940).

and was administered for the first time in 1969 (Vinovskis, 1998). NAEP has been used for 50 years and currently tests across 10 content areas in Grades 4, 8, and 12 (National Center for Education Statistics, 2019). Tyler, who was born in 1902, continued to contribute to the field through lecturing and consulting until his death in 1994. Because of his influence in the fields of assessment and evaluation, Ralph Tyler is referred to as the "Father of Evaluation" (Mukhongo, 2019).

While Tyler stands out as perhaps the most influential figure in early evaluation, the launching of Sputnik by the Soviet Union in 1957 helped propel the field of evaluation to where it is today. At the time, the United States thought itself the superpower of the world, yet the Soviet Union beat the Americans into space. Even with the United States following up with a successful launch of the Explorer 1 in 1958, the realization that the United States was not leading the space race called in to question the effectiveness of the American education system in its ability to create top scientists. Sputnik led to the founding of the National Aeronautics and Space Administration (NASA) and initiated a new focus across America on technological and scientific discovery (Garber, 2007).

In addition to Sputnik, the postwar economy of the late 1940s through the 1960s was also an important factor in the development of the evaluation field. Along with the economic growth during this time came a greater call for social programs to bridge the gap between those who benefitted from current society and those who were suffering, living in poverty, and marginalized. In response to this call, some existing federal social programs were expanded and others created anew. As part of the Social Welfare History Project, Marx (2011) provides an overview of American social policy during the 1960s, including the following programs created and laws enacted during that time:

- The Juvenile Delinquency and Youth Offenses Control Act of 1961 funded programs aimed at reducing juvenile crime.

- In 1962, amendments to the Social Security Act created programs to aid families with dependent children.

- The Manpower Development and Training Act of 1962 created new job training programs.

- The Community Mental Health Centers Act of 1963 facilitated the creation of community mental health centers to provide preventive services.

- The Civil Rights Acts of 1964 and 1965 changed federal policy regarding the enforcement of sanctions for civil rights violations.

- In 1965, Medicare and Medicaid programs enabled senior citizens and those living in poverty to have access to health care.

- The Older Americans Act of 1965 formed a national network of organizations to serve the aging population with health and nutrition programs.

- The Elementary and Secondary Education Act of 1965 provided financial assistance to low-income schools.

- The Economic Opportunity Act of 1965 provided alternative training and job programs to youth.

Other social programs created during the 1960s included the federal Food Stamp Act, the Work Incentive program, the Work-Study program, and Head Start (Marx, 2011). It was during the second half of the 20th century, when social programs exploded and the focus on education expanded, that the field of evaluation was born.

2.1.3 Late 20th Century to Early 21st Century

Due to calls for educational reform following Sputnik and the proliferation of social programs in the 1960s, the need for critical examination of the effectiveness and impact of these reforms and programs became apparent. However, it also became apparent that professionals with the necessary evaluation skills were scarce. Further, the field lacked evaluative tools and methodologies with which to examine programs and policies. Thus, during the 1970s and born from a dearth of knowledge, the evaluation profession emerged. As the field developed, assessment remained a method to measure outcomes, but evaluation progressed beyond assessment to include additional methods and approaches.

During the 1970s, professionals from many domains contributed to the development of evaluation as a field in its own right. Psychologists, including Ralph Tyler, Lee Cronbach, and Donald Campbell, brought quantitative methods to evaluation. Sociologists, such as Michael Quinn Patton and Carol Weiss, developed qualitative and theory-based approaches to evaluation. Other early evaluators from the realms of philosophy, communications research, educational psychology, and statistics helped shape the wealth of evaluation tools and approaches we have today. See Table 2.1 for a list of important contributors to the field of evaluation, as well as where they were employed (if applicable) in 2019, where they studied, and their field of study. This table is not meant to be exhaustive and surely there are important contributors to the field that are not included, but it serves as a starting point for understanding the convergence of many disciplines to shape evaluation as a profession. The particular contributions of individuals to the field of evaluation, as well as a discussion of evaluation approaches, will be addressed in more detail in Chapter 4.

The first university courses on evaluation were also developed in the 1970s. Some of the pioneering institutions were Stanford University, Western Michigan University, and the University of Illinois (Hogan, 2007). While funding for program evaluation at the federal level was cut in the 1980s, the field continued to develop and expand. In the mid-1980s, the **American Evaluation Association (AEA)** was created when two smaller associations merged. The AEA is an international professional association of evaluators focused on sharing knowledge of evaluation approaches and methods. The group hosted its first annual conference in 1986. The AEA now has about 7,300 members across more than 80 countries (see www.eval.org).

During the 1990s, the U.S. government increased funding for and amplified focus on program and policy evaluation of federal initiatives. States and local organizations began to look to evaluation as a way to improve their programming. The states of Massachusetts and South Carolina as well as the city of Chicago included evaluation

American Evaluation Association (AEA): an international professional association of evaluators focused on sharing knowledge of evaluation approaches and methods.

TABLE 2.1 ⬢ Early Contributors to the Field of Evaluation			
Evaluator	Employment (if applicable, as of 2019)	Degree Received From/Date	Degree/Field of Study
Donald T. Campbell	Deceased 1996	University of California, Berkeley (1947)	PhD, Psychology
Huey T. Chen	Mercer University	University of Massachusetts—Amherst[1]	PhD, Sociology
Thomas D. Cook	Northwestern University	Stanford University (1967)	PhD, Communications Research
Lee J. Cronbach	Deceased 2001	University of Chicago (1940)	PhD, Educational Psychology
Stewart I. Donaldson	Claremont Graduate University	Claremont Graduate University (1991)	PhD, Psychology
David M. Fetterman	Fetterman & Associates	Stanford University (1981)	PhD, Educational and Medical Anthropology
Jennifer C. Greene	University of Illinois	Stanford University (1976)	PhD, Educational Psychology
Gary T. Henry	University of Delaware	University of Wisconsin–Milwaukee (1982)	PhD, Political Science
Ernest R. House	University of Colorado Boulder	University of Illinois at Urbana-Champaign (1968)	EdD, Education
Mark W. Lipsey	Vanderbilt University	Johns Hopkins University (1972)	PhD, Psychology
Mel M. Mark	Pennsylvania State University	Northwestern University (1979)	PhD, Psychology
Michael Quinn Patton	Consultant, Utilization-Focused Evaluation	University of Wisconsin–Madison (1973)	PhD, Sociology
Peter H. Rossi	Deceased 2006	Columbia University (1951)	PhD, Sociology
Michael J. Scriven	Claremont Graduate University	Oxford University (1956)	PhD, Philosophy
William R. Shadish	Deceased 2016	Purdue University (1978)	PhD, Clinical Psychology
Robert E. Stake	University of Illinois at Urbana-Champaign	Princeton University (1958)	PhD, Psychology

(Continued)

Evaluator	Employment (if applicable, as of 2019)	Degree Received From/Date	Degree/Field of Study
TABLE 2.1 ⬢ (Continued)			
Daniel L. Stufflebeam	*Deceased 2017*	Purdue University (1964)	PhD, Statistics and Measurement
William M. K. Trochim	Cornell University	Northwestern University (1980)	PhD, Methodology and Evaluation Research
Ralph W. Tyler	*Deceased 1994*	University of Chicago (1927)	Educational Psychology
Carol H. Weiss	*Deceased 2013*	Columbia University (1977)	PhD, Sociology
Joseph S. Wholey	University of Southern California	Harvard University[1]	PhD, Philosophy

1. Unable to locate year of degree.

in their human services programs (Weiss, 1998). Many evaluation texts and journal articles were published in the 1990s, adding to the wealth of resources available to evaluation professionals. Due to the diverse backgrounds of early evaluators (see Table 2.1), the approaches and methods of evaluation varied considerably, which sparked debate over the merit and worth of different approaches. These debates continue today, but it is through this debate and dialogue that evaluators have formed a community of professional learning where divergent thinking can be discussed, critiqued, advanced, and, most important, respected. Evaluation approaches, including their strengths and critiques, will be reviewed in Chapter 4.

2.1.4 Hogan's Framework

While the historical evolution of evaluation can be explored by century, it can also be examined at a finer level. Hogan's framework of evaluation development provides a rich conceptualization of how and when the field developed. He divides the progression of program evaluation into seven time periods, beginning in the late 1700s:

1. Age of Reform (1792–1900s)

2. Age of Efficiency and Testing (1900–1930)

3. Tylerian Age (1930–1945)

4. Age of Innocence (1946–1957)

5. Age of Development (1958–1972)

6. Age of Professionalization (1973–1983)

7. Age of Expansion and Integration (1983–present)

Hogan describes the Age of Reform as the time when the first recorded evaluation took place. As mentioned above, higher education institutions in England and the United States began to use quantitative methods to evaluate students, partially in an effort to increase income by teaching a greater number of students. Similar measures were used to assess the performance of civil servants and in hiring practices for military recruits. Beyond evaluating people, measures of student learning were used to examine the performance of educational programs and systems. After the turn of the 20th century, during what Hogan calls the Age of Efficiency and Testing, Taylor's scientific management further facilitated the movement toward objective measurement and assessment as a form of evaluation. Ralph Tyler, the "Father of Evaluation," has his own era, the Tylerian Age. It was during this time that objectives were used as a foundation for evaluation. Tyler's work on national assessments across multiple content areas is still evident today.

The Age of Innocence, during the mid-1900s, is aptly labeled by Hogan, as it refers to the time when many programs were created and investments made in the United States, without thought to whether they were worth the time and money allocated to them. That is, the postwar economy spurred both intense need and rapid growth across many sectors, in what some might call an irresponsible rollout of actions without regard to long-term consequences. Hogan's label of "innocence" is nicer than mine of "irresponsibility." The Age of Development propelled the United States further into growth mode; however, conversations arose regarding accountability and the effectiveness of the many investments made in the preceding decades.

My favorite of Hogan's ages, the Age of Professionalization, is the time during which the field took on its modern contours. Due to the clear need to examine the effectiveness of government spending and associated programs, as well as the call for evaluation from private foundations and organizations, researchers across many fields converged and joined forces to develop the new field. Professional organizations were formed, evaluation methodologies generated, methods of dissemination (such as journals) created, and university programs focused on producing evaluation professionals developed. Finally, the Age of Expansion and Integration continues to this day. Evaluation is now recognized as a profession and, further, infrastructure to support the field of evaluation has been developed. Yet evaluation is still a relatively young field and there are many opportunities for discovery and growth.

IN THE REAL WORLD...

The Cambridge-Somerville Youth Study (CSYS) was described earlier in the chapter (see "In the Real World"). About 325 boys received counseling, family guidance, academic assistance, medical assistance, and other community-based services over a five-year period between 1939 and 1944.

Findings after 15 years as analyzed by McCord and McCord (1959) showed little evidence that the program had reduced criminal behavior. They concluded that the intervention provided to treatment boys through CSYS was ineffective at crime prevention. However, from subsequent analyses, they did find that boys who began treatment earlier (before 10 years of age) and those who had more interaction with their counselor/social worker (weekly visits) had less criminal behavior than boys who started treatment later and had less frequent contact with their social worker.

Findings after 30 years, as analyzed by McCord (1978), not only showed no evidence that the CSYS program reduced crime, but revealed that boys who participated in the program had poorer later life outcomes than boys in the control group. As adults, boys who participated in the program were more likely to commit a second crime, more likely to show signs of alcoholism and serious mental illness, more likely to have a stress-related disease, and more often reported dissatisfaction with their job. McCord hypothesizes that interaction with a counselor during childhood may foster dependency upon outside services and create expectations of success that were not realized. She concludes that social work interventions, such as CSYS, actually increase risk of poor later life outcomes for the youth they are designed to help.

Criticisms of McCord's analyses and subsequent conclusion came from many fronts. Researchers believed her study lacked rigor and neglected to use more sophisticated analyses that might have been more informative (Vosburgh & Alexander, 1980). Conclusions based on treatment versus control boys have also been criticized because the control group was not a "no treatment" group, but more likely a group of boys who received other services that were not documented in the study.

Other hypotheses as to why the treatment boys had poorer long-term outcomes include McCord's (2003) peer deviancy theory. She believed the CSYS intervention component in which treatment boys were brought together at a camp fostered social connections that may have allowed deviant youth to bond and reinforce deviant behavior (McCord, 2002). Other researchers point to subsequent research on protective factors, social influences, and institutional influences (Welsh, Zane, & Rocque, 2017).

Sources: McCord (1978, 2002, 2003); McCord & McCord (1959); Vosburgh & Alexander (1980); Welsh et al. (2017).

    QUICK CHECK

1. Who is considered the "Father of Evaluation" and why?

2. What event occurred in the 1950s that helped to jump-start the field of evaluation? What occurred during the 1960s that further brought to bear the need for qualified evaluators?

3. During what time frame was evaluation recognized as a profession? What fields did the early contributors to evaluation approaches come from?

4. What is the primary professional association for evaluators?

2.2 THE HISTORY OF ETHICS IN RESEARCH AND EVALUATION

Much of what we know about modern medicine, human behavior, and effective practices is due to research. As stated in Chapter 1, research and evaluation are necessary to ensure that the programs and policies, as well as treatments and interventions, we use work for the people they are designed to help. In a sense, it is an ethical obligation of researchers, whether they are basic scientists or program evaluators, to examine whether resources are being spent wisely on methods that are effective. As researchers, we seek to increase and share knowledge to the betterment of human beings. However, what trumps this knowledge-generation process is that no harm is done along the way. Unfortunately, in the United States and around the world, there have been numerous experiments done on humans, perhaps aimed at the greater good, but without regard for the human beings that were exploited. In some cases, the harm to humans has been deliberate and callous, where individuals were dehumanized and seen solely as test subjects. In other cases, researchers may have been more neglectful than outright malicious, but the end result was the same: harm to people. Because of the sometimes horrific and always troubling abuses of humans in the name of research, guidelines and protections for humans involved in research have been established in the last 50 years. Researchers and evaluators alike are bound by these ethical guidelines. Guidelines and protections for humans involved in research are discussed in Chapter 4; this chapter will examine the history of unethical treatment of humans during research that led to the need for ethical guidelines and oversight.

2.2.1 Human Experimentation Outside of the United States

Nazi Germany Experiments. Experiments conducted by Nazis during World War II were inarguably the worst abuses of humans in history. Nazis experimented on millions of individuals, including men, women, and children. Experiments were conducted on humans without their consent and without regard to pain and suffering. Individuals were exposed to freezing temperatures, poison, tuberculosis, sterilization, joint transplants, toxic gas, and infections (Tyson, 2000).

Japanese Unit 731. During and after World War II, it is reported that Japan experimented on potentially hundreds of thousands of men, women, and children using chemical and biological warfare. These experiments, called Japanese Unit 731, also included vivisection, limb amputations, and freezing experiments similar to those performed in Nazi Germany (Kristoff, 1995).

Soviet Chamber. Prior to World War II and operating until at least the 1950s, the Soviet Union had a secret laboratory called the Chamber. The Chamber was used to experiment on humans with deadly poisons (Central Intelligence Agency, 1993).

Aversion Project. During the 1970s and 1980s, South Africa conducted experiments to convert homosexuals to heterosexuals. Lesbian and gay soldiers were forced to undergo hormone treatments and even chemical castration. In addition, gender reassignment surgery was performed, without consent, on nearly a thousand men and women (Kaplan, 2004). This massive experiment on homosexuals is commonly referred to as the Aversion Project.

2.2.2 Human Experimentation Within and By the United States

Tuskegee Syphilis Experiments. For 40 years beginning in 1932, the U.S. Public Health Service and the Tuskegee Institute in Tuskegee, Alabama, experimented on poor African American farmers to learn about the progression of and treatments for syphilis. Six hundred men, about 400 with syphilis and 200 without, were given free medical care in return for their participation in the study. Even when penicillin became recognized as an effective treatment for syphilis in 1947, study participants were not offered this treatment. In 1997, President Bill Clinton apologized to the eight surviving participants of the Tuskegee experiments (Physicians Committee for Responsible Medicine, 2019).

Monster Study. To test his theory that the diagnosis of stuttering can itself cause stuttering, a University of Iowa researcher, Wendell Johnson, conducted a study in 1939 with children at an orphanage. Orphaned children with normal speech patterns were told they had poor speech, including a stutter. These children, who did not have speech problems prior to the study, developed stutters and suffered negative psychological and behavioral effects (Silverman, 1998).

U.S. Radiation Experiments. From the mid 1940s until the 1980s, the U.S. government conducted a research program focused on the effects of radiation on humans. Hundreds of experiments were sponsored across the United States; subjects included the elderly, prisoners, pregnant women, and terminally ill patients. These experiments were conducted at multiple sites, and in many cases subjects received radiation doses up to 98 times greater than what was known at the time to be tolerable (Faden, 1996; Knight-Ridder, 1994; U.S. Department of Energy, 1995; U.S. House of Representatives, 1986).

Guatemala Syphilis Experiments. In 2010, while examining documents from the Tuskegee syphilis study, a researcher discovered that a similar experiment was performed by the U.S. government between 1946 and 1948 in Guatemala. Over 1,300 people were intentionally infected with venereal diseases, including syphilis, to examine how effective penicillin was in treating the diseases. Only a portion of the subjects were administered penicillin and over 80 individuals died from participation in the study (Resnick, 2019). President Barack Obama apologized to the Guatemalan people on behalf of the U.S. government.

Project MK-Ultra. The Central Intelligence Agency (CIA) conducted mind control experiments called MK-Ultra, beginning during the Cold War in the 1950s and continuing through the 1960s. Participants were exposed to hallucinogenic drugs such as LSD, hypnosis, radiation, toxins, chemicals, electroshock, and lobotomy as part of the CIA's research into behavior modification. While some subjects agreed to participate, many were coerced or did not even know they were involved in an experiment. Subjects included mentally impaired boys, American soldiers, mental hospital patients, and prisoners. Due to the records being destroyed by the CIA in 1973, the government was unable to identify all who participated (Budiansky & Goode, 1994; Nofil, 2019).

Holmesburg Prison Experiments. Beginning in the early 1950s, a researcher from the University of Pennsylvania School of Medicine, Albert Kligman, paid prisoners at Holmesburg Prison a small fee in order to perform a variety of experiments on them. Prisoners were infected with ringworm, herpes, and staphylococcus; were exposed to toxic drugs and chemicals; participated in commercial testing for products such as detergents and dyes; and were used by pharmaceutical companies to test drugs, including tranquilizers and antibiotics. Inmates suffered many side effects including hallucinations, scan lesions, scars, memory loss, and cognitive impairment. Even with ethical codes being established due to the atrocious experiments by the Nazis, these experiments continued until they were finally stopped in the mid-1970s (Hornblum, 1998).

Milgram Obedience Experiments. In an effort to understand why German military personnel followed orders and took part in the horrendous Nazi experiments during World War II, in 1961 Stanley Milgram, a psychologist at Yale University, undertook a series of "obedience" experiments. The Milgram experiments studied how far people would go to obey authority. Study participants were told to shock a "learner" for incorrect answers; however, the study participants did not know the learner was not a real person, but rather a recording. After each shock, the participant was instructed to increase the voltage of the next shock, despite the learner's call for them to stop. If the study participant hesitated, the authority figure prodded the participant to continue with the experiment. Nearly two thirds (65%) of participants obeyed the authority figure to the point of maximum shock. While Milgram debriefed participants after the experiment about the deception and the true purpose of the experiment, these experiments have been highly criticized and are deemed by most to be ethically questionable and by many to be unethical (Miller, Collins, & Brief, 1995).

Tearoom Trade. In 1970, Laud Humphreys conducted a study to understand impersonal sex in public restrooms, called "tearooms." Humphreys, a doctoral student at Washington University in St. Louis, Missouri, documented the encounters through field notes while serving as the lookout, or "watchqueen," during these impersonal sexual encounters (Humphreys, 1975). Subjects did not know Humphreys was a researcher, that he was taking field notes, or that he followed the men to their cars in order to record their license plate numbers. Using public records, he located their home addresses and visited their homes a year later under the guise of a mental health interviewer. Of the 134 men for whom he had located home addresses, 50 agreed to an interview. Humphreys's tactics have received much criticism, regardless of whether some believe his findings to be informative (Nardi, 1995).

Stanford Prison Experiments. In 1971, Philip Zimbardo from Stanford University conducted an experiment to study people's psychological reactions to being held captive. Participants were male college students who volunteered, in exchange for financial compensation, to be in a psychological study simulating a prison. The study was designed to last two weeks, but was terminated after six days due to abusive conditions and psychological distress. While most agree that the experiment violated ethical standards, there is continuing discussion as to why participants who were assigned to be prison guards so quickly took on inhumane, power-hungry behaviors, and why the subjects who were assigned to be prisoners accepted this treatment. Some believe it was due to the power inherent in the simulated situation, while others believe personal disposition was a factor. Regardless, the student volunteers suffered psychologically as a result of their participation in this experiment (Carnahan & McFarland, 2007).

2.2.3 Human Experimentation Today

The experiments described above are certainly not all of the unethical experiments conducted in the United States and beyond over the past century; however, they are some of the most notorious. They shaped a history of ethical violations in research on humans that led to explicit protections of humans and clear guidelines for researchers. These guidelines apply to all researchers, including evaluators. The history of legislation related to human-subject protections and ethical conduct of researchers will be reviewed in Chapter 4.

Even with all that has been done to humans in the name of research, and our ability to retrospectively identify ethical violations, have we really learned? There are always new areas of research that may not be explicitly addressed in current ethical standards, for example, in gene research and modification. As researchers, it is important that we always be reflective and deliberate in our actions. In 2015, the National Institutes of Health (NIH) declared that it would not fund research that employs gene editing of human embryos (NIH, 2015). Three years later, the director of the NIH, Francis Collins, released a statement expressing concern over human-genome editing. A Chinese researcher had just released news that the first gene-edited twin babies had been born in China (NIH, 2018). The NIH reaffirmed its position of not supporting gene editing of human embryos. In 2019, Collins and the NIH called for an international moratorium on human-gene editing and the alteration of DNA before implantation. Other countries have joined this moratorium, but it is not yet a policy supported by all nations (NIH, 2019).

I had the pleasure of hearing Frances Collins speak several months back and was struck by his strong ethical convictions. He clearly supports science and research, but not without a firm grasp of the implications that scientific advances may have on the future. He is not asking researchers to never explore this area, but he is asking researchers worldwide to have a discussion about how laboratory-modified genes might affect humans. Science may allow us to create a genetically modified baby, but that baby will grow up and until we have a clear understanding of how our interfering with the creation of human life might affect that human life (and all human life), we should proceed with measured steps and the utmost caution. Perhaps if some of the earlier researchers had taken a step back before embarking on an experiment, and really weighed the potential intended and unintended consequences, we would not have such a checkered past of ethical shortcomings. We should conduct research, not because we can, but because it is right.

2.3 CURRENT ISSUES IN EVALUATION

There are many relevant and timely issues in evaluation that will be covered throughout the text. In this section, we will discuss the common issues in evaluation and infrastructure supports that address these issues.

2.3.1 Shadish's Common Threads

In his editorial "The Common Threads in Program Evaluation," William Shadish (2006) identified five concerns that appear throughout the program evaluation literature:

Concern 1: How do evaluators construct knowledge about programs?

Concern 2: How do evaluators place value on evaluation results?

Concern 3: How do programs change and how can evaluation be used to influence that change?

Concern 4: How do evaluators use evaluation results to influence policy making?

Concern 5: How can evaluators organize their practice to address concerns 1–4?

These concerns, or "common threads," have arisen from and helped to shape the field of evaluation, and these concerns still permeate every meeting of the American Evaluation Association. Concern 1 speaks to how we conduct evaluation, including what we can and cannot measure and the approaches and designs we use to understand a program's operation and impact. Concern 2 relates to the theoretical frameworks and practical methods that help evaluators make sense of evaluation results and value results such that they can inform recommendations. Concern 3 is one of the primary differences between basic research and program evaluation. Program evaluation is intended for practical use and application such that program activities can be improved. The usefulness and use of evaluation findings are necessary for change to occur. Concern 4 is similar to concern 3, but relates to leveraging evaluation results to influence the policy process. In order to leverage findings, evaluators need to identify facilitators and barriers to use by policy-makers and work to share results in such a way that capitalizes on facilitators, overcomes barriers, and ultimately advances the use of data in the policy-making process. Finally, concern 5 is about organizing our practice as evaluators, to balance the methods used in conducting an evaluation, the way in which results are communicated, how these results are used for program improvement, and the extent to which findings can influence the policy process.

2.3.2 Resource Sharing and Dissemination

The Cochrane Collaboration is an international organization that provides synthesized research evidence around topics in health care. Cochrane was created in 1993 in the United Kingdom as a way to facilitate the sharing and promote the use of evidence-based practices and interventions in health care decision making. Cochrane can be accessed at https://www.cochrane.org/.

The Campbell Collaboration was created in 2000 based on the Cochrane Collaboration model. It is named after Donald Campbell, a psychologist who helped shape the field of scientific inquiry in the social sciences. Just as the Cochrane Collaboration focuses on systematic reviews in the medical and health fields, the Campbell Collaboration focuses on systematic reviews of social and behavioral interventions and programs. The Campbell Collaboration can be accessed at https://campbellcollaboration.org/.

The What Works Clearinghouse (WWC) is a resource provided by the Institute of Education Sciences (IES). It was created in 2002 with the involvement of some of the same researchers who helped to start the Campbell Collaboration. The WWC includes evidence-based practices and programs in many education-related areas, including early-childhood education, literacy, behavior, and mathematics. The clearinghouse creates intervention reports through a rigorous review process based on rating studies according to a set of standards and then summarizes findings for studies that do meet standards. The WWC can be accessed at https://ies.ed.gov/ncee/wwc/. See Figures 2.1 and 2.2 for information on the WWC and how it rates evaluation studies. The WWC provides a resource for evaluators to examine what research has already been done on topics and for practitioners to understand what evidence-based practices and programs exist on a given topic.

FIGURE 2.1 ⬡ What Works Clearinghouse

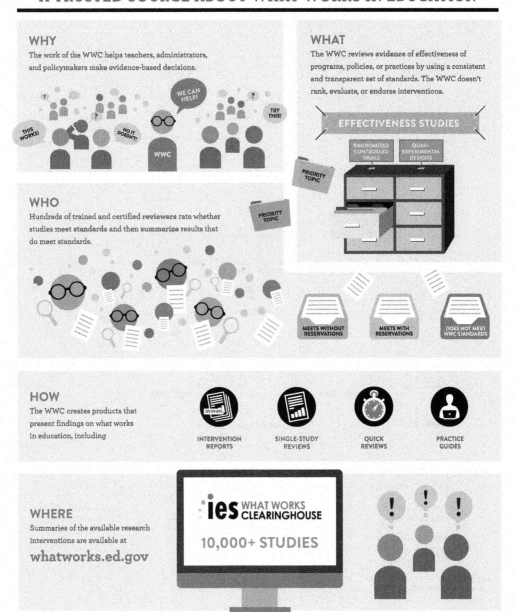

Source: What Works Clearinghouse on IES website at https://ies.ed.gov/blogs/ncee/post/five-reasons-to-visit-the-what-works-clearinghouse

FIGURE 2.2 ● What Works Clearinghouse Rating Process

HOW THE WWC RATES A STUDY

──── RATING GROUP DESIGNS ────

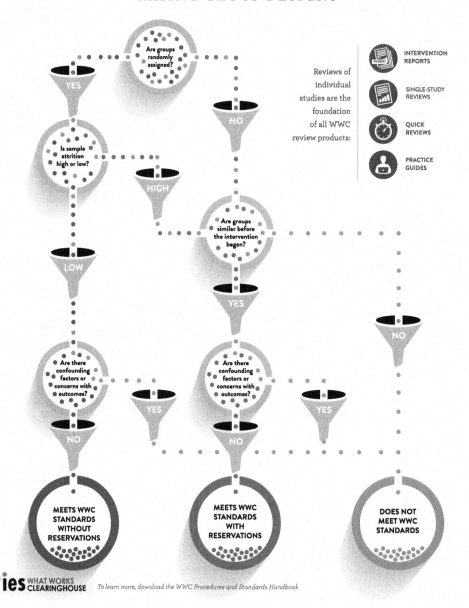

Are groups randomly assigned?

YES

NO

Is sample attrition high or low?

HIGH

Are groups similar before the intervention began?

LOW

YES

NO

Are there confounding factors or concerns with outcomes?

Are there confounding factors or concerns with outcomes?

YES

YES

NO

NO

MEETS WWC STANDARDS WITHOUT RESERVATIONS

MEETS WWC STANDARDS WITH RESERVATIONS

DOES NOT MEET WWC STANDARDS

Reviews of individual studies are the foundation of all WWC review products:

INTERVENTION REPORTS

SINGLE-STUDY REVIEWS

QUICK REVIEWS

PRACTICE GUIDES

ies WHAT WORKS CLEARINGHOUSE   *To learn more, download the WWC Procedures and Standards Handbook*

Sources: What Works Clearinghouse on IES website at https://ies.ed.gov/blogs/ncee/post/five-reasons-to-visit-the-what-works-clearinghouse

QUICK CHECK

1. What experiments are considered the worst ethical violations in human history? Who conducted the experiments? How many people were affected?

2. What do the Tuskegee and Guatemala experiments have in common?

3. In comparing experiments such as the Holmesburg and MK-Ultra to experiments such as the Stanford Prison and Milgram, what are your thoughts on medical harm versus psychological harm?

4. Explain the five concerns of evaluators that Shadish summarized from the evaluation literature.

Finally, the American Evaluation Association provides critical infrastructure and support for the field of evaluation. AEA provides guiding principles for evaluators (see Chapter 4); core competencies for evaluation professionals; content- and methodology-focused topical interest groups as a means for evaluators to share ideas and collaborate; links to resources and evaluator blogs; professional development opportunities, including summer institutes and webinars, for evaluators to learn new skills; evaluator recognition; journals to disseminate best practices and professional advances; discussion forums; and events for evaluators to network, learn, and share, such as the annual meeting. AEA can be accessed at https://www.eval.org/.

2.4 CHAPTER SUMMARY

In this chapter, the history of evaluation was discussed from two perspectives: development of the field of evaluation and development of research ethics that affect how evaluations are conducted. While evaluation as a human activity has been around as long as humans have walked the Earth, evaluation as a method of examining programs is rather new. Two primary events shaped the field of evaluation, namely the launching of Sputnik by the Russians in 1957 and the proliferation of social programs in the 1960s. Sputnik forced the United States to accelerate its space program and reexamine the ways in which scientists are prepared. The American education system, in particular, became a focus for improvement.

Investment in numerous social programs eventually prompted a focus on whether the programs were cost-efficient and cost-effective. Both created a need for evaluators of programs. Individuals from many fields came together to shape the field of evaluation, including psychologists, educators, and sociologists. In the 1970s and 1980s, universities began to offer courses in evaluation and the **American Evaluation Association** was created. AEA is an international professional association of evaluators focused on sharing approaches and methods.

Ethical guidelines in evaluation are based on research ethics. There is a disturbing world history of ethical violations in research. The experiments by Nazi Germany during World War II are perhaps the worst example of humans abusing humans in the name of research, though the United States government has also conducted numerous unethical experiments on humans, including the Tuskegee syphilis experiments and the sponsorship of widespread radiation experiments. There are also numerous examples of unethical treatment of human subjects by American researchers. Two of the best known are the Stanford prison experiments and the Milgram experiments.

Along with the history of evaluation and this history of ethical violations in research, common concerns of evaluators regarding program evaluation are presented, as well as infrastructure supports to address these concerns. Five concerns are explained: (1) the methods evaluators use to conduct evaluations, (2) the way in which results are communicated, (3) how these results are used for program improvement, (4) the extent to which findings can influence the policy process, and (5) how evaluation practice can be organized to address issues of design, reporting, use, and influence. Finally, professional organizations, such as the AEA, and resources, such as the What Works Clearinghouse, are infrastructure supports that can aid evaluators in addressing, discussing, and building knowledge about some of these common concerns.

Reflection and Application

1. In the chapter, the human radiation experiments conducted by the United States were introduced. The U.S. Department of Energy documented at least 425 such experiments, including a study conducted at Vanderbilt University in which over 800 pregnant women were given radioactive iron to test its absorption. A 1995 document by the U.S. Department of Energy summarizes these experiments (https://www.osti.gov/opennet/servlets/purl/16141769/16141769.pdf). Go to this document and choose one experiment; search the internet to see if you can find additional information on this experiment.

   a. What was the purpose of the experiment?

   b. When was it conducted?

   c. Who participated in the experiment?

   d. Did the subjects know they were participants in a study?

   e. Was there any resolution, settlement, or apology as a result of the experiment?

2. Go to the What Works Clearinghouse (https://ies.ed.gov/ncee/wwc/). Choose a topic and explore the research on this topic. How can evaluators use the WWC to address some of the concerns presented by Shadish in his "common threads" editorial?

EVALUATION ETHICS

Irrespective of whether we are believers or agnostics, whether we believe in God or karma, moral ethics is a code which everyone is able to pursue.

—Dalai Lama

Upon completion of this chapter, you should be able to

- Explain the interconnected relationship between research ethics and evaluation ethics.
- Describe the timeline and content of research legislation nationally and internationally.
- Identify the ethical responsibilities of an evaluator.
- Explain the interface between the ethical responsibilities of the agency/organization and the ethical responsibilities of the evaluator.
- Distinguish between ethical and unethical behavior.

3.1 ETHICS DEFINED

Merriam-Webster online defines **ethics** as "the discipline dealing with what is good and bad; a set of moral issues or aspects." Ethics are moral obligations that guide us in determining whether a certain behavior is right or wrong. The 20th and 21st centuries have seen breakthroughs in the understanding and regulation of research ethics. Because evaluation is a form of research, the ethical responsibilities of researchers extend to the field of evaluation. The principles guiding evaluation ethics were introduced in Chapter 1 and will be further explored in this chapter. And while Chapter 2 introduced ethics by providing the history of abuse, this chapter will explain the ethical standards that guide

> **Ethics:** moral obligations guiding the determination of behavior as right or wrong.

the profession of evaluation as well as the legislative mandates that affect evaluation. For the purposes of this chapter, the words "evaluation," "study," and "experiment" will be used interchangeably throughout the discussion of research ethics, regulations, and participant protections.

Ethical behavior in the context of program evaluation is complex, perhaps more complex than in other types of research. Research in general is deeply systematic with protocol structures that reflect the consistency and accuracy the investigator believes will yield the highest quality of knowledge. By envisioning and enacting an experiment with clear procedures, meticulous data collection, and rigorous analysis, researchers seek to create the greatest possible contribution to their field. Researchers, in general, hope to favorably alter outcomes for health and well-being, the environment, or commerce. Similarly, evaluators, by designing and implementing a thorough and sound evaluation, seek to generate findings that will contribute to decisions regarding program improvement and accountability.

While evaluation includes all the complexities of research, evaluators also have to be cognizant of the intricacies inherent in real-world settings where programs operate and policies function. The ethics of evaluation reflect the complexities of a scientific approach to understanding the efforts related to programs, policies, and processes designed to make life better for participants and populations. Such efforts are continually changing as they are affected by context, content, communities, and funding as they are being delivered, received, and measured. Recognizing and operating within this real-world context requires nimble response and balance. In keeping with the real world of evaluation design and implementation, ethical considerations are a constant companion—requiring preparation, vigilance, and prompt response to challenges and changes. This chapter will address ethics from two perspectives: the greater field of research ethics and the more focused domain of ethics as it relates to the evaluation profession, particularly with regard to values and cultural competence.

3.2 RESEARCH ETHICS GUIDELINES AND LEGISLATION

Research ethics are the foundation of evaluation ethics. The previous chapter began the conversation of research ethics, making clear the case for regulation of the research fields. This section starts with a condensed history of important events impacting research ethics in the 20th century through to the 21st.

3.2.1 Nuremberg Code

In response to the atrocities committed by German physicians during World War II, criminal proceedings were brought against those who conducted the Nazi experiments on concentration camp prisoners. The initial trials were held from November 1945 to

October 1946 and sentences were determined using a tribunal of judges from multiple countries. Additional trials were held between 1946 and 1949 by U.S. military tribunal (History.com Editors, 2018). The Nazi defendants argued that the experiments conducted in the concentration camps were no different from experiments conducted before the war and, further, that there was no international code or law to guide what was considered legal research on humans (United States Holocaust Memorial Museum, 2019). In 1947, as a result of the Nuremberg trials, a document delineating 10 points to guide experiments involving humans was drafted. These 10 points are referred to as the Nuremberg Code (as cited by the Office of Human Research Protections [OHRP], 2019b). There is some debate as to the author of the Nuremberg Code. Some claim it was an American doctor, Andrew Ivy, who served as an adviser to the Nuremberg tribunal and some believe it was an English physician, Maurice Pappworth, who was in communication with Ivy. Others claim it was an Austrian American tribunal judge, Leo Alexandar (Gaw, 2014). Regardless, while the code (see Figure 3.1) provided guidance to researchers,

---

FIGURE 3.1 ● Nuremberg Code (as cited by OHRP, 2019b)

1. The voluntary consent of the human subject is absolutely essential.

2. The experiment should be such as to yield fruitful results for the good of society, unprocurable by other methods or means of study, and not random and unnecessary in nature.

3. The experiment should be so designed and based on the results of animal experimentation and a knowledge of the natural history of the disease or other problem under study that the anticipated results will justify the performance of the experiment.

4. The experiment should be so conducted as to avoid all unnecessary physical and mental suffering and injury.

5. No experiment should be conducted where there is an a priori reason to believe that death or disabling injury will occur; except, perhaps, in those experiments where the experimental physicians also serve as subjects.

6. The degree of risk to be taken should never exceed that determined by the humanitarian importance of the problem to be solved by the experiment.

7. Proper preparations should be made and adequate facilities provided to protect the experimental subject against even remote possibilities of injury, disability, or death.

8. The experiment should be conducted only by scientifically qualified persons. The highest degree of skill and care should be required through all stages of the experiment of those who conduct or engage in the experiment.

9. During the course of the experiment the human subject should be at liberty to bring the experiment to an end if he has reached the physical or mental state where continuation of the experiment seems to him to be impossible.

10. During the course of the experiment the scientist in charge must be prepared to terminate the experiment at any stage, if he has probable cause to believe, in the exercise of the good faith, superior skill and careful judgment required of him that a continuation of the experiment is likely to result in injury, disability, or death to the experimental subject.

it had no legality and could not be enforced (Mandal, Acharya, & Parija, 2011). It did, however, lay the foundation for the ethical guidelines we have today (Fischer, 2006).

3.2.2 Declaration of Helsinki

The newly established World Medical Association (WMA) began deliberating the role of ethics in research around the same time the Nuremberg Code was written. However, due to debate over how restricting ethical principles should be in the research field, reaching a consensus around a set of shared ethical principles was difficult (Wiesing, 2014). Finally, about 15 years after the Nuremberg Code was released, in June 1964, the Declaration of Helsinki was adopted by the 18th World Medical Association General Assembly, in Helsinki, Finland. The declaration is intended to be a living document that is revised as the field of research evolves (Carlson, Boyd, & Webb, 2004). The first revision was in Tokyo, Japan, in 1975; subsequent revisions were made in Venice, Italy, in 1983; Hong Kong in 1989; Somerset West, Republic of South Africa, in 1996; Edinburgh, Scotland, in 2000; Washington, D.C., in 2002; Tokyo again in 2004; and Seoul, Republic of Korea, in 2008. The declaration was most recently updated during the 64th WMA General Assembly, in Fortaleza, Brazil, in October 2013 (WMA, 2013).

Like the Nuremberg Code, the Declaration of Helsinki includes guidelines for research involving human subjects. A human subject is a living individual who participates in a research study; this participation may be directly through intervention or interaction, or by the researcher having access to private data that would allow identification of the individual. While the declaration specifically refers to the responsibilities of physicians, the intent is that this same responsibility extends to any researcher who participates in human subjects research. Thus, the ethical principles outlined in the Declaration of Helsinki apply to all research involving human beings—not just biomedical research that may happen in a laboratory at a bench—but also social research, psychological research, health research, and educational research, as well as evaluation across all these fields.

Human subject: a living individual who participates in a research study; this participation may be directly through intervention or interaction, or by the researcher having access to private data that would allow identification of the individual.

The declaration includes 13 general ethical principles, as well as specific principles related to risks and benefits to research participants, guidelines for research with vulnerable groups and individuals, scientific requirements and research protocols, research ethics committees, privacy and confidentiality, informed consent, use of placebos, posttrial provisions, research registration and dissemination of results, and unproven interventions in clinical practice. In total, the Declaration of Helsinki includes 37 principles to guide research involving human subjects (WMA, 2013).

3.2.3 National Research Act

Even after the Declaration of Helsinki, violations of the ethical principles of human subjects research occurred within and outside of the United States. One of the most well-known examples of research misconduct occurred with the Tuskegee syphilis study.

Researchers from the U.S. Public Health Service started the Tuskegee syphilis experiments in Alabama in 1932, in collaboration with the Tuskegee Institute. The purpose of the study was to understand the progression of syphilis to help develop treatments. Over 600 black men took part in the study over a 40-year period from 1932 to 1972. More than half of the men had syphilis, while the others did not. Participants were not informed that the study was about syphilis, but rather the men were led to believe they were being treated for "bad blood." At the time, "bad blood" was understood to include several ailments, including syphilis but also anemia and fatigue. While the study was initially scheduled for 6 months, it continued for decades (Centers for Disease Control and Prevention, 2015b).

Thirteen years into the study, in 1945, a treatment for syphilis became available. However, study participants who had syphilis were not told of or offered the treatment, as doctors continued to study the progression of their disease. Even when concerns were raised by a study participant in 1969, the U.S. Centers for Disease Control (CDC) and the America Medical Association (AMA) affirmed the need for the study. Finally, in 1972, after a news article was published about the experiment, an advisory panel recommended an immediate stop to the study. Multiple lawsuits and settlements have occurred as a result of the Tuskegee syphilis study (CDC, 2015a).

The National Research Act was passed in 1974, mainly in reaction to the ethics violations of the Tuskegee experiments. The act created the National Commission for the Protection of Human Subjects of Biomedical and Behavioral Research. The commission, in turn, set guidelines for human subjects research, including the requirement of voluntary informed consent of any research participant (Research and Economic Development, 2019). Informed consent is an individual's voluntary agreement to participate in a study, only after being provided with and understanding information about the study, including the research purpose and research risks.

In an effort to enforce this requirement, the National Research Act also requires research on human subjects to be reviewed by an **Institutional Review Board (IRB)**. An IRB is a committee that is charged with protecting human subjects in research; IRBs review all proposals prior to research being conducted to ensure adequate protections and safeguards are in place.

3.2.4 Belmont Report

The commission established under the National Research Act drafted the seminal document guiding human subjects research to this day. This document was released in 1979 and is formally titled *Ethical Principles and Guidelines for the Protection of Human Subjects of Research* (National Commission for the Protection of Human Subjects of Biomedical and Behavioral Research, 1979). However, the guide is commonly referred to as the Belmont Report, named after the Belmont Conference Center in Maryland, where the commission meetings took place.

Informed consent: an individual's voluntary agreement to participate in a study after being provided with and understanding information about the study, including the research purpose and research risks.

Institutional Review Board (IRB): a committee that is charged with protecting human subjects in research. IRBs review all research prior to the research being conducted to ensure adequate protections and safeguards are in place.

The Belmont Report outlines the ethical principles for conducting research with human subjects: Respect for Persons, Beneficence, and Justice. It also gives guidance for researchers regarding informed consent, assessment of risk and benefits, and selection of subjects. Figure 3.2 provides selected text describing each principle from the Belmont Report.

The first principle, respect for persons, requires researchers to treat research participants as individuals entitled to and capable of making their own decision regarding participation. The principle addresses informed consent, in that research participants are entitled to the information necessary to make an informed, voluntary decision about participating in research. Further, it states that if a person is unable to make autonomous decisions, researchers are charged with enacting additional procedures to ensure populations that are vulnerable, such as children and prisoners, are adequately protected in research.

FIGURE 3.2 ● Belmont Report (selected text)

1. **Respect for Persons**: Respect for persons incorporates at least two ethical convictions: first, that individuals should be treated as autonomous agents, and second, that persons with diminished autonomy are entitled to protection. The principle of respect for persons thus divides into two separate moral requirements: the requirement to acknowledge autonomy and the requirement to protect those with diminished autonomy.

2. **Beneficence**: Persons are treated in an ethical manner not only by respecting their decisions and protecting them from harm, but also by making efforts to secure their well-being. Such treatment falls under the principle of beneficence. The term "beneficence" is often understood to cover acts of kindness or charity that go beyond strict obligation. In this document, beneficence is understood in a stronger sense, as an obligation. Two general rules have been formulated as complementary expressions of beneficent actions in this sense: (a) do not harm and (b) maximize possible benefits and minimize possible harms.

3. **Justice**: Who ought to receive the benefits of research and bear its burdens? This is a question of justice, in the sense of "fairness in distribution" or "what is deserved." An injustice occurs when some benefit to which a person is entitled is denied without good reason or when some burden is imposed unduly. Another way of conceiving the principle of justice is that equals ought to be treated equally. However, this statement requires explication. Who is equal and who is unequal? What considerations justify departure from equal distribution? Almost all commentators allow that distinctions based on experience, age, deprivation, competence, merit and position do sometimes constitute criteria justifying differential treatment for certain purposes. It is necessary, then, to explain in what respects people should be treated equally. There are several widely accepted formulations of just ways to distribute burdens and benefits. Each formulation mentions some relevant property on the basis of which burdens and benefits should be distributed. These formulations are (a) to each person an equal share, (b) to each person according to individual need, (c) to each person according to individual effort, (d) to each person according to societal contribution, and (e) to each person according to merit.

Source: National Commission for the Protection of Human Subjects of Biomedical and Behavioral Research (1979).

The second principle, beneficence, includes two distinct rules: do no harm and weigh benefits against risks. Research should maximize the potential benefits to participants, while minimizing potential harm. In addition, research should not be undertaken at the detriment to some for the benefit of others.

Lastly, the third principle, justice, further instructs researchers to treat all individuals fairly and equally. Research should not be undertaken on vulnerable populations because they are convenient or because the researcher has easy access. Likewise, research should strive to involve participant groups who are likely to benefit from the findings, rather than focusing on groups unlikely to benefit.

Three additional areas are addressed in the Belmont Report: informed consent, assessment of risks and benefits, and selection of subjects. These are applications of the three principles. For instance, respect for persons requires informed consent. Consent should focus on providing adequate information, ensuring comprehension of that information, and voluntary participation. Beneficence is based upon an assessment of research risks and benefits. The nature and scope of risks and benefits should be considered, along with a systematic assessment of risks and benefits. Finally, justice relates to the selection of subjects for research. Selection of subjects should be fair, as should the distribution of outcomes of the research. Institutionalized, marginalized, and diminished populations are especially vulnerable and research with these populations must adequately substantiate how it is fair to include the population in the research and how research outcomes will benefit the population.

3.2.5 Common Rule

The Belmont Report is the cornerstone of the federal policy for the Protection of Human Subjects (2018), referred to as the Common Rule. The Common Rule was first published in 1991 and, similar to the Declaration of Helsinki, has been updated as the field of research progresses. The Revised Common Rule became effective in 2018. The 2018 revision includes changes to reduce the burden on researchers, including a new categorization that excludes some projects from IRB review, a change in the continuing review process to alleviate recurring reviews for some research, and a simplification of the consent process aimed at making consent forms more readable and less cumbersome for participants. An additional recommendation that was not implemented with the 2018 revisions, but may be implemented in coming years, is the creation of a single IRB (sIRB) process governing cooperative research across organizations (Gearhart, 2018; National Institutes of Health, 2019; OHRP, 2019d).

Regulations set forth in the Common Rule must be followed by any organization receiving federal funds for human subjects research. Such organizations are required to file an assurance with the Office of Human Research Protections, formalizing their commitment

Federalwide Assurance (FWA): an agreement between the government and an organization stating that it will comply with the Common Rule; includes designation of an Institutional Review Board (IRB) to review all research to ensure adequate protection for human subjects.

Minimal risk: a criterion for human subjects research that involves the determination as to whether the research involves more risk to an individual than would be encountered in everyday life.

Exempt: human subjects research that falls under one of eight exempt categories and is determined to pose no more than minimal risk; exempt from IRB review.

Expedited review: human subjects research that is reviewed by a member of the IRB and determined to fall under one of nine categories.

Full review: human subjects research that does not fall under one of the eight exempt or nine expedited categories and thus is reviewed by the full IRB.

to follow the guidelines of the Common Rule. The Federalwide Assurance (FWA) states that the organization will comply with human subjects research regulations. Part of this compliance is designating an Institutional Review Board (IRB) to review all research to ensure adequate protection for human subjects (OHRP, 2019a). Violation of the FWA can jeopardize the organization's ability to pursue and conduct research with federal funding.

An important component of the federal rule is the concept of **minimal risk**. Minimal risk is a criterion for human subjects research that involves the determination as to whether the research involves more risk to an individual than would be encountered in everyday life. An organization's IRB determines the type of review necessary for the research based on the minimal risk criteria.

When a study is submitted for IRB review, the first decision is whether it is indeed human subjects research. Human subjects research involves systematic investigation intended to contribute to the greater knowledge-based research that involves collecting and/or accessing identifiable data from living subjects (human subjects). If the study does not meet these criteria, it is categorized as nonhuman subjects research. In this case, researchers are still obligated to follow ethical guidelines, but do not have to submit protocol changes to the IRB (unless those modifications might change whether the study is indeed human subjects research). On the other hand, if the study is determined to be human subjects research, it will fall under one of three review types: exempt, expedited, or full review.

The first review type is "exempt." Exempt studies are considered human subjects research, but do not need to follow all Common Rule procedures. A research study can be **exempt** from the Common Rule regulations if it falls into one of eight categories. Often, program evaluation falls into one of the exempt categories. For example, if the research is a study of normal educational practices (category 1); data collected from interviews or observations of public behavior (category 2); research involving benign behavioral interventions (category 3); or data collected for evaluation or improvement of public service programs (category 5), it may be considered exempt (Protection of Human Subjects, 2018).

Research that is not exempt from federal human subjects regulations will undergo either an **expedited review** or **full review** by the IRB. Expedited reviews are conducted by one member of the IRB, rather than the full IRB. Expedited reviews fall into one of nine categories; the two categories that are most relevant to evaluators are the collection of data from recordings for research purposes (category 6) and research on individual or group behavior and research using surveys, interviews, focus groups, or program evaluation (category 7). Many evaluations that are not considered exempt qualify for expedited review under category 6 or 7. If the study is not considered exempt and does not qualify for an expedited review, it must be reviewed by the full IRB (OHRP, 2019c). Table 3.1 includes a list of the major ethics documents and legislation as well as a link to the full text.

TABLE 3.1 ● Links to Ethics Documents		
Document	**Year**	**Web Link**
Nuremberg Code	1947	https://history.nih.gov/research/downloads/nuremberg.pdf
Declaration of Helsinki	1964 (last revised 2013)	https://www.wma.net/wp-content/uploads/2016/11/DoH-Oct2013-JAMA.pdf (2013 revision)
National Research Act	1974	https://history.nih.gov/research/downloads/PL93-348.pdf
Belmont Report	1979	https://www.hhs.gov/ohrp/sites/default/files/the-belmont-report-508c_FINAL.pdf
Federal Policy for the Protection of Human Subjects/Common Rule	1991 (last revised 2018)	https://www.hhs.gov/ohrp/regulations-and-policy/regulations/common-rule/index.html (2018 revision)

 QUICK CHECK

1. What international documents laid the foundation for ethics legislation in the United States?
2. What are the three ethical principles outlined in the Belmont Report? How do you think these ethical principles relate to evaluations?
3. What is the Common Rule? How does the establishment of IRBs relate to the Common Rule?
4. What different ways might research be categorized by an IRB?

3.3 IRB PROTOCOLS AND AMENDMENTS

Planning and designing a research study can seem daunting enough, but add to that the responsibility to submit the study through an IRB prior to conducting any research, and the process may become overwhelming. My graduate students often fret the most over IRB requirements, even though I tell them it is not that difficult (while reminding them that they have no choice). Our most important responsibility as evaluators is to do no harm, and submitting our studies through the IRB ensures that we have adequate human protections.

IRBs require that researchers complete training prior to engaging in research. Many organizations provide in-person IRB training for researchers. There are also individual online training programs that detail the responsibilities of the researcher. The Collaborative Institutional Training Initiative (CITI) is one such program. CITI has modules in human subjects protections and the responsible conduct of research. Upon completion of the online CITI modules, the researcher is provided with a certificate that is valid for three years. Note that some funding organizations have additional training requirements beyond the basic IRB human subjects protections module; it is important to check the educational requirements that are particular to a research funder.

The first task I give any undergraduate, graduate, or researcher who works with me is to complete IRB training. I also have the students in my evaluation course complete IRB training as part of the course requirements—perhaps you have the same requirement as part of your evaluation course! Before engaging in research, check with your institution to see if it offers IRB training. Larger organizations might contract with an online training program.

Once training is complete, you are ready to start working on your IRB submission. The heart of the submission is the **IRB protocol**. The IRB protocol is a document that details the purpose and design of your research study. It includes the participants and how they were selected, what information will be collected from them and how it will be collected, how the data will be used, and how the data will be stored. Your organization will likely have a template with the required information that you complete and submit to your IRB. Accompanying the IRB protocol should be any consent forms, communication with participants, and data collection instruments.

IRB protocol: a document that details the purpose and design of your research study; the protocol is submitted to the IRB along with any consent forms, communication with participants, and data collection instruments.

Once your protocol is submitted to the IRB, you wait. Depending upon the IRB and the number of submissions in the queue ahead of you, approval might take days, weeks, or months. Your organization will likely be able to give you an estimate of what to expect. However, because there is always some wait, it is good to submit your protocol well in advance of when you hope to start your study. You cannot enroll participants in your study or collect any data until you have IRB approval. Often, the IRB will come back to you with questions and ask for revisions; if this should happen, do not be alarmed, simply revise the documents and resubmit. Typically, you will not lose your spot in the queue. Once again, I would like to emphasize, you wait. Waiting is difficult and it may take longer than you expect, but the consequences of not waiting can be dire for you and your organization. See "In the Real World" for more information on what might happen if you do not wait for IRB approval before beginning your study.

Amendment: a document that details proposed changes to your current research protocol; the amendment should include any accompanying documents, just like the initial protocol.

Once you have the approval and your study is underway, you might decide to conduct an additional survey, enroll more participants, add additional data collection, or expand to another site. If this is the case, you can create an amendment to your protocol. An **amendment** is an additional document detailing the proposed changes to your protocol. As with your initial protocol, the amendment should include any accompanying data collection instruments, consents, or other documentation. Also, you *must* wait for approval of the amendment before putting any of the proposed changes into place.

IN THE REAL WORLD . . .

Years back, when I was a relatively new evaluator, a doctoral student in my department had finished all his coursework, passed his comprehensive exams, completed IRB training, defended his dissertation proposal, and was anxious to finish his dissertation and graduate. The student had been in graduate school for five years and was ready to move to the next stage in his life.

In collaboration with his adviser, he completed all of the required paperwork for the IRB and submitted the protocol along with a survey that would be administered to all students in a local school district. Because he already had the finalized version of the survey and was anxious to collect data, he sent the survey to the school district. They distributed the surveys to teachers for their students to complete.

The parent of one of the students saw the survey and was curious about it. They were not concerned and had no problems with the survey, but rather they were excited about it and wanted to learn more. They called the university to get more information. Because the protocol had not yet been approved by the IRB, information about the study and the accompanying survey were not in the Research Office files. This alerted the Research Office to a survey administration that had not been approved. After looking into the matter, the Research Office found that the protocol had been submitted to the IRB and was in the queue to be reviewed, but had not yet been reviewed and thus had not yet been approved. This constituted a breach in the ethical obligations of the researcher and a violation of the agreement the university had made with the federal Office of Human Research Protections.

Because no data had been returned, the university was able to stop the study, avoiding serious repercussions. The doctoral student was dismissed from the program. I remember seeing him one day and he was gone the next. I often wonder what happened to him. I imagine the experience was devastating, especially after years of education and then not being able to finish your degree, not to mention the embarrassment of such a serious infraction. The disturbing irony of the situation is that the survey would have been approved within a matter of weeks.

This is a cautionary but true story. As anxious as you may be to begin a study, wait to get the proper approvals. Proceeding without approval can have serious, and long-lasting, consequences to you as a researcher and to your organization.

3.4 ETHICAL RESPONSIBILITIES OF ORGANIZATIONS

Because of the history of abuse in research involving human subjects, individuals and organizations that engage in human subjects research have an ethical responsibility and are legally required (by federal law 45 C.F.R. Part 46) to submit all research involving humans through an IRB. Organizations must have procedures in place to follow federal law and individuals must adhere to those procedures prior to conducting any research involving humans.

Organizations have an ethical responsibility to understand and follow the regulations set forth under the Federal Policy for the Protection of Human Subjects. Large organizations, including universities, typically operate their own IRB, under their FWA (Federalwide Assurance). Smaller research organizations that do not have the capacity to have their own IRB can join an independent IRB. Independent IRBs can be accredited by the Association for the Accreditation of Human Research Protection Programs (AAHRPP). On the AAHRPP website, individuals or organizations can search for accredited IRBs by city and state. Independent IRBs can also register with the Office for Human Research Protections (OHRP).

Many organizations have management systems that facilitate the tracking and review of research. The university where I work uses a web-based system called IRBNet; however, there are many other systems, including eProtocol, Mentor IRB, IRBManager, IRBco, and so on. IRB management systems facilitate the submission of new studies, locating and completing of forms, creating amendments to studies, and collaborating with other researchers on studies.

In all, the primary ethical responsibilities of an organization are to create the infrastructure and provide the tools for researchers to comply with human subjects regulations. This includes facilitating training on the conduct of research with human subjects, assisting researchers with understanding the ethical obligations of research, creating systems to manage IRB protocols and study amendments, monitoring compliance, and reporting any unanticipated problems or adverse events.

3.5 ETHICAL RESPONSIBILITIES OF EVALUATORS

Albert Schweitzer, winner of the Nobel Peace Prize in 1952, said "the first step in the evolution of ethics is a sense of solidarity with other human beings." As evaluators, we have a responsibility to know and abide by the regulations required of research with human subjects. However, we also have a responsibility to our fellow humans in that we view all individuals as people first, and research participants second. The discipline of evaluation also has its own set of guiding principles that align well with Albert Schweitzer's sentiment. As such, evaluators have an ongoing responsibility to follow the ethical guidelines in their field, especially as they relate to values and cultural competence.

3.5.1 AEA Guiding Principles for Evaluators

As introduced in Chapter 1 and explained more thoroughly in Chapter 2, the primary professional association for the discipline of evaluation is the American Evaluation Association (AEA). AEA serves evaluators in the United States and internationally. In addition to linking evaluators with resources and facilitating collaborations, AEA provides a set of guiding principles for evaluators. The **AEA Guiding Principles for Evaluators** (AEA, 2018b) were last updated in 2018 and are intended to encourage evaluators to consider the deeper ethical concerns present in evaluation. AEA challenges evaluators to consider what is right and just in their pursuit of pragmatic knowledge about the usefulness, effectiveness, and impact of a program or policy. The principles are systematic inquiry, competence, integrity, respect for people, and common good and equity (AEA, 2018b). Each principle is summarized below; a complete description of the principles, as well as definitions of key terms, can be found at the end of Chapter 1.

3.5.1.1 Systematic Inquiry

The principle of *systematic inquiry* charges evaluators to conduct systematic, well-planned evaluations that are data-based, comprehensive, and relevant to the context in which the program is implemented. The AEA lays out six components to address this principle, summarized as follows.

Evaluators should

1. Adhere to the highest technical standards.

2. Include stakeholders in determining evaluation questions and methods.

3. Report their methods with enough detail such that others can critique their work.

4. Clearly delineate the limitations of the study and its findings.

5. Disclose the assumptions and theories that affect their interpretation of findings.

6. Consider the ethical implications of using new technologies in their evaluations.

3.5.1.2 Competence

The principle of *competence* requires evaluators to be capable and skilled in the services that they provide. The AEA lays out four components to address this principle, summarized as follows.

Evaluators should

1. Have the relevant education and skills necessary to conduct evaluation.

2. Disclose any areas where competencies are weak and make efforts to remediate.

3. Pursue the necessary skills and knowledge for the cultural context of the evaluation.

4. Stay current in their field through regular education and training.

3.5.1.3 Integrity

The principle of *integrity* requires evaluators to conduct their work with honesty and transparency. The AEA lays out seven components to address this principle, summarized as follows.

Evaluators should

1. Be honest and open with clients about the evaluation and its limitations.

2. Disclose any conflicts of interest before conducting an evaluation.

3. Communicate in a timely manner any changes to the evaluation plan.

4. Work with stakeholders to clarify expectations regarding the evaluation process and outcomes.

5. Accurately and honestly report evaluation processes and findings.

6. Address evaluation concerns openly and decline the evaluation if necessary.

7. Report all funding sources and the client who requested the evaluation.

3.5.1.4 Respect for People

The principle of *respect for people* requires evaluators to value and honor the dignity of persons and populations involved in the evaluation and to take into account the cultural context when conducting evaluations. The AEA lays out four components to address this principle, summarized as follows.

Evaluators should

1. Adhere to the ethical standard of respect for persons, by working to understand and respect the opinions and perspectives of all stakeholder groups.

2. Adhere to the ethical standard of beneficence, including informed consent, confidentiality, and do no harm.

3. Adhere to the ethical standard of beneficence by minimizing risks and maximizing benefits.

4. Adhere to the ethical standard of justice by ensuring voluntary and fair participation.

3.5.1.5 Common Good and Equity

The principle of *common good and equity* requires evaluators to make concerted efforts to make contributions to the good of all and the advancement of a society that is equitable, fair, and just. The AEA lays out five components to address this principle, summarized as follows.

Evaluators should

1. Balance stakeholder interests, the common good, and the integrity of the evaluation.

2. Work to address potential negative impacts of the evaluation on the common good.

3. Work to address potential risks of the evaluation perpetuating historic inequities.

4. Balance transparency and dissemination with confidentiality and respect for people.

5. Work to minimize bias and possible power imbalances resulting from the context within which the evaluation is conducted.

3.5.2 AEA Evaluator Competencies

In addition to the Guiding Principles for Evaluators that address ethical conduct in evaluation, the American Evaluation Association has developed a set of evaluator competencies. The intention of outlining evaluator competencies is to clarify the expectations of evaluators and the essential aspects of professional practice. To date, evaluators have no common certification or credentialing, and in the absence of accepted qualifications, the field has struggled with what it means to be an evaluator. Medical doctors require board certification to practice, accountants test to become CPAs, teachers take the PRAXIS exam to achieve certification, and engineers can seek a Professional Engineering license. Yet evaluators simply call themselves evaluators. In an effort to define what makes an individual an evaluator, AEA has identified five core competencies. The **AEA Evaluator Competencies** (AEA, 2018a) define the expectations of a competent evaluator across five domains: professional practice, methodology, context, planning and management, and interpersonal skills.

The *professional practice* domain describes a competent evaluator as one who is knowledgeable of and uses the Guiding Principles for Evaluators, the Program Evaluation Standards, and the AEA Statement on Cultural Competence. Note that AEA's Statement of Cultural Competence is described in the next section.

The *methodology* domain outlines that a competent evaluator uses systematic inquiry, adopts appropriate evaluation designs, and produces credible evaluations. Competent evaluators are also described as those who involve stakeholders in all aspects of evaluations, as appropriate, as well as who use program logic and theory-based approaches, if applicable. Further, competent evaluators do not merely present evaluation findings, but interpret those findings within the context of the program.

The *context* domain explains that a competent evaluator is one who takes the time to understand the context of the program, including the environment, stakeholders, culture,

AEA Evaluator Competencies: a set of competencies across five domains that define the expectations of a competent evaluator; domains are

- professional practice,
- methodology,
- context,
- planning and management, and
- interpersonal skills.

values, and history. Competent evaluators also engage multiple stakeholder groups in the evaluation and promote evaluation use within the context of the program.

The *planning and management* domain addresses the necessity that evaluators tend to the managerial aspects of evaluation. That is, competent evaluators plan appropriately, safeguard data, supervise evaluation processes, monitor progress, and are mindful of resources and timelines.

Finally, the interpersonal domain speaks to the importance of *interpersonal skills*, including oral and written communication and cultural competence. A competent evaluator builds positive relationships for stakeholders, policymakers, and practitioners and works to build trust with stakeholders and incorporate multiple perspectives into the evaluation.

The AEA Evaluator Competencies document is reproduced in Figure 3.3, with permission from the AEA, at the end of this chapter.

3.5.3 AEA Cultural Competence Statement

The **AEA Statement on Cultural Competence in Evaluation** (AEA, 2011) is intended to clarify AEA's expectations for evaluators in the area of cultural competence. Cultural competence is an awareness and understanding of the needs of stakeholders. It is also the ongoing development of a set of skills that enable evaluators to effectively communicate with stakeholders from different cultural groups. Cultural competency includes awareness, attitude, knowledge, and skills. It is also a value-laden construct and one that AEA has purposefully chosen as being critical to evaluation. In fact, AEA states that being culturally competent is an ethical obligation of an evaluator. Remember our discussion of values in Chapter 1? People from different cultures have different values and it is imperative that evaluators conduct evaluations that are respectful and of value to program stakeholders. As such, it should be a conscious effort of evaluators to understand stakeholder values, in order to be fair and equitable. The AEA Statement on Cultural Competence identifies four essential practices for culturally competent evaluators:

- Acknowledge the complexity of cultural identity.
- Recognize the dynamics of power.
- Recognize and eliminate bias in language.
- Employ culturally appropriate methods.

The full AEA Statement on Cultural Competence, including an explanation of why cultural competence is important in evaluation and a detailed description of the essential practices for cultural competences, can be found on AEA's website at https://www.eval.org/d/do/154.

AEA Statement on Cultural Competence in Evaluation: a set of four essential practices to guide evaluators in being culturally competent:

- Acknowledge the complexity of cultural identity.
- Recognize the dynamics of power.
- Recognize and eliminate bias in language.
- Employ culturally appropriate methods.

3.5.4 Values and Ethics

Individuals from different cultures have different values, and those values influence communication, decision making, and relationships. Evaluators have values and stakeholders have values, and these values may be in conflict. In fact, the value systems of multiple stakeholders within the same program will likely differ. However, like unconscious biases we may have, it is important to understand and recognize values in order to address them appropriately. Is it ethical to impose our values in the evaluation of a program? Is it even possible to set aside values when conducting an evaluation? Or are values so ingrained in all that we do that it is nearly impossible to deviate from them? Likewise, is ignoring or overlooking the values of stakeholders ethical? To what extent should an evaluator be expected to understand and adapt to stakeholder values and culture? In the same vein, to what extent should stakeholders be expected to cooperate in an evaluation that does not acknowledge and respect value differences? AEA, the most prominent professional organization for evaluators, promotes and fosters attention to values and believes that incorporating cultural competencies into an evaluation is indeed an ethical obligation of evaluators. If you are wondering how you might do this, return to the previous section and read the guiding documents that AEA provides for evaluators.

In an evaluation of a program focusing on increasing the rates of early screening for developmental delays among low-income families in urban areas, we were fortunate to have the opportunity to discuss the checklists being used with participants. It surprised us to find that some of the questions on the checklist were confusing and a little off-putting. It surprised us because this checklist had been used nationally for screening children. However, it had never been used with low-income families in urban areas. Two particular questions that stood out asked parents if their child had mastered the skills of riding a tricycle or using safety scissors. Families told us that even if they could afford a tricycle, they would not let their child ride one in the city. As for safety scissors, some of the parents felt this was an oxymoron. They informed us that scissors were not safe for children under 3, so why would we even imply that they were safe. The safety scissors question referred to the child-sized, dulled scissors sold at office stores, though some parents were not aware of such scissors. In both cases, the child had not yet met the milestone, but it was because they had not had nor would they have the opportunity to meet the milestone. We were able to give feedback to the creators of the survey in hopes that it would be modified for the future. Sometimes we simply do not know what we do not know. However, we can also strive to learn more and use that information to improve our evaluations. I do not believe having unfamiliar questions on a survey is unethical, but I would say it is unethical to not act upon information received, especially when it affects the quality and validity of data.

Many years ago, I was asked to conduct an evaluation focused on understanding the conflict between administrators at a school and a large group of students for whom English was their second language. We decided to conduct focus groups with the students because we believed they would be more comfortable speaking alongside their peers. Instead of my conducting the focus group and expecting the students to understand and respond in English, I worked with a colleague who conducted the focus groups in the students' native language. As an evaluator, I valued the comfort of participants and importance of gathering the best feedback possible. As participants, I would imagine the students felt more respected and comfortable without any language barrier in the discussion. It was clear from the student discussions that they were trusting us to provide feedback to the administration without revealing their identities. As administrators, it was clear they valued evaluative information that would help them improve the school's climate. In this study, I believe we had an ethical obligation to protect student identity while providing accurate, useful information to school administrators.

I will also add that in this evaluation the findings were controversial and challenging to present. And some findings could not be relayed because they would have allowed identification of participants in our focus groups, and protection of privacy and upholding the trust of students was valued higher than providing the most useful information. Had we breached confidentiality, I do believe it would have been an ethical violation. Would we have been charged with a crime? No. Would we have lost our jobs? Probably not. Would we have lost credibility? Perhaps. But the reason we protected the privacy of individuals is that, as evaluators, we valued our obligation to participants over disclosing all findings. You may be wondering if it is ethical to not disclose all findings from a study. This goes back to values and, fortunately, there are principles and ethical codes to guide us in making these sorts of decisions. I would say every effort should be made to accurately disclose all findings, *unless* that disclosure would violate confidentiality, put participants at risk, and potentially harm participants.

I will reiterate here what was said in Chapter 1 about values. Our own values affect all aspects of evaluation, from the research designs and methods we choose to use, to how we interact with stakeholders and the way in which we interpret our findings. Stakeholder values and the political context in which a program operates also affect how an evaluation is conducted and how data are used.

Understanding stakeholder values and the context in which a program operates can aid you in designing an evaluation that meets stakeholder needs and is more likely to be used to influence decision making. Understanding our own values can help us to examine how they might impact our evaluations, as well as increase awareness such that we can improve our practice. Understanding and adhering to professional guidelines, standards, and codes of conduct, as well as being mindful of the core competencies of an evaluator, can only serve to strengthen the work that we do as evaluators.

3.6 ADDITIONAL CONSIDERATIONS

Before we close this chapter on evaluation ethics, there are few additional considerations that are important for evaluators. The first is confidentiality and privacy. Both are common terms in research and evaluation, and they are critically important to maintaining respect for persons and beneficence. The second is handling unanticipated or adverse events. Conflict of interest will also be discussed.

3.6.1 Confidentiality and Privacy

As mentioned above, confidentiality and privacy are critically important in maintaining respect for persons and beneficence. Privacy refers to the protection of people, while confidentiality refers to the protection of data. In fact, confidentiality is an extension of **privacy** in that if data are not adequately protected, neither are people. Privacy is a participant's right to control who has access to their personal information. Privacy can be maintained by securing the proper consent before a person is interviewed, as well as by keeping information on an individual confidential.

When a researcher is able to connect an evaluation participant and their data, **confidentiality** becomes an important consideration. Confidentiality refers to how private information provided by participants is safeguarded; evaluators should take precautions to protect the identity of participants from others. Typically, evaluation participants are assured confidentiality of their data when they participate in a study.

Individuals involved in an evaluation may have some form of vulnerability if their confidentiality is compromised. It is an evaluator's responsibility to create procedures for protecting confidentiality even in the event of a data breach. For instance, the release of confidential program participant information for an evaluation of a treatment to decrease drug use might allow employers to identify them as substance users, which could in turn affect their employment or health benefits. In this example, however, participant names or other identifiable information should never have been stored with data on the participant. In order to protect confidentiality and provide safeguards in the event of a data breach, a nonidentifiable ID should be linked to the data. A separate file could link this identifier to the actual participant.

Confidentiality also comes into play when reporting data. While it may be straightforward and obvious to not report data at the individual level with identifying information, confidentiality can also be breached through **deductive disclosure**. Deductive disclosure occurs when a person's identity can be determined through responses or a combination of responses. Suppose mathematics achievement data were being reported at the district level by race, gender, and achievement level. If there are a small number of individuals comprising a racial group, it may be reasonable for a reader to deduce who they are and

Privacy: refers to a participant's right to control who has access to their personal information.

Confidentiality: refers to how private information provided by participants is safeguarded; evaluators should take precautions to protect the identity of participants.

Deductive disclosure: occurs when a person's identity can be determined through responses or a combination of responses.

thus what they scored. An example would be if there were ten Haitian Creole (HC) students in the district, four males and six females. Suppose the report showed two HC females scored Advanced, three HC females scored Proficient, four HC males scored Basic, and one HC female scored Below Basic on the mathematics assessment. Since all HC males scored Basic, it would be easy to deduce the achievement score of the HC boy who attends your neighborhood school.

Confidentiality is also important when reporting qualitative data. Evaluators should thoroughly review qualitative reports to ensure that comments supporting conclusions from interviews or focus groups do not inadvertently reveal the identity of the person who made the comment.

3.6.2 Unanticipated or Adverse Events

For evaluators, the process of dealing with unanticipated situations that may arise during data collection or analysis is grounded in the *American Evaluation Association's Guiding Principles for Evaluators*, as well as legislation related to research ethics and IRB regulations. Respect for people should be at the center of any handling of adverse or unanticipated events. Whenever in doubt, contact your IRB for guidance on handling situations that may increase the risk for participants or change the nature of the study. An example is an evaluation I participated in several years back. Health data were needed for the evaluation and per the approved IRB, data were to be de-identified. Upon opening the file received from the health department, it was quickly apparent that the file included data we were not supposed to have, for example, names and addresses. We notified the IRB and they instructed us how to complete and submit the necessary unanticipated event form and how to handle the file we received. They also reached out to the health department to determine what further action was needed. In addition to notifying the IRB, we briefed the program leadership so they were aware of the issue.

Problems may also be encountered outside of the evaluation that affect the evaluation, for example, data theft or disclosure during the evaluation of potentially illegal activity. Suppose after collecting personally identifiable information (PII) on consent forms for participants of an addiction treatment program, the briefcase of the evaluator is stolen on his way back to work. Again, as with the case presented above, both the IRB and the program leadership should be notified. The IRB will require a completed unanticipated/ adverse event form describing the incident and in most cases a change in the protocol to prevent a similar problem from occurring in the future. The IRB may also require that the participants be notified. In another example, information regarding sexual misconduct was disclosed during an interview being conducted by the evaluator. The misconduct was in no way related to the program but was rather something that occurred during the time the individual was participating in the program. In such cases, it is important to remember that the evaluator is not in a position to determine if criminal behavior did

QUICK CHECK

1. What is an IRB protocol and why is it important?

2. What are the five guiding principles for evaluators, per the American Evaluation Association?

3. While training a teaching assistant on how to administer a test that is part of the evaluation, the assistant reveals that she is concerned one of her students is being abused. What should the evaluator do?

4. What responsibilities does an evaluator have regarding confidentiality? If data are reported without personally identifiable information, how might confidentiality still be breached?

or did not occur, but they are obligated to report the information to the IRB and to any other entity required by their organization per mandated reporter guidelines. The IRB will advise the evaluator on how to manage the interview data that contain information regarding the alleged behavior. The organization will advise on the necessary reporting regarding the disclosed behavior. As you can see from these examples, the evaluator should not deal with adverse or unanticipated events alone, but should reach out to the IRB for guidance and to ensure that the required procedures are followed, including unanticipated event reporting, data management, and potential changes in protocol.

3.6.3 Conflict of Interest

The usability of evaluation findings is highly dependent on the credibility of the evaluator and the evaluation methodology. Conflicts of interests, such as the evaluator or a family member of the evaluator financially benefitting from the program being evaluated, bring credibility into question. For this reason, any conflict of interest (COI) must be acknowledged. Most IRB application protocol forms entail a description of any actual or potential COI and most IRB training includes a section covering the topic. In addition, any COI should be clearly stated in the evaluation report.

3.7 CHAPTER SUMMARY

Evaluators abide by the ethical guidelines of human subjects research. **Ethics** are moral obligations that guide us in determining whether a certain behavior is right or wrong. A **human subject** is a living individual who participates in a research study; this participation may be directly through intervention or interaction, or by the researcher having access to private data that would allow identification of the individual. Research is a voluntary process, and for research that requires individual consent, evaluators need to follow informed consent procedures. **Informed consent** is an individual's voluntary agreement to participate in a study after being provided with and understanding information about the study, including the research purpose and research risks. An **Institutional Review Board (IRB)** governs human subjects research. An IRB is a committee that is charged with protecting human subjects in research; IRBs review all research prior to the research being conducted to ensure adequate protections and safeguards are in place. Evaluation protocols must be submitted through the IRB prior to the collection of any data.

The ethical principles for conducting research with human subjects are detailed in the Belmont Report and include respect for persons, beneficence, and justice. Federal regulations for human subjects research, referred to as the Common Rule, are based on the Belmont Report. Any organization receiving federal funds for human subjects research must follow the Common Rule, as set forth in their Federalwide Assurance. A **Federalwide Assurance (FWA)** states that the organization will comply with human subjects research regulations and establish an IRB.

Minimal risk is a criterion for human subjects research that involves the determination as to whether the research involves more risk to an individual than would be encountered in everyday life. Based on this criterion, human subjects research is determined to be **exempt** from the Common Rule, **expedited** through the IRB process, or subject to the IRB's **full review**. An **IRB protocol** is a document that details the purpose and design of a research study. It describes the participants and how they were selected, what information will be collected from them and how it will be collected, how the data will be used, and how the data will be stored. Evaluators have several documents to guide them in protecting human subjects in research, including the **AEA Guiding Principles for Evaluators**, the **AEA Evaluator Competencies**, and the **AEA Statement on Cultural Competence in Evaluation**.

Reflection and Application

1. Why are evaluators required to abide by research ethics guidelines?

2. How are the ethical principles as outlined in the Common Rule similar to or different from the Guiding Principles for Evaluators as outlined by the American Evaluation Association?

3. When designing a new evaluation, what procedures need to be followed *before* any data are collected?

4. When putting a new protocol through the IRB, what are the four determinations that the IRB might make? (Hint: Three of these four determinations are the type of IRB review.)

5. Suppose you are conducting an evaluation focused on gathering employees' views of several new human resources policies. Findings indicate unfavorable opinions of a new employment policy. After reading the evaluation report that details these findings, the agency director wants to know which employees expressed these opinions. What should the evaluator do?

FIGURE 3.3 ● AEA Evaluator Competencies

1.0

DOMAIN

PROFESSIONAL PRACTICE

focuses on what makes evaluators distinct as practicing professionals

Professional practice is grounded in AEA's foundational documents, including the Program Evaluation Standards, the AEA Guiding Principles, and the AEA Statement on Cultural Competence.

The competent evaluator...

1.1 Acts ethically through evaluation practice that demonstrates integrity and respects people from different cultural backgrounds and indigenous groups.

1.2 Applies the foundational documents adopted by the American Evaluation Association that ground evaluation practice.

1.3 Selects evaluation approaches and theories appropriately.

1.4 Uses systematic evidence to make evaluative judgments.

1.5 Reflects on evaluation formally or informally to improve practice.

1.6 Identifies personal areas of professional competence and needs for growth.

1.7 Pursues ongoing professional development to deepen reflective practice, stay current, and build connections.

1.8 Identifies how evaluation practice can promote social justice and the public good.

1.9 Advocates for the field of evaluation and its value.

2.0

DOMAIN

METHODOLOGY

focuses on technical aspects of evidence-based, systematic inquiry for valued purposes

Methodology includes quantitative, qualitative, and mixed designs for learning, understanding, decision making, and judging.

The competent evaluator...

2.1 Identifies evaluation purposes and needs.

2.2 Determines evaluation questions.

2.3 Designs credible and feasible evaluations that address identified purposes and questions.

2.4 Determines and justifies appropriate methods to answer evaluation questions, e.g., quantitative, qualitative, and mixed methods.

2.5 Identifies assumptions that underlie methodologies and program logic.

2.6 Conducts reviews of the literature when appropriate.

2.7 Identifies relevant sources of evidence and sampling procedures.

2.8 Involves stakeholders in designing, implementing, interpreting, and reporting evaluations as appropriate.

2.9 Uses program logic and program theory as appropriate.

2.10 Collects data using credible, feasible, and culturally appropriate procedures.

2.11 Analyzes data using credible, feasible, and culturally appropriate procedures.

2.12 Identifies strengths and limitations of the evaluation design and methods.

2.13 Interprets findings/results in context.

2.14 Uses evidence and interpretations to draw conclusions, making judgments and recommendations when appropriate.

AEA Evaluator Competencies

SPRING-SUMMER 2016 A series of virtual and in-person focus group discussions using a structured guide with leadership & members of TIGs & affiliates • Targeted efforts to engage international members, who make up 20% of AEA's membership (reviewed proposed domains, specific items for each domain, & discussed pros & cons of defining evaluator competencies) • A guide for AEA Affiliate leaders to use at their annual meetings to solicit member feedback

2016 AEA SUMMER INSTITUTE (ATLANTA) Follow-up listening post

2016 AEA CONFERENCE (ATLANTA) Second series of listening posts

DECEMBER 2016 An aea365 week on the draft competencies in highlighting the dedicated feedback link on the AEA website

2016

(Continued)

FIGURE 3.3 **(Continued)**

3.0

DOMAIN
CONTEXT

focuses on understanding the unique circumstances, multiple perspectives, and changing settings of evaluations and their users/stakeholders

Context involves site/location/environment, participants/stakeholders, organization/structure, culture/diversity, history/traditions, values/beliefs, politics/economics, power/privilege, and other characteristics.

The competent evaluator . . .

3.1   Responds respectfully to the uniqueness of the evaluation context.

3.2   Engages a diverse range of users/stakeholders throughout the evaluation process.

3.3   Describes the program, including its basic purpose, components, and its functioning in broader contexts.

3.4   Attends to systems issues within the context.

3.5   Communicates evaluation processes and results in timely, appropriate, and effective ways.

3.6   Facilitates shared understanding of the program and its evaluation with stakeholders.

3.7   Clarifies diverse perspectives, stakeholder interests, and cultural assumptions.

3.8   Promotes evaluation use and influence in context.

4.0

DOMAIN
PLANNING & MANAGEMENT

focuses on determining and monitoring work plans, timelines, resources, and other components needed to complete and deliver an evaluation study

Planning and management include networking, developing proposals, contracting, determining work assignments, monitoring progress, and fostering use.

The competent evaluator . . .

4.1   Negotiates and manages a feasible evaluation plan, budget, resources, and timeline.

4.2   Addresses aspects of culture in planning and managing evaluations.

4.3   Manages and safeguards evaluation data.

4.4   Plans for evaluation use and influence.

4.5   Coordinates and supervises evaluation processes and products.

4.6   Documents evaluation processes and products.

4.7   Teams with others when appropriate.

4.8   Monitors evaluation progress and quality and makes adjustments when appropriate.

4.9   Works with stakeholders to build evaluation capacity when appropriate.

4.10 Uses technology appropriately to support and manage the evaluation.

5.0

DOMAIN
INTERPERSONAL

focuses on human relations and social interactions that ground evaluator effectiveness for professional practice throughout the evaluation

Interpersonal skills include cultural competence, communication, facilitation, and conflict resolution.

The competent evaluator . . .

5.1   Fosters positive relationships for professional practice and evaluation use.

5.2   Listens to understand and engage different perspectives.

5.3   Facilitates shared decision making for evaluation.

5.4   Builds trust throughout the evaluation.

5.5   Attends to the ways power and privilege affect evaluation practice.

5.6   Communicates in meaningful ways that enhance the effectiveness of the evaluation.

5.7   Facilitates constructive and culturally responsive interaction throughout the evaluation.

5.8   Manages conflicts constructively.

SEPTEMBER 2017 Member survey on the content of the latest draft (roughly 1200 responses/16% response rate, including nearly 1100 separate comments)

2017 AEA CONFERENCE (WASHINGTON, DC) Two sessions to gather additional feedback from members

2017

Source: American Evaluation Association, https://www.eval.org/p/cm/ld/fid=472

EVALUATION IDEOLOGIES AND APPROACHES

One ideology, one system is not sufficient. It is helpful to have a variety of different approaches. . . . We can then make a joint effort to solve the problems of the whole of humankind.

—Dalai Lama

Upon completion of this chapter, you should be able to

- Describe common evaluation approaches.
- Identify the evaluator(s) associated with common evaluation approaches.
- Explain how multiple approaches might be used in an evaluation.
- Describe how evaluation designs and evaluation approaches are used in an evaluation.
- Explain the rationale for using theory-based evaluation approaches.
- Relate embedded evaluation to other evaluation approaches.

4.1 INQUIRY AND IDEOLOGY

As discussed in Chapter 2, evaluation as we know it emerged in the 1960s and took shape in the 1970s with the contributions of researchers from an array of disciplines. Many of these individuals are still active in the field and other great thinkers have joined them in continuing the growth and development of evaluation as a profession. Because of the diversity in background of many of those in the field of evaluation, the modes of inquiry and ideologies with which evaluators frame their quest for knowledge are also varied. This variation has cultivated and continues to foster deep thinking, constructive debate, and consequently a wealth of resources and information from which new evaluators can explore and develop their own modes of inquiry and ideology.

In organizing this chapter, I struggled with a framework that would be most useful for those not familiar with evaluation to make sense of the various methodologies and approaches. My students often have difficulty understanding how to differentiate between a design, an approach, an ideology, and a method. One of my "go-to" resources for various perspectives and theories of evaluation is *Evaluation Roots* (Alkin, 2013). In his text, Alkin presents evaluation theory as a tree, with three foundational elements, or roots:

- social accountability

- social inquiry

- epistemology

and three branches:

- use

- methods

- valuing

The three roots of the tree represent the facilitators of the growth of evaluation as a discipline. As seen in Chapter 2, evaluation became a focus when a host of government programs were created in the 1960s, without built-in accountability mechanisms. Thus, early evaluators were prompted by calls to study these programs in an effort to determine effectiveness; their focus on the **social accountability** of programs is an important root of evaluation as we know it today. Likewise, systematic **social inquiry** is the root that led to methods focusing on measuring effectiveness for accountability purposes. Finally, the **epistemology** root is centered on the study of knowledge. This root adds a critical dimension to evaluation, reminding us that while the rationale and methods of evaluation are important, just as important is consideration of how the knowledge gained through evaluation can most effectively be used to inform policy and practice.

The three branches of evaluation represent how the evaluation roots have evolved and grown. Alkin (2013) places key theorists along these branches. Other important theorists, many of whom are listed in "Early Contributors to the Field of Evaluation," Table 2.1 in Chapter 2, are included as underbranches.

Social accountability: the need to investigate the effectiveness of social programs in order to hold program leadership accountable; social accountability relates to the development of the "use" branch of evaluation.

Social inquiry: the need to develop methodologies to evaluate the effectiveness of social programs; social inquiry relates to the development of the "methods" branch of evaluation.

Epistemology: the need to understand the value we place on knowledge in making judgments about worth; epistemology relates to the "valuing" branch of evaluation.

The "use" branch relates to the social accountability root. The major evaluation theorists on the use branches, underbranches, and leaves focus their work on evaluation approaches that facilitate the use of evaluation by stakeholders. Early contributors to the use branch include Daniel Stufflebeam and Michael Patton. The "methods" branch relates to the social inquiry root. Theorists along these branches have contributed to evaluation designs and methodology. Early contributors to the methods branch include Donald Campbell and Peter Rossi.

Finally, the "valuing" branch relates to the epistemology root. At the base of this root is Michael Scriven, a philosopher and one of the most prominent early influencers of evaluation. I find this branch the most difficult to explain, due to its philosophical underpinnings. Perhaps it is because of my engineer brain, but wrapping my mind around deep constructs such as the meaning of truth and knowledge is a struggle; I would rather solve a math problem. However, as my daughter tells me when I get stuck in my head, "Use your words, mom." So, here goes. Theorists along the valuing branches focus on the role of an evaluator. As with the other branches, there is a diversity of thinking along this branch, with some theorists believing it is the role of the evaluator to make an objective judgment about the worth of a program. On the other hand, some theorists along this branch recognize that all measurement is subject to error, and thus, as evaluators, we cannot make objective assertions. They argue that we should instead strive to capture the complexities of a program and engage stakeholders in the valuing process. Early contributors to the valuing branch include Michael Scriven and Robert Stake.

While many of the evaluators mentioned above figure prominently in the development of evaluation in the United States, Figure 4.1 shows Alkin's expanded theory tree that includes American as well as international evaluation theorists (Alkin, Christie, & Vo, 2013).

While I find this depiction of evaluation theory extremely helpful in understanding the development of the field and varying perspectives of evaluation, I have also found that the blending of evaluation approach and design within the same tree can be confusing and limiting. Part of this is due to the natural tendency for us to "find" ourselves on a branch, as opposed to viewing evaluation as a blending of branches. Part of this is also due to our minds often thinking linearly and not conceptualizing the overlap or influence between branches. Alkin (2013) addresses this in *Evaluation Roots* and explains how the proximity of evaluators on branches in relation to neighboring branches is reflective of the interrelationships among branches. However, even taking into account proximity does not account for how theories across branches might work together within the same evaluation. Regardless, if you pursue evaluation as a career, I highly recommend including his text in your personal evaluation library. The depth of knowledge presented on and by prominent evaluators, the growth of evaluation as described by the many contributors to

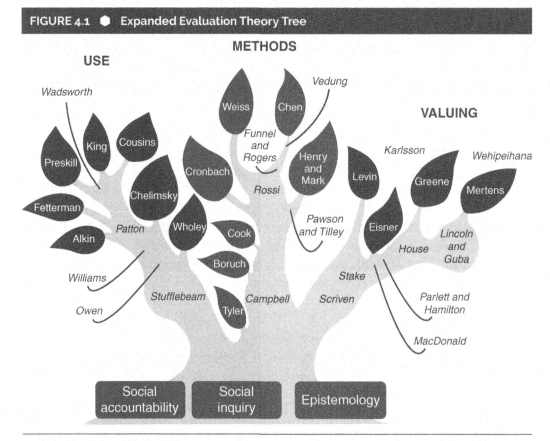

FIGURE 4.1   ●   Expanded Evaluation Theory Tree

Source: Alkin et al. (2013, p. 388).

his text, and the wealth of information on the evaluation approaches developed by those contributors is surpassed by none.

The remaining sections of this chapter will clarify how evaluation perspectives include both approaches and designs and how our own ideologies influence our perspectives toward evaluation. I will introduce theorists on Alkin's evaluation tree using a blend of design and approach, stemming from ideology.

4.2 EVALUATION IDEOLOGY

Ideology: a system of beliefs that we use to explain and develop solutions; a philosophy or a way of thinking about a certain topic or issue.

An **ideology** is a system of beliefs that we use to explain and develop solutions. An ideology is a philosophy or a way of thinking about a certain topic or issue. Our ideologies are shaped by life experiences, cultural beliefs, traditions, and those around us whose opinions we value. Ideologies help us to frame our thinking and, in turn, determine our actions. Ideologies are often unspoken and may be difficult to articulate, but they influence the way in which we view the world and the choices we make. As with any field, there are particular issues that help to define our ideology. I will refer to these issues as calibrators, taken from multiple definitions of the term. Calibrators divide or mark a scale with gradations to determine the degree of something along that scale. Likewise, calibrators can also be plans that have a specific use or application.

A **calibrator**, used in the context of evaluation, is a continuum upon which we can consider where our beliefs fall and through which we can apply those beliefs in a particular context. The calibrators presented in this section are not meant to be dichotomous, that is, either-or, but rather a range with the extremes presented as a way to consider where your beliefs might fall along the continuum, as well as the strength with which you hold that belief. Three areas of calibrators are discussed: design calibrators, role calibrators, and methods calibrators. These categories and the calibrators within them are not mutually exclusive, as you will notice some similarities. But, taken as a whole, they should provide you with considerations to shape and focus your own ideology.

4.2.1 Design Calibrators

Design calibrators help us to organize our thinking around the overarching research design used in evaluation. Evaluation design is covered in detail in Chapter 8, though considerations regarding how you make design choices will be presented below. It should be noted, however, that other factors often determine what evaluation design we can and cannot use in a specific situation. Thus, regardless of our thinking about these calibrators, it does not necessarily mean that we will be in a position to use any design we choose or make unilateral decisions regarding evaluation design. The design we use will be influenced by the resources, both people and financial, available to the evaluation and the context in which the evaluation is implemented. For instance, in some contexts, the environment might facilitate or even promote stakeholder involvement and foster evaluator access to program participants. In other contexts, the environment might present barriers to evaluation.

Calibrator D1: Design Structure. At one extreme on the design structure calibrator is the medical model of research. At the other extreme is the anthropological model of research. Important questions include the following:

- To what extent can and should evaluation be conducted in a controlled environment, using research designs closely aligned to the medical model of research?

- To what extent can and should evaluation be conducted in natural settings, much like research designs used in anthropological research?

Calibrator: a continuum upon which we can consider where our beliefs fall and through which we can apply those beliefs in a particular context.

- In what ways is there a trade-off between causation in controlled settings versus correlation in natural settings?

- What is the ideal design structure for program evaluation? To what extent does this design structure vary by the purpose of the evaluation being primarily formative or primarily summative?

Some evaluators believe that unless the underlying research design is of sufficient rigor to make causal conclusions, there is little value in utilizing resources to conduct the evaluation. Other evaluators believe that the controls necessary to implement an experiment based on the medical model create an unrealistic environment within which to evaluate the program, thus limiting the generalizability of findings. There is no doubt that veteran evaluators have already formed ideologies in this area and have strong preferences for design structure in various evaluation environments. Honestly, I understand and respect the arguments at both extremes, and I hesitate to share my ideologies for fear of influencing your own deliberations. However, I will say two things: If the ability to relate a program's strategies to its goals is compromised, generalizability is a moot issue. Likewise, if the effort for program staff to conduct an evaluation is so cumbersome due to environmental changes necessary to create a controlled environment, evaluation is less likely to occur. Oh—and one more thing—making decisions based on some information is better than decisions made without data (either because evaluation is too cumbersome or not valued), yet even the "some information" needs to be valid and credible. All in all, if I had to take a stand on the design structure, it would be to develop as rigorous of an evaluation as possible (i.e., aim toward the medical model of research), while taking into account stakeholder preferences and contextual constraints.

Calibrator D2: Design Purpose. Design purpose relates to the process and intent of the evaluation. At one extreme is keeping the program or intervention "pure," that is, not making any changes to the program during the evaluation. At the other extreme is continuous program improvement, such that the program is adjusted on an ongoing basis throughout the evaluation based on formative data. An argument for the former is that if the program is continuously changing, it is difficult to know what the program really is and the extent to which results are "muddied" by strategies that are not consistently implemented. However, an argument on the other extreme is that it is a missed opportunity, and perhaps even unethical, to not make programmatic improvements that would likely improve results for program participants. Important considerations include the following:

- In what ways do mid-evaluation program changes affect the interpretability of findings?

- In what ways do mid-evaluation program changes affect the replicability of the program?

- To what extent should a program make adjustments during an evaluation based on formative data?

- In what ways should formative evaluation be used during an evaluation to improve a program?

As with all calibrators described in this section, I understand the arguments for and against the extremes. On many calibrators, like design structure, my preference is a range and highly situational. However, with regard to design purpose, I have a strong preference. You do not need to agree with me, and I hope you will develop your own preferences over time with careful consideration and experience. My preference with regard to design purpose is that program evaluation should focus on continuous improvement. I believe it is one of the features of program evaluation that sets it apart from other forms of research. Evaluation is about improving programs and policies, and I think we have the best chance of doing so if we make continual, deliberate programmatic changes based on data, all while carefully documenting those changes.

4.2.2 Role Calibrators

Role calibrators help us to organize our thinking around the function and responsibility of the evaluator. As mentioned in the above section, the context of the evaluation can influence the extent to which an evaluator can implement an evaluation in the preferred manner. However, the two calibrators discussed below can help shape your own ideology around your preferred role as an evaluator.

Calibrator R1: Evaluator Involvement. Early evaluation viewed the evaluator as a dispassionate, pietistic expert, brought in to pass judgment. While this may seem harsh, evaluators were not seen as partners, collaborators, or friendly visitors. Evaluators were fairly hands-off when it came to the program. Remnants of this view can still be seen in how evaluator visits are perceived by program staff. Evaluators can make program staff nervous, just as we are nervous anytime we feel evaluated. Even though the evaluation is of a program and not an individual, program staff still have a stake in the findings. If the program is not functioning well, program staff may lose responsibility or even their job. However, more recently, evaluators are often partners with program staff. This partnership can take many forms, from the evaluator working only in an advisory capacity to the evaluator working closely with program staff during all phases of the evaluation. Thus, the evaluator involvement calibrator addresses the role of the evaluator and how the evaluator fits within the program. Important considerations include the following:

- What role and relationship should an evaluator have with program staff?

- To what extent should the evaluator keep firm boundaries between the evaluation and the program? What are the benefits and drawbacks to keeping such boundaries?

- To what extent should the evaluator be a full partner with program staff in determining the direction of the program?

A former colleague of mine liked to refer to an evaluator as a critical friend. Evaluators can be a critical friend, a trusted partner, or an external consultant. The difficulty is determining what the most appropriate role is for any given evaluation.

Calibrator R2: Evaluator Responsibility. An important consideration with regard to evaluator role is the responsibility the evaluator has to a program and to the organization within which that program is implemented. On the one hand, evaluation can be an external activity, with the evaluator's responsibility to come in, complete the evaluation, provide a report, and leave. On the other end of the spectrum, the evaluator can view evaluation as a capacity-building activity. In such cases, the evaluator seeks to build processes and facilitate data-driven practices that are still in place when the formal evaluation is complete. Important considerations include the following:

- To what extent should an evaluation be external/peripheral to the program?

- To what extent should evaluators collect the data necessary for the evaluation without interfering with program processes?

- How much should an evaluation try to change program processes to incorporate data collection as an ongoing process?

- In what ways can and to what extent should evaluators build structures into programs to facilitate a reliance upon data by program staff post-evaluation?

As with design purpose, evaluator responsibility is a calibrator about which I have strong opinions. You may disagree with my opinion and I encourage you to form your own opinion. However, I will share that I believe evaluators have a responsibility to make a difference, not just in the report or recommendations that they leave behind, but in the systems they create during the evaluation. If, as evaluators, we are truly committed to promoting the use of data to make programmatic decisions, we will work to build capacity within programs such that staff are not dependent upon an external evaluator for data-based decision making. We should facilitate an environment of continuous improvement so that data use remains even as the evaluator moves on.

4.2.3 Methods Calibrators

Methods calibrators help us to organize our thinking around the types of data collection methods we value and how we use the methods to orient our evaluation. The two calibrators discussed below can help shape your own ideology around your views on methods and evaluation focus.

Calibrator M1: Data Collection Methods. A common debate in evaluation, and in all research, is the value of quantitative and qualitative methods. Many evaluators have a strong preference for one over the other, though I daresay most evaluators recognize the usefulness of employing mixed methods, that is, including both quantitative and qualitative methods in an evaluation. Quantitative methods typically allow evaluators to capture information more quickly from more individuals, and large volumes of quantitative data can be analyzed much more quickly than qualitative data. Quantitative measures are also more reliable, whereas it is much more time-consuming for qualitative researchers to ensure adequate reliability in qualitative data. However, qualitative measures can have adequate reliability with structured and consistent data analysis procedures. An example of quantitative analysis is how the multiple-choice items on your SATs can be scored quickly by a machine, and regardless of how many times they are scored, the results would be the same. In addition, the SAT multiple-choice data from thousands of people can be scored at the same time. On the other hand, analysis of the SAT writing responses is more time-consuming and multiple raters are used to score each essay. Yes, any individual scorer can only score one essay at a time. In addition, these raters must go through extensive training to ensure they are consistent in their scoring. The analysis of qualitative data requires similar techniques that might be used to score an essay and such techniques include inter-rater reliability considerations that are not present in quantitative analysis. However, while quantitative methods allow you to analyze more data, more quickly, and with more reliability, they do not provide the kind of rich detail and description that is inherent in qualitative data. Thus, qualitative data can be used to illuminate quantitative findings, such that we can better understand the meaning behind responses and calculations. Quantitative data can help us to determine the generalizability of findings from qualitative data, by enabling us to create closed-ended items on a topic that can be asked of a larger group of people. Thus, important considerations include the following:

- To what extent do quantitative methods restrict the ability of evaluators to understand a program's operation and impact at a deeper level?

- To what extent do the smaller samples involved in studies using qualitative methods portray a skewed view of a program? How can samples in qualitative studies be constructed so that findings are representative of a larger stakeholder group?

- In what ways can both quantitative and qualitative methods be used to provide both depth and breadth to an evaluation?

Calibrator M2: Methods Focus.   With regard to evaluation methods, another consideration for evaluators is how to focus their evaluation. At the heart of methods focus is whether evaluation designs should be constrained by program goals. Ralph Tyler, first introduced in Chapter 2 as the "Father of Evaluation," laid the groundwork for what most consider to be the first program evaluation approach: **objectives-oriented evaluation**. While there were other methods that people used to make decisions prior to focusing on objectives, such as expertise-oriented evaluation based on expert opinion and consumer-oriented evaluation intended to make evaluative judgments for public good, objectives oriented was the first evaluation approach geared toward making a value judgment for a specific stakeholder group (Fitzpatrick, Sanders, & Worthen, 2011). Objectives-oriented evaluation focuses on the goals and objectives of a program. Methods are chosen to measure data based on these objectives, and findings are analyzed to determine the extent to which those objectives were met. On the other end of the methods-focus spectrum is Michael Scriven's **goal-free evaluation**. Unlike objectives-oriented evaluation, goal-free evaluation is not designed around the specified goals and objectives of a program. Instead, the stated goals and objectives of a program are viewed as incomplete, potentially biased, and a barrier to fully evaluating the program (Scriven, 1991, 2013). Scriven recommends that evaluators examine the program in its entirety, such that both intended and unintended outcomes are measured. So, while there is some element of measuring objectives in a goal-free evaluation, it is not the sole focus to the extent that additional important outcomes are overlooked. For instance, focusing solely on measuring achievement changes based upon a program to increase the rigor of courses might overlook an increase in the number of students who drop out due to frustration. On the other hand, measuring only a program's goal of increasing youth participation in summer programs might miss the decrease in neighborhood crime by youth during the summer months. Important considerations regarding the methods-focus calibrator include the following:

- To what extent are a program's goals worded as strategies the program intends to implement versus the outcomes that would result if those strategies were implemented as planned? What is an evaluator's responsibility to work with program staff to truly understand a program's goals, beyond those stated by the program?

- How likely is it that the program will have unintended consequences, either positive or negative?

Objectives-oriented evaluation: an approach to evaluation where the focus of the evaluation is on how well the program met a set of predetermined objectives.

Goal-free evaluation: an approach to evaluation where the evaluation is not constrained by program goals, but rather focuses on the measurement of outcomes, whether intended or unintended; developed by Michael Scriven.

IN THE REAL WORLD . . .

Revisiting the Cambridge-Somerville Youth Study (CSYS): Ideology. The CSYS was introduced in Chapter 2. The purpose of CSYS (Cabot, 1940) was both to prevent juvenile delinquency among boys as well as to study the effectiveness of juvenile delinquency interventions. It is revisited here to illustrate how ideology relates to design, role, and methods.

While it is impossible to truly know what Cabot's **ideology** was with regard to evaluation, we can surmise from descriptions of the study where his beliefs might fall along each calibrator continuum. With regard to the **design calibrators**, the design indicates he favored the medical model of research design and it does not appear that findings were used for program improvement. With regard to **role calibrators**, the evaluators were external and do not appear to have had much involvement with the program beyond data collection. There is no evidence that CSYS was a capacity-building evaluation. With regard to **methods calibrators**, while some qualitative methods may have been used, the predominant methods appear to have been quantitative and focused on the objectives of the CSYS.

What if the CSYS evaluators had had a different ideology? Consider each scenario and identify ways that the change may have affected the findings from the study.

SCENARIO 1: Suppose the evaluators chose to forgo a control group and included all youth in the program.

SCENARIO 2: Suppose findings were used throughout the program to improve services for the children involved.

SCENARIO 3: Suppose the evaluator was someone internal to the program.

SCENARIO 4: Suppose the evaluators worked closely with stakeholders throughout the program, building processes for them to collect and analyze their own data.

SCENARIO 5: Suppose the youth were observed and data were collected from these observations, instead of from instruments designed to measure behavior.

SCENARIO 6: Suppose the evaluators did not use the stated objectives of the program to drive the study, but instead examined any potential outcome of the program.

- What is an evaluator's responsibility with regard to evaluation focus? To what extent is an evaluator only obligated to evaluate the objectives of a program as stated by program leadership? To what extent does an evaluator have a responsibility to study other potential impacts of a program beyond the intended goals?

Ideally, the relationship between evaluators and stakeholders would be a partnership, such that decisions regarding the focus of an evaluation can be jointly determined. See "In The Real World" for a discussion of how ideology may have influenced the Cambridge-Somerville Youth Study.

4.2.4 Calibrators and Ideology

The six calibrators discussed above are provided for you as areas to reflect upon as you develop your own ideology around evaluation. Figure 4.2 includes a graphical

FIGURE 4.2 ● Evaluation Ideology Calibrators and Influencers

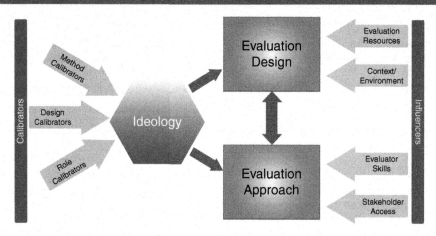

representation of how these calibrators shape ideology—and how ideology, in turn, guides our choices regarding evaluation designs and approaches. On the right side of the diagram are additional influencers that affect our use of evaluation designs and approaches. For instance, resources and context can constrain the types of research designs that might be employed. Evaluator skills and experiences, as well as the degree of access we have to stakeholders, influence the approaches that we are able to take with regard to a particular evaluation. The following two sections will address evaluation design and approaches. The section on designs focuses on how they were shaped by early evaluators and only includes a brief explanation of their purpose (Chapter 8 provides detailed information on evaluation design). Evaluation approaches describe some common evaluation approaches in the field and who contributed to the development of each approach.

 QUICK CHECK

1. How does an evaluator's ideology affect their choice of evaluation designs and approaches?

2. Do you think an evaluator should build evaluation capacity among the staff of the program they are evaluating? Why or why not?

3. If you had limited resources for an evaluation, would you use qualitative or quantitative methods? Explain your reasoning.

4. Explain the six calibrators that affect an evaluator's ideology. What are your thoughts on each calibrator? Do you have strong preferences regarding any of the calibrators?

4.3 EVALUATION DESIGN

Ideology influences the evaluation designs we choose to use. In particular, our philosophy regarding the design and methods calibrators drives the overall structure of our evaluation. While there are additional factors that affect and constrain choices regarding evaluation design and methods, our underlying ideology shapes the extent to which we view different research designs as strong or weak. In this section, major contributors to evaluation design will be discussed, within the framework of the evaluation designs themselves. Chapter 8 will explore evaluation design in more detail.

4.3.1 Experimental Designs

Donald Campbell. Donald Campbell was one of the most critical pioneers in the call for social experimentation in the field of evaluation (Rossi, Lipsey, & Henry, 2018). His groundbreaking work pioneered the application of the experimental model used in psychological research to the evaluation field (Christie & Alkin, 2013). The experimental model of research includes random assignment of subjects to a program/intervention or to a control condition. Campbell's perspective was that decisions about policy and programs should be made on the basis of experimental research. His perspectives are detailed in his 1969 article "Reforms as Experiments." For over half a century, his work has guided social science researchers and evaluators on how to conduct rigorous research aimed at establishing causal inference. **Causal inference** is the ability of evaluators to claim that the program they are evaluating is responsible for the outcomes they measured. One of the most influential books in the field was written by Campbell and his coauthor Julian Stanley. Campbell and Stanley's (1963) seminal work *Experimental and Quasi-Experimental Designs for Research* is one that every researcher and evaluator should have in their library. They detail design considerations for randomized controlled experiments, quasi-experiments, and nonexperimental studies. Their work has had a lasting impact on the field of evaluation and has facilitated the use of both experimental and quasi-experimental designs (Shadish & Luellen, 2013). It began a shift in the field, which led to randomized experiments being considered the "gold standard" design for establishing causal inference (Christie & Alkin, 2013).

Robert Boruch. Similar to Campbell's legacy, Robert Boruch has been instrumental in furthering the use of randomized experiments in the evaluation field. One of Boruch's (1997) most influential works, *Randomized Experiments for Planning and Evaluation*, provides a practical guide to randomized experiments for evaluators. Boruch is a strong proponent of using randomized experiments, promotes them as the most effective method for evaluating a program's effects, and argues that any program can employ randomized experiments to determine their effectiveness. As stated by Christie and Alkin (2013),

Causal inference: the ability of an evaluator to claim that the program they are evaluating is responsible for the outcomes they measured; causality can be claimed with experimental designs.

> Mosteller and Boruch (2002) edited *Evidence Matters: Randomized Trials in Education Research*, arguing for the increased implementation of randomized trials in educational research to identify effective educational interventions. . . . These two publications [*Evidence Matters* and the National Research Council's *Scientific Research in Education* (Shavelson & Towne, 2002)] have been cited as offering key arguments for RCTs [randomized controlled trials] in educational research and have been noted for shaping the ways in which funding for educational research has been awarded under the No Child Left Behind legislation. (pp. 22–23)

Additionally, Boruch (2013) argues that evaluation organizations are critical to ensure the production and use of evaluation evidence. As such, he is a staunch advocate for the development of local, state, federal, and multinational evaluation organizations. Boruch was one of my advisers in graduate school; he has a wealth of knowledge and has experience with evaluation in many fields, including education and criminal justice. He was instrumental in shaping the Campbell Collaboration, an organization dedicated to generating systematic reviews of research, particularly with regard to social programs. Boruch was involved with the Campbell Collaboration in its earliest days and, deservedly, the Campbell Collaboration has instituted a Robert Boruch Award for Distinctive Contributions to Research That Informs Public Policy. When I think of Boruch, I can hear him say that the purpose of evaluation is to determine "What works? What works better? For whom? Under what conditions?" These four questions guide my work as an evaluator.

4.3.2 Quasi-Experimental Designs

Critics of experimental designs argue that they are difficult, and at times impossible, to implement in many real-world contexts. This is because experimental designs require random assignment of subjects to either a program or a control condition. For many social programs, restricting access or making a random determination as to who receives the program raises both ethical and logistical concerns. If half of the eligible youth in a school were randomly assigned to a new school counseling program designed to improve the coping skills of youth experiencing trauma in their lives, families as well as teachers might believe it is unjust to deny services to the other half of the students in order to have a control group. In addition, the school counselor might feel uncomfortable providing this new program to only some students and not use the new techniques with all students. Proponents of randomized controlled experiments might suggest, as an alternative, assigning whole schools to the intervention or control group, as opposed to groups of students within a single school, at least until data show the program to be effective. However, unless you have multiple schools willing to participate in the study that accept that they may or may not be chosen to receive the new program, it would be impossible to assign at the school level. Opponents to randomized controlled experiments would likely suggest that the evaluator consider finding an existing comparison group, or creating one through nonrandomized methods. For example, a neighboring school with similar demographics could be used as an existing comparison group, or allowing students or schools to self-select to participate in the program might enable those who do not select to participate to approximate a control group. Designs that have a nonrandomly assigned comparison group are called quasi-experimental designs. As you will read in Chapter 8, using existing groups or nonrandomized groups for the program and comparison, as opposed to forming new groups through random assignment, lacks the controls necessary to draw causal conclusions between the program and measured outcomes. Thus, even though such designs are perhaps more feasible and viewed as more ethical, attributing outcomes to the program is more difficult.

Thomas Cook. While Campbell and Boruch believe randomized controlled experiments to be superior to other designs, they also contributed to our understanding of quasi-experimental designs. Thomas Cook partnered with Campbell during the 1970s to expand the work on quasi-experimental designs (Christie & Alkin, 2013). While during the course of his career Campbell focused increasingly on purely experimental designs, Cook devoted his efforts to examining quasi-experimental designs for program evaluation. In fact, Cook and Campbell (1979) coauthored a text on quasi-experimental designs. Cook was known for criticizing the use of randomized controlled experiments in evaluation, arguing that randomization is unrealistic because contextual factors often cannot be controlled in an evaluation (Christie & Alkin, 2013). He encouraged evaluators to choose designs that consider the context of the evaluation, rather than applying randomized experiments across the board.

Lee Cronbach. Lee Cronbach made many contributions to the fields of evaluation, statistics, measurement theory, and research methods. He was a student of Ralph Tyler and is perhaps best known for Cronbach's coefficient alpha (Cronbach, 1951). In the evaluation field, he is best known for two publications: *Toward Reform of Program Evaluation* (Cronbach & Associates, 1980) and *Designing Evaluations of Educational and Social Programs* (Cronbach, 1982). Cronbach offered a different perspective from purely experimental researchers such as Campbell. Where Campbell focused on maximizing a study's ability to rigorously examine causal relationships, Cronbach stressed the importance of being able to generalize results beyond the evaluation (Chen, 2013).

Peter Rossi. Peter Rossi was a sociologist by training. His early work was heavily influenced by Campbell, though in later years he evolved from preferring randomized experiments to promoting a more theory-driven approach to evaluation (Chen & Rossi, 1983; Christie & Alkin, 2013). One of Rossi's greatest contributions to the field is his textbook titled *Evaluation: A Systematic Approach* (Rossi et al., 2018), now in its eighth edition. This was the textbook I used in graduate school; however, it was a much earlier edition and Rossi's only coauthor was Howard Freeman. Rossi states that he believes the best contribution that the field of evaluation can make to the world is to establish which social programs are effective and which are not (Rossi, 2013).

4.3.3 Nonexperimental Designs

Michael Bamberger. Nonexperimental designs either do not have a comparison group or have a poor comparison group, and as such are considered to be weaker designs than experimental or quasi-experimental designs. Due to his work with complex, international programs in developing areas, Michael Bamberger has worked to develop methodologically rigorous nonexperimental designs. Bamberger has written several books to guide evaluators in creating evaluation designs under realistic conditions of time, budget, and data constraints (Bamberger, Rugh, & Mabry, 2011; Bamberger, Vaessen, & Raimondo, 2015). Bamberger recommends repeated implementations of single-case evaluation designs as a way to examine treatment effects. He also supports approaches such as longitudinal analyses, in-depth case studies, concept mapping, and multiple case studies to increase the rigor of nonexperimental designs.

4.4 EVALUATION APPROACH

Ideology influences our approach to evaluation. Specifically, our views concerning role calibrators shape the approaches we choose to use. Within the design of an evaluation, whether that design be experimental, quasi-experimental, or nonexperimental, evaluators employ different approaches. These approaches are chosen based on how evaluators view the role of stakeholders and how evaluators envision the use of evaluation findings. However, there are additional factors that affect our choice of evaluation approach, such as our skills and experiences, as well as our access to stakeholders. In this section, common evaluation approaches will be introduced, along with the evaluators who developed those approaches. Objectives-oriented (Tyler), goal-free (Scriven), and theory-based (Chen and Weiss) approaches to evaluation will be explained. In addition, approaches such as responsive evaluation (Stake), CIPP evaluation (Stufflebeam), utilization-focused evaluation (Patton), participatory evaluation (Cousins), and empowerment evaluation (Fetterman) will be described. This list of approaches is not exhaustive and there are many additional evaluation approaches throughout the literature you may want to explore; however, these are some of the more common approaches to evaluation and will provide a good foundation as you learn about evaluation, begin to shape your own ideology, and identify your preferred designs and approaches.

4.4.1 Objectives-Oriented Evaluation

Ralph Tyler. Objectives-oriented evaluation, based on Ralph Tyler's work with educational reform, was discussed earlier in the chapter. As a recap, it is an approach to evaluation that focuses on the goals and objectives of a program. Methods are chosen to measure data based on these objectives, and findings are analyzed to determine the extent to which those objectives were met.

4.4.2 Goal-Free Evaluation

Michael Scriven. Goal-free evaluation, developed by Michael Scriven, was also described earlier in the chapter. Goal-free evaluation is based on the premise that focusing an evaluation on objectives provides an incomplete picture of the impact of a program. Instead, Scriven advocates that evaluators examine programs in their entirety, such that both intended and unintended outcomes are measured.

4.4.3 Theory-Based Evaluation

Huey Chen. While the beginnings of basing evaluation on a program's theory can be seen with objectives-oriented evaluation, theory-based evaluation did not really come into its own as an evaluation approach until the 1990s (Coryn, Noakes, Westine, & Schroeter, 2011). For the most part, Huey Chen is credited with developing the theory-driven evaluation approach (Chen, 1990; Christie & Alkin, 2013). In their article "Evaluating With Sense," Chen and Rossi (1983) promoted the use of theory in evaluation. Chen (2013) argues that theory-driven evaluation incorporates both Campbell's focus on internal validity and Cronbach's focus on external validity, as well as Scriven's recognition that unintended outcomes are just as important as intended goals. Theory-driven evaluation is an approach that can be used within an evaluation design, whether that design be a randomized controlled experiment, quasi-experiment, or nonexperiment (Chen, 1990, 2015). Note that the terms theory-driven evaluation and theory-based evaluation are often used interchangeably, as both refer to evaluations that are premised upon program theory.

Theory-based evaluation (TBE): an approach to evaluation that explicitly relates what a program does to its intended outcomes, based on the underlying logic of why and how a program works. TBE involves identifying the early and intermediate objectives through which program strategies function to achieve program goals.

Carol Weiss. My favorite textbook in the field is Carol Weiss's (1998) *Evaluation*, with the exception of the one you are reading now, of course! Unfortunately, with her passing in 2013, Weiss's textbook will never be updated. Mathison (2005) refers to Weiss as the "Founding Mother" of evaluation (p. 449). Weiss was a pioneer in the work on **theory-based evaluation (TBE)**. Theory-based evaluation is an approach to evaluation that explicitly relates what a program does to its intended outcomes, based on the underlying logic of why and how a program works. TBE involves identifying the early and intermediate objectives through which program strategies function to achieve program goals.

Weiss believed the purpose of evaluation was to improve social programs and spent much of her career studying evaluation use (Weiss, 2013). She promoted using theory to guide evaluation and stated that evaluators should seek to understand the assumptions underlying the relationship between a program and its desired outcomes (Weiss, 1998). While Chen termed the approach theory-driven evaluation, Weiss referred to it as theory-based evaluation. Theory-based evaluation seems to be the more common nomenclature. The theory-based evaluation approach is one that will be used throughout this book.

4.4.4 Responsive Evaluation

Robert Stake.   Robert Stake was a pioneer in the field of qualitative evaluation. While working on educational program evaluation in the 1960s, Stake (2011) developed the **responsive evaluation** approach. The premise of the approach is that evaluation information should be useful to stakeholders, and that observing a program in operation, without artificial controls, is the best way to make it useful. Yet, while he values stakeholder perspectives, he does not advocate stakeholder involvement in all aspects of the evaluation (Christie & Alkin, 2013). Several tenets of responsive evaluation are as follows:

> **Responsive evaluation:** an approach to evaluation that focuses on program activities, responds to stakeholder needs, and values the perspectives of all those involved in the program.

1. A focus on what the program does, rather than intended outcomes

2. A responsiveness to stakeholder needs for information

3. An acknowledgment of multiple perspectives in reporting findings

Stake believes an evaluator should become very involved with the program, and exercise flexibility in observing activities, rather than focusing narrowly on stated program goals. He is an advocate of frequent observations, interviews, and document reviews (Stake, 2011, 2013). Stake is a proponent of using case studies in evaluation and is known for his recommendation that evaluators construct "thick description" of stakeholder values and evaluation findings (Christie & Alkin, 2013, p. 34).

4.4.5 CIPP Evaluation

> **CIPP evaluation:** an approach to evaluation that incorporates four types of evaluation: context evaluation, input evaluation, process evaluation, and product evaluation. The CIPP model is used to improve programs and aid decision making.

Daniel Stufflebeam.   Daniel Stufflebeam advocated for the use of partnerships in evaluation (Rossi et al., 2018). Stufflebeam (2013) believed, "evaluation's purpose is not only to prove but also to improve" (p. 244). He viewed evaluation as a critical component for effective decision making. His work on partnerships and program improvement led to the development of the **CIPP evaluation** approach. CIPP includes four components: context, input, process, and product.

Stufflebeam began his development of the CIPP model in the mid-1960s, as a response to his dissatisfaction with other evaluation designs and approaches available at the time. He believed experimental designs were not appropriate for the complexity of his evaluations and he was not a fan of objectives-oriented approaches to evaluation. In his evaluations of many school improvement grants, he listened to stakeholders and identified the four important areas where evaluation could inform decision making. The CIPP model has many similarities to theory-based evaluation in that strategies, process objectives, and goals are key components of the evaluation. Stufflebeam's (2013) CIPP includes four types of evaluation:

1. Context evaluation relates to a program's needs and contextual conditions.

2. Input evaluation relates to the planning of activities that are part of the program.

3. Process evaluation relates to the implementation of those activities.

4. Product evaluation relates to the intended and unintended outcomes.

CIPP is intended to be a comprehensive approach to evaluation that uses both qualitative and quantitative methods. Stufflebeam (2011) also values stakeholder involvement in evaluation, but believes that to maintain integrity, evaluators should retain control of the evaluation process.

4.4.6 Utilization-Focused Evaluation

Michael Quinn Patton. Michael Quinn Patton is a sociologist turned evaluator. He developed **utilization-focused evaluation (UFE)**, an approach that asserts an evaluation's value is in its utility to stakeholders. Patton (2013) explains that at the heart of UFE is "intended use by intended users" (p. 293). Like responsive evaluation, UFE is a very hands-on approach to evaluation where the evaluator works very closely with intended users of the evaluation. Also, like responsive evaluation, the evaluator takes the role of a facilitator in guiding stakeholders to determine what they need from the evaluation.

Like Stufflebeam, Patton's perspectives on evaluation were shaped by his real-world experience working in complex settings. Serving in the Peace Corps in the 1960s, Patton worked as a community development generalist in very poor, rural villages. In this setting, Patton learned the critical importance of grounding evaluation efforts in the perspectives, values, and interests of the local people who "were there before I came and would be there after I left" (Patton, 2011, p. 4).

Patton also developed **principles-focused evaluation (PFE)**. PFE is similar to developmental evaluation, a method of evaluating complex programs in diverse environments. PFE is appropriate for evaluating policies or strategies in open systems, where there is uncertainty and complexity. Unlike UFE, where the focus is on use by intended users,

Utilization-focused evaluation (UFE): a collaborative approach to evaluation in which the evaluator prioritizes the perspectives and values of the individuals who will be most affected by evaluation findings.

Principles-focused evaluation (PFE): an approach to evaluation that focuses on evaluating the implementation and outcomes of principles.

with PFE the focus is on principles. In such evaluations, core principles are identified and the evaluation focuses on how those principles are implemented, as well as outcomes and broader impacts. PFE focuses on three questions (Patton, 2018):

1.   What are the principles?

2.   How are those principles being implemented?

3.   What outcomes are associated with the implemented principles?

4.4.7 Participatory Evaluation

J. Bradley Cousins. As a way to address the nonuse of evaluation findings, J. Bradley Cousins advocated for stakeholder engagement. Like responsive and utilization-focused evaluation, **participatory evaluation** is an approach that relies on stakeholder involvement. Like Stufflebeam, Cousins supports partnerships between stakeholders and evaluators. However, Cousins's participatory evaluation approach also stresses the importance of using rigorous evaluation methods. His rationale for this, like his motivation for building partnerships with stakeholders, is to facilitate evaluation use (Christie & Alkin, 2013).

Cousins sees the evaluator role as a coordinator who engages stakeholders in all aspects of the program, from design to data collection to analysis and reporting. His partnership model charges both stakeholders and evaluators with the joint responsibility of conducting the evaluation. Thus, like Stake, Cousins advocates for stakeholder involvement, but unlike Stake, Cousins broadens the role of the stakeholder and blurs the distinction between stakeholder and evaluator. Stakeholders in participatory evaluation are a focused group of collaborators who work closely with the evaluator in partnership. In a participatory partnership, stakeholders engage in capacity building in order to learn how to conduct the study (Cousins, 2013; Cousins & Earl, 1992).

Participatory evaluation: an approach to evaluation that relies on a partnership between stakeholders and evaluators.

4.4.8 Empowerment Evaluation

David Fetterman. David Fetterman's ideas for **empowerment evaluation** were inspired while writing his book *Speaking the Language of Power: Communication, Collaboration and Advocacy* (Fetterman, 1993). Like many of the approaches described above, the empowerment evaluation approach is collaborative. It also promotes the use of both quantitative and qualitative methods, as well as capacity building among stakeholders. However, what sets it apart from other approaches is its focus on self-determination (Fetterman, 1994).

Empowerment evaluation: an approach to evaluation that is focused on self-determination as a way to empower stakeholders to use evaluation findings and conduct their own evaluations.

Empowerment evaluation is based on community psychology and empowerment theory and the premise that if stakeholders are involved in evaluation, they are more likely to use the findings. The approach is about stakeholders taking ownership of the evaluation

> ✓ **QUICK CHECK**
>
> 1. How did Cook and Campbell view evaluation design? How were their views similar? How were they different?
> 2. How did Campbell and Cronbach differ in their views toward causality and generalizability?
> 3. How did Scriven approach evaluation? How is this different from Tyler's approach?
> 4. Compare and contrast utilization-focused, participatory, and empowerment approaches to evaluation. Who developed each approach?

process, as a way to foster data-informed decision making, and empowering them to work together to make changes. The evaluator's role is to build capacity so that stakeholders can become self-sufficient in conducting their own evaluations (Fetterman, 1994, 2013). In Fetterman's (1994) words, empowerment evaluation is a method that enables evaluators to "give voice to the people" (p. 1). Fetterman believes that building capacity among stakeholders to conduct evaluations of their own programs is a form of empowerment (Christie & Alkin, 2013).

4.5 EMBEDDED EVALUATION

Embedded evaluation, as introduced in Chapter 1, is an evaluation approach based on continuous improvement, in which program processes and practices are examined and refined in order to improve outcomes. The **embedded evaluation (EMB-E)** approach is really a combination of approaches, based on continuous improvement principles. At its core, embedded evaluation is theory-based; however, the methods used in explicating the theory are a little different from Weiss's method. In embedded evaluation, early and intermediate objectives are worded as measurable outcomes, to facilitate the development of indicators. Further, an evaluation matrix is used to expand on each component of the logic model to guide data collection and analysis. Embedded evaluation also includes elements of the participatory evaluation approach. Stakeholders are involved in every aspect of the evaluation process. However, while capacity building is a hopeful extension of embedded evaluation, it is not as explicit and intentional as in Cousins's participatory model. Other approaches could also be incorporated into an embedded approach, depending upon ideology, including responsive evaluation and empowerment evaluation. See "In The Real World" for considerations about how different evaluation approaches might have affected the Cambridge-Somerville Youth Study.

Embedded evaluation (EMB-E): an evaluation approach based on continuous improvement, in which program processes and practices are examined and refined to improve outcomes.

IN THE REAL WORLD . . .

Revisiting the Cambridge-Somerville Youth Study (CSYS): Design and Approach. The CSYS (Cabot, 1940) was based on an experimental research design. The predominant evaluation approach was objectives oriented, in that the evaluation focused on the goals and objectives of the program. It is revisited here to illustrate how a different ideology may have affected the study.

What if the CSYS evaluators had chosen a different **research design**? How do you think a quasi-experimental or nonexperimental design would have impacted the findings? How do you think a different design would have affected the credibility of the findings? How do you think a different design would have affected the usability of the findings? Do you think we would still be talking about the study today if it had used a nonexperimental design?

What if the CSYS evaluators had a different **evaluation approach**? Consider each scenario and identify ways that the change may have affected the findings from the study.

SCENARIO 1: If goal-free evaluation was used, would we still have data on the same outcomes?

SCENARIO 2: If theory-based evaluation (TBE) was used, what other indicators might have been tracked? What was the theory underlying the CSYS program?

SCENARIO 3: If responsive evaluation was used, would the design have still been experimental? What might have been learned from examining program activities more closely?

SCENARIO 4: If CIPP evaluation was used, would the design have still been experimental? If the evaluation was focused on information for stakeholder decision making, how might the program have evolved?

SCENARIO 5: If utilization-focused evaluation (UFE) was used, would the design have still been experimental? If the evaluation was focused on collecting information that was valued by and useful to program stakeholders, would we still have data on the same outcomes? What other data might have been collected in a UFE?

SCENARIO 6: If participatory evaluation was used, how might stakeholder perspectives have been incorporated into how the experimental design was carried out?

SCENARIO 7: If empowerment evaluation was used, would the design have still been experimental? How might stakeholder capacity building have been built into the evaluation?

SCENARIO 8: If embedded evaluation was used, how might the focus on improving program processes and practices have affected program implementation?

4.6 CHAPTER SUMMARY

This chapter discusses evaluation ideologies and approaches. **Ideologies** are a system of beliefs that we use to explain and develop solutions. Six **calibrators** are suggested that shape our ideology. Design, use, and methods calibrators are each a continuum upon which we can consider where our beliefs and preferences fall. Ideology, in turn, guides our choices regarding evaluation designs and approaches.

Experimental, quasi-experimental, and nonexperimental designs are briefly introduced and will be covered in more detail in Chapter 8. While many researchers have contributed to our knowledge and use of these designs, some of the most prominent evaluators are introduced: Campbell and Boruch (experimental); Cook, Cronbach, and Rossi (quasi-experimental); and Bamberger (nonexperimental).

Within an evaluation design, evaluators use a variety of approaches in the way in which they structure and conduct the evaluation, interact with stakeholders, and use evaluation findings. **Objectives-oriented evaluation** (Tyler) is an approach to evaluation where the focus of the evaluation is on how well the program met a set of predetermined objectives. **Goal-free evaluation** (Scriven) is an approach to evaluation where the evaluation is not constrained by program goals, but rather focuses on the measurement of outcomes, whether intended or unintended. **Theory-based evaluation** (Chen and Weiss) is an approach to evaluation that explicitly relates what a program does to its intended outcomes, based on the underlying logic of why and how a program works; TBE involves identifying the early and intermediate objectives through which program strategies function to achieve program goals. **Responsive evaluation** (Stake) is an approach to evaluation that focuses on program activities, responds to stakeholder needs, and values the perspectives of all those involved in the program. The **CIPP evaluation** (Stufflebeam) approach to evaluation incorporates four types of evaluation: context evaluation, input evaluation, process evaluation, and product evaluation. **Utilization-focused evaluation** (Patton) is a collaborative approach to evaluation in which the evaluator prioritizes the perspectives and values of the individuals who will be most affected by evaluation findings. **Principles-focused evaluation** (Patton) is an approach to evaluation that focuses on evaluating the implementation and outcomes of principles. **Participatory evaluation** (Cousins) is an approach to evaluation that relies on a partnership between stakeholders and evaluators. **Empowerment evaluation** (Fetterman) is an approach to evaluation that is focused on self-determination as a way to empower stakeholders to use evaluation findings and conduct their own evaluations. Finally, **embedded evaluation** is an evaluation approach based on continuous improvement, in which program processes and practices are examined and refined to improve outcomes.

Reflection and Application

1. Suppose you are planning to evaluate the effectiveness of the first-year orientation program for freshman at your school in helping students assimilate into the university environment. What evaluation design would you choose? What evaluation approach(es) would you choose? Why did you select that design and approach?

2. Your local YMCA has consulted you about evaluating a tutoring program that partners senior citizens with young children in local schools. They want to know how the program has impacted senior citizens' feelings of connectedness to the community. What evaluation approach would you recommend?

3. Create a matrix comparing the various evaluation approaches on the dimensions of stakeholder involvement, types of methods advocated, role of the evaluator, and purpose of the method.

4. Choose one approach to evaluation described in this chapter. Research the approach and the evaluator who developed the approach.

DEFINE, PART 1

Understanding the Program

By failing to prepare, you are preparing to fail.

—Benjamin Franklin

Upon completion of this chapter, you should be able to

- Describe the purpose of embedded evaluation.
- Discuss resources you can use to understand your program.
- Create program goals worded as outcome statements.
- Identify a program's primary strategies.
- Explain a program's theory, linking strategies to goals.
- Describe contextual conditions necessary for a program to be successful.
- Explain the difference between a theory of change (ToC) and a theory of action (ToA).

5.1 EMBEDDED EVALUATION

Charles Darwin said, "It is not the strongest of the species that survive, not the most intelligent, but the one most responsive to change." Being responsive to change acknowledges that learning is required to improve and perfect. Planning is not a one-time, up-front activity; it is a continual process of refining and adapting. Such planning and adaptation are not unique to living creatures, but are also a necessity for the programs and processes that human beings rely upon. Programs across many fields focus on improving services for people. For example, a higher-education program might focus on increasing access to college for low-income youth; a behavioral health program might implement a new counseling intervention intended to decrease seasonal affective disorder; an environmentally focused program might establish recycling centers at local schools to increase the volume of recycling within a community; and a nutrition program might include a new campaign to encourage youth to reduce fast-food consumption. Programs in many areas, including education, health, social services, and criminal justice, are aimed at helping people. As such, the leaders of such programs have a responsibility to understand what the program does, why it does it, and how the program is affecting the people involved, so that the program can be continually improved to benefit the people it serves. The purpose of evaluation is to determine if programs are indeed helping people, including the extent to which they are effective and for whom, as well as under what conditions and in what ways they work best. Chapters 5–11 of this textbook present a framework to aid you in embedding evaluation into program planning, design, and decision making to foster such continuous improvement.

5.1.1 Continuous Improvement Centered, Theory Based, Utilization Focused

As introduced in Chapter 1 and described in Chapter 4, **embedded evaluation (EMB-E)** is a comprehensive approach aimed at building evaluation into a program's design and operations. EMB-E is founded upon continuous-improvement principles (Deming, 2018) and is a theory-based approach to evaluation (Weiss, 1998). Because of its focus on continuous improvement and its consequent reliance upon partnerships with stakeholders to focus data collection on metrics that enable continuous improvement, EMB-E also incorporates aspects of participatory (Cousins & Earl, 1992) and utilization-focused evaluation (Patton, 2013).

EMB-E is an approach and also a framework. The framework includes defining objectives and goals as measurable outcomes during theory explication, building a logic model to represent the program's theory, creating indicators based on logic model components, and developing an evaluation matrix. The evaluation matrix is an extension of the logic model that drives data collection and analysis. Finally, the framework includes stakeholder-focused interpretation and use-intended recommendations to inform the continuous-improvement cycle.

Over the next few chapters, you will be led step-by-step through EMB-E, from documenting how and why your program works to using your evaluation results. It may be useful at this point to refer back to the embedded evaluation framework presented in Chapter 1. This framework is based on the following five steps:

Step 1. DEFINE: What is the program?

Step 2. PLAN: How do I plan the evaluation?

Step 3. IMPLEMENT: How do I evaluate the program?

Embedded evaluation (EMB-E): a comprehensive continuous-improvement-centered, theory-based, utilization-focused approach; a framework to build evaluation into a program's design and operations, making information and data the basis upon which the program operates and thus fostering continuous improvement.

Step 4. INTERPRET: How do I interpret the results?

Step 5. (a) INFORM and (b) REFINE: How do I use the results?

Step 1 will be covered in this chapter (Understanding the Program) and in Chapter 6 (Modeling the Program). Step 2 will be addressed in Chapters 7 (Planning the Evaluation) and 8 (Evaluation Design). Chapter 9 (Implementing the Evaluation) and Chapter 10 (Analyzing the Data) will focus on Step 3. Chapter 11 (Interpreting the Results) and Chapter 12 (Using Evaluation Results) will concentrate on Steps 4 and 5, respectively. The embedded evaluation model is provided in Figure 5.1.

5.1.2 Dynamic and Cyclical

By now in your study of evaluation, I am sure you would agree that evaluation is a dynamic process. While the embedded evaluation framework leads the evaluator through a stepped process, these steps are not meant to be items on a checklist. Evaluation is not a linear process

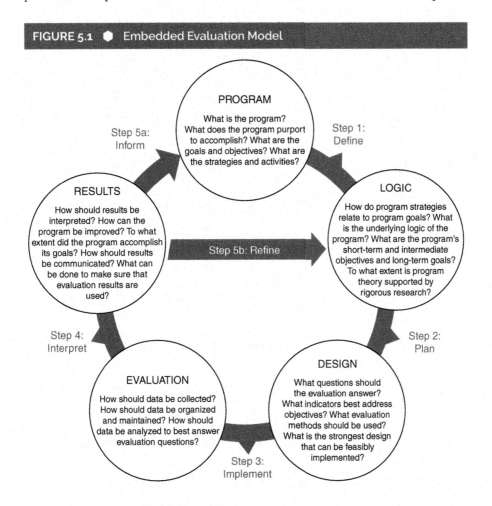

FIGURE 5.1 ● Embedded Evaluation Model

and EMB-E steps are not rungs on a ladder culminating with the final step. As long as a program is in operation, evaluation should not end. Evaluation is not *one and done*. The context within which a program operates is ever changing, just as the world we live in is ever changing. Evaluation findings for a certain group of people, in a particular context, at one point in time may not be relevant for another group of people, in a different context, at a later date.

The steps of EMB-E are components of the evaluation process that impact and influence each other. Information learned in one step may lead to refinement in a previous step. Thus, as information is gathered and lessons are learned, the program is improved. That is, EMB-E is a cyclical approach; it is grounded in continuous improvement cycles. Embedded evaluation aims to enable program staff to build and implement high-quality programs that are continuously improving, as well as to determine when programs are not working and need to be discontinued.

5.1.3 EMB-E Steps and Nodes

Before moving on to Step 1 (Define), I would like to explain the EMB-E graphical illustration in a little more detail. As described above, there are five steps. There are also five nodes in Figure 5.1. Each node is the result of the preceding step; it is the product of the step. For instance, defining the program (Step 1) results in the program's logic (node). At the conclusion of planning the evaluation (Step 2), the evaluation design is created (node). Once this design is implemented (Step 3), evaluation data are collected (node). Once the data are interpreted (Step 4), evaluation results are available (node). Finally, these data are used to inform program staff regarding effectiveness and to refine the program for continuous improvement purposes (Step 5). It should be noted, however, that refinement can occur at any step. For simplicity's sake, Step 5 links results to both program and logic, yet lessons learned during implementation of the evaluation may prompt you to return to planning, or findings during interpretation may raise questions that indicate a need to reexamine program definition. Thus, the model is meant to be a resource for you and it is my attempt to illustrate the ongoing, continuous cycle of evaluation with some simplicity, but it should not be seen as an inflexible ideal that constrains how an evaluation is implemented. As evaluators, we need to be flexible, and even creative, as we strive to understand the program, listen to the needs of stakeholders, and design an evaluation that provides a program's leadership with the information they need for decision making.

5.2 UNDERSTANDING THE PROGRAM

Because understanding the program is the foundation to understanding its effectiveness, the first step in conducting your evaluation is to understand what you want to evaluate. Whether you are evaluating a new program or a program that has been operating for some time, it is important to begin with the basics, that is, understanding how the program works. Do not rely on what you already know about the program or what you believe the program intends to accomplish. Instead, take what you know, and build on it with information from multiple sources. By doing this, you will gain a full understanding of the program, including multiple perspectives and expectations, as well as basic underpinnings and complex inner workings.

5.2.1 Previous Evaluations and Program Documentation

So, how do you find out more about the program? You may want to investigate whether the program has undergone any rigorous *previous evaluations*. If well designed and well carried out, previous evaluations can provide useful information regarding how a program operates. Start by searching the literature and internet for both published and unpublished evaluation reports of the same or similar programs. Such reports can not only inform you of important elements of the program, but can also give you valuable information regarding lessons learned, issues to consider, and potential evaluation instruments or methods that might be used in your evaluation.

For an existing program, a source from which you can learn more about the program is *existing documentation*. Documents such as strategic plans; training materials; meeting minutes; and federal, state, or local requirements may have useful information for understanding the program and the context in which it was implemented. It is also a good idea to familiarize yourself with any program materials. If the program is funded by a grant, an important place to start is the grant application. Grantors typically require applicants to delineate program goals and strategies. You will need to read the application carefully to tease out the goals and strategies. Often, stated goals are not really goals but rather strategies, while goals themselves may be indirectly alluded to in a project narrative. For instance, an applicant might have "provide families with healthy food alternatives" as a goal. In reality, this is a strategy meant to address a goal such as "increased intake of healthy foods" or "improved eating habits" or "improved health."

Another good source of information on an existing program is the *internet*, including a program or organization's website. Like grant applications, however, you will need to read through all information on the site to ascertain the program's true goals and strategies, and perhaps distinguish them from the program's stated goals and strategies. Very rarely does program documentation have strategies and goals clearly articulated. As the evaluator, you will need to pay careful attention to text that seems to describe a program activity or strategy and information that alludes to the reasons why a program was implemented.

5.2.2 Conversations, Interviews, and Group Discussions

Further, you may want to *talk with people* who have experience with the program, such as community members or partnering organizations, as well as program staff from agencies that have implemented the program. One of the best pieces of advice I received as an early evaluator was "work the phone." At the time, the internet was still fairly sparse and certainly not the amazing resource it is today. Do not be afraid to reach out to people, even if they seem out of reach. I am sure you have heard the phrase "we all put our pants on the same way." You might be surprised by the response you receive from the leader of a large organization, the president of a nonprofit, a high-ranking public official, or an established, well-known researcher.

I find it very productive to email individuals and typically receive timely responses to my inquiries. Though, as my daughter reminds me, email is *so yesterday*. What?! Maybe to the younger generation it is an outdated mode of communication, but for the workplace, it is still very relevant and effective. In this day and time, perhaps it would be more appropriate to say, "Work your social media," but do not forget that the phone (and email) can be your friend.

If you have experience with the program, you should absolutely document what you know, but also include others in your information gathering. Consider conducting *interviews and group discussions* with program staff to learn more about their insights into the program, how it operates, and what goals it intends to achieve. Instead of asking staff to recite the program's stated goals and strategies, discuss what the program hopes to change and what the program does or intends to do to bring about that change. Interviews with people familiar with a program are invaluable to understanding program expectations and activities.

5.3 DELINEATING GOALS AND STRATEGIES

Once you have a good understanding of the program, the next step is to document more systematically what you know about the program. The first component in explaining the program is to describe the program's goals; the second component is to delineate the program's strategies.

5.3.1 Documenting Program Goals

A **program goal** is a broad, general statement of what a program intends to accomplish or its desired result. Goals should reflect a shared understanding among program stakeholders as to what the program should achieve. What does the program intend to accomplish? How would you know if it worked? If the program were a success, what would have happened? What would have changed?

Program goal: a general statement of what a program intends to accomplish or its desired results.

Goal statements should reflect the overall intent of the program or a shared vision of what the program is supposed to accomplish. In comparison, objectives tend to be more specific and are often short term or intermediate in time span. If objectives are known, record them; however, at this point in program planning, broad, long-term goal statements are sufficient.

A program may have one or two goals, or it may have many goals. For example, a program focused on community conflict resolution may have a primary goal of improving community relations. On the other hand, for a program focused on at-risk youth, goals might be to decrease risky behavior, decrease youth arrests, and increase the high school graduation rate. Goals can focus on any facet of life. For instance, goals may have to do with changing the behavior of individuals, altering their quality of life, impacting knowledge of program participants, affecting attitudes, adjusting living or environmental conditions, or shifting the level of involvement or safety in the community.

In EMB-E, program goals should be worded as **outcome statements**. Later, the indicators and targets you create to address program goals will be SMART (specific, measurable, agreed upon, realistic, and time bound). I mention this because many of you have likely heard of SMART goals. The SMART framework (Doran, 1981) will be described in Chapter 7 in the discussion on creating indicators for goals and objectives. However, for our purposes program goal statements should begin with an outcome word (such as increase, decrease, improve, etc.) that indicates what the program should accomplish. Avoid starting goal statements with nondescript words, such as help, show, and make. Outcome words should focus on what the program itself will *do* as part of its strategies and activities, not on what the program *affects*. Thus, program goals should focus on what will be achieved after implementation of the program.

When documenting the program's primary goals, ask yourself the following: If the program were successful, what observable change would likely be seen? Once again, programs should be designed not around what the program does, but on what the program intends to accomplish. The services provided by the program, its strategies and activities, are important and will be the focus of the next section. However, it is important to note that what the program does is a means to an end. This end is the program's goal or goals. The program's design, its implementation, and its evaluation should all focus on these goals. That is, a program should be designed around its goals, not its strategies. The goals are the destination; the program design maps out the program's route to reach this destination. Table 5.1 displays some sample goal statements.

5.3.2 Identifying Program Strategies

Once you have documented what the program intends to accomplish, the next component is to document the program's strategies. How will the program accomplish its goals? What strategies will be used to achieve the goals? What activities will need to be put in place for the program? Does the program have activities that occur in the community, in the home, at the workplace, or in a combination of these settings?

Program strategies are activities or clusters of activities. Strategies might be access to financial and other resources, or provision of support services, professional guidance,

Outcome statement: a statement of what the program intends to accomplish that begins with an outcome word. While goals are worded many different ways, embedded evaluation is based on goals being worded as outcome statements.

Program strategies: activities the program puts into place to accomplish its goals. Strategies might include services, materials, training, resources, or a cluster of activities.

TABLE 5.1 ● Goal Statement Examples	
If I want to	**The goal(s) might be to**
Change the behaviors of community members	Improve community self-monitoring Increase community involvement Improve civic leadership
Change the attitudes of community members toward their own community	Improve attitudes toward community Decrease atomization within the community Increase feelings of community ownership

training, skill development, mentoring, or counseling. Strategies might be ongoing throughout the program or drawn on at various stages during the program's operation. Listing all strategies used as part of the program is important to explaining later how and to what extent the program's goals were met.

If you are embedding evaluation into an existing program, examine what the program does. If you are embedding evaluation into a new program, examine what the program proposes to do. Either way, document the major strategies of the program put in place to accomplish the program's goals. Whether you are working with a new program or an existing program, the process of understanding the program is the same. Spending the time to understand the program and to document its strategies designed to meet goals is critical not only to operating the program, but also to designing an effective evaluation.

Documenting strategies may appear to be a simple inventory of things to do. It is important to note, however, that the strategies a program implements are not stand-alone activities on a checklist, but rather interconnected activities designed to work together to meet a common goal or goals. We will have more on this interconnectedness later when we discuss implementation evaluation in Chapter 7. For now, to understand the program for the purpose of designing the evaluation, the task is simply to identify and document the strategies. For an example of how to document a program's goals and strategies, see the "In The Real World" example on the next page.

If you are following along with your own program, at this point you have documented your program's goals, as well as the strategies that will be employed as part of the program to meet these goals. The next task is to relate program strategies to program goals. Important questions at this stage are: Why should the program work? Why should implementing this set of strategies meet the goals set for the program?

IN THE REAL WORLD . . .

The **DC Central Kitchen** provides thousands of free meals every day to homeless shelters, transitional homes, and nonprofit organizations in and around Washington, D.C. The program has three primary goals: (1) reduce hunger; (2) increase employment; and (3) increase access to healthy foods.

The DC Central Kitchen has five primary strategies it uses to address these goals: (1) meal distribution to area organizations; (2) culinary job training for homeless adults; (3) food recycling to use leftover and surplus food; (4) providing school meals to low-income children; and (5) distributing fresh produce and healthy snacks to corner stores in area food deserts.

Sources: http://www.dccentralkitchen.org/.

 QUICK CHECK

1. The first step in program evaluation is to

   a. Collect your data

   b. Design your evaluation

   c. Outline your evaluation report

   d. Understand your program

2. Once you have researched and found out as much information as you can about the program, the next task should be to

   a. Collect your data

   b. Design your evaluation

   c. Document your program's goals

   d. Determine if the program is effective

3. A program intends to impact the anxiety college students feel at exam time. What might be a goal for this program? What strategies might the program use to address this goal?

Answers: 1-d; 2-c; 3-answers will vary (example goal: decreased anxiety among college students; example strategies: coping strategies workshops and on-call counseling services)

5.4 EXPLAINING THE PROGRAM THEORY

The linkages between program strategies and program goals are assumptions about why the program should have the desired outcomes. These underlying assumptions, taken together, are the basis of the program theory. That is, the **program theory** is the reasoning behind why the program should work. Suppose it is believed that holding town meetings and

Program theory: the theory as to why the program should work. It is a set of underlying assumptions that explain the linkages between program strategies and program goals.

providing conflict-resolution training to community members would improve community relations. Or suppose it is assumed that creating a youth community center, providing engaging and relevant after-school and summer activities, employing counselors to work with youth on interpersonal skills, and making tutors available for homework help will improve the outcomes for at-risk youth, including reducing risky behavior and decreasing the high school drop-out rate.

In documenting the program's theory, take each program strategy and examine how it relates to the program's goals. What makes you believe that the strategy will result in the intended outcomes? What changes should occur during and after implementation of strategies that will lead to reaching the program goals?

Take the first example above, of implementing the strategy to hold town meetings. It is hoped that this would lead to the early outcome of residents attending those meetings. If the outcome of residents attending the meetings is achieved, what intermediate outcome might this lead to? If residents attend the meetings, it might be hoped that they increase their communication with one another. If there is increased communication, it could be that residents will have an increased sense of belonging to the community.

Likewise, why would the strategy of providing training to community members to resolve conflicts peacefully lead to improved community relations? It is hoped that if conflict-resolution training is offered residents will participate. If more community members are trained, it is logical to believe that the conflict-resolution skills among residents will improve.

Finally, theoretically the increased feelings of belongingness and improved conflict-resolution skills among community members realized through the town meetings and training strategies will likely lead to improved community relations. As you can see through this example, program theory can be flushed out by continually asking the question, "If I implement this strategy or achieve this objective, what outcome should I see next?" See the framework in Figure 5.2 for relating program strategies to program goals.

When examining the linkages between program strategies and goals, try to determine the basis for these assumptions. Are the assumptions grounded in solid research? Or are

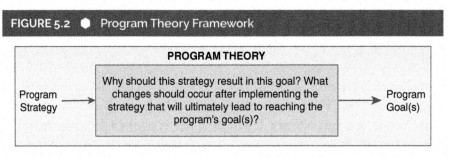

FIGURE 5.2 ● Program Theory Framework

QUICK CHECK

Try documenting the program theory for the following program:

The strategies include

- Creating a youth community center,
- Providing engaging and relevant after-school and summer activities,
- Employing youth counselors to mentor at-risk youth,
- Working with youth on interpersonal skills, and
- Making tutors available for homework help.

The goals are

- Reducing risky behavior among at-risk youth and
- Decreasing the high school drop-out rate among at-risk youth.

Answers: Answers will vary. An example of a program theory for the first strategy is as follows. Creating a community youth center for at-risk youth will lead to more at-risk youth attending the youth center. More youth attending the youth center will result in decreased time spent unsupervised. Decreased time spent unsupervised will lead to decreased opportunity to engage in risky behavior. A decreased opportunity to engage in risky behavior will lead to a reduction in risky behavior among at-risk youth.

they based on emerging knowledge or personal experience? Documenting the relationship between a program's strategies and its goals explains the program design and is the basis for embedding evaluation into the program. Additionally, understanding whether this relationship is based on solid research or emerging knowledge will aid you when designing your evaluation. Programs that are based on emerging knowledge or are innovative in their approach should have a more extensive and rigorous evaluation than a program that is developed on solid research and shaped from previous evaluation evidence.

The process of describing the program's theory and delineating the assumptions that underlie the program will be further explored in Chapter 6, when the program's theory is documented using a logic model. See the case study on the following page for an example of documenting program theory.

5.5 DETERMINING CONTEXTUAL CONDITIONS

Most programs rely upon certain **contextual conditions** being met and resources being readily available to operate the program. If the program you are evaluating assumes that a certain infrastructure is in place or that specific materials are available, you should identify and list these conditions and resources when planning your evaluation. If a program is built upon the presumption that trained counselors, or other skilled professionals, are

Contextual conditions: resources, infrastructure, facilities, services, or any other conditions that are necessary for the program to be successful, but are not part of the program itself.

available for hiring in the area in which the program will be implemented, this should be listed as a contextual condition. Further, if the program operation assumes that facilities are available for convening people or providing education or that a partnering organization will provide services critical to the program, these should be included as contextual conditions as well. Any resource that is necessary for the program to be successful, but that is not part of the program itself, should be clearly documented.

In the previous section, a program was introduced to improve community relations. Two of the primary strategies were to hold town meetings and provide conflict-resolution training to community members. Contextual conditions, or resources necessary to implement the program that are not part of the program itself, might be a facility in which to hold town meetings and a location in which to provide conflict-resolution training. Another contextual condition might be the availability of trainers skilled in conflict resolution. If the location of town meetings and/or training is such that community members cannot walk to the facility, the availability of transportation is another important contextual condition to consider. If you find that the necessary contextual conditions are not in place, such as the availability of convenient public transportation, including the provision of transportation as a strategy of the program itself might be a consideration.

Note that contextual conditions are different from contextual influences. Contextual conditions are assumptions about what resources and infrastructure are necessary for a

CASE STUDY
Youth Abstinence-Plus (YAP) Program

For decades, researchers and practitioners have debated the use of abstinence-only programs versus sexual education programs as a means to decrease the incidence of unintended pregnancy and the spread of sexually transmitted infections (STIs) among youth. Even with the growing evidence that abstinence-only programs are not effective at delaying sexual activity or reducing STIs, these programs became very popular during the early 2000s. In fact, some researchers found that abstinence-only programs had negative unintended consequences related to denying youth access to information about safe sex and protection from disease. On the other hand, sexual education programs have been criticized as promoting sexual activity, though little evidence supports this claim.

An alternative to these two approaches is an abstinence-plus program that combines safe sex education with a strong message that promotes abstinence. Over the next few paragraphs, we will design a program called Youth Abstinence-Plus (YAP) that includes a focus on abstinence, education regarding safe sex for those youth who find themselves in sexual situations, and access to contraceptives for youth who plan to engage in sexual activity.

From the above description, we can determine that the YAP program goals are as follows:

1. Decrease the pregnancy rate among youth.
2. Decrease the spread of STIs among youth.
3. Increase the number of youth who choose sexual abstinence.

The YAP program strategies are provision of the following:

1. Materials on the benefits of abstinence
2. Education regarding safe sex
3. Access to contraception

So, our initial program theory is as follows:

- Providing materials on and a message about the benefits of sexual abstinence among youth will increase the number of youth who choose sexual abstinence, which will lead to a decrease in the pregnancy rate among youth and a decrease in the spread of STIs.

- Providing youth with education regarding safe sex practices will decrease the pregnancy rate among youth and decrease the spread of STIs.

- Providing youth access to contraceptives will decrease the pregnancy rate among youth and decrease the spread of STIs.

The next step is to expand on the program theory, make the objectives leading from the strategies to the goals more specific, and explicitly state the program's underlying logic. Ideally, the program staff, key stakeholders, and evaluation staff would hold a series of meetings to discuss why the program's strategies will result in the goals that were specified. The following is the expanded logic that might evolve from such meetings:

- Providing **materials on promoting sexual abstinence** and a message about the benefits of sexual abstinence among youth will increase access to materials on abstinence, leading to an increased number of youth who receive the message about the benefits of abstinence, leading to an increased number of youth who understand the benefits of abstinence. An increase in the number of youth who understand the benefits of abstinence will lead to an **increase in the number of youth who choose sexual abstinence**, which will lead to a **decrease in the pregnancy rate among youth** and a **decrease in the spread of STIs**.

- Providing youth with **education regarding safe sex practices** will increase access to education regarding safe sex practices, leading to an increase in the number of youth who receive education regarding safe sex practices, which will lead to an increase in the number of youth who understand the benefits of safe sex practices. An increase in the number of youth who understand the benefits of safe sex practices will lead to improved safe sex practices among youth who are sexually active. Improved safe sex practices among sexually active youth will **decrease the pregnancy rate among youth** and **decrease the spread of STIs among youth**.

- Providing youth with **access to contraceptives** will increase the number of youth who have access to contraceptives, which will increase the number of sexually active youth who obtain contraceptives. An increase in the number of sexually active youth who obtain contraceptives will increase the use of contraceptives among sexually active youth, leading to improved safe sex practices among sexually active youth. Improved safe sex practices among sexually active youth will **decrease the pregnancy rate among youth** and **decrease the spread of STIs among youth**.

program to reach its goals. **Contextual influences** are factors in the environment that may affect the program's operations and success. Contextual influences may be political, economic, social, or technological (PEST). The PEST framework is a structured method of examining the various influences within the program's environment and considering how they might impact the program (Aguilar, 1967). At this point in EMB-E, we are focusing on contextual conditions. However, it is always a good idea for program staff to conduct a PEST analysis prior to a new program being implemented and routinely during program operation.

5.6 PROGRAM THEORY AND OTHER THEORIES

The term "theory" is used in many fields and in multiple contexts. At its core, a theory is simply a proposition or an explanation, describing why you think something occurs the way that it does. However, because the term is used so frequently and across disciplines, it is hoped that this section will clarify how program theory relates to and differs from other types of theory.

A **theory** is a system of beliefs intended to explain how something works. Merriam-Webster online adds that a theory is "a hypothesis assumed for the sake of argument or investigation." Theories are common in science and are typically developed after a series of hypotheses have been tested. Thus, theories are often based on more than a hunch or an educated guess. Rather, findings from previous work or research are the foundation for the development of a theory. Innovation is founded on promising theories and based on promising practices.

Some well-developed theories in psychology are personality theory, cognitive-behavioral theory, developmental theory, and social-cognitive theory. Engineers use systems theory. Managers use motivational theory and leadership theory. Biologists have feedback theory. Sociologists have many theories, including symbolic interaction theory, conflict theory, critical theory, feminist theory, and game theory. The field of philosophy abounds with theories, including theories about truth and power. There are even theories related to political change, fiscal behavior, and communications.

Theories are not static; they are dynamic. Developing theory is a process. Hence, theories should evolve and improve as we learn more about how and why something works. Additionally, some theories have more evidence to support them than others, and it is important to know what kinds of evidence a theory is based upon. The stronger the evidence and the more tested the theory, the more confident you can feel in using the theory as the basis for a program. However, this does not mean that untested theories should not be used as the basis for a program. Rather, untested theories can lead to innovative programs. For programs based on untested theory, however, rigorous evaluation designs

Contextual influences: factors in the environment that may affect the program's operations and success; context can be examined using a PEST analysis, which explores political, economic, social, and technological influences.

Theory: a system of assumptions or beliefs intended to explain how something works.

are critical to shaping the program and determining its effectiveness. Evaluation design will be discussed in Chapter 8.

5.6.1 Program Theory Revisited

Programs and policies that are intended to improve the lives of people are based on a theory, though this theory is not always explicitly stated. If we view a program or policy as fact and do not question how well it works and for whom it works best, we could potentially do more harm than good in our effort to help people. Thus, evaluation is the science of understanding what works so that we can be confident the programs and policies we are using are indeed accomplishing what we set out to accomplish. Evaluation can be viewed as a systematic way of testing a theory related to how we can best serve people. The theory we are testing is called program theory.

As stated earlier in this chapter, program theory is focused on program goals. Program theory is helpful in understanding why the program should work (that is, why the program's strategies should result in the program's goals). Program theory is an outcomes-based description of the logic fundamental to the program.

Program theory has been used to explain programs for nearly half a century. Many evaluators have their own preferred way of writing the program's theory and representing the theory graphically. While a logic model is the most common way of illustrating program theory, logic models also vary in their detail and format (logic models will be discussed Chapter 6). Regardless of the way program theory is written or the format and detail of its accompanying model, the purpose is primarily the same: Program theory outlines the assumptions underlying why a program should work, linking what the program does (strategies) to its long-term goals (worded as outcomes).

5.6.2 Theories of Change

A **theory of change** (ToC) describes how change occurs. A ToC can be narrative or pictorial. However, it is typically a general representation of how strategies relate to goals. ToCs are also referred to as causal models, as the model shows the theorized causal linkages between a program and its intended outcomes. However, the term causal is misleading. While the model can appear to show causal linkages between strategies, objectives, and goals, causality can only be claimed based on the design of the evaluation. That is, certain evaluation designs, due to the way in which participants are included in the evaluation, can approximate cause-and-effect relationships between program strategies and the outcomes of the program.

Theories of change are just that—theories. The evaluation design is used to test that theory by providing evidence, to the extent possible, that a relationship exists between what the program does and what is accomplished. Theories of change show theorized

Theory of change (ToC): a theory that describes how a change occurs; program theory is a theory of change.

associations; the evaluation design can potentially provide evidence of causal relationships. Causality will be further explored in Chapter 8.

Program theory is a theory of change. Program logic models, as mentioned above and covered in more detail in Chapter 6, are a graphical representation of a ToC, providing detailed outcome-focused information about how and why the change should occur. Theories of change are very useful in explaining *why* a program does what it does, as well as in designing the program's evaluation; they do not explain *how* the program is implemented. Thus, it is important to remember that a ToC, including program theory, is based on outcomes, results we would like to see, and not on how services are provided or activities implemented to reach those outcomes. If you would like to read more on ToCs, the Annie E. Casey Foundation has a useful guide that describes creating and using theories of change (Organizational Research Services, 2004).

5.6.3 Theories of Action

A **theory of action (ToA)** is the operationalization of a theory of change. While sometimes a ToA is used synonymously with a ToC, there are important distinctions. A ToA describes the processes through which change occurs and explains the means through which strategies are implemented. It focuses on the services provided to reach our intended outcomes.

Implementation theory is a theory of action. Implementation theory focuses on the service delivery aspect of a program (Nilson, 2015; Weiss, 1998). That is, it relates the objectives within the program's theory to program activities that must occur to address that objective. Implementation theory is a more operational theory and is intended for program delivery, as opposed to a program theory's representation of the intended outcomes of strategies throughout program implementation. Program theory and implementation theory work together to explain why and how a program works. While this text focuses on program theory as a way to embed evaluation into a program, the strategies that are part of a program's theory could be represented using implementation theory. A model of a program's implementation theory would guide program staff regarding what activities to deliver and at what stage in the program operation to deliver them.

5.7 CONSIDERING ALTERNATIVE THEORIES

Theory of action (ToA): a theory that describes how a program is delivered.

Implementation theory: a theory of action that describes the activities that precipitate change.

If you are using Chapters 5–8 as a guide to design an evaluation, at this point, you have documented the program, including the strategies that will be part of the program and the intended goals of the program. You have also considered the assumptions as to why the strategies should result in achieving the program's goals. As mentioned in the previous section, these assumptions explain why the program should work and are the basis of the program's theory. Before defining the program any further, this would be a good place to pause for a moment and reflect on the program theory that you have documented. Ask

QUICK CHECK

1. A group of assumptions that, taken together, explain why a program should work is called the program's

   a. Context

   b. Implementation

   c. Strategy

   d. Theory

2. For the program in the previous Quick Check aimed at reducing risky behavior and decreasing the high school drop-out rate, describe at least two contextual conditions.

3. Explain how a theory of change differs from a theory of action.

Answers: 1-d; 2-answers will vary (example: a facility to house the youth community center and the availability of mentors); 3-answers will vary (example: a ToC describes why change occurs, while a ToA describes how change occurs)

yourself again why you think your assumptions of the program should work. Are your assumptions based on a solid research foundation? That is, do you have reason to believe based on results from evaluations conducted by others or more general research in the field that the program will work? Or are your assumptions based on emerging knowledge in the field, a hypothesis, or your own experience?

Understanding the basis of the program's theory is important to designing a rigorous evaluation. Implementation assessment should always be central to your evaluation design; however, the less evidence there is to support the program's theory, the more carefully you will want to monitor the implementation of the program and gather early and intermediate information on program effectiveness. If there is evidence from methodologically sound past evaluations that is contrary to your proposed theory, you will want to think carefully about what is different about the program to inspire those who are developing the program to think it will work. In such cases, documenting alternative theories may prove useful to you in understanding and interpreting program results. It is important to note that there is nothing wrong with a sound, well-documented theory that has little existing information to support its effectiveness, as the information you obtain from your evaluation may be the foundation of innovation.

5.8 CHAPTER SUMMARY

Embedded evaluation is a comprehensive approach to build evaluation into your program's design and operations. The first step in conducting an evaluation is to understand what you want to evaluate, beginning with the program's goals and strategies. A **program goal** is a broad, general statement of what a program intends to accomplish or its desired result. Program goals should be worded as **outcome statements**. **Program strategies** are activities the program puts into place to accomplish its goals. Strategies might include services, materials, training, resources, or a cluster of activities. The next step is to relate program strategies to program goals. **Program theory** is the theory as to why the program should work. It is a set of underlying assumptions that explain the linkages between program strategies and program goals. Documenting the program using program theory will aid program staff and evaluators in describing the program's goals, delineating the program's strategies, and explicitly stating the logic that relates the program's strategies to its goals. It is also important to identify the **contextual conditions** necessary for the program to operate. A contextual condition is any resource, infrastructure, facility, service, or other condition that is necessary for the program to be successful, but that is not part of the program itself. **Contextual influences** are factors in the environment that may affect the program's operations and success; context can be examined using a PEST analysis examining political, economic, social, and technological influences.

A **theory** is a system of beliefs intended to explain how something works. A **theory of change (ToC)** describes how change occurs. A ToC can be narrative or pictorial. However, it is typically a general representation of how strategies relate to goals. Program theory is a ToC. A **theory of action (ToA)** is the operationalization of a theory of change that describes how a program is delivered. **Implementation theory** is a ToA that describes the implementation of program activities.

Reflection and Application

1. Choose a program or policy in your community and identify its stated program goals. Are these goals worded as measurable outcomes? If not, read through the documentation of the program and rewrite the program goals as measurable outcomes.

   a. Next, identify the program's strategies.

   b. Brainstorm the theory that relates the program's strategies to the program's goals (worded as measurable outcomes).

   c. Using the brainstormed theory, word the early and intermediate objectives as measurable outcomes.

   d. What contextual conditions are necessary for the program to be successfully implemented?

2. Choose a social problem important to you. Develop goals indicating the necessary change to address this problem. What strategies might you use for a program focused on these goals?

DEFINE, PART 2

Modeling the Program

He who asks a question is a fool for five minutes;
he who does not ask a question remains a fool forever.

—Chinese proverb

Upon completion of this chapter, you should be able to

- Explain what a logic model is and its purpose.
- Describe the benefits of stakeholder involvement in the logic modeling process.
- Create a logic model to represent a program.
- Use logic modeling to facilitate the creation of program theory.
- Explain your program's theory using a logic model.
- Describe how a logic model can be used with stakeholders.

6.1 CHAPTER IN CONTEXT

In Chapter 5, the first step of the embedded evaluation model was introduced—*define*. This chapter continues the process of defining the program you intend to evaluate by building upon the program theory delineated in Chapter 5.

In this chapter, logic modeling will be introduced as a way to graphically represent a program's theory. The logic model you create will be the foundation of the program's

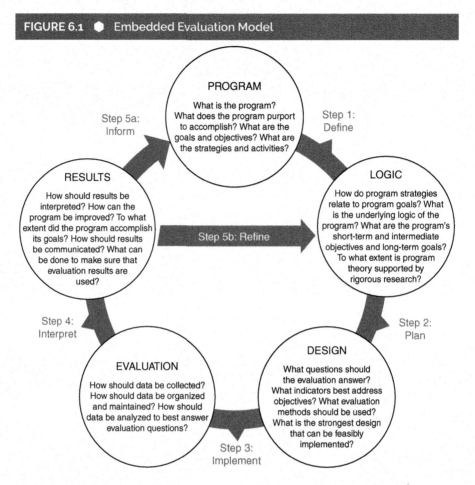

FIGURE 6.1 ● Embedded Evaluation Model

evaluation, guiding you through the remaining steps of embedded evaluation. As a reminder, the define step is the most important step of the embedded evaluation process—the strength and precision of your evaluation is dependent upon you spending the time to accurately represent the program during program definition.

6.2 WHAT IS A LOGIC MODEL?

Logic model: a graphical representation of a program's theory.

Developing the program's theory and modeling the program's logic are part of the same overall process of understanding the program. A **logic model** graphically displays the program's theory and explains how you believe the program works. For that reason, Chapters 5 and 6 work together but are not necessarily sequential. That is, developing your program's theory *using* logic modeling is helpful in determining early and intermediate objectives. It is recommended that logic modeling be used to facilitate the development of the program theory.

A logic model shows the relationships between a program's strategies and the intended effects of those strategies on the program. In the logic model you create in this chapter, these intended effects will be represented as objectives. You will focus on these objectives throughout the evaluation to determine the extent to which the program is working as envisioned. Your logic model is the cornerstone of the program and its evaluation and should be continually used to check progress throughout the program's implementation, to help discover problems with the program, and to make necessary corrections and improvements while the program is in operation.

In that regard, *logic modeling is a process*, not simply an end result. While you will create a tangible logic model for the program—a model that will be a critical component of the program's operation and evaluation—the power is in the creation process. The process of logic modeling has many uses, from understanding an existing program to designing a new project to fostering shared ownership of a plan to teaching others how a program is intended to work.

6.2.1 Stakeholder Involvement in Logic Modeling

Putting a new idea into practice involves change, and change is dependent upon people. Furthermore, change takes time. The people involved in a program, called program stakeholders, are critical to successful and timely change. Stakeholders were defined in Chapter 1, but in this section stakeholder involvement in program definition and evaluation planning will be addressed. A **program stakeholder** is anyone who has an interest or stake in the operation or success of a program. Key stakeholder groups often include program staff, community members, program participants, and policymakers. Logic modeling can facilitate change by building a shared vision and ownership among stakeholders from the outset, but only if creating the logic model is a shared process. This does not mean that you need to include every stakeholder in every phase of logic modeling. The initial creation of a logic model works best if done by a small group, perhaps a subcommittee of the larger evaluation team. However, once this group creates a draft, including others in the process will likely enrich the model, improve the program's subsequent implementation, and increase the likelihood of successful change.

Program staff are a key stakeholder group. Including program staff in the logic modeling process can help to ensure everyone involved with operating the program is working toward a common goal and that all staff understand and support what the program is trying to accomplish. Program staff can provide significant insight into why a strategy might be successful and offer valuable information regarding examination of the implementation of strategies. Programs are more likely to be successful when the staff feel ownership of the program. Further, evaluations are more likely to

Program stakeholder: anyone who has an interest or stake in the success of a program. Key stakeholders include program staff, community members, program participants, and policymakers.

be an integral part of program improvement if program staff have a shared understanding of and commitment to goals and objectives that have been mutually set for the program.

Community members are another important stakeholder group. The community of the program includes those in the environment in which the program will operate. Thus, the community will vary depending upon the program. For a program intending to improve outcomes for at-risk youth in the community, the community would be the town or neighborhood in which the program is implemented. For a program intending to improve the achievement of students with disabilities, the focus will likely be on the school community, especially parents and teachers. Including community members in the logic modeling process can help foster a culture in which those in the environment in which the program will operate understand and embrace what the program staff are trying to accomplish. The success or failure of a program can depend upon the degree to which program efforts are supported in the community in which the program is implemented.

Program participants are the focus of a program and inarguably one of the most important stakeholder groups. Including program participants in the logic modeling process, when possible, invites them to be active participants in program planning and development. However, for new programs, the actual program participants often have not been determined. In such cases, including individuals who are similar to those who would be the focus of a program can provide valuable insight into program strategies, as well as objectives and goals.

Policymakers are a fourth important stakeholder. Including policymakers in the logic modeling process can foster mutual understanding of the program and its goals. Policymakers provide a unique perspective on the evidence a program must generate in order to receive continued support and future funding.

The logic modeling process should include the person or people who will have primary responsibility for the program, as well as those who are critical to its success. Because the logic model you are creating will be used for evaluation purposes, your model will not simply describe the program or project, but it will also inform indicators that you will use to measure your program's success throughout its operation. For this reason, someone with evaluation expertise, perhaps you, should be part of the logic modeling team.

It is important to note that the inclusion of stakeholders is not a symbolic, one-time effort to garner support. Stakeholder involvement should not end once the logic model is drafted. When a true commitment to stakeholders is made, those who are affected by or have an investment in the program are involved in every aspect of the evaluation, from defining the program to planning the evaluation to interpreting findings. The purpose of including stakeholders throughout is to ensure that the information produced from the evaluation is useful, to make program improvements, and to foster program success. To accomplish this, evaluators should endeavor to engage stakeholders in an ongoing partnership to continually

QUICK CHECK

1. A logic model explains
   a. When program activities should be implemented.
   b. What the program staff will do at the start, middle, and end of the program.
   c. How you expect a program's **strategies** to result in the program's goals.
   d. How each program stakeholder is related to the program.
2. What is a program stakeholder? Why is it important to include program stakeholders in the logic modeling process?

Answers: 1-c; 2-a person who has a stake in the program

improve the program's design and operation. With regard to defining the program, the more key stakeholders that can be substantively involved in the logic model development process and the more people who truly understand how the program is intended to work, the more likely the program and its evaluation will be effective. Once you have the logic modeling team assembled, the following sections will take you through the process of creating the model.

6.3 CREATING THE LOGIC MODEL

In Chapter 5, you completed the most important part of program design and evaluation—you defined the program, documenting what the program intends to accomplish (its goals) and what the program will do to accomplish those goals (its strategies). You have also begun to examine *why* the program should work (the program's theory). Next is the process of refining this theory and making the linkages between strategies and goals operational. Using the program's theory and underlying assumptions as the foundation, you will begin to create a model that depicts the program's inner workings.

6.3.1 Breaking Open the Black Box

At the heart of your logic model are the linkages between what is done as part of the program and what will be accomplished with the program. The linkages explain how the program works. While there are many variants of logic models, in embedded evaluation (EMB-E) the logic model linkages will focus on the program's short-term and intermediate objectives. Short-term and intermediate objectives are critical to improving the implementation of the program as well as to establishing the association, supported by data, that the program's strategies are theoretically related to the program's goals. Without short-term and intermediate indicators that reflect the program's underlying theory, your evaluation would be a Black Box with inputs (strategies) and outputs (goals). The purpose of program theory and logic modeling is to break open this box and create a model that is representative of the logic behind why the program should work. In Chapter 5, an initial program theory framework was introduced (see Figure 6.2). The logic model expands the inside of the box, answering the questions of why the strategy should result in the goals and what changes need to occur that will lead to reaching the program's goals. The answers to these questions will allow you to monitor the program's operation and enable you to make assertions about the success of the strategies that are part of the program.

If the program theory is well defined, you may find that creating the logic model is a breeze. If the program theory still needs some explanation of how the program should work, the process of creating your logic model will aid you in further refining it. Logic modeling is an opportunity to really think through the assumptions laid out in the program's theory, to consider again what resources and supports are needed to implement the program effectively, and to lay out a plan indicating what will be achieved at various stages during the program's operation.

6.3.2 Logic Model Components

Your logic model will be a living model, in that the theory underlying your model and the indicators informing your model are not static but will change as your understanding changes. Start with the program theory; your logic model will represent this theory. However, as information is obtained through the program's implementation and evaluation, you will need to revise and improve the model so that it is always an accurate representation of the program. The logic model is your road map and reflective of your initial understanding of the program, as well as the knowledge you acquire during the program's operation.

Logic models take on many shapes and sizes. Some logic models are tabular, with columns listing the strategies, objectives, and goals. Some of the more common logic models used for evaluation are a combination of tabular and graphical. However, even with boxes and arrows that might show overall flow between all strategies, objectives, and goals of a program, these models often do not break down the logic for each individual strategy. Without examining the specific theory for each strategy, a model cannot show relationships between strategies, nor does it show the interconnectedness of how strategies work together to meet long-term goals.

Additionally, some logic models use different terminology for model components. A common framework is inputs, activities, outputs, outcomes, and impacts. This framework is explained

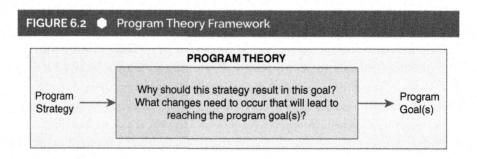

FIGURE 6.2 ● Program Theory Framework

well by the W.K. Kellogg Foundation (2004) in its *Logic Model Development Guide* and is used by many organizations, including the Centers for Disease Control and Prevention (Ladd et al., 2005) and the World Bank (Roberts & Khattri, 2012). In such models,

- *inputs* are available resources used to implement the program,

- *activities* are the planned strategies that are conducted using the inputs,

- *outputs* are the products resulting from the activities,

- *outcomes* are the short- and long-term participant-level changes anticipated as a result of the program, and

- *impacts* are the intended and unintended systems changes resulting from the program.

The logic modeling process in EMB-E uses a graphical approach to model the theory behind the relationships between *each* strategy and the long-term goals. It is similar to the above approach in that it examines relationships between program activities and the anticipated changes that result from those activities. It is also similar in that early results are typically product based (i.e., the availability of whatever it is the program is providing), with participant-level and system-level results occurring as the program progresses. However, it differs in terminology as well as in how outputs, outcomes, and impacts are categorized. In EMB-E, the availability of outputs (i.e., what the program creates or offers, such as a resource guide or training session) is viewed as an early objective of the program. Further, the distinction between outcomes and impacts being participant versus systems related, respectively, is not one that is recognized in EMB-E. Because the terms "outcomes" and "impacts," as well as "objectives" and "goals," are often used interchangeably by stakeholders, I have found that the subtle differences in definitions are not meaningful or relevant to stakeholders. Instead, the term "objectives" is used for theorized early and intermediate effects or impacts of the program, with long-term impacts being referred to as long-term "goals." The nomenclature of "goals" is preferred over "objectives" for longer-term impacts because of stakeholder familiarity with the term "goals." It should be noted, however, that I do work with stakeholders to define their goals as outcomes, rather than as an activity or output of a program. As such, a program's stated goals are a starting point for defining the long-term and important *why* of the program.

The components used in EMB-E logic modeling are strategies, early objectives, intermediate objectives, and long-term goals. As you gain more experience with logic modeling, you may decide to modify the process described in this text, perhaps by using another display approach or different model components. Regardless of approach or method of display, logic modeling is an incredibly useful tool for evaluations. I would encourage you to use logic modeling in your evaluations because of the program clarity it facilitates, as well as the scaffolding it provides within which to structure your evaluation.

The primary components of an EMB-E logic model, in order of development, are as follows:

1. Defining long-term goals

2. Delineating program strategies

3. Detailing early objectives

4. Outlining intermediate objectives

5. Listing necessary contextual conditions or resources

Long-term goals are the primary reason for the program, focusing on the change the program would like to see. *How* long-term the goals are will depend on the scope of the program. For a small, short-term program, long-term goals may reflect what the program would like to change in six months or a year. For a larger program with more lofty goals, long term might be two to five years. For a policy, long term could be looking at as much as 10 to 20 years into the future.

Strategies are activities that a program puts into place to accomplish its goals. Strategies may be a single activity or a cluster of activities. For example, while one strategy for a program intended to increase the college enrollment rate of newly graduated seniors may be providing text messages during the summer (to promote continued involvement); another might be providing college financial planning assistance for families. Financial planning assistance for families is a cluster of activities, including workshops to help students fill out the FAFSA® (Free Application for Federal Student Aid) forms, scholarship awareness seminars, and grant-seeking and grant-writing activities.

Early objectives are short-term changes or outcomes associated with the program. Early objectives focus on early implementation of strategies. However, instead of relating to *how* the strategy was implemented, they measure the early outcomes of that implementation. For a program that offers FAFSA completion workshops, an early objective might be related to attendance at the workshop. In Chapter 5, a program was introduced to improve community relations. An early objective of that strategy was to make town meetings available and to encourage community members to participate.

Intermediate objectives are changes or outcomes you would expect to see after the verification that early objectives were met. For instance, if attendance at the FAFSA completion workshops was high, an intermediate objective might focus on the number of FAFSAs completed. Similarly, if town meetings were indeed made available to community members and community members attended these town meetings, intermediate objectives might be increased communication among community members and increased feelings of belongingness to the community. See Figure 6.3 for an example of how providing financial planning assistance to families through FAFSA completion workshops might lead to increased college enrollment.

Long-term goals: the intended results of the program.

Strategies: activities put into place to accomplish program goals.

Early objectives: short-term outcomes associated with the program.

Intermediate objectives: mid-term outcomes associated with the program.

FIGURE 6.3 ● College Enrollment Program Theory

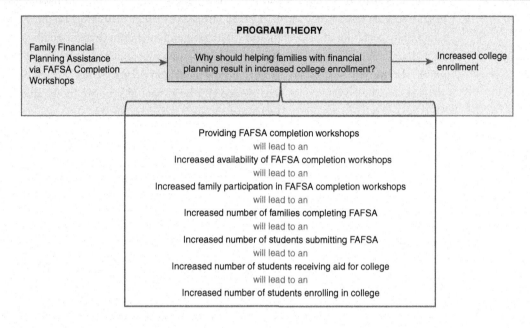

Contextual conditions are resources, infrastructure, facilities, services, or any other conditions that are necessary for the program to be successful, but are not part of the program itself. See Chapter 5 for more information on contextual conditions.

Finally, logic modeling and program theory are two sides of the same coin. Program theory includes the underlying assumptions of the program made explicit; logic modeling is the representation of this theory graphically. Thus, logic modeling is an illustration of the program theory discussed in Chapter 5. Early objectives, intermediate objectives, and long-term goals are the beginning, middle, and end expectations of the theory, respectively. For this reason, logic modeling can be used as a tool to develop the program's theory, as it is helpful to *see* the interconnections within the program's theory as it is being delineated.

6.3.3 Logic Model Graphics

To make it easy to distinguish between strategies, objectives, and goals in your logic model, it is helpful to represent each using consistent shapes. While you may decide to depict your logic model using your own preferred shapes, in this text the following shapes will be used:

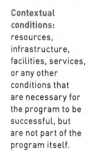

- Strategies will be denoted by rounded rectangles.

- Early and intermediate objectives will be denoted by rectangles.

- Long-term goals will be represented by elongated ovals.

Contextual conditions: resources, infrastructure, facilities, services, or any other conditions that are necessary for the program to be successful, but are not part of the program itself.

Start by stating the program's long-term goals on the right-hand side of your logic model. A program's goals are its destination. When describing a program, focus on what the program is striving toward, not what it does. So, instead of saying, "This program provides a community center for at-risk youth," say, "This program intends to decrease youth crime in the community." Then, you can add, "by providing a community center for at-risk youth." In this vein, goals should go first on the model (on the right-hand side) and then strategies (on the left-hand side). Next, work on the logic that links the two (in the middle).

Including contextual conditions and resources on your model is a helpful reminder of what needs to be in place for the program to operate. If you decide to add contextual conditions or resources to your model, you can list these conditions on the far left-hand side of your model (before your strategies). See Figure 6.4 for an example of how to structure your logic model headings.

Once you have listed your contextual conditions and necessary resources, strategies, early and intermediate objectives, and long-term goals, it is time to translate the program's theory (set of assumptions) into your logic model. It is important to think carefully about what needs to occur in the short term, intermediate term, and long term. Map out your assumptions, carrying each strategy through to a long-term goal. Some strategies may share early and intermediate objectives, and some objectives may branch out to one or more other objectives. Check to be sure that all strategies ultimately reach a goal and that no short-term or intermediate objectives are dead ends (meaning that they do not also carry through to a long-term goal). Remember, every component of your model is put into place to achieve the program's long-term goals. As mentioned earlier, it is your road map, keeping you on track until you reach your destination.

The theory for a program intending to increase the college enrollment rate was shown in Figure 6.3. Contextual conditions, or resources necessary for the program to be successful, include the assumption that facilities will be available where the workshops can be held. Another contextual condition is that there will be FAFSA specialists available to conduct the workshops. Finally, the program assumes that families will have access to transportation to and from the workshop. An example of the logic model for one strategy of the college enrollment program, FAFSA completion workshops, is shown in Figure 6.5.

Seeing a fully completed logic model with multiple strategies and long-term goals may be helpful at this point. The following pages continue the case study of the Youth Abstinence-Plus program, a fictitious program intended to decrease the pregnancy rate among youth, decrease the spread of STIs, and increase the number of youth who choose abstinence by combining education for youth regarding safe sex practices with promoting abstinence from sexual activity.

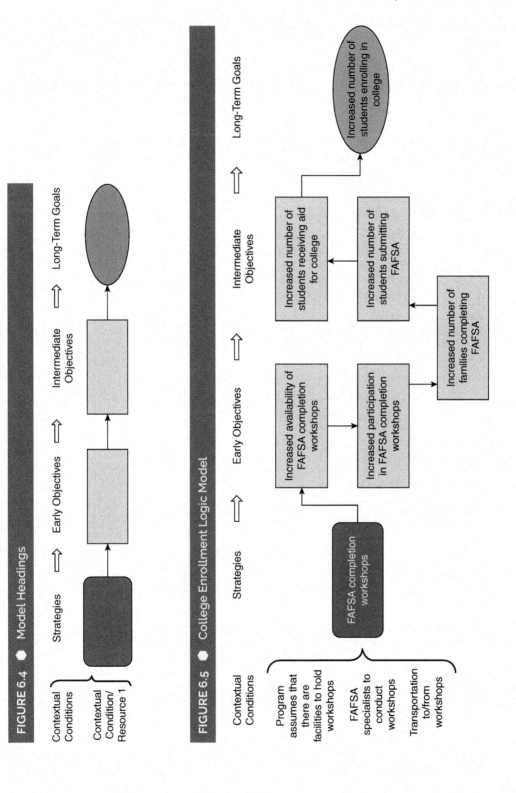

FIGURE 6.4 ● Model Headings

FIGURE 6.5 ● College Enrollment Logic Model

CASE STUDY
Youth Abstinence-Plus (YAP) Program

For decades, researchers and practitioners have debated the use of abstinence-only programs versus sexual education programs as means to decrease the incidence of unintended pregnancy and the spread of sexually transmitted infections (STIs) among youth. Even with the growing evidence that abstinence-only programs are not effective at delaying sexual activity or reducing STIs, these programs became very popular during the early 2000s. In fact, some researchers found that abstinence-only programs had negative unintended consequences related to denying youth access to information about safe sex and protection from disease. On the other hand, sexual education programs have been criticized as promoting sexual activity, though little evidence supports this claim.

An alternative to these two approaches is an abstinence-plus program that combines safe sex education with a strong message that promotes abstinence. Over the next few paragraphs, we will design a program called Youth Abstinence-Plus (YAP) that includes a focus on abstinence, education regarding safe sex for those youth who find themselves in sexual situations, and access to contraceptives for youth who plan to engage in sexual activity.

From the above description, we can determine that the YAP program goals are as follows:

1. Decrease the pregnancy rate among youth.
2. Decrease the spread of STIs among youth.
3. Increase the number of youth who choose sexual abstinence.

The YAP program strategies are the provision of the following:

1. Materials on the benefits of abstinence
2. Education regarding safe sex
3. Access to contraception

So, our initial program theory is as follows:

- Providing materials on and a message about the benefits of sexual abstinence among youth will increase the number of youth who choose sexual abstinence, which will lead to a decrease in the pregnancy rate among youth and a decrease in the spread of STIs.

- Providing youth with education regarding safe sex practices will decrease the pregnancy rate among youth and decrease the spread of STIs.

- Providing youth access to contraceptives will decrease the pregnancy rate among youth and decrease the spread of STIs.

The next step is to expand on the program theory, make the objectives leading from the strategies to the goals more specific, and explicitly state the program's underlying logic. Ideally, the program staff, key stakeholders, and evaluation staff would hold a series of meetings to discuss why the program's strategies will result in the goals that were specified. The following is the expanded logic that might evolve from such meetings:

- Providing **materials on promoting sexual abstinence** and a message about the benefits of sexual abstinence among youth will increase the availability of materials on abstinence, leading to an increased number of youth who receive the message about the benefits of abstinence, leading to an increased number of youth who understand the benefits of abstinence. An increase in the number of youth who understand the benefits of abstinence will lead to an **increase in the number of youth who choose sexual abstinence**, which will lead to a **decrease in the pregnancy rate among youth** and a **decrease in the spread of STIs**.

- Providing youth with **education regarding safe sex practices** will increase the availability of education regarding safe sex practices, leading to an increased number of youth who receive education regarding safe sex practices, which will lead to an increase in the number of youth who understand the benefits of safe sex practices. An increase in the number of youth who understand the benefits of safe sex practices will lead to improved safe sex practices among youth who are sexually active. Improved safe sex practices among sexually active youth will **decrease the pregnancy rate among youth** and **decrease the spread of STIs among youth**.

- Providing youth with **access to contraceptives** will increase the number of youth who have access to contraceptives, which will increase the number of sexually active youth who obtain contraceptives. An increase in the number of sexually active youth who obtain contraceptives will increase the use of contraceptives among sexually active youth, leading to improved safe sex practices among sexually active youth. Improved safe sex practices among sexually active youth will **decrease the pregnancy rate among youth** and **decrease the spread of STIs among youth**.

With the theory expanded and the logic explicitly stated, a logic model can be developed to graphically represent the assumptions that underlie the YAP program. Figure 6.6 shows the start of the YAP logic model.

Figure 6.7 shows the full logic model for the YAP program.

FIGURE 6.6 ⬡ Case Study: YAP Logic Model Framework

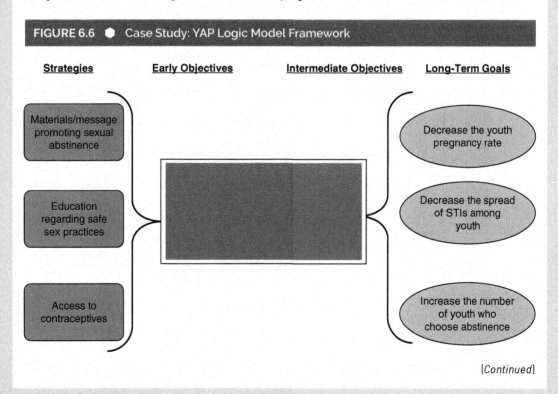

(*Continued*)

(Continued)

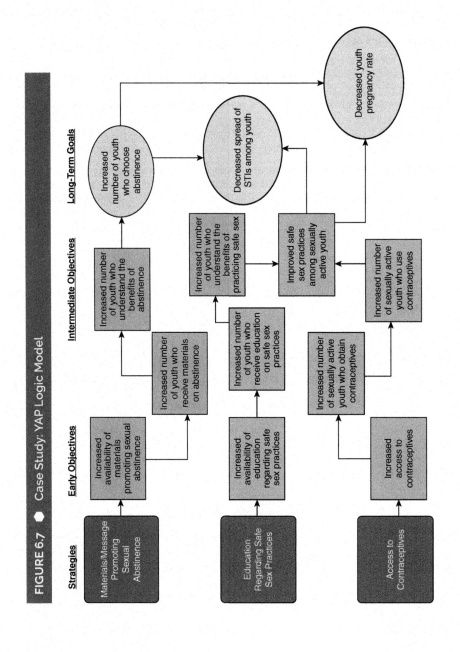

FIGURE 6.7 ⬡ Case Study: YAP Logic Model

QUICK CHECK

1. What is Black Box evaluation? How does logic modeling address the limitations of Black Box evaluation?

2. A logic model includes
   a. An implementation plan for your program.
   b. Program strategies, objectives, and goals.
   c. Program strategies and their associated costs.
   d. The results of your evaluation.

3. What are contextual conditions? Why are contextual conditions important for evaluators to consider?

4. If a program has two strategies and one long-term goal, how might you describe the program?

Answers: 1-an evaluation that only looks at strategies and long-term goals; 2-b; 3-any resource that is necessary for the program to be successful, but that is not part of the program itself; 4-the program intends to reach its *goal* by implementing *strategy 1* and *strategy 2*

6.3.4 Updating the Logic Model

The process of creating your logic model offers an additional opportunity for you to examine whether important strategies or objectives are missing. However, this opportunity does not end once the initial model is developed. A program's logic model should be a living model that is updated and adapted as you learn more about the theory underlying the program. As you create and think through the assumptions of your logic model, continue to ask yourself if it makes sense that the program's strategies would result in the long-term goals of the program. Is the logic of how strategies relate to early and intermediate objectives and long-term goals sound? Are additional strategies needed? Are additional objectives needed? It is important to use the logic modeling process to reaffirm or refine your program's theory, as the model will be the basis of the program's design and evaluation.

6.4 USING THE PROGRAM'S LOGIC MODEL

Once you have a draft logic model, you can share the draft with key program stakeholders, such as program staff, community members, program participants, policymakers, and funders. Talking through your model with stakeholders and asking for input and feedback can help to improve your model as well as *foster a sense of responsibility and ownership* for the program. Even the best ideas take many hands to achieve success. The more key stakeholders you can substantively involve in the logic model development process and the more key people who truly understand how the program is intended to work, the more likely it is that you will succeed. Once complete, your model can be used to *facilitate a mutual understanding* among stakeholders of what the program looks like, as well as what the program intends to accomplish.

Logic modeling as an exercise can facilitate program understanding, while the resulting logic model can be a powerful tool to document a program, tracking a program's progress and communicating a program's status and findings. Using a logic model to *communicate progress toward goals* has the added benefit of reminding stakeholders of the purpose of and theory behind a program. Stakeholders, including the funding agency, will want to know the extent to which their resources, time and financial, were effectively used to improve outcomes for people and communities.

As evaluators, perhaps the most important use of a logic model is to *focus the evaluation design*. The logic model that you create to depict the program's theory is the foundation of the program and also the scaffolding for the evaluation. The program's evaluation will be embedded within the program through the logic model. The logic model can then be used as a guide throughout the program's operation to record the degree to which early and intermediate objectives have been met in order to monitor program implementation and impact. Chapters 7 and 8 will guide you through evaluation planning and design, using the logic model as the guiding framework.

QUICK CHECK

1. What are some uses of a logic model? Why is it important to have stakeholder involvement in the logic modeling process?

2. How often should you update a logic model?
    a. About once a year
    b. At least every month
    c. Never—once it is developed, it should be followed
    d. When the program changes

3. How does a program's logic model relate to the program's evaluation?

Answers: 1-answers will vary; 2-d; 3-it is used to embed the evaluation into the program's design

6.5 MORE ON LOGIC MODELS

Logic models can be simple or quite sophisticated, and can represent small projects as well as large systems. This chapter presents a method for creating logic models based on 20 years of experience working with stakeholders. When I started working on logic models in the 1990s, we referred to them as "causal maps." However, I quickly realized that such naming confused the intent and use of the model. While the intent was to show theorized causal relationships, its use could only test those causal linkages with very specific research designs. Further, I felt one of the strengths of explicitly stating the theoretically causal relationships underlying a program was to enable the systematic collection of data to provide evidence of relationships between strategies and goals, when causality could not be determined. As a result, we began to refer to the models as "logic maps" and then on to "logic models." Logic model is the most accepted terminology today, though you will still hear people refer to them as causal maps or logic maps from time to time.

There are many great resources on developing logic models. Some of these show logic models in tabular form and some graphically. I prefer a graphical to tabular representation, because typically when logic models are shown as tables, they do not explicitly link specific strategies to specific objectives. Instead, the strategies are listed in a column with objectives and goals as separate columns. Such a depiction does not show how strategies work together toward a long-term goal. However, they are still useful, especially when the precise linkages between strategies, objectives, and goals have not yet been established.

As mentioned earlier in the chapter, many other logic models use the inputs, activities, outputs, outcomes, and impacts framework. This is also a fine method for depicting theory; however, I have found the distinction between inputs, activities, and outputs was not always intuitive to stakeholders, nor the determination of when an outcome becomes an impact. At times, I felt I spent valuable time explaining the terminology when that time instead could have been spent working together to explicate the theory. That said, I cannot say I have never used the framework, as some stakeholders are familiar with it and prefer to work with what they already know. Once you feel comfortable with the intent of logic modeling and know how to create a model using the method described in this chapter, I would encourage you to explore different frameworks and find the model that best works for you and your stakeholders.

If you would like to know more about logic models or logic modeling, some good resources are the *Logic Model Guidebook* (Knowlton & Phillips, 2009) and *Logic Modeling*

Methods in Program Evaluation (Frechtling, 2007). Weiss (1998) also provides a good explanation of logic models and their uses. It also bears reiterating that the W.K. Kellogg Foundation (2004) provides a terrific online resource for logic modeling called the *Logic Model Development Guide.*

6.6 CHAPTER SUMMARY

A **logic model** graphically displays a program's theory and explains how you believe the program works. While the logic model is tangible, logic modeling is a process. The process of logic modeling has many uses, from understanding an existing program to fostering shared ownership of a plan to being the framework for the program's evaluation design. The people involved in a program, including anyone who has an interest or stake in the operation or success of the program, are **program stakeholders**. Key stakeholders include program staff, community members, program participants, and policymakers.

There is no "one way" to create a logic model. In this text, we use an approach that includes long-term goals, strategies, early objectives, intermediate objectives, and contextual conditions. **Long-term goals** are the intended results of the program. **Strategies** are activities put into place to accomplish program goals. **Early objectives** are short-term outcomes associated with the program, focusing on indicators reflecting successful program implementation. **Intermediate objectives** are mid-term outcomes associated with the program. Each of the components in a logic model is put in place to achieve the long-term goals of the program. **Contextual conditions** are resources, infrastructure, facilities, services, or any other conditions that are necessary for the program to be successful, but are not part of the program itself.

Logic modeling is an ongoing process of refinement as more is learned about the program during implementation. This process and the resulting logic model can be used to foster a sense of ownership of and responsibility to a program, facilitate a mutual understanding of a program, and communicate a program's progress toward long-term goals. The logic model is also the framework upon which the program's evaluation is designed.

Reflection and Application

1. Refer back to the program or policy you chose in the Reflection and Application in Chapter 5.

   a. Create headings for your logic model, including strategies, early objectives, intermediate objectives, and long-term goals.

   b. Add your program's long-term goals to the right side of your model.

   c. Add your program's strategies to the left side of the model.

   d. Using the theory you developed in Chapter 5, translate the theory to the logic model. It may be helpful to use the YAP case study as an example.

   e. In using your theory to create your logic model, did you identify or clarify objectives in your model? If so, how?

2. Choose one strategy on your model. Try reading through your model from left to right, using the following template:

   This program is based on the theory that *Strategy* will lead to *Early Objective*. *Early Objective* will lead to *Intermediate Objective*. *Intermediate Objective* will lead to *Long-Term Goal*.

   You will need to include statements for each early and intermediate objective.

PLAN, PART 1

Planning the Evaluation

We thought we had the answers; it was the questions we had wrong.

—Bono

Upon completion of this chapter, you should be able to

- Formulate relevant and clear evaluation questions.
- Embed evaluation questions into a program's logic model.
- Construct evaluation questions for program strategies, short-term and intermediate objectives, and long-term goals.
- Create specific and measurable indicators to address evaluation questions.
- Estimate realistic targets for indicators.
- Organize evaluation questions and indicators into an evaluation matrix.

7.1 CREATING EVALUATION QUESTIONS

The French philosopher Voltaire said that a man should be judged by his questions rather than his answers. Likewise, an evaluation should be appraised, at least in part, by the quality, practicality, and feasibility of its questions. This chapter begins Step 2 in embedded evaluation, planning the evaluation, and is centered on creating evaluation questions that will shape the program's evaluation.

FIGURE 7.1 ● Embedded Evaluation Model

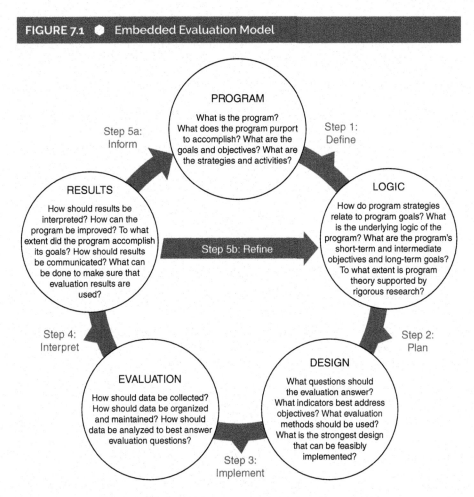

Evaluation questions provide a structure for focusing the evaluation. The questions will guide data collection efforts and analysis of data. Thus, evaluation questions are critical to the usefulness of evaluation information to program stakeholders. Asking irrelevant or impractical evaluation questions will yield ineffective and inadequate answers.

While many evaluations ill-advisedly begin with creating evaluation questions, the first step should always be understanding the program. How can you create important and informed evaluation questions until you have a solid understanding of the theory that underlies a program? Because you have already created a logic model during the process of understanding the program, generating evaluation questions is a natural progression from the model. By relying on the logic model to create evaluation questions, you are *embedding* the evaluation into the program's theory. Embedding evaluation questions helps to avoid some of the typical pitfalls with evaluation questions, such as asking questions irrelevant to program stakeholders or inadequately tied to the program itself. Building the evaluation around logic model components that have been agreed upon with stakeholders during logic model development will tie every question asked back to the fundamental logic underlying the program.

There are many useful texts and guides to help create evaluation questions. However, few adequately follow the question-writing guidelines that will be outlined in this chapter and even fewer tie the questions directly to the program's logic model. Yet there are several resources that can be very helpful in understanding what types of questions are most beneficial to stakeholders and in understanding how the answers to those questions can drive program development.

Western Michigan University's Evaluation Center has many useful and practical checklists for evaluators when designing and implementing evaluations. One such checklist is the *Evaluation Questions Checklist for Program Evaluation* (Wingate & Schroeter, 2016). All checklists from the Evaluation Center can be found at wmich .edu/evaluation/checklists. A guide that is particularly helpful because of its attention to program theory is *A Step-by-Step Guide to Evaluation* (www.wkkf.org/resource-directory/resource/2010/w-k-kellogg-foundation-evaluation-handbook) by the W.K. Kellogg Foundation (2017). Another worthwhile resource is UNICEF's *Overview of Impact Evaluation* (Rogers, 2014) from its Impact Evaluation Series (www.unicef-irc .org/KM/IE/impact.php). In addition, BetterEvaluation (www.betterevaluation.org) provides several materials for developing evaluation questions and for assistance with evaluation in general, including its *Rainbow Framework* (2013) for monitoring and evaluation (www.betterevaluation.org/rainbow_framework/), links to all 13 briefs in UNICEF's Impact Evaluation Series (www.betterevaluation.org/en/resources/guide/ unicef_impact_evaluation_series), and access to the *Looking Back, Moving Forward* evaluation manual (www.betterevaluation.org/resources/guide/sida_evaluation_manual) by Sida, the Swedish International Development Cooperation Agency (Molund & Schill, 2007). Finally, the RWJF Evaluation Series' *A Practical Guide for Engaging Stakeholders in Developing Evaluation Questions* (www.rwjf.org/en/library/ research/2009/12/a-practical-guide-for-engaging-stakeholders-in-developing-evalua .html) by the Robert Wood Johnson Foundation (Preskill & Jones, 2009) provides a five-step process, with accompanying worksheets, to guide evaluators in how to include stakeholders in the development of evaluation questions.

The following sections will detail the process of writing evaluation questions, including guidelines for "good" questions and strategies for structuring meaningful evaluation questions.

7.1.1 Examining Evaluation Questions

The Centers for Disease Control and Prevention (2013) outline four criteria for examining evaluation questions. These are stakeholder engagement, appropriate fit, relevance, and feasibility. **Stakeholder engagement** refers to the degree to which stakeholders were involved in creating the questions and are committed to answering the questions. **Appropriate fit** refers to how consistent the evaluation questions are with the program's theory and how directly linked they are to the program's goals and objectives. Because the logic model you developed in the previous chapter was built from the program's goals and objectives developed during the delineation of the program's theory, the process described in the following sections will ensure that your evaluation questions meet this criterion. The third criterion is **relevance**, which relates to the degree to which the evaluation questions are tied to the purpose of the evaluation and the usefulness of the answers to stakeholders. Finally, **feasibility** speaks to the extent that the process through which the evaluation questions will be answered is ethical and respectful, as well as whether resources are available to answer the questions. Feasibility also implies a cost-benefit relationship between the resources and effort necessary to answer the evaluation questions and the usefulness of the information that will be provided by their answers. These four criteria should be in the forefront of your mind during question development.

7.1.2 Structuring Evaluation Questions

In addition to the aforementioned criteria, here are more recommendations for drafting sound evaluation questions. For instance, when drafting evaluation questions, they should be *open-ended*. Avoid yes/no questions, as closed-ended responses limit the information you can obtain from the evaluation. Instead of asking, "Does my program work?" you might ask,

- To what extent does the program work?

- How does the program work?

- In what ways does the program work?

- For whom does the program work best?

- Under what conditions does the program work best?

Keep in mind that these questions are very broad and should be tailored to your specific program. For instance, the term "work" should be clarified for your program's intended

Stakeholder engagement: the extent to which stakeholders are committed to answering the evaluation questions.

Appropriate fit: the extent to which the evaluation questions are consistent with the program's theory.

Relevance: the extent to which answers to the evaluation questions will be useful to stakeholders.

Feasibility: the extent to which there are adequate resources available to answer the evaluation questions.

outcomes. Further, evaluation questions should be *clear* and *direct*. Avoid complex questions that are multipart. These are also called double-barreled questions. Instead, unpack compound questions into multiple, simpler questions. For example, instead of asking, "How did the program affect the achievement and attitudes of fifth-grade students?" you might create two questions:

- To what extent did the achievement of fifth-grade students improve?

- In what ways did the attitudes of fifth-grade students change?

Also, instead of asking, "Did the program improve confidence and job skills of unemployed workers?" you might split this into the following questions:

- To what extent did the confidence of unemployed workers increase?

- In what ways did the job skills of unemployed workers improve?

It is also important to note that the original question in both examples was not only compound (including two outcomes), but also complex in that it tied the program to the outcome causally. Causal questions can only be answered (and causal assertions can only be made) with experimental research designs. For now, unless you know you will use an experimental evaluation design, avoid such complex questions in favor of more straightforward questions. In evaluations that do not use experimental designs, theory-driven evaluation and logic modeling, coupled with a strong evaluation design, can aid in providing evidence that the measured outcomes are associated with the program's activities. Evaluation designs, including experimental and nonexperimental designs, will be explored later in the text.

Evaluation questions are often improved by providing *subquestions*. Hence, you could create one primary question with several subquestions. For example, instead of solely asking, "To what extent did the achievement of fifth-grade students improve?" you might also ask,

- How did student achievement for fifth graders vary by gender, race, home language, and socioeconomic status?

- How did achievement for fifth-grade students differ by initial testing quartile?

Further, instead of only asking, "To what extent did the number of unemployed workers decrease (i.e., the number employed increased)?" you might also ask:

- In what ways did confidence relate to employment status?

- How did employment status vary by gender, race, age, and type of employment sought?

7.2 EMBEDDING EVALUATION QUESTIONS INTO YOUR LOGIC MODEL

Evaluation questions tend to fall into three categories taken from your logic model: measuring the implementation of strategies (process evaluation/implementation assessment), identifying the progress toward short-term and intermediate objectives (formative evaluation), and recognizing the achievement of long-term program goals (summative evaluation). Both implementation assessment and process evaluation are types of formative evaluation; the findings from formative evaluation are intended to improve the program. Summative evaluation includes both outcome and impact evaluation; the findings from summative evaluation are used to make decisions regarding the program's future. See Chapter 1 for more information on implementation assessment, as well as process, formative, and summative evaluation. The following paragraphs will lead you through question development in each of these areas and present some important aspects to consider while creating evaluation questions.

7.2.1 Evaluating the Implementation of Program Strategies (Process Evaluation)

How do you know if the program contributed toward achieving (or not achieving) its goals if you do not examine the implementation of its strategies? It is important for evaluation questions to address the program's key strategies and activities. Evaluation does not take place in a controlled laboratory but rather in real-world settings, which require justification of why it is believed the program strategies will result in the measured outcomes. A program's underlying theory, represented by its logic model, shows the linkages between the strategies and the goals. The evaluation of a program's operation will set the stage to test the program's theory. And more important, asking evaluation questions about how strategies were applied can tell you the degree to which the program had the opportunity to be successful.

This examination of the implementation of strategies is called **process evaluation** (Chen, 1996). Process evaluation examines operations and assesses implementation. As such, it can help you understand the fidelity with which the program strategies were implemented. Process evaluation findings can also aid you in interpreting the impact of a program. If the evaluation shows that program strategies were not implemented as planned,

Process evaluation: evaluation aimed at understanding the operations of a program and assessing the fidelity with which program strategies were implemented.

attributing outcomes to the intended strategies would be inappropriate. Further, when evaluating a program that is implemented in several sites, process evaluation findings would allow examination of the outcomes in relation to variations in implementation.

It is never a good idea to measure outcomes before assessing implementation. If you find down the road that long-term goals were not met, is it because the program did not work or because key components of it were not applied properly or at all? Suppose you find that the long-term goals were successfully met. Do you have enough information to support that the program contributed to this success? It is a waste of resources to expend valuable time and money evaluating program outcomes if important program components were never put into place. This is referred to as **implementation failure** (Rossi, Lipsey, & Henry, 2018). Implementation failure occurs when the program is not implemented as planned. This failure might be related to program materials not being received, appropriate staff not being hired, necessary training not being available, or other issues that result in the program not being implemented at all, implemented partially, or implemented in a way that was not intended. It is important for an evaluator to examine strategies in order to provide feedback to program leadership early and often about how program implementation is occurring.

Program implementation may not occur for many reasons. I evaluated a program designed to improve youth practices with regard to internet safety. It relied on using social robots to present scenarios to the children. However, shortly after receiving funding, the program found out that the company making the robots went out of business. The evaluation was put on hold until a new technology could be found. In evaluating a program designed to improve achievement through increasing learning time, by way of home- and classroom-based gaming programs, we found out too late that the program was not implemented as planned. Our process evaluation focused primarily on the home component, which was operating well. However, nearly nine months into the program, when doing end-of-year teacher interviews, we found that some schools had not even opened the software for classroom use. We further found that teachers were never trained, so they did not know how to install or use the software. This evaluation was very early in my career and it taught me quite a bit about examining very early indicators of implementation. More recently, a program I was brought on to evaluate had seen a steady decrease in attendance at webinars over the last year. Initially, my thinking was that the topics were not relevant to potential participants or that participants were too busy to participate. However, process evaluation revealed that participants at three of the four institutions involved in the program were not receiving emails regarding the webinars. Apparently, a year prior, firewall changes were made at the institution sending out the webinar announcements. This firewall prevented the announcements from even reaching participants at the other three institutions. These three examples all resulted in

Implementation failure: occurs when the program is not implemented as planned.

TABLE 7.1 ● Evaluation Questions: Strategies	
If my strategy is to	**Evaluation questions might be**
Create a youth community center	Where was the community center located? How did youth travel to and from the community center? Did the facilities meet the needs of the youth?
	How was the community center staffed? What were the qualifications of staff? How were staff trained? How did staff interact with youth?
	What activities were offered to youth at the community center? How were activities offered to youth? To what extent did the activities offered meet the needs of the youth?
Provide affordable fresh fruits and vegetables to inner-city families	What fresh fruits and vegetables were provided? How were fresh fruits and vegetables provided? Who provided the fruits and vegetables?
	What was the quality of the produce? What was the price of the produce? To what extent did the type, quality, and cost of produce vary by location within the city?

implementation failure, but for various reasons. The failure of the first was temporary and out of the program's control, the second was due to service delivery failure, and the third due to unanticipated technological barriers. The lesson learned in all of these examples is that frequent communication between program leadership and evaluators as well as deliberate and systematic assessment of the implementation are critical to the appropriate use of program resources and ultimately program success.

While you will likely want to create evaluation questions that are specific to the strategies of the particular program being evaluated, a fundamental evaluation question at this stage is: What is the fidelity with which program activities have been implemented? Table 7.1 provides several examples of evaluation questions based on implementation.

Process evaluation findings, if provided to program staff in a timely manner, can help to shape a program. If findings show that program staff are struggling with the implementation of a strategy, information can be provided to the program management to further explore why implementation is not occurring as planned and to make any necessary adjustments to the program. Using process evaluation findings to shape the program is formative evaluation.

7.2.2 Evaluating Progress Toward Short-Term and Intermediate Objectives (Formative Evaluation)

Evaluating a program's *opportunity* to be successful, by examining its implementation, is the initial step toward determining the program's success. It is a type of formative evaluation because it is focused on program improvement. The second category of evaluation questions will address how the program is working. That is, how do you know if a program is on track to meeting its long-term goals? Findings from these questions are also used to inform improvement and thus are also a type of formative evaluation. Measuring progress toward short-term and intermediate objectives plays a significant role in determining how a program is working. By examining progress, early problems with the program can be caught and remediated before they become critical impediments to the program's success. Program staff can use interim evaluation findings to plan, shape, and improve the program prior to the evaluation of final outcomes. Originally introduced by Scriven (1967), evaluation used to shape the program is called **formative evaluation**.

Like implementation assessment, very early program objectives often relate to the opportunity of the program to be successful. That is, they focus on early indicators of implementation. If you use the input-activity-output terminology of logic modeling, you might call these very early indicators of opportunity *outputs*. For instance, if a program strategy is training for government leaders in a developing country, implementation assessment might examine what the training looked like, including its focus, modules, length of time, and mode of delivery. However, the output of the strategy is the actual training and an early indicator of this output would examine if the training was made available to government leaders. In EMB-E, early objectives include access or availability, as well as participation or use. In the government training example, both the content and structure of the training, as well as the availability of training and subsequent participation, are critical to the program being able to meet its intermediate and long-term objectives.

It is much easier and more cost-effective to uncover problems or issues early in a program's implementation. If early findings show the program is implemented, but that people are not taking advantage of the program, information can be provided to the program management to further explore why participation is low so they can make any necessary adjustments to the program.

Formative evaluation provides program staff with the necessary information for them to be able to understand the degree to which the program is on course, so that they can make mid-course adjustments and refinements as needed. It should be noted that early and intermediate objectives are focused on program outcomes. The way in which data from these objectives are used determines whether the evaluation is intended to be formative or summative. That is, data are not inherently formative or summative. While we may refer to data as formative data or summative data, it is not the data themselves that are formative or summative. Rather, it is their use or intended purpose that determines the type of evaluation. Because EMB-E is focused on continuous improvement, I have classified early and intermediate objectives as formative evaluation because of their role in program refinement. They could just as well be used for summative purposes, in which decisions about a program's status, resources, expansion, and so forth are made based upon findings. Thus, it is important to keep in mind that outcome-related data and data on program implementation can be used for both formative and summative purposes (Weiss, 1998).

Formative evaluation: evaluation used to shape the program; program staff can use interim evaluation findings to plan, shape, and improve the program prior to the evaluation of final outcomes.

Evaluation questions at this stage should focus on a program's specific short-term and intermediate objectives. However, an overarching evaluation question at this stage might be: To what extent is the program on track to achieving its long-term goals? Use the program's logic model to guide the creation of evaluation questions pertaining to early and intermediate objectives, just as strategies from the logic model were used to create the first set of evaluation questions. Table 7.2 provides several examples of formative evaluation questions.

TABLE 7.2 ● Evaluation Questions: Early and Intermediate Objectives	
If my early objective is to	**Evaluation questions might be**
Increase youth access to the community center	To what extent was a community center made available to youth? When did youth have access to the community center?
Increase the number of youth participating in community center activities	To what extent did the number of youth participating in community center activities increase? How did the participation rate differ by demographics?
	In what ways did youth participate in the community center? How did participation differ by age, gender, ethnicity, socioeconomic status, and home language? How did participation differ by time of day, day of week, and time of year?
Increase access to fresh fruits and vegetables	To what extent and in what ways did inner-city families have access to fresh fruits and vegetables? To what extent were fresh fruits and vegetables affordable to inner-city families?
	Where were fresh fruits and vegetables made available to families? How did the availability of fresh fruits and vegetables vary by section of the city?
Increase the consumption of fresh fruits and vegetables	To what extent were fresh fruits and vegetables purchased by families? Who purchased the fresh fruits and vegetables? When and where were the fresh fruits and vegetables purchased?
	To what extent did the amount of fresh fruits and vegetables consumed by inner-city families increase?
If my intermediate objective is to	**Evaluation questions might be**
Decrease the time youth spend unsupervised	To what extent did the time youth spend unsupervised decrease?
	To what extent did risky behavior among youth decrease?
Decrease risky behavior among youth	In what ways did youth reduce their risky behavior?
Improve healthy eating habits	To what extent did healthy eating habits improve? To what extent did consumption of fast foods decrease?

While you created your logic model starting with the program's long-term goals, it is often easier to craft evaluation questions left to right. Begin with your strategies and work your way toward early and intermediate objectives and then long-term goals. Some evaluation questions may address more than one objective, while some objectives may have more than one evaluation question. That is, there does not need to be a one-to-one correspondence between objectives on the logic model and evaluation questions. However, you should have at least one evaluation question that addresses each objective. Later, the evaluation team can prioritize evaluation questions. In doing this, it is possible that you will decide, based on your priorities and resource constraints, not to address certain questions and objectives in your evaluation.

7.2.3 Evaluating Progress Toward Long-Term Goals (Summative Evaluation)

Finally, a third set of evaluation questions should focus on a program's long-term goals. While evaluation findings at this stage in the program's operation can still be used to improve the program's implementation, assessment of long-term goals is typically used for summative decision making. That is, results from the measurement of long-term goals are often used to make decisions about whether program funding should be extended and if a program should be continued, expanded, scaled down, or discontinued. Thus, evaluation focused on measuring a program's impact in order to make decisions about the program's future is called **summative evaluation** (Scriven, 1967).

Summative evaluation: evaluation focused on a program's impact; summative evaluation findings are used to make decisions about program funding and continuance.

Your questions will be specific to the program's goals, though they should address the following: To what extent does the program work? For whom does the program work best? Under what conditions does the program work best? Another important question relates to the cost-effectiveness of the program. Cost-effectiveness will be further explored in Chapter 11. Table 7.3 provides several examples of summative evaluation questions. If you

TABLE 7.3 ● Evaluation Questions: Long-Term Goals	
If my long-term goal is to	**Evaluation questions might be**
Decrease youth crime in the community	To what extent did crimes committed by youth decrease? To what extent did the number of youth arrests decrease? To what extent was the program cost-effective in decreasing crime in the community?
Improve health among inner-city families	To what extent did the health of inner-city families improve? To what extent was the program cost-effective in improving health among inner-city families?

do not have the resources to focus on all of your evaluation questions, you may need to prioritize. The next section will discuss considerations when prioritizing evaluation questions.

7.2.4 Prioritizing Evaluation Questions

When prioritizing evaluation questions, it is important to keep in mind the purpose of the evaluation. For a comprehensive evaluation, there should be at least some measurement in all three categories: implementation of strategies, short-term/intermediate objectives, and long-term goals. In doing this, you will be addressing process, formative, and summative evaluation needs.

For a new program, the evaluation may focus on process and formative evaluation questions, with summative evaluation questions being delayed until it is reasonable to assume the program may have had the time and opportunity to have a longer-term impact. For a more mature program, there may be little value in formative evaluation, especially if the program is unlikely to be modified based on findings. Rather, the focus might be on data for summative decision making. If program leadership is interested in best practices and lessons learned in order to replicate an existing, successful program in another location, the evaluation might be focused on process and how implementation of the existing program relates to outcomes to inform the new implementation. It is important to listen to stakeholders so that evaluation questions are prioritized according to their needs.

It is tempting to ask many questions about a program's implementation and impact in order to know as much as possible about the program and how to make improvements. However, every question asked involves data collection and analysis. Collecting data in and of itself can be time-consuming and costly. More important, data collection asks something of staff and clients of the program. Weiss (1998) warns that if the evaluation asks too much of staff and clients in terms of time, energy, or information, the evaluator risks alienating them and losing their assistance and support. Out of respect for client and staff time, it is important to only ask those questions that are critical to program understanding, improvement, and impact. Similarly, every question asked and all data collected also involve analyzing those data. Preparing data to be analyzed can be time-consuming. Quantitative data will likely involve data entry, quality checks for accuracy, and statistical analysis. Qualitative data can be even more time-consuming, in that the data need to be organized, coded, and themed, as well as assertions developed and supported through the data. When designing your evaluation and creating evaluation questions, evaluators should keep in mind the burden those questions might place on staff and clients, as well as the resources necessary to collect and analyze data. While not all decisions regarding prioritization need to be made when evaluation questions are developed, it is good to keep in mind that these decisions will need to be made prior to finalization of the evaluation plan.

QUICK CHECK

1. Evaluation of program strategies is called . . .
   a. External evaluation.
   b. Formative evaluation.
   c. Process evaluation.
   d. Summative evaluation.

2. Evaluation of early and intermediate objectives is to <u>formative evaluation</u>, as the evaluation of long-term goals is to . . .
   a. Formative evaluation.
   b. Implementation evaluation.
   c. Process evaluation.
   d. Summative evaluation.

3. Which of the following evaluation questions is worded best?
   a. To what extent did depression decrease among adolescents?
   b. Did depression decrease among adolescents?
   c. To what extent did depression, anxiety, and ADHD decrease among adolescents?
   d. In what ways did the program cause a decrease in depression among adolescents?

4. Write an evaluation question for the following strategy: Provide conflict resolution training for teachers.

5. Write an evaluation question for the following early objective: Increase the number of teachers trained in conflict resolution.

6. Write an evaluation question for the following intermediate objective: Improve teacher knowledge of conflict resolution strategies.

7. Write an evaluation question for the following long-term goal: Decrease the number of student conflicts.

8. What sub-questions might you add to your evaluation questions for number 4–7?

Answers: 1-c; 2-d; 3-a; 4-answers will vary (example:In what ways was conflict resolution training provided to teachers?); 5-answers will vary (example:To what extent did the number of teachers trained in conflict resolution decrease?); 6-answers will vary (example:To what extent did teacher knowledge of conflict resolution strategies improve?); 7-answers will vary (example:To what extent did student conflict decrease?)

7.2.5 Examining Unintended Consequences

Many times, evaluations focus so intently on the intended outcomes that important unintended consequences of the program may go unnoticed. A study of nearly three million students in the United States found that the implementation of a more rigorous science and mathematics program of study was associated with an increase in high school drop-out rates (Plunk, Tate, Bierut, & Grucza, 2014). Further, an Austrian study of health promotion programs intended to improve the skills of health care workers found that the unintended negative side effects of the program were stronger and more prominent than the intended positive impact (Gugglberger, Flaschberger, & Teutsch, 2014). Health care workers who participated in the program, while improving their skills, also suffered increased work stress, work overload, and job frustration. Similarly, a program may have unidentified positive effects that might be missed if evaluation questions are defined too narrowly. For instance, Pokémon Go, in its effort to get more people hooked on its game, had the unintended effect of increasing the physical activity of its players (Bucher, 2016).

Chen (2015) calls the exclusive focus of an evaluation on a program's goals a goal trap, and asserts that it is more problematic for policies or large programs of broad scope. To combat omitting both unidentified positive and negative impacts of a program, Scriven (1972) recommended *goal-free evaluation* be considered, a type of evaluation in which evaluators are unaware of the program's stated goals. However, such evaluation may be impractical, as well as impossible, for internal evaluations where all staff are likely aware of their organization's programs and their intended outcomes. Weiss (1998) recommends that evaluators brainstorm possible unintended outcomes using their own knowledge and understanding of the program, as well as similar programs. Program staff would also be a useful resource to help identify potential program effects that were not measured, whether they be positive or negative effects. In addition, particularly when examining negative effects, program critics and opponents may be able to shed light on important unintended consequences.

Oliver, Lorenc, and Tinkler (2019) identify three primary challenges for evaluators, as well as policymakers, when examining the unintended effects of programs and policies: identifying unintended consequences, evaluating unintended consequences, and explaining unintended effects. Their recommendations were also threefold: Use a range of both qualitative and quantitative methods to examine the implementation and impacts of programs and policies, use theory-based methods to plan evaluations, and include stakeholders in discussions of methods and theory.

Goal trap: Focusing exclusively on the goals of the program such that unintended consequences, either positive or negative, are missed.

CASE STUDY 7.1
Youth Abstinence-Plus (YAP) Program: Evaluation Questions

After (1) learning about the program, (2) identifying the program's strategies and goals, (3) brainstorming the theory underlying the program, and (4) developing the YAP program logic model, the evaluation design process now turns to creating evaluation questions. Refer to Chapter 6 for the YAP logic model.

Creating a table with a separate row for each component on the logic model is recommended. Categorizing and labeling the components by strategies, early and intermediate objectives, and long-term goals will help to easily align components and questions in the table with the logic model. Questions are created directly from the YAP logic model. Remember, questions should be open-ended. However, they should also be very straightforward and address the logic model component clearly. There is no need to be especially creative with evaluation questions or to worry about the repetitive nature of the question prompts. The important part is making sure your questions cover the relevant aspects of the logic model component so that program staff can make effective decisions regarding the program's implementation, operation, and impact. Table 7.4 presents evaluation questions for each logic model component.

TABLE 7.4 ● Case Study: YAP Evaluation Questions

	Logic Model Component	Evaluation Question(s)
Strategies	Materials promoting sexual abstinence	What were the content and format of materials promoting abstinence? In what ways were materials promoting abstinence made available to youth?
	Education regarding safe sex practices	What were the content and format of education regarding safe sex practices? In what ways was education provided?
	Access to contraceptives	In what ways, from whom, and at what locations were contraceptives available to youth? What types of contraceptives were made available to youth?
Early and Intermediate Objectives	Increase availability of materials on abstinence	To what extent did youth have access to materials on abstinence?
	Increase the number of youth who receive materials on abstinence	To what extent did the number of youth who received materials on abstinence increase? In what ways did youth obtain materials related to abstinence?
	Increase availability of education regarding safe sex practices	To what extent was education regarding safe sex practices made available to youth?

	Logic Model Component	Evaluation Question(s)
Early and Intermediate Objectives	Increase the number of youth who receive education regarding safe sex practices	To what extent did the number of youth who received education regarding safe sex practices increase? How did youth receive education regarding safe sex?
	Increase the number of youth who have access to contraceptives	To what extent did the number of youth with access to contraceptives increase? To what extent were youth aware of their access to contraceptives?
	Increase the number of sexually active youth who obtain contraceptives	To what extent did the number of sexually active youth who obtain contraceptives increase? Where did youth obtain contraceptives? What types of contraceptives did youth obtain?
	Increase the number of youth who understand the benefits of abstinence	To what extent did the number of youth who understand the benefits of abstinence increase? What did youth understand about abstinence?
	Increase the number of youth who understand the benefits of practicing safe sex	To what extent did the number of youth who understand the benefits of practicing safe sex increase? What did youth understand about safe sex practices?
	Increase the number of sexually active youth who use contraceptives	To what extent did the number of sexually active youth who use contraceptives increase? What types of contraceptives did youth choose to use? How often did youth use contraceptives in sexual situations?
	Improve safe sex practices among sexually active youth	To what extent did safe sex practices among sexually active youth improve? In what ways did safe sex practices improve?
Long-Term Goals	Increase the number of youth who choose abstinence	To what extent did the number of youth who choose abstinence increase?
	Decrease the spread of STIs among youth	To what extent did the spread of STIs, including HIV, decrease?
	Decrease the youth pregnancy rate	To what extent did the youth pregnancy rate decrease?

IN THE REAL WORLD . . .

The **United Nations World Food Programme (WFP)** provides food aid to millions of people in order to improve the lives of the poorest people in the world. It uses food aid to "support economic and social development, meet refugee and emergency food needs, and to promote world food security." The WFP conducts ongoing evaluations of its programs.

In 2013, nearly half of Armenian children lived below the poverty line. The WFP's Armenian Development Project was created to support capacity building in developing a sustainable, locally based, school feeding program. In 2015, an independent organization was contracted to evaluate the Armenian program. The school feeding activities of the program focused on about 900 primary schools.

The process evaluation of the United Nations World Food Programme project focused in Armenia found that its Sustainable School Feeding Strategy was not implemented as was intended. Instead of being a school feeding policy promoting capacity building, it was implemented primarily as a food service to schoolchildren.

Evaluation results of the Armenian program were used formatively to strengthen the school feeding strategy during implementation. Formative evaluation results also led the program to focus more on improving gender equality, specifically focusing on outcomes for the engagement of males in school feeding activities.

The summative evaluation found that the Armenian food program met its goal of reaching 50,000 individuals. In addition, the program was able to provide schoolchildren with meals five days a week during the entire school year (180 days).

Sources: United Nations World Food Programme (2015, 2019).

7.3 WHAT DATA SHOULD I COLLECT?

Now that you have developed a logic model and decided on evaluation questions, the next task is to plan how you will answer those questions. Your logic model is your road map during this process. Just as you used the key components of the logic model as a guide to develop evaluation questions, evaluation questions will drive the data that will be collected through the evaluation.

Indicator: a statement that can be used to gauge progress toward program goals and objectives; can be derived from evaluation questions and used to measure change or growth. An evaluation question may have one or more indicators. An indicator is SMA:

- Specific
- Measurable
- Agreed upon

The answers to evaluation questions will give you the information you need to understand the program's implementation, as well as provide feedback to program staff to improve the program and make critical program decisions. The following paragraphs will take you through the process of creating indicators for evaluation questions that relate to program strategies, short-term objectives, intermediate objectives, and long-term goals. These indicators will dictate what data should be collected to answer the evaluation questions.

7.3.1 Indicators and Targets

Indicators are statements that can be used to gauge progress toward program goals and objectives. An **indicator** is a guide that lets you know if you are moving in the right direction. Your indicators will be derived from your evaluation questions; for some evaluation questions, you might have multiple indicators. Indicators are the metrics that will be tied to targets or benchmarks, against which to measure the performance of the program. After identifying indicators, the next step is to clarify the indicators by agreeing upon realistic and time-bound targets. Thus, a **target** is a clarification of an indicator. A target provides a yardstick and timeline for your indicator, specifying how much progress should be made and by when in order to determine to what extent goals and objectives have been met.

Indicators and targets should be SMART: specific, measurable, agreed upon, realistic, and time bound. SMART goals were originally introduced by Doran (1981) and used in the field of management. The following description adapts the SMART framework for indicators and targets developed for evaluation purposes.

Specific refers to *what* will be measured to answer the evaluation question. Specific may also refer to descriptive information that provides additional details about the indicator in order to better understand *how* the program was implemented.

Measurable refers to the extent to which the indicator can be observed, quantified, or collected. Measurable does not mean that the indicator must be quantitative in nature, just that it be something that can be clearly described, observed, and interpreted in a meaningful way.

Agreed upon refers to the extent that key program stakeholders understand and support the indicator chosen to answer the evaluation question. The indicator should also be available to the evaluation team, or at least able to be collected. Doran (1981) refers to the "A" of SMART as attainable, while it is also sometimes referred to as achievable. Both should be considered when being agreed upon. The indicator should be feasible to measure with the resources available, including time and financial resources. However, these two characteristics, attainable and achievable, are more aptly covered in the "R" of SMART.

Realistic addresses the degree to which the amount of change that would constitute success is achievable. Identifying the extent of the expected change may involve some research into what is typical or what past experience has to tell us regarding to what extent and how quickly an indicator can be affected. Some refer to the "R" of SMART as relevant, which is also important. Relevance speaks to the degree to which what is being measured accurately reflects what is addressed by the evaluation question. Relevance is also something that should be discussed when an indicator is agreed upon.

Time bound refers to when the indicator will be measured and within what time frame the observed change is expected to occur. If the indicator is a one-time measurement, then this would specify when the indicator will be measured. If the indicator reflects change during a period of time, for example, a percentage increase or decrease, keep in mind that a baseline measurement would be required to measure the change in the indicator. In this case, the time frame of the baseline measurement as well as the future date by which change is expected to occur should be specified.

Target: a clarification of an indicator, specifying how much progress should be made and by when in order to determine to what extent goals and objectives have been met; targets should provide a realistic timeline and yardstick for indicators.

A target is RT:

- Realistic
- Time bound

To summarize, indicators are derived from evaluation questions and used to measure progress toward program goals and objectives. Targets provide a realistic timeline and yardstick for indicators. Indicators and targets should have the following characteristics:

- An indicator is SMA:

  Specific

  Measurable

  Agreed upon

- And a target is RT:

  Realistic

  Time bound

Together, indicators and targets are **SMART**.

It should be noted that program objectives are often discussed in reference to the SMART criteria. However, rarely do objectives have enough detail to be truly considered SMART. Often an objective is SMA, with the RT criteria being omitted. For this reason, it is recommended to explicitly expand upon program objectives to be sure they are indeed SMART. Creating indicators and targets can provide greater assurance that the program data collected for evaluative purposes do indeed answer the evaluation questions and address the program objectives in a specific, measurable, agreed upon, realistic, and time-bound manner.

7.3.2 Some Examples of Indicators and Targets

Returning to the example of a program intended to decrease the number of youth arrests in the community by providing an after-school and summer youth community center, one of the objectives was to "Increase the number of youth participating in the community center." The evaluation question was twofold: To what extent did the number of youth participating in community center activities increase? How did the participation rate differ by demographics? In this case, the original objective of *increasing the number of youth participating in the community center* could be considered SMA, but it lacks the RT. Because the objective is already specific and measurable, the indicator may be the objective slightly reworded as "the number of youth participating in activities at the community center." In order to address the second evaluation question, a second indicator might be added to collect demographic data of the youth who participate in the center activities. The target would clarify these indicators, making it realistic and time bound. An example might be "Within three months of program start, participation in community center activities will increase by 20%."

Another example relates to the aforementioned program to improve healthy eating by providing fresh fruits and vegetables to inner-city families. Two evaluation questions were developed for the program goal to "Improve healthy eating habits": To what extent did eating habits improve? To what extent did consumption of fast foods decrease? The program goal and first evaluation question are broad and need some clarification. Healthy eating habits can be defined multiple ways. Healthy eating may mean eating more fruits and vegetables. It may mean eating less fast food or fewer carbohydrates. Another way it might be defined is reduced consumption of processed foods. The indicator would need to specify exactly what will be measured to answer the evaluation question. As stated previously, this indicator should be specific, measurable, and agreed upon by key stakeholders. The target would specify the time frame during which the change should occur and how much change would constitute success for the program.

A third example relates to a state policy aimed at improving the quality of classroom teachers by addressing teacher recruitment and retention. An objective on the logic model states, "Increase the number of highly qualified teachers in the state" and a corresponding evaluation question asks: To what extent was the number of highly qualified teachers increased in the state? However, there are several ways that a "highly qualified teacher" can be defined, such as by certifications, education, content knowledge, and so on. The indicator would specify the definition(s) that the evaluator chooses to use, providing critical information to determine the data element(s) that will be collected. For example, to be specific and measurable, the indicator might be twofold: "the number and percentage of teachers who are state certified" and "the number and percentage of teachers who hold National Board certification." Targets might include "Within three years, all of the teachers in the state will be state certified" and "Within five years, 50% of teachers in the state will have National Board certification."

For some programs, it is possible that reasonable targets cannot be set prior to the program's operation. For instance, consider a program that is intended to decrease the incidence of major depression among the elderly participants in a program, and the chosen indicator is the number of older adults with major depression. In this case, the evaluation team might like to see results of baseline depression screenings prior to setting their target. In this case, an initial screening may be done at the start of the program and, once baseline scores are known, targets can be determined.

7.4 CREATING THE EVALUATION MATRIX

Now that you have created evaluation questions with accompanying indicators and targets for each component of the logic model, how do you organize that information into a usable format for evaluation? One method is to use an **evaluation matrix**.

An evaluation matrix represents the logic model components, evaluation questions, indicators, and targets by logic model strategies, early and intermediate objectives, and long-term goals. Information for completing the data source, data collection, and data

Evaluation matrix: a tabular representation of the

- evaluation questions,
- indicators,
- targets,
- data sources,
- data collection techniques, and
- data analysis methods

embedded within and associated with each component of a program's logic model.

analysis columns will be covered next. Evaluation matrices can be created in Google Docs, Microsoft Word, Microsoft Excel, or another word processing or spreadsheet software package. Table 7.5 shows an example shell of an evaluation matrix.

At this point in your evaluation design, you should be able to complete the first four columns of the evaluation matrix: logic model component, evaluation questions, indicators, and targets. The remaining three columns will be explained in Chapter 8. An example matrix is shown in the case study on the following pages.

TABLE 7.5 ⬡ Evaluation Matrix Example Shell							
	Logic Model Component	Evaluation Questions	Indicators	Targets	Data Source	Data Collection	Data Analysis
Strategies/ Implementation							
Short-Term and Intermediate Objectives							
Long-Term Goals							

 QUICK CHECK

1. Evaluation questions should be developed from
   a. Data sources.
   b. Logic model components.
   c. Indicators.
   d. Targets.

2. Targets should be developed from
   a. Data sources.
   b. Logic model components.
   c. Indicators.
   d. Evaluation questions.

3. Indicators should be specific, measurable, and agreed upon, while targets should be
   a. Routine and time sensitive.
   b. Realistic and time bound.
   c. Qualitative.
   d. Quantitative.

4. Write an indicator for the following early objective: Increase the number of teachers trained in conflict resolution. What might an appropriate target be for this indicator?

5. Write an indicator for the following intermediate objective: Improve teacher knowledge of conflict resolution strategies. What might an appropriate target be for this indicator?

6. Write an indicator for the following long-term goal: Decrease the number of student conflicts. What might an appropriate target be for this indicator?

7. Suppose a program at a local elementary school intends to decrease student absences. The indicator decided upon is average daily attendance as a percentage of enrollment. The target set is, Within three months, the average daily attendance as a percentage of enrollment will be 100%. Evaluate this indicator and target using the SMART criteria described in this chapter.

8. For question 7 above, what might be a target that meets the SMART criteria? What other indicators and targets might be used to address the goal of decreased student absenteeism?

Answers: 1-b; 2-c; 3-b; 4-answers will vary (example: Number of teachers trained); 5-answers will vary (example: Teacher knowledge of conflict resolution); 6-answers will vary (example: Number of teacher-reported student conflicts); 7-answers will vary (It is specific, measurable, potentially agreed upon, and time bound, but it is NOT realistic that all students always be present and NOT appropriate that the program be held accountable for an unachievable target); 8-answers will vary (example: Within six months, average daily attendance will improve by 10%)

CASE STUDY 7.2

Youth Abstinence-Plus (YAP) Program: Partial Evaluation Matrix

Table 7.6 shows the beginning, partial evaluation matrix for the YAP program.

TABLE 7.6 ⬡ Case Study: Partial Evaluation Matrix

	Logic Model Component	Evaluation Question(s)	Indicators	Targets
Program Strategies/Implementation	Materials promoting sexual abstinence	What were the content and format of materials promoting abstinence? In what ways were materials promoting abstinence made available to youth?	Content and format of abstinence materials Method of delivering abstinence materials to youth	By program start, materials promoting sexual abstinence are developed and implemented with fidelity
	Education regarding safe sex practices	What were the content and format of education regarding sex practices? In what ways was education regarding safe sex provided?	Content and format of education regarding safe sex practices Method of delivering education regarding safe sex to youth	By program start, education regarding safe sex practices is implemented with fidelity
	Access to contraceptives	In what ways, from whom, and at what locations were contraceptives available to youth? What types of contraceptives were made available to youth?	Distribution method of contraceptives to youth Types of contraceptives available to youth	By program start, methods of access to contraceptives will be implemented with fidelity

	Logic Model Component	Evaluation Question(s)	Indicators	Targets
Early and Intermediate Objectives	Increase the availability of materials on abstinence	To what extent did youth have access to materials on abstinence?	Availability of abstinence materials to youth	Within one week of program start, abstinence materials will be available to all youth
	Increase the number of youth who receive materials on abstinence	To what extent did the number of youth who received materials on abstinence increase? In what ways did youth obtain materials related to abstinence?	Number of youth receiving abstinence materials; *Method of receiving abstinence materials*	With three months of program start, all youth will have received materials on abstinence
	Increase the availability of education regarding safe sex practices	To what extent was education regarding safe sex practices made available to youth?	Availability of education regarding safe sex practices	Within one week of program start, education regarding safe sex will be available to all youth
	Increase the number of youth who receive education regarding safe sex practices	To what extent did the number of youth who received education regarding safe sex practices increase? How did youth receive education regarding safe sex?	Number of youth receiving education on safe sex practices; *Method of receiving education on safe sex practices*	Within three months of program start, all youth will have received education on safe sex practices
	Increase the number of youth who have access to contraceptives	To what extent did the number of youth with access to contraceptives increase? To what extent were youth aware of their access to contraceptives?	Number of youth who have access to contraceptives; Number of youth who are aware of their access to contraceptives	Within three months, all youth will have access to contraceptives; Within six months, all youth will be aware of their access to contraceptives

(Continued)

TABLE 7.6 ● (Continued)

Logic Model Component	Evaluation Question(s)	Indicators	Targets
Increase the number of sexually active youth who obtain contraceptives	To what extent did the number of sexually active youth who obtain contraceptives increase? Where did youth obtain contraceptives? What types of contraceptives did youth obtain?	Number of sexually active youth who obtain contraceptives *Demographics of youth who obtain contraceptives* *Method and location of receiving contraceptives* *Types of contraceptives received*	Within one year, there will be a 25% increase in sexually active youth who obtain contraceptives
Increase the number of youth who understand the benefits of abstinence	To what extent did the number of youth who understand the benefits of abstinence increase? What did youth learn about abstinence?	Number of youth who understand the benefits of abstinence *Nature of youth's understanding about the benefits of abstinence*	Within six months of the start of the program, all youth will be able to describe the benefits of abstinence
Increase the number of youth who understand the benefits of practicing safe sex	To what extent did the number of youth who understand the benefits of practicing safe sex increase? What did youth learn about practicing safe sex?	Number of youth who are able to describe the benefits of practicing safe sex *Nature of youth's understanding about the benefits of practicing safe sex*	Within six months, all youth will be able to describe the benefits of practicing safe sex
Increase the number of sexually active youth who use contraceptives	To what extent did the number of sexually active youth who use contraceptives increase? What types of contraceptives did youth choose to use? How often did youth use contraceptives in sexual situations?	Number of sexually active youth who use contraceptives *Demographics of youth who use contraceptives* *Types of contraceptives used* *Frequency with which contraception is used*	Within one year, there will be a 20% increase in the number of sexually active youth who use contraceptives

20% Long-Term Goals

Logic Model Component	Evaluation Question(s)	Indicators	Targets
Improve safe sex practices among sexually active youth	To what extent did safe sex practices among sexually active youth improve? In what ways did safe sex practices improve?	Number of sexually active youth who practice safe sex; *Demographics of youth who practice safe sex*; *Nature of safe sex practices used*; *Frequency with which contraception is used*	Within one year of program start, there will be a 20% increase in sexually active youth who practice safe sex
Increase the number of youth who choose abstinence	To what extent did the number of youth who choose abstinence increase?	Number of youth who choose abstinence; *Demographics of youth who choose abstinence*; *Self-reported reason for youth choosing abstinence*	Within one year of program start, there will be a 20% increase in the number of youth who choose abstinence
Decrease the spread of STIs among youth	To what extent did the spread of STIs, including HIV, decrease?	Number of youth diagnosed with STI/HIV; *Demographics of youth diagnosed with STI/HIV*	Within two years of program start, there will be a 20% decrease in the number of youth diagnosed with STI/HIV in the community
Decrease the youth pregnancy rate	To what extent did the youth pregnancy rate decrease?	Number of youth who become pregnant; *Demographics of youth who become pregnant*	Within two years of program start, there will be a 20% decrease in the number of youth in the community who become pregnant

7.5 CHAPTER SUMMARY

Evaluation questions should be developed *after* you have a thorough understanding of the theory that underlies the program. Begin with the program's logic model and develop evaluation questions for each model component. Examination of the implementation of strategies is called **process evaluation**, and the corresponding questions should focus on the degree to which the program had the opportunity to be successful. Questions addressing early and intermediate objectives are intended to shape the program and are part of **formative evaluation**. These interim evaluation findings can help to determine if the program is on track to meet long-term goals and aid in making mid-course adjustments and improvements to the program. Questions focusing on long-term goals are used to determine the program's impact so that decisions can be made regarding program funding. Such decisions are part of **summative evaluation**. Evaluation questions should be *open-ended* and include *subquestions*; questions should *avoid compound structure and causal language*. Evaluation questions will need to be prioritized to avoid asking too much of stakeholders and to set reasonable expectations for data collection and analysis resources. It is also important to remember that there may be unintended positive or negative consequences of a program that might be missed if evaluation questions are defined too narrowly.

Indicators and targets should be developed from evaluation questions. An **indicator** is a metric that will be tied to targets to measure performance of the program. Indicators should be specific, measurable, and agreed upon. A **target** is a clarification of an indicator that specifies how much progress should be made within a certain time frame to claim adequate progress. Targets should be realistic and time bound.

An **evaluation matrix** is a tool to organize your evaluation design, including program strategies, objectives, and goals, as well evaluation questions, indicators, and targets. Your evaluation matrix will be expanded upon in subsequent chapters as decisions are made regarding measures, data collection, and data analysis.

Reflection and Application

1. Describe process, formative, and summative evaluation. Find a real-world example of each.
2. Refer to the program or policy you chose for the Reflection and Application at the end of Chapter 6.
   a. From the logic model you created, choose one each of the program's strategies, objectives, and goals.
   b. For each of these logic model components, create an evaluation question.
   c. For each evaluation question, create an accompanying indicator and target.
   d. Analyze how well your indicators and targets address the SMART criteria.
3. Explain why unintended consequences are important and why evaluators should be concerned about them.
4. Describe why prioritizing evaluation questions is important. What might happen if an evaluator does not prioritize evaluation questions?

PLAN, PART 2

Designing the Evaluation

Research is creating new knowledge.

—Neil Armstrong

Upon completion of this chapter, you should be able to

- Identify common evaluation designs, including nonexperimental, quasi-experimental, and experimental.
- Compare and contrast evaluation designs in terms of evaluation rigor.
- Describe methods to strengthen evaluation designs.
- Categorize evaluation methods as quantitative and qualitative.
- Define reliability and validity, as they relate to evaluation.
- Describe the advantages and disadvantages of various evaluation tools and methods.

8.1 EVALUATION DESIGN

The famous German philosopher Immanuel Kant once said, "Experience without theory is blind, but theory without experience is mere intellectual play." Even the best theory is useless if it is not assessed in operation. By this definition, the theory outlined in Chapters 5–6 and the questions developed in Chapter 7 to examine this theory are intellectual play until they are implemented. The evaluation design within which this theory will be

FIGURE 8.1 ● Embedded Evaluation Model

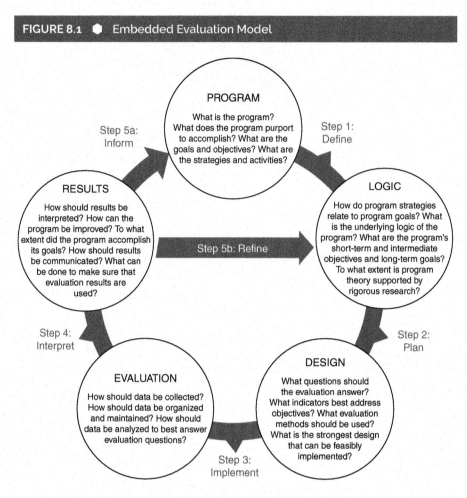

implemented is the framework for examining experience. The more rigorous the evaluation design, the more confident one can be in attributing this experience to the program itself.

We evaluate because it is important and ethical to know to what extent a program works, under what conditions or with what supports it works, for whom it works best, and how to improve the program. In the previous two chapters, we defined the program and what it means to say the program "works." A strong evaluation design can help you to rule out other plausible explanations as to why a program may or may not have met the expectations set through its indicators and targets. How many programs are continued with little examination of how they are benefiting the participants? How often do we "experiment" on people by putting a new program into effect without following up to see if there was any benefit (much less any adverse effect)? When do we make our decisions based on data, and how often do we accept anecdotal stories or simple descriptions of use as though they were evidence of effectiveness (because we have nothing else on which to base our decisions)? Evaluation can provide us with the necessary information to make sound decisions regarding the strategies we use within programs.

8.1.1 Attribution and Design Rigor

Evaluation built into a program can aid an evaluator in continually monitoring a program to foster continuous improvement, as well as to provide program staff with information to determine whether participants are benefiting (or not). The design of the evaluation also determines the extent to which an evaluator can confidently and appropriately assert the program influenced results. Suppose you are evaluating a mathematics program and your results show that student scores in mathematics, on average, increased twofold after the program was put into place. But upon further investigation, you find that half of the students had never used the program, and that the students who used the program in fact had much lower scores than those who did not. What if you had not investigated? This program may have been hindering, rather than helping, student learning.

The example in the preceding paragraph is intended to show that while evaluation is important, it is *good* evaluation (ones that provide valid information as to how the program is working) that really matters. Evaluation relies on **attribution**. And the more directly you can attribute evaluation findings to program strategies, the more meaningful evaluation findings will be—and the more useful your findings will be to program staff as they work to improve their program. A strong evaluation design coupled with positive findings is what you might hope for, but even a strong evaluation that provides findings showing dismal results from a program provides valuable and important information. Evaluation results that help you to discontinue programs that do not work are just as valuable as findings that enable program staff to continue to build upon those programs that do improve participant outcomes.

Attribution: the action of crediting measured outcomes to a program.

The strength of an evaluation design, or the **design rigor**, directly impacts the degree to which an evaluation can provide the program with valid ongoing information on implementation as well as long-term goals regarding the success of the program. A strong evaluation design is one that is built to provide credible information for program improvement, as well as to rule out competing explanations for summative findings. Some evaluation designs provide stronger evidence of **causation** than others. So, how do you choose the strongest possible design and methods to answer your evaluation questions, taking into account any constraints that you may have? This will partly depend upon the extent to which you have control over the implementation setting and other, similar settings. The following sections will build upon the information

Design rigor: the extent to which an evaluation design merits attribution of strategies to measured outcomes.

Causation: the attribution of a program (the cause) to the measured outcomes (the effect).

introduced in Chapter 4 on evaluation design and further explore the most common designs, including nonexperimental designs, quasi-experimental designs, and experimental designs.

8.1.2 Nonexperimental and Single-Group Designs

If you are implementing a project at only one site, your evaluation will likely focus on a single group. In a **single-group design**, one group participates in the program and that same group is evaluated. There is no comparison group that does not receive the program included in the evaluation. While a single-group design is the simplest evaluation design, it is also the weakest evaluation design. This is because there may be many competing explanations as to why the evaluation measured the results it did. If the evaluation showed promising results, could it be because of something else that was affecting participants at the same time? Or perhaps the participants would have had the same results without the program?

Single-group design: an evaluation design focused on examining the effects of a program on one group of participants; an evaluation design without a comparison group. Single-group designs are also referred to as *nonexperimental designs*.

Using your logic model along with a single-group design can help to improve the credibility of your findings. For instance, suppose you are evaluating a new program in a classroom or school focused on improving reading comprehension among third graders. If the evaluation results are promising, the principal has agreed to incorporate the funding for the program into the ongoing budget. If you do not have another classroom or school against which to compare progress (i.e., you have a single-group design), you can explain how the program operates by using your logic model and the data collected at each stage of operation. You can give evidence showing that the program's activities were put into place, use data from your early and intermediate objectives to show change in teacher practice and student progress, and present long-term outcomes showing how reading comprehension changed. While you cannot claim that the program *caused* the change in reading comprehension, you can use your logic model and its associated indicators to demonstrate a theoretical association between the program and long-term outcomes. A great resource for designing rigorous, nonexperimental evaluations, taking into account time and budget constraints, is *RealWorld Evaluation* by Bamberger, Rugh, and Mabry (2011).

Comparison-group design: an evaluation design that includes the examination of program effects in two or more groups, at least one of which receives the program and at least one of which does not. Strong comparison-group designs are also referred to as *quasi-experimental designs*.

8.1.3 Quasi-Experimental and Comparison-Group Designs

If you are able to have more than one group participate in your evaluation, typically you can improve the usability of your findings. Using multiple groups in an evaluation, referred to as a **comparison-group design**, can help to rule out some of the other competing explanations as to why a program may have worked (Campbell & Stanley, 1963; Cook & Campbell, 1979; Cronbach, 1982; Rossi, Lipsey, & Henry, 2018). The *program group* is the group that receives the program. The *comparison group* is the group that does not receive the program being evaluated. However, the groups must be comparable.

Comparing test scores from a district that used a new program to test scores from another district that did not use the new program would not yield meaningful information if the demographics, resources, and size of the two districts are not comparable.

The rigor of a comparison-group design will vary with how closely matched the comparison group is with the group that will be implementing the program. Convenience groups, such as a community chosen because it neighbors your community, will likely not yield results that are as meaningful as would a comparison community that is purposefully chosen to match your community based on multiple key indicators that you believe might influence outcomes, such as gender, ethnicity, and socioeconomic composition.

Just because a good comparison group does not readily exist for a program, an evaluator should not give up on the possibility of finding or creating one. Evaluators should use some creativity when creating an evaluation design and identifying comparison groups. Suppose you have been asked to evaluate a domestic violence intervention program that your county plans to implement in conjunction with local police. If you have flexibility such that you could work with townships across the county to vary the timing of the implementation, you could create a comparison group using a staggered implementation. For instance, several townships could implement the program in one year, leaving the remaining townships as a comparison group. If evaluation results are promising, the comparison townships could be brought on board in the following year.

Another example is a classroom-based program that two teachers are interested in using with their students. One teacher could use the program in their classroom in the fall semester, and the other in the spring semester. The two teachers could compare the results not only within the program classroom from one semester to the next, but also between the two classrooms in the evaluation. Or suppose a program is implemented at a local community center. A few towns away you find a demographically comparable community that also has a community center. In such a case, you might consider using the neighboring community center as a comparison group. Another example is a drug rehabilitation program that can only accommodate a set number of individuals. Once the program meets capacity, instead of turning away other potential participants, program staff can refer them to other providers as well as invite them to participate in the evaluation. The program could follow these individuals as a comparison group, along with program participants. Similarly, a program that provides job skills training for individuals with disabilities can invite applicants who cannot be accommodated once the program is full to participate in the evaluation, as well as to be placed in the next training course to be offered. These individuals would serve as a comparison group for the training program, as well as provide a baseline for future evaluation when they begin the training course. Thus, there are many ways that comparison groups can be incorporated into an evaluation.

Strong comparison-group designs are often referred to as *quasi-experimental designs*. When considering a comparison group, seek to identify or create a group that is as similar as possible to the group that will be implementing the program, especially on the key variables that might influence the results. However, the only way to make certain, to the extent possible, that groups are equivalent is through random assignment. Random assignment is discussed in the following section.

8.1.4 Experimental Designs

The most rigorous evaluation design is a *true experiment*. Comparison-group designs, discussed above, attempt to approximate a true experiment. However, in a true experiment, the comparison group is not an existing group, but rather one created as part of the evaluation. This type of design is an **experimental design**, in which participants are randomly assigned to the program or to a nonprogram control group (Boruch, 1997; Campbell, 1969; Mosteller & Boruch, 2002). True experiments are also referred to as *randomized controlled experiments* or *randomized controlled trials* (RCTs). The *program group*, sometimes called the intervention group, is the group that receives the program. The group that does not receive the program is the *control group*.

In a true experiment, participants are randomly assigned to either participate in the program or an alternative condition (such as a different program or no program at all). Theoretically, the process of random assignment creates groups that are equivalent across both observable and unobservable characteristics (Campbell & Stanley, 1963). By randomly assigning program participants, you can rule out other explanations for changes in the outcomes you measure; any differences in groups would be due to chance alone and theoretically would not differentially impact the findings for one group more than the other.

For some programs, random assignment may align well with program resources. For instance, for programs that do not have the resources to include all participants from the start, randomly assigning participants to the program would address in a fair manner who participates in the program and would allow you to draw causal conclusions from your evaluation findings. For example, suppose you have been asked to evaluate the effectiveness of a charter school. In talking with school staff, you find that the charter school receives approximately twice as many applicants as they can admit for their 200 spots. Instead of admitting the first 200 students or the 200 students with the strongest academic record, you might encourage school staff to consider randomly assigning applicants to the charter school spots. In doing so, you would be creating a control group of the applicants who were not admitted and could potentially follow up with them on the same outcomes you examine for the charter school group. With such a design, the evaluator can compare outcomes of the two groups and attribute any significant differences to the charter school intervention.

Experimental design: an evaluation design in which participants are randomly assigned to receive the program or to a nonprogram control group. Experimental designs are also called *randomized controlled trials* (RCTs).

Another example of when an RCT might be possible is a lottery with staged implementation. For instance, instead of a program allowing individuals to self-select to participate or deciding that program staff can purposefully assign participants to the program, recommend the program consider a lottery at the start to determine who will participate and when. In such cases, if results are promising for the first cohort that participates, additional resources could be sought to expand the program to include the second cohort.

8.1.5 Choosing the "Best" Design for Your Program

Designing evaluations of existing programs often comes with more constraints than when an evaluator is brought in at the very beginning of program design. There is no right or wrong evaluation design, but evaluators should strive to utilize the most rigorous design they can, taking into account any constraints. Regardless of design, you will address the same evaluation question and measure the same indicators as set forth in Chapter 7. However, the rigor of your design will limit or support the confidence one can have in the evaluation's findings.

Be creative when designing your evaluation and determining comparison or control groups. You might find that, with a little resourcefulness at the design stage, you can implement a stronger evaluation than you originally thought (see Bamburger, Rugh, & Mabry, 2011).

Finally, some evaluators might tell you the *best* design is a randomized controlled trial, while other evaluators may be of the opinion that findings from such designs are not generalizable to other populations and thus question the additional time and effort involved in creating and examining a control group. Both arguments have merit. However, no evaluator would likely dismiss the importance of understanding the strengths and weaknesses of different evaluation designs, as well as understanding the extent to which you can claim your program caused certain outcomes based on your evaluation design (see Campbell & Stanley, 1963).

8.1.6 Enriching Your Evaluation Design

Whether you have chosen to evaluate using a single-group, comparison-group, or experimental design, there are several methods and approaches you can use to *enrich your evaluation design*. **Evaluation enrichments** are added supports in your evaluation design that can increase the usefulness of your results and credibility of your findings, make your evaluation more manageable, and expand upon information obtained throughout program implementation. These methods include using repeated measures, longitudinal data, and sampling. Logic modeling too can enrich your evaluation, as it can be used to construct a reasoned explanation for your evaluation findings. Supplementing your evaluation design with a case study could also enrich your evaluation design by providing in-depth information regarding implementation and participant experiences.

Evaluation enrichments: added supports to your evaluation design that can increase the usefulness of results and credibility of findings. Some enrichments include using repeated measures, longitudinal data, and sampling, as well as logic modeling and case studies.

Using **repeated measures**, collecting the same data elements at multiple time points, can also help to strengthen your evaluation design (Minitab Blog Editor, 2015). If the program you are evaluating is intended to improve critical thinking skills over a specified time period (e.g., one year), taking repeated measurements (perhaps monthly) of indicators that address critical thinking skills will not only provide you with baseline and frequent data with which to compare end-of-year results, but also enable program staff to use midterm information to make midcourse corrections and improvements.

Using **longitudinal data**, data collected over an extended period of time, can enable you to follow program participants in the long term and examine post-program changes (Caruana, Roman, Hernández-Sánchez, & Solli, 2015). Longitudinal data can also enable you to examine a program's success using a time series analysis. For example, suppose a school district made the change from half-day to full-day kindergarten 5 years ago, and you are asked whether the program positively affected student learning. The district has been using the same reading assessment for kindergarteners for the past 10 years. The assessment is given in September and May of each year. You examine the September scores over the past 10 years and find that there has been little variability in mean scores. Mean scores by gender, ethnicity, and English language learner (ELL) status have all been fairly steady. You conclude the kindergarteners have been entering school at approximately the same mean reading level for the past 10 years.

Next, you examine the May reading scores for the past 10 years. You notice that for the first 5 years, the mean end-of-year scores (overall and by subgroup) were significantly higher than the September scores, but varied little from year to year. However, for the past 5 years, the May scores were about 15% higher than in the previous 5 years. The increase by gender and ethnicity was similar and also consistent over the past 5 years, while reading scores for ELL students were over 30% higher in the spring, after the full-day program was instituted. After ruling out other possible explanations for the findings to the extent possible, you conclude that the full-day kindergarten program appears to have been beneficial for all students, and particularly beneficial for the district's ELL students.

If a program has many program participants or if you lack the funds to use all of a program's participants in your evaluation, **sampling** to choose a smaller group from the larger population of program participants is an option. Random sampling selects evaluation participants randomly from the larger group of program participants, and may be more easily accepted by stakeholder groups. Whether you are using random sampling or purposeful sampling, you should select a sample group that is as representative as possible of all of your participants (i.e., the population). Typically, the larger the sample you use, the more precise and credible your results will be. See "sampling" in Salkind's (2010) *Encyclopedia of Research Design* for information on selecting unbiased samples.

Repeated measures: collecting the same data elements at multiple time points.

Longitudinal data: data collected over an extended period of time.

Sampling: choosing a smaller group to participate in the evaluation from the larger population of program participants.

QUICK CHECK

1. When would it be appropriate to causally attribute program outcomes to strategies?
   a. When your logic model is really good
   b. When you involved stakeholders in logic modeling
   c. When you have a single-group evaluation design
   d. When you have an experimental evaluation design

2. What is the difference between nonexperimental, quasi-experimental, and experimental evaluation designs? Which design is considered the most rigorous and why?

3. What are some ways you can strengthen your evaluation designs?

Answers: 1-d; 2-the number of groups and the way in which subjects are placed in groups; experimental; 3-including repeated measures, longitudinal data, and so on

Using **logic modeling** in your evaluation can also help to strengthen the credibility of your findings (Weiss, 1998). By examining the implementation of strategies and activities as well as the measurement of progress on early, intermediate, and long-term indicators, a logic model can provide interim data that can be used to adjust and improve the program during its operation (Frechtling, 2007; Knowlton & Phillips, 2009; W.K. Kellogg Foundation, 2004). As described with the reading comprehension example in the single-group design section, logic modeling can help to show a theoretical association between the strategies and outcomes in even the weakest of evaluation designs.

Finally, a **case study** is an in-depth examination of a person, group of people, or context (Yin, 2017). Case studies can enrich your understanding of a program, as well as provide a more accurate picture of how a program operates. More information on case studies will be provided in the next section.

8.2 EVALUATION METHODS AND TOOLS

Logic modeling: the process of determining indicators for program objectives and goals based on program theory.

Two of the most important components of embedded evaluation are building evaluation indicators into the logic model and determining what design to use for the evaluation. Using the analogy of a treasure map within a home, the logic model is the map within the evaluation design. A strong evaluation design will preserve the findings derived using the logic model, just as a strong home will preserve the map within. A weak evaluation design, like a weak house, will make its contents vulnerable to outside forces. However, the sturdier the map, the more likely it will provide some useful information should the house not protect it from the elements. That is, a strong logic model within a weak

Case study: an in-depth examination of a person, group of people, or context.

evaluation design will still yield useful information. Yet a strong logic model within a rigorous evaluation design will enable much stronger conclusions regarding program effectiveness and impact. As you have likely surmised, a weak logic model within a strong evaluation design provides little useful information, just as an unreadable treasure map within a sturdy home brings you no closer to the treasure. That said, in this section you will add strength and depth to your logic model by continuing to build upon the evaluation matrix you began in Chapter 7. Methods and tools will be identified or developed for each indicator on your logic model, addressing the question, *How will you collect your data?*

Although there are many evaluation methods, most are classified as qualitative, quantitative, or both. **Qualitative methods** rely primarily on noncategorical, free response, observational, or narrative descriptions of a program, collected through methods such as open-ended survey items, interviews, or observations. **Quantitative methods**, on the other hand, rely primarily on discrete categories, such as counts, numbers, and multiple-choice responses. Qualitative and quantitative methods reinforce each other in an evaluation, as qualitative data can help to describe, illuminate, and provide a depth of understanding to quantitative findings. For this reason, you may want to choose an evaluation design that includes a combination of qualitative and quantitative methods, commonly referred to as **mixed methods**. Some common evaluation methods are discussed below and include assessments and tests, surveys and questionnaires, interviews and focus groups, observations, existing data, portfolios, and case studies. Rubrics are also included as an evaluation tool that is often used to score, categorize, or code interviews, observations, portfolios, qualitative assessments, and case studies.

Qualitative methods: evaluation methods that rely on noncategorical data and free response, observational, or narrative descriptions.

Quantitative methods: evaluation methods that rely on categorical or numerical data.

Mixed methods: evaluation methods that rely on both quantitative and qualitative data.

Before delving in to different methods, it is worth mentioning the ways in which the terms assessment and survey are sometimes used and misused. First, while the term "survey" is sometimes used synonymously with "evaluation," evaluation does not mean survey. A survey is a tool that can be used in an evaluation and it is perhaps one of the most common tools used in evaluation, but it is just one tool nonetheless.

Another terminology confusion is between "assessment" and "evaluation." These too are often used interchangeably. However, many in the field of evaluation would argue that assessment has a quantitative connotation, while evaluation can be mixed method.

Similarly, the term "measurement" is often used synonymously with "assessment," and measurement too has a quantitative connotation. I believe the confusion lies in the terms "assess," "evaluate," and "measure"; they are synonyms. So, it only makes sense that assessment and evaluation, and sometimes measurement, are used synonymously. And while there is nothing inherently wrong with using these terms interchangeably, it is a good idea to ask for clarification when the terms assessment and measurement are used. Some major funders use the term "assessment plan" to mean "evaluation plan," but others may use the term assessment as an indication that they would like quantitative measurement. The takeaway from this is to communicate with stakeholders such that the evaluation (or assessment) you design meets their information needs and expectations.

8.2.1 Qualitative Methods

Qualitative methods focus on noncategorical, observational, or narrative data. Evaluation using qualitative methods is primarily inductive, in that data are collected and examined for patterns. These patterns are then used to make generalizations and formulate hypotheses based on these generalizations. Qualitative methods include interviews and focus groups, observations, some types of existing data, portfolios, and case studies. Each method is described in the following paragraphs.

Interviews and *focus groups* (qualitative) are typically conducted face-to-face or over the phone. We also conduct individual interviews using video conferencing software. Focus groups are group interviews and can also be conducted using video conferencing software, but I have found it is difficult to maintain the richness of discussion found in face-to-face focus groups when conducted using video. However, I have no doubt as we become more skilled with facilitating group discussions where individuals are in varied locations, video focus groups will become an important and invaluable mode of research. The list of interview and focus group questions is referred to as a protocol; an interview protocol can be created with questions to address your specific information needs. The interviewer can use follow-up questions and probes as necessary to clarify responses. However, interviews and focus groups take time to conduct and analyze. Due to the time-consuming nature of interviews and focus groups, sample sizes are typically small, and research costs can be expensive. See *Interviews in Qualitative Research* (King, Horrocks, & Brooks, 2018) and *Focus Groups* (Krueger & Casey, 2014) for more information on designing and conducting interviews and focus groups.

Observations (usually qualitative but can be quantitative) can be used to collect information about people's behavior, such as teacher's classroom instruction or students' active engagement. Observations can be scored using a rubric or through theme-based analyses, and multiple observations are necessary to ensure that findings are grounded. Because of this, observational techniques tend to be time-consuming and expensive, but can provide an extremely rich description of program implementation. See the observation section of Robert Wood Johnson Foundation's *Qualitative Research Guidelines Project* (Cohen & Crabtree, 2006) for more information and a list of resources on using observation in research.

Existing data (usually quantitative but can be qualitative) are often overlooked but can be an excellent and readily available source of evaluation information. Using existing data such as school records (e.g., student grades, test scores, graduation rate, truancy data, and behavioral infractions), work samples, and lesson plans, as well as documentation regarding school or district policy and procedures, minimizes the data collection burden. However, despite the availability and convenience, you should critically examine the quality of existing data and whether they meet your evaluation needs.

Portfolios (typically qualitative) are collections of work samples and can be used to examine the progress of the program's participants throughout the program's operation. Work samples from before (pre) and after (post) program implementation can be compared and scored using rubrics to measure growth. Portfolios can show tangible and powerful evidence of growth and can be used as concrete examples when reporting program results. However, scoring can be subjective and is highly dependent upon the strength of the rubric and the training of the portfolio scorers; in addition, the use of rubrics in research can be very resource intensive (Herman & Winters, 1994).

Case studies (mostly qualitative but can include quantitative data) are in-depth examinations of a person, group of people, or context. Case studies can include a combination of any of the methods reviewed above. Case studies look at the big picture and investigate the interrelationships among data. For instance, a case study of a school might include interviews with teachers and parents, observations in the classroom, student surveys, student work, and test scores. Combining many methods into a case study can provide a rich picture of how a program is used, where a program might be improved, and any variation in findings from using different methods. Using multiple, mixed methods in an evaluation allows for a deeper understanding of a program, as well as a more accurate picture of how a program operates and its successes. See Yin (2017) for more information on case study research.

8.2.2 Quantitative Methods

Quantitative methods focus on categorical or numerical data. Evaluation based on quantitative data is primarily deductive, in that it begins with a hypothesis and uses the data to make specific conclusions. Quantitative methods include assessments and tests, as well as surveys and questionnaires, and some types of existing data. Each method is described in the following paragraphs.

Assessments and *tests* (typically quantitative but can include qualitative items) are often used prior to program implementation (pre) and again at program completion (post), or at various times during program implementation, to assess program progress and results. Assessments are also referred to as tests or instruments. Results of assessments are usually objective, and multiple items can be used in combination to create a subscale, often providing a more reliable estimate than any single item (see Wright, 2007). If a program is intended to decrease depression or improve self-confidence, you will likely want to use an existing assessment that measures depression or self-confidence. If you want to measure knowledge of organizational policies, you may decide to create a test based on the policies specific to the organization. However, before using assessment or test data, you should be sure that the assessment adequately addresses what the program intends to achieve. You would not want the success or failure of the program to be determined by an assessment that does not accurately measure the program's outcomes.

The reliability and validity of an instrument are important considerations when selecting and using instruments such as assessments and tests (as well surveys and questionnaires). **Reliability** is the consistency with which an instrument measures whatever it intends to measure. There are three common types of reliability: internal consistency reliability, test–retest reliability, and inter-rater reliability. See Figure 8.2 for a description of each type of reliability.

Reliability: the consistency with which an instrument measures something.

Validity is the accuracy with which an instrument measures a construct. The construct might be anxiety, aptitude, achievement, alcoholism, or self-confidence. There are four types of validity: content validity, construct validity, criterion-related validity, and consequential validity. See Figure 8.2 for more information on each type of validity.

Validity: the accuracy with which an instrument measures a construct.

FIGURE 8.2 ● Reliability and Validity

Reliability is the consistency with which an instrument assesses whatever it assesses. Reliability may refer to any of the following elements:

- The extent to which a respondent gives consistent responses to multiple items that are asking basically the same question in different ways (internal consistency reliability)

- The extent to which individuals' scores are consistent if given the same assessment a short time later (test–retest reliability)

- The extent to which different raters give consistent scores for the same open-ended response or different observers using an observation protocol give consistent scores for the same observation (inter-rater reliability)

Validity refers to how well an instrument measures what it is supposed to or it claims to measure. An assessment is not simply valid or not valid but rather valid for a certain purpose with a certain population. In fact, the same assessment may be valid for one group but not for another. For example, a reading test administered in English may be valid for many students but not for those in the classroom who are ELLs.

Traditional views of validity classify the validity of a data collection instrument into three types: content validity, construct validity, and criterion-related validity.

Content validity addresses whether an instrument asks questions that are relevant to what is being assessed.

(Continued)

FIGURE 8.2 ● (Continued)

Construct validity is the degree to which a measure accurately represents the underlying, unobserved theoretical construct it purports to measure.

Criterion-related validity refers to how well a measure predicts performance. There are two types of criterion-related validity—concurrent and predictive. Concurrent validity compares performance on an assessment with that on another assessment. For example, how do scores on the statewide assessment correlate with those on another nationally normed, standardized test? Predictive validity indicates the degree to which scores on an assessment can accurately predict performance on a future measure. For instance, how well do SAT scores predict performance in college?

A fourth type of validity that is sometimes noted is *consequential validity.* Consequential validity refers to the intended and unintended social consequences of using a particular measure, for example, using a particular test to determine which students to assign to remedial courses.

When choosing an assessment or creating your own instrument, you should investigate the technical qualities of reliability and validity to be sure the test is consistent in its measurement and to verify that it does indeed measure what you need to measure. Further, taking a subset of items from a validated instrument to create a new instrument does in fact create a new instrument, with untested reliability and validity. Results from an instrument that is not valid are, in turn, not valid. That is, using an instrument that has not been validated through the examination of reliability and validity can result in erroneous and costly decisions being made based upon those data.

Surveys and *questionnaires* (typically quantitative but can include qualitative items) are often used to collect information from large numbers of respondents. They can be administered online, on paper, in person, or over the phone. In order for surveys to provide useful information, the questions must be worded clearly and succinctly. Survey items can be open-ended or closed-ended.

Open-ended survey items allow respondents to provide free-form responses to questions and are typically scored using a **rubric**. A rubric is a scoring guide used to categorize text-based or observational information based upon set criteria or elements of performance. See Figure 8.3 for more information on rubrics. Closed-ended items give the respondent a choice of responses, often on a scale from 1 to 4 or 1 to 5. Surveys can be quickly administered, are usually easy to analyze, and can be adapted to fit specific situations.

Rubric: a guideline that can be used objectively to examine subjective data.

Building a survey in conjunction with other methods and tools can help you to understand your findings better. For instance, designing a survey to explore findings from

---

FIGURE 8.3 ● Scoring Rubrics

Rubrics as an evaluation tool provide you with a way to identify, quantify, categorize, sort, rank, score, or code portfolios, observations, and other subjective data.

Rubrics are used to score student work, such as writing samples or portfolios, as well as to examine classroom implementation of a program. When rubrics are used to examine behavior or performance, observers rely on the rubric definitions to determine where the behavior or performance lies on the rubric scale. Rubrics are typically scaled 1 to 4 or 1 to 5, with each number representing a level of implementation or a variation of use.

Observers or rubric scorers must be highly trained so that scoring is consistent among scorers (referred to as inter-rater reliability) and over multiple scoring occasions.

Rubrics can also be used to facilitate program implementation. Providing those implementing a project or program with a rubric that indicates variations in implementation, as well as what the preferred implementation would look like, can help to promote fidelity of implementation. For instance, just as students are provided with a scoring rubric before they complete a writing assignment (so they know what is expected and what constitutes an ideal response), teachers or administrators could be provided with a rubric regarding how to use or operate a program or how to conduct an activity.

---

observations or document reviews can enable you to compare findings among multiple sources. Validating your findings using multiple methods gives the evaluator more confidence regarding evaluation findings.

Using a previously administered survey can save you time, may give you something to compare your results to (if previous results are available), and may give you confidence that some of the potential problems have already been addressed. Two notes of caution, however, in using surveys that others have developed: (1) Be sure the instrument has been tested and demonstrated to be reliable and valid for the intended population, and (2) be sure the survey addresses your evaluation needs. It is tempting to use an already developed survey without thinking critically about whether it will truly answer your evaluation questions. Existing surveys may need to be adapted to fit your specific needs.

See *Survey Research Methods* (Fowler, 2013) for more information on designing, administering, and analyzing surveys.

8.2.3 Mixed Methods

Mixed-method studies combine both qualitative and quantitative methods. For example, an evaluation of a program intended to increase the retention of faculty from underrepresented groups in the STEM fields (science, technology, engineering, and math) might utilize a survey (quantitative) to examine faculty satisfaction among all faculty, as well as focus groups (qualitative) with a sample of faculty to explore more in-depth faculty experiences. Just as it is not good practice to base a student's final grade in a course on one test, it is also poor practice to base an evaluation on one measure. Using multiple measures, both quantitative and qualitative, provides for a much more valid determination of impact. Table 8.1 presents an overview of evaluation methods and tools used to collect data, noting advantages and disadvantages.

TABLE 8.1 ◆ Evaluation Methods and Tools			
Methods and Tools	**Basic Information**	**Advantages**	**Disadvantages**
Assessments and Tests	• Usually quantitative but can be qualitative • Can be administered online or in person • Can be administered individually or in groups	• Multiple items may be used in combination to create a subscale, often providing a more reliable estimate than any single item. • Can be used pre- and post-program implementation to measure growth	• If assessment is not aligned well with the program, data may not be a meaningful indicator of program success. • If reliability and validity are not adequate, the data will be poor quality, and inaccurate conclusions may be drawn.
Surveys and Questionnaires	• Typically quantitative but can be qualitative • Can be administered in person, over the phone, online, or through the mail	• In-person surveys can be a quick method to collect data. • If conducted with a captive (in-person) audience, response rates can be high. • Electronic or internet-based surveys can save time and costs with data entry and can improve data quality by reducing data entry errors.	• Due to postage costs and multiple mailings, mail surveys can be expensive. • Response rates of mail surveys can be low. • If during data analysis it is found that questions were not worded well, some data may be unusable.
Interviews	• Qualitative method • Can be conducted in person or over the phone	• Follow-up questions can be used to obtain more detail when needed.	• Time-consuming to conduct • Time-consuming to analyze data

		• Follow-up probes can be used to determine how interviewees are interpreting questions. • Nonverbal communication during in-person interviews aids in response interpretation.	• Limited number of participants • Can be expensive, depending on the number of people interviewed
Focus Groups	• Qualitative method • Multiple people can be interviewed at the same time.	• Follow-up questions can be used to obtain more detail when needed. • Follow-up questions can be used to determine how interviewees are interpreting questions. • Participants can build on each other's responses. • Often more cost-effective than interviews • Nonverbal communication during in-person focus groups can aid in response interpretation.	• Group setting may inhibit participants from speaking freely. • Difficult to coordinate schedules with multiple people • Participants may focus on one topic, limiting exploration of other ideas. • Requires a skilled facilitator • Time-consuming to analyze data
Observations	• Typically qualitative but can be quantitative • Can be done in person, via video, through one-way glass, or from a distance	• Provides a good sense of the use of the program • Allows the researcher to gain a full understanding of the environment of participants • Helps to provide a context for interpreting data	• Sometimes need many observations to gain a realistic sense of the use of a program • Time-consuming to observe, thus expensive • Time-consuming to analyze • Participant behavior may be affected by observer presence

(Continued)

TABLE 8.1 ● (Continued)			
Existing Data	• Can be qualitative or quantitative • Might include school records (electronic or paper based), work samples, lesson plans, or existing documentation (such as meeting minutes or attendance sheets)	• Low burden on participants to provide data • Relatively inexpensive to collect • Electronic data may facilitate analysis • Interpretation of existing data is often objective. However, interpretation of existing data such as documents or meeting minutes can be subjective.	• May not correspond exactly to evaluation needs • May be incomplete or require additional interpretation • May need special permission or consent to access and use • If not electronic, may be time-consuming to analyze
Portfolios	• Primarily a qualitative method • Can be captured and stored electronically	• Can provide a representative cross-section of work • If portfolio work is used pre-program and post-program, data can be used to examine growth.	• Scoring of qualitative work is often subjective. • Objectivity of results relies on strength of scoring rubric and training of scorers. So, reliability and validity should be considered.
Case Studies	• Primarily a qualitative method • Can include both qualitative and quantitative data • Can include a mixture of many methods, including interviews, observations, existing data, etc.	• Provides a multimethod approach to evaluation • Often allows a more in-depth examination of implementation and change than other methods	• Analyses of data can be subjective • Expensive to conduct and analyze; as a result, sample sizes are often small
Rubrics	• Quantitative method • Guidelines to objectively examine and score subjective data such as observations, portfolios, open-ended survey responses, student work, etc.	• Powerful method to examine variations of program implementation • Well-defined rubrics can be used not only for evaluation purposes but also to facilitate program implementation.	• Objectivity of results relies on strength of scoring rubric and training of scorers.

IN THE REAL WORLD ...

The **Perry Preschool Project** intended to improve the educational outcomes for three- and four-year-old African American children who were living in poverty and at high risk for school failure. Strategies included morning preschool sessions taught by certified teachers, low student–teacher ratios, an active learning preschool curriculum, and weekly home visits. The project began in 1962 and ran through 1967, though outcomes for the participants continue to be monitored.

The **evaluation design** was a randomized controlled experiment, in which 128 children were randomly assigned to either the Perry Preschool or a no-preschool control group. The evaluation also employed a longitudinal design to examine the long-term impact of the program on life outcomes.

Prior to receiving the program, there were no significant differences in terms of intellectual performance or demographic characteristics between the Perry Preschool children and the control group children.

The Perry Preschool Project used multiple measures to determine impact, including educational attainment, teen pregnancy rate, employment status, income, and criminal activity and incarceration.

The children have been followed into adulthood. At the age 27 follow-up, the Perry Preschool group had a 44% higher high school graduation rate than the control group. In addition, the Perry Preschool group had 50% fewer teen pregnancies than did the control group. At the age 40 follow-up, the Perry Preschool group had a 42% higher median monthly income than the control group. Further, the Perry Preschool participants were 46% less likely to have spent time in jail than the control group.

Source: Social Programs That Work (2019).

 QUICK CHECK

1. How do quantitative and qualitative methods differ? What are some quantitative evaluation methods? What are some qualitative evaluation methods?

2. Which of the following is NOT a type of reliability?

    a. Construct

    b. Internal consistency

    c. Inter-rater

    d. Test–retest

3. When might an evaluator use a rubric?

    a. When administering a survey

    b. When categorizing observed behavior

    c. When giving a test

    d. When conducting a focus group

4. Which evaluation method would be most appropriate to gain an in-depth understanding of individual experiences in a drug treatment program?

(Continued)

(Continued)

   a. An assessment

   b. A focus group

   c. A one-on-one interview

   d. Observation

5. Which evaluation method would be most appropriate for measuring the self-confidence of a large group of people?

   a. An assessment

   b. A focus group

   c. A one-on-one interview

   d. Observation

Answers: 1-in the type of data collected; 2-a; 3-b; 4-c; 5-a

TABLE 8.2 ● Evaluation Matrix Example Shell							
	Logic Model Component	Evaluation Questions	Indicators	Targets	Data Source	Data Collection	Data Analysis
Strategies							
Early and Intermediate Objectives							
Long-Term Goals							

8.3 EVALUATION MATRIX: IDENTIFYING DATA SOURCES

In Chapter 7, an evaluation matrix was introduced as a way to build evaluation into each component of your logic model. At that time, the first four columns were completed: logic model component, evaluation questions, indicators, and targets. The fifth column defines the quantitative and qualitative methods that will be used to measure evaluation indicators. Table 8.2 shows an example shell of an evaluation matrix. As highlighted, the data source column will identify the type of data to be collected for each indicator.

Table 8.3 will be helpful in identifying appropriate methods to use as data sources. In the youth community center example from Chapter 7, one of the indicators was "the number of youth participating in the community center." How might you collect the necessary

CASE STUDY

Youth Abstinence-Plus (YAP) Program

Table 8.3 shows the evaluation matrix for the YAP program showing data sources for each indicator.

TABLE 8.3 ⬡ YAP Partial Evaluation Matrix

	Logic Model Component	Evaluation Question(s)	Indicators	Targets	Data Source	Data Collection	Data Analysis
Program Strategies/Implementation	Materials promoting sexual abstinence	What were the content and format of materials promoting abstinence? In what ways were materials promoting abstinence made available to youth?	Content and format of abstinence materials Method of delivering abstinence materials to youth	By program start, materials promoting sexual abstinence are developed and implemented with fidelity	Fidelity of implementation rubric		
	Education regarding safe sex practices	What were the content and format of education regarding safe sex practices? In what ways was education regarding safe sex provided?	Content and format of education regarding safe sex practices Method of delivering education regarding safe sex to youth	By program start, education regarding safe sex practices is implemented with fidelity	Fidelity of implementation rubric		
	Access to contraceptives	In what ways, from whom, and at what locations were contraceptives available to youth? What types of contraceptives were made available to youth?	Distribution method of contraceptives to youth Types of contraceptives available to youth	By program start, methods of access to contraceptives will be implemented with fidelity	Fidelity of implementation rubric		

(Continued)

TABLE 8.3 ● (Continued)

	Logic Model Component	Evaluation Question(s)	Indicators	Targets	Data Source	Data Collection	Data Analysis
Early and Intermediate Objectives	Increase the availability of materials on abstinence	To what extent did youth have access to materials on abstinence?	Availability of abstinence materials to youth	Within one week of program start, abstinence materials will be available to all youth	Program records		
	Increase the number of youth who receive materials on abstinence	To what extent did the number of youth who received materials on abstinence increase? In what ways did youth obtain materials related to abstinence?	Number of youth receiving abstinence materials *Method of receiving abstinence materials*	Within three months of program start, all youth will have received materials on abstinence	Inventory of materials		
	Increase the availability of education regarding safe sex practices	To what extent was education regarding safe sex practices made available to youth?	Availability of education regarding safe sex practices	Within one week of program start, education regarding safe sex will be available to all youth	Program records Training schedule		
	Increase the number of youth who receive education regarding safe sex practices	To what extent did the number of youth who received education regarding safe sex practices increase? How did youth receive education regarding safe sex?	Number of youth receiving education on safe sex practices *Method of receiving education on safe sex practices*	Within three months of program start, all youth will have received education on safe sex practices	Training sign-in sheets		

Increase the number of youth who have access to contraceptives	To what extent did the number of youth with access to contraceptives increase? To what extent were youth aware of their access to contraceptives?	Number of youth who have access to contraceptives Number of youth who are aware of their access to contraceptives	Within three months, all youth will have access to contraceptives Within six months, all youth will be aware of their access to contraceptives	Program records
Increase the number of sexually active youth who obtain contraceptives	To what extent did the number of sexually active youth who obtain contraceptives increase? Where did youth obtain contraceptives? What types of contraceptives did youth obtain?	Number of sexually active youth who obtain contraceptives *Demographics of youth who obtain contraceptives* *Method and location of receiving contraceptives* *Types of contraceptives received*	Within one year, there will be a 25% increase in sexually active youth who obtain contraceptives	Inventory of contraceptives
Increase the number of youth who understand the benefits of abstinence	To what extent did the number of youth who understand the benefits of abstinence increase? What did youth learn about abstinence?	Number of youth who understand the benefits of abstinence *Nature of youth's understanding about the benefits of abstinence*	Within six months of the start of the program, all youth will be able to describe the benefits of abstinence	Youth survey

(Continued)

TABLE 8.3 ● (Continued)

	Logic Model Component	Evaluation Question(s)	Indicators	Targets	Data Source	Data Collection	Data Analysis
Early and Intermediate Objectives	Increase the number of youth who understand the benefits of practicing safe sex	To what extent did the number of youth who understand the benefits of practicing safe sex increase? *What did youth learn about practicing safe sex?*	Number of youth who are able to describe the benefits of practicing safe sex *Nature of youth's understanding about the benefits of practicing safe sex*	Within six months, all youth will be able to describe the benefits of practicing safe sex	Youth survey		
	Increase the number of sexually active youth who use contraceptives	To what extent did the number of sexually active youth who use contraceptives increase? *What types of contraceptives did youth choose to use? How often did youth use contraceptives in sexual situations?*	Number of sexually active youth who use contraceptives *Demographics of youth who use contraceptives* *Types of contraceptives used* *Frequency with which contraception is used*	Within one year, there will be a 20% increase in the number of sexually active youth who use contraceptives	Youth survey		
	Improve safe sex practices among sexually active youth	To what extent did safe sex practices among sexually active youth improve? *In what ways did safe sex practices improve?*	Number of sexually active youth who practice safe sex *Demographics of youth who practice safe sex* *Nature of safe sex practices used* *Frequency with which contraception is used*	Within one year, there will be a 20% increase in sexually active youth who practice safe sex	Youth survey		

20% Long-Term Goals

Goal	Evaluation Question	Indicators	Objective	Data Source
Increase the number of youth who choose abstinence	To what extent did the number of youth who choose abstinence increase?	Number of youth who choose abstinence *Demographics of youth who choose abstinence* *Self-reported reason for youth choosing abstinence*	Within one year of program start, there will be a 20% increase in the number of youth who choose abstinence	Youth survey
Decrease the spread of STIs among youth	To what extent did the spread of STIs, including HIV, decrease?	Number of youth diagnosed with STI/HIV *Demographics of youth diagnosed with STI/HIV*	Within two years of program start, there will be a 20% decrease in the number of youths diagnosed with STI/HIV in the community	Youth survey Public health records
Decrease the youth pregnancy rate	To what extent did the youth pregnancy rate decrease?	Number of youth who become pregnant *Demographics of youth who become pregnant*	Within two years of program start, there will be a 20% decrease in the number of youth in the community who become pregnant	Youth survey Public health records

information to measure this indicator? Most programs track attendance at events and activities. Thus, for this indicator, it is likely the program would have daily attendance records indicating the number of youth who participate. If such data are not already collected, a simple log could be created for the community center to track this information.

An indicator for the healthy eating example might be consumption of fast food. It is unlikely that existing records would capture this information, so new data would need to be collected. A possible data source might be a weekly log (short survey) on which participants can record their fast food consumption. Another possible way to address this indicator is through participant interviews; however, asking participants to reflect back over a certain time period to estimate their fast food consumption would likely be less reliable than having participants keep a weekly log. With busy schedules, it is challenging to ask participants in a program to accurately recall past behaviors and practices.

Finally, in the teacher quality example, an indicator was the number of teachers who are state certified. Schools would most certainly have this information in their current records. For the same program, you might also have an indicator to examine teacher satisfaction. To understand teacher satisfaction, evaluation methods such as teacher interviews or surveys would be most appropriate. The case study on the following pages provides multiple examples of data sources for different types of indicators.

8.4 CHAPTER SUMMARY

The usefulness of evaluation relies on the extent to which it is appropriate to assume that data collected through the evaluation are valid measures of the impact of the program. **Attribution** is the crediting of outcomes to a program. The degree of attribution is determined by the evaluation design; the ideal is for an evaluation to be able to assert **causation** (that the program is responsible for the measured impact). **Design rigor** is the extent to which an evaluation design merits attribution of strategies to measured outcomes.

There are three primary categories of evaluation designs. Nonexperimental or **single-group designs** are evaluation designs that include one group of participants. **Comparison-group designs** are evaluation designs that include two or more groups, with at least one group receiving the program and at least one group not receiving the program. Quasi-experiments are strong comparison group designs. **Experimental designs** are evaluation designs in which participants are randomly assigned to the program or to a nonprogram control group. Experimental designs are also called randomized controlled trials (RCTs). **Evaluation enrichments**, such as repeated measures, longitudinal data, and sampling, are supports that can be included in your evaluation design to increase the rigor of the design.

The data collection methods used in an evaluation can be classified as qualitative, quantitative, or mixed. **Qualitative methods** rely on noncategorical, text-based data and include interviews, focus groups, observations, portfolios, and case studies. **Quantitative methods** rely on categorical or numerical data and include assessments, tests, and surveys. **Mixed methods** combine both quantitative and qualitative methods. Reliability and validity are important considerations when choosing evaluation methods. **Reliability** is the consistency with which an instrument measures whatever it measures; **validity** is the accuracy with which an instrument measures the intended construct. **Rubrics** are guidelines that can be used to objectively examine subjective data and are used to convert qualitative information into quantitative measures.

Reflection and Application

1. Explain why attribution is important in evaluation.

2. Refer to the program or policy you chose for the Reflection and Application in Chapters 6 and 7.

    a. For each indicator in your evaluation matrix, identify one or more data sources.

    b. For each data source, determine if the data already exist or if they require the development of a new instrument or data collection measure.

3. Refer to the Perry Preschool Project described in "In the Real World." Look up the project on the internet. Individuals participated in the program when they were in preschool; how old are they now? What are some of the outcomes measured in the last follow-up?

4. Choose two evaluation methods from Table 8.1. Research more about the advantages and disadvantages of the methods. Find an example evaluation where each method was used.

IMPLEMENT, PART 1

Implementing the Evaluation

Coauthored With Katrina Morrison

Science is fun. Science is curiosity. Science is a process of investigating. It's posing
questions and coming up with a method. It's delving in.

—Sally Ride

Upon completion of this chapter, you should be able to

- Identify components of a strong, informed consent letter in embedded evaluations.
- Create an informed consent letter for an embedded evaluation.
- Describe various methods for collecting data in embedded evaluations.
- Summarize strategies for checking and organizing your data after data collection.

9.1 CHAPTER IN CONTEXT

You have built the boat, now it's time to set sail. In other words, you've prepared your
study: You've taken ethical considerations into account and designed a thoughtful evaluation project. The next step is to implement the evaluation. However, before proceeding
with guidance on how to conduct the evaluation, a brief review of how we got to this
point may be helpful. First, there was a call to evaluate. This request may have come

FIGURE 9.1 ● Embedded Evaluation Model

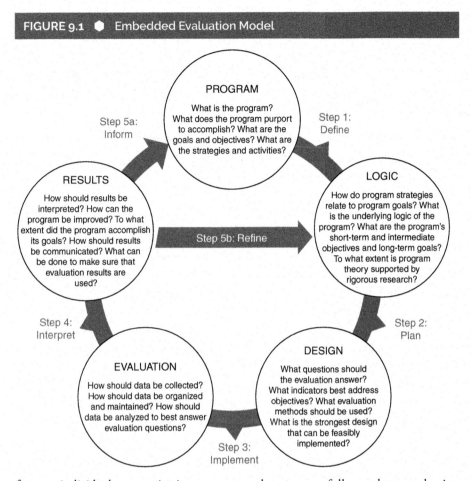

from an individual or organization, or you may have purposefully sought an evaluation contract or grant by responding to a request for proposal (RFP). See Chapter 1 for more information on RFPs. The evaluation request may have come through informal or formal means. That is, you may have been directly asked to conduct the evaluation or asked to partner with a colleague on an evaluation. On the other hand, you may have had to submit a formal proposal, explaining the approach and methods you would use and detailing the budget. Finally, you may have your own resources that you decided to dedicate to evaluating a program or policy of interest. In any event, whether the call to evaluate came informally from existing partnerships or formally through an RFP, the program or policy you are evaluating has stakeholders. See Chapter 1 for information on stakeholders.

Once you have decided to embark on an evaluation, whether it be an existing program or a new program, the first step was to understand your program (see Chapters 5 and 6). This process was conducted in conjunction with stakeholders using theory-based methods and logic modeling. The result of this process was a model of your program. Next, you used this model to embed evaluation indicators into your program's theory and began to build an evaluation matrix that captures information related to evaluating these embedded indicators (Chapter 7). Finally, you chose, in partnership with stakeholders, the best research design within which to evaluate your program (Chapter 8). Your evaluation plan, including the program's logic model, evaluation matrix, and research design, is your boat. Let's set sail.

This chapter provides guidance on conducting an evaluation by building on previous chapters' discussions on ethics and design. It provides practical information regarding informed consent, collecting data, and organizing data.

9.2 INFORMED CONSENT

Before collecting data from evaluation participants, it is important to determine whether **informed consent** is necessary. Informed consent is an individual's agreement to participate in an evaluation with full knowledge of potential benefits or risks. If your institution has an Institutional Review Board (IRB), it can give you guidance on informed consent requirements. If you do not have access to an IRB, you can visit the U.S. Department of Health and Human Services, Office for Human Research Protections (www.hhs .gov/ohrp/regulations-and-policy/index.html) for guidance. As explained in Chapter 3, some evaluations are not considered human subjects research and thus do not require informed consent. Additionally, many evaluations are exempt from Common Rule regulations based on one of the eight exemption categories (see Chapter 3). In these cases, informed consent should be considered; however, the consent may be more informal than required under nonexempt human subjects research. In either case, exempt or nonexempt, informed consent represents a key tenet in the fundamental principles of research ethics. It reflects the principle of *respect for persons* and it recognizes an individual's autonomy by empowering participants to make free decisions with all the necessary information for them to make those decisions. Informed consent acknowledges one's right and capacity to decide and values their dignity as a participant.

When obtaining informed consent, an evaluator tells the participant that they have the right to choose to participate in the study and that they can stop participating at any time with no consequence. For evaluations that require informed consent, informed consent must be given and documented before any data are collected. If informed consent is necessary, the process usually occurs as follows: (1) first, the evaluator introduces themselves; (2) next, the evaluator verbalizes a general summary of the project's aims, what they will ask of the participant, and how findings will be used; and (3) then, the evaluator hands

Informed consent: an individual's agreement to participate in an evaluation with full knowledge of potential benefits or risks.

an informed consent form to the individual(s), gives them time to read it, invites them to ask questions, and presents them a consent form for signature.

9.2.1 Consent Forms

A consent form is a document used to obtain informed consent and is included in a project's Institutional Review Board (IRB) submissions (see Chapter 3). See Figure 9.2 for an example of a consent form. The consent form usually lists statements describing the following:

- Purpose(s) of the study

- What participants will be asked to do

- Potential risks and benefits to participants

- Confidentiality of information collected

- Participant's right to withdraw without penalty

- Participant's voluntary participation

Consent form: a document used to obtain informed consent from a potential evaluation participant.

FIGURE 9.2 ●   Informed Consent Form Example

INFORMED CONSENT TO PARTICIPATE IN RESEARCH

Title of Project: *New Method* Evaluation

Principal Investigator(s):   Jane C. Doe, PhD (include address)

You are being invited to participate in a research study. This consent form tells you about the study including its purpose, what you will be asked to do if you decide to take part, and the risks and benefits of being in the study. Please read the information below and ask us any questions you may have before you decide whether or not you agree to participate.

PURPOSE OF THIS STUDY

The purpose of this study is to evaluate the implementation and impact of *New Method*. *New Method* is a program that [insert a few sentences about what this study will do/ contribute]. You are being asked to participate because your organization will be using *New Method*.

WHAT YOU WILL BE ASKED TO DO

As part of this study you will be asked to complete or participate in the following ways:

- Basic demographic and background information survey

- Interview(s) related to your experiences with *New Method*

(Continued)

FIGURE 9.2 ◗ (Continued)

POSSIBLE RISKS AND DISCOMFORTS

- There are no risks to you beyond those that might be encountered in your everyday life.

WHAT ARE THE POTENTIAL BENEFITS?

You will not benefit directly from taking part in this research. However, the knowledge gained from this study may contribute to program improvement for future use of *New Method*.

HOW WILL CONFIDENTIALITY BE MAINTAINED? WHO MAY KNOW THAT YOU PARTICIPATED IN THIS RESEARCH?

Any potential loss of confidentially will be minimized by protecting your confidentiality in these ways:

- All data on paper will be stored in a locked file cabinet in the Research Institution's office suite, and all electronic data (documents and audio files) will be kept on a secure server on the department's network.

- Transcripts and electronic copies of audio recordings will be identified by a unique ID created by the Principal Investigator; only members of the research team will be able to match IDs to participant names.

- Data will only be shared among researchers on the project for analysis purposes.

- Presentations or reports of any data and analyses will not include participants' names or other identifiable information.

- The confidentiality of your records will be protected to the extent permitted by law. Your research records may be viewed by the Institutional Review Board, a committee formally designated to approve, monitor, and review biomedical and behavioral research involving humans. Records relating to this research will be kept for at least three years after the research study has been completed.

The research data we will be collecting from you during your participation in this study may be useful in other research studies in the future. Your choice about future use of your data will have no impact on your participation in this research study. **Do we have your permission to use in future studies data collected from you?** (Please write your initials next to your preferred choice.)

➡️   _____ YES _____ NO

WILL THERE BE ANY COSTS TO YOU FOR PARTICIPATING IN THIS RESEARCH?

- There will be no costs to you for participating in this research.

DO YOU HAVE TO TAKE PART IN THIS STUDY?

Taking part in this research study is entirely voluntary. You do not have to participate in this research. If you choose to take part, you have the right to stop at any time. If you decide not to participate or if you decide to stop taking part in the research at a later date, there will be no penalty or loss of benefits to which you are otherwise entitled.

Your decision to stop participation, or not to participate, will not influence current or future relationships with the Research Institution.

WHO SHOULD YOU CALL IF YOU HAVE QUESTIONS OR CONCERNS?

If you have any questions about this study, please contact the Principal Investigator, Jane Doe, at (555) 555-5555 or jcdoe@researchinstitution.org.

If you have any questions or concerns about your rights as a research participant, you may contact the Research Institution's Institutional Review Board at irb@reearchinstitution.org or (555) 555-1111.

Your signature on this form means that:

1. **You are at least 18 years old.**

2. **You have read and understand the information given in this form.**

3. **You have asked any questions you have about the research and the questions have been answered to your satisfaction.**

4. **You accept the terms in the form and volunteer to participate in the study. You will be given a copy of this form to keep.**

➡ _____ _____   ___ /___ /___

    Printed Name of   Signature of Participant   Date
    Participant

_____ _____   ___ /___ /___

    Printed Name of   Signature of Person   Date
Person Obtaining Consent   Obtaining Consent

9.2.2 Assent Forms

At some point, your evaluation might involve data collection from children under the age of 18 or other individuals who are not legally able to give informed consent. In the event that you are conducting an evaluation with persons who cannot give legal consent, you must secure consent from their parent or guardian *and* assent from that person directly. Assent for that individual asserts that they agree to participate in an evaluation with full knowledge of the potential benefits or risks.

Potential participants who cannot legally sign a consent form are asked to sign an **assent form**. An assent form looks very much like a consent form, except it might use words more appropriate for the targeted age group or population. While a consent form would be directed to the parent or guardian giving consent for their child to participate in the study, an assent form would be directed at the individual who cannot give legal consent. Both parents or guardians and the individual being invited to participate in the evaluation must sign the consent and assent forms, respectively, prior to any data collection.

Assent: for persons under the age of 18 or another individual who is not able to give legal consent, an agreement to participate in an evaluation with full knowledge of potential benefits or risks. Note that informed consent from a parent or guardian, in addition to assent from a youth under age 18, must be granted prior to a youth's participation in an evaluation.

Assent form: a document used to obtain assent from a potential evaluation participant.

9.2.3 Distribution of Consent and Assent Forms

When possible and to facilitate data collection, informed consent and assent forms can be provided in advance, through email or regular mail, giving the potential participant time to read and consider before talking with the evaluator. We regularly email consent forms to potential participants as an attachment to give the participant a chance to review. We also tell them that reading the form beforehand is not required, but that it would give them an early opportunity to prepare any questions in advance.

If you are conducting a focus group and plan to distribute forms at the focus group, the evaluator can follow the same procedures outlined previously: verbally describing the study, inviting questions, and distributing the consent forms to the group. If you are able to get to the focus group location early, consider distributing consent forms and pens onto seats prior to the arrival of participants. That way, as people trickle in and sit, they have a chance to read over the form. Once you have collected consent forms, start the focus group. However, if new people arrive late to the focus group, you should pause to explain the study again and give the new participant(s) the consent form to review. If there is a research assistant available to attend focus groups, that person could attend to new attendees, field questions, and secure consents prior to the new arrival joining the focus group.

In the case of phone or video conference interviews, we often email the consent letter in advance and have the participant sign, scan, and email the form back to us prior to the interview.

9.2.4 Active Versus Passive Consent

The consent described above is **active consent**. Active consent involves documenting the consent of individuals prior to their participation in an evaluation. This is in contrast to **passive consent**. Passive consent involves informing individuals of their right not to participate in an evaluation, but does not require them to sign a consent form. In some cases, a letter is sent to participants informing them of the study and asking them to sign and return the form if they do not consent. If the form is not returned, consent is assumed.

An example of active versus passive consent can also be seen in California's Active Consent law that requires students on college campuses to actively consent before any sexual activity. While no form needs to be signed to comply with this law, a verbal or clear "yes" must be provided prior to sexual contact. Passive consent, or the assumption that sexual contact is consensual because an individual does not resist or object, is illegal under California's law. Another common example of passive consent is when a researcher conducting a study with schoolchildren sends a letter home to parents informing them of the study and asking them to call the school if they do not want their child to participate. Table 9.1 provides some takeaways regarding informed consent.

Active consent: consent that is documented through the signing of a consent form.

Passive consent: consent that is assumed due to an individual's voluntary participation after being informed about the evaluation.

TABLE 9.1 ● Informed Consent Processes

Be sure consent processes	Avoid consent processes that
✓ Allow potential participants to sign or initial all pages of the consent letter.	⊗ *Only* require participants to sign the last page of a multipage letter.
✓ Use accessible language and short sentences.	⊗ Use formal terms and overly long passages in writing and jargon when speaking.
✓ Provide the principal investigator's (PI) contact information.	⊗ Overlook including PI contact information on the consent form.
✓ Formally ask participants if they have any questions about the research.	⊗ Forget to verbally check if participants have questions.
✓ Provide participants with a copy of the consent form.	⊗ Neglect to provide participants with a copy of the consent form.

Many individuals view passive consent as unethical, while some believe it to be ethically questionable. In addition, some IRBs are very hesitant to approve passive consent studies and will only do so with compelling evidence that obtaining active consent would jeopardize the study and that not obtaining active consent meets the minimal risk criteria. In pure research, the ethics of passive versus active consent are typically clear, with active consent being the preferred and often required method of consent. However, we do want to clarify the issue of active and passive consent when it comes to evaluation.

Evaluation is a form of applied research and, as mentioned in Chapter 1, is intended to foster improvement in programs and policies. As such, it is often conducted as part of normal operations within an organization or program. An evaluator is typically invited to study a program so that an organization can understand how the program is being implemented, how it could work better, what its impact is, and if the dollars spent are worth the cost. Whether or not the evaluation is a study of normal operations within an organization and whether the evaluation is intended for program improvement are important factors in determining if an evaluation is considered human subjects research. As discussed in Chapter 3, evaluations are many times considered exempt from further review by the IRB or do not meet the criteria for research with human subjects. For instance, evaluation in educational settings, evaluation of behavioral interventions, and secondary research studies are many times considered exempt. Please note, however, the evaluation design and methods still need to be submitted through an organization's IRB. It is the IRB's determination whether the study qualifies as exempt. For exempt studies, consent may not be required. Yet it is still good practice and ethically sound, when possible, to provide potential participants with a description of the study and acquire some form of consent for participation.

For interviews conducted within studies that are not considered human subjects research, we typically audio record the interviewees' verbal consent. For surveys, we provide a cover sheet that explains the study, indicates that participants are not obligated to participate and can withdraw at any time, and asks them to check a box indicating their consent prior to completing the survey. See Figure 9.3 for an example of how informed consent might be collected for an electronic survey conducted as part of an evaluation that is not considered human subjects research.

We use a consent form similar to that in Figure 9.3 for an evaluation of a program focused on reducing unconscious bias and improving diversity and inclusion policies and practices among faculty. We also use this method of consent for a translational research evaluation that is considered nonhuman subjects research.

In summary, informed consent is an evaluator's ethical duty. It is obtained through interacting with a participant about the study, then securing their consent in verbal or written form. Obtaining consent should involve giving the potential participant all the information they need to make their decision. Information should be presented in a clear and accessible way and the evaluator should prepare to answer any questions.

FIGURE 9.3 ● Example of an Informed Consent Form for an Exempt Evaluation

Directions: This survey asks about your experiences with the Building Bridges program. Your responses will be used to improve the program. Completion of this survey is voluntary; you may choose not to complete this survey. Clicking on the Electronic Consent "Agree" button indicates your consent to participate.

Clicking on the "Agree" button below indicates that you have read the above information and you voluntarily agree to participate in this survey. Please select your choice below:

☐ Agree

☐ Do not agree (exit survey)

 QUICK CHECK

1. What are the components of a strong informed consent letter?

2. How are consent and assent similar? How are they different?

9.3 COLLECTING THE DATA

The types of data you collect depend on how you design your study (see Chapter 8 regarding research design). Evaluators use a number of strategies for data collection. This section includes descriptions of common methods of data collection, including survey instruments, existing data, interviews, focus groups, observations, and document reviews.

9.3.1 Survey Instruments and Existing Data

Survey instruments are questionnaires that give your participants a standard set of questions and response categories. They represent an efficient strategy for collecting data because they are straightforward, can yield data from many people in a short amount of time, and can be done at a low cost. It is important that researchers identify their target population for the survey as well as how they will administer the survey. A researcher can administer a survey by mail, over the phone, during interviews, and through email. With electronic survey tools like Qualtrics and SurveyMonkey, researchers can even send participants links to surveys directly to their smartphones! The mode chosen depends on the cost, the amount of time for data collection, and the respondents. In some studies, researchers use more than one mode to administer a survey. Also, they make accommodations for people with disabilities or those whose dominant language is not English, such as using larger print or translation.

The survey instrument itself should be easy for the survey-taker to answer. The survey should begin with questions that help build rapport with the respondent (Henry, 2005), such as questions about the respondent's educational background or years of work experience. It should be organized in a way that questions that ask about the same topic are grouped together. The instrument should include the most important questions the researcher needs to ask. When using an electronic survey, we often structure it such that the most important questions appear earlier in the survey, in case respondents do not complete the entire survey. This is especially important if the survey is long. If your survey is particularly long, ask yourself, "If I were asked to complete this survey, would I?" If the answer is no, that is a sign that you should try to streamline your questions and shorten your survey. While it is tempting to ask every question you are interested in, there is definitely a trade-off between length of survey and **response rate**. Response rate is the number of surveys completed divided by the number of surveys distributed. For instance, if you email a survey to 150 people and 62 respond, your response rate is 41.3% (62/150). Few people have the patience to complete a long survey (even us), so longer surveys typically yield lower response rates.

Follow-up is key in survey research. If a survey is administered electronically, it is in the researcher's best interest to monitor how many respondents have taken the survey. This is especially important if the researcher wants a particular number of respondents (Henry, 2005).

Survey instruments: questionnaires that give your participants a standard set of questions and response categories.

Response rate: the percentage of people who complete your survey as a function of the number of surveys distributed. Response rate = Number of surveys completed / Number of surveys distributed.

Existing data: data collected on an ongoing basis by a particular institution or agency.

Data-sharing agreement: an agreement between an evaluator and an organization that stipulates how data necessary to the evaluation will be shared, protected, and used.

Interviews: verbal exchanges guided by questions that focus on a particular topic.

Structured interview: a predetermined set of questions to ask the interviewee during the interview.

Interview protocol: a predetermined set of questions to ask the interviewee during the interview.

Probe: a follow-up question used to explore responses in more detail.

Unstructured interview: an interview during which questions and probes are added following up on questions that emerge during the interview.

Semi-structured interview: an interview that includes some predetermined questions, but also retains the flexibility to include probes or follow-up questions as topics emerge.

Emailing or mailing reminders to survey-takers can improve the response rate. However, we have found that after about three reminders, it is unlikely that the response rate will increase significantly.

Several resources that are particularly useful in designing survey instruments are *Asking Questions: The Definitive Guide to Questionnaire Design* (Bradburn, Sudman, & Wansink, 2004), *Your Opinion, Please! How To Build the Best Questionnaires in the Field of Education* (Cox & Cox, 2008), and *Survey Research Methods* (Fowler, 2008). The W.K. Kellogg Foundation (2017) also provides a nice checklist for use during survey design in *A Step-By-Step Guide to Evaluation*.

Evaluators also use **existing data** collected on an ongoing basis by a particular institution or agency, especially for measuring outcomes. Examples of these data are students' standardized test scores, annual district survey data, or patients' behavior scores on a periodic assessment completed by medical staff. Prior to the start of the study, the evaluator should inform the institution that collects the data that the data are needed for the evaluation. The institution and evaluator will negotiate a **data-sharing agreement** that outlines which data will be shared, how the evaluator will acquire the data, how data will be organized to protect privacy, how the data will be secured, and how the data will be used.

9.3.2 Interviews and Focus Groups

Interviews are verbal exchanges guided by questions that focus on a particular topic. Often, interviews are distinguished as structured, unstructured, or semi-structured. An interview that is based on a series of predetermined questions that the evaluator asks the participant, also known as the interviewee, is considered a **structured interview**. The predetermined questions are called an **interview protocol**. An interview protocol typically has primary questions, as well as a series of related questions called probes. A **probe** is a follow-up question used to explore responses in more detail. In **unstructured interviews**, the researcher shapes the interview around the unique perspective of each respondent, probing and following up on questions that emerge during the interview. In unstructured interviews, the researcher might not follow a scripted protocol, but might come to the interview with ideas about the topics to be discussed. A primary difference between structured and unstructured interviews is the degree of flexibility the researcher has in exploring topics and asking follow-up questions. In a structured interview, the interviewer adheres to the protocol in terms of both questions asked and the order in which they are asked.

Semi-structured interviews blend the predetermined questions of a structured interview with the flexibility of adding probes or follow-up questions as topics emerge.

Interviews can take place in person, over the telephone, or over video conference. They are usually recorded using an audio-recording device. Typically, audio is typed, or transcribed, into a program like Microsoft Word.

Depending on the study, for long (one hour or more) over-the-phone interviews, you may want to email the protocol to the interviewee ahead of time. This gives the interviewee a chance to read the questions in case it is difficult to hear over the phone. It also helps keep interviewees engaged without face-to-face interaction, as they know what is being asked and how many questions will be asked.

A focus group is a small group of individuals, typically six to eight, brought together to answer questions regarding a specific topic. The group is usually homogenous in some way. For instance, it could be students in the same grade, teachers of the same subject, leaders of similar nonprofits, or professionals at the same level who are program participants. Who participates depends on their availability, interest, and qualifications. Focus groups can be used for many purposes in evaluation, including to

1. understand a program, problem, or phenomenon from a certain group's point of view;

2. inform logic model development or refinement;

3. provide formative feedback for a particular program; and

4. inform future research efforts, such as helping to determine topics for a future survey.

As with interviews, the evaluator uses a set of questions to guide the conversation; that is, focus groups also follow a protocol. The focus group protocol is used to guide the discussion in an orderly manner. Focus groups also have a facilitator whose role mirrors that of the interviewer in an individual interview. The facilitator is responsible for following the protocol while encouraging all participants to voice their opinions. The facilitator is a moderator of discussion and ensures that hesitant or quieter speakers get opportunities to share their viewpoints. Depending on the question, the facilitator may ask for a response from every participant in the focus group. For instance, if the question is "How has your school district helped each of you become a better administrator?" then each person would have an opportunity to share. But for a question such as "How has the community liaison improved relationships in your neighborhood?" the facilitator may not need to hear answers from each participant. However, after a few participants share their experiences, the facilitator may ask of the remaining participants, "Do you agree or disagree?" In this way, focus groups are able to explore both similar and conflicting views.

Individual and group interviews should take place in settings that are comfortable and where participants feel they can speak honestly. For focus groups, the facilitator should remind participants that while participants are discouraged from repeating what is said during the focus group, they cannot promise confidentiality because other focus group participants will hear what everyone says. However, the facilitator can ask participants

Focus group: a small group of individuals, typically six to eight, brought together to answer questions regarding a specific topic.

Facilitator: the interviewer in a focus group, who is responsible for not only following the protocol, but also moderating the discussion in a productive and constructive way.

to respect one another's opinions and experiences and to keep the conversation within the room by not sharing the discussion with others. Thus, focus group facilitators have many responsibilities. They are tasked with creating an atmosphere in which participants feel comfortable and safe sharing their views and experiences, elaborating on other respondents' answers, or disagreeing with other participants, all while collecting valuable information to inform program improvement. Becoming a skilled facilitator takes practice; it requires

1. strong listening skills,

2. an ability to manage group discussions,

3. experience with conflict resolution, and

4. an understanding of nonverbal communication.

We would tell you about an early experience one of us had when facilitating a focus group as a young evaluator, but it would likely make you laugh out loud and should you be reading this text in public, we would not want to make others stare at you. We will tell you that a practice that has helped us is spending time studying the protocol before an interview or focus group. Being comfortable with the protocol helps a facilitator to concentrate on the interview responses and make eye contact, which in turn helps to make the interviewees more comfortable. Testing your audio-recording equipment prior to the interview or focus group is important, too, as is making sure you have the correct address of the location in which the focus group or interview will take place. Yes, we have learned both of these things the hard way, too.

Deciding whether to include interviews or focus groups in your evaluation may depend on several factors. First, consider whether you have the resources and necessary skills to conduct and analyze data from interviews and focus groups. Data from interviews and focus groups typically take more time to collect and to analyze than existing data or data from surveys. The skill set needed to analyze the qualitative data collected from interviews and focus groups is also very different from the skill set needed to analyze quantitative or categorical data.

Second, consider the comfort of participants in being interviewed face-to-face versus in a group. Some individuals simply do not like to talk in person and would prefer a survey. Others may prefer talking individually. In a recent evaluation, we decided to conduct individual interviews. However, several of the participants purposely requested that they be interviewed together. We accommodated this request because the quality of data collected is typically related to how comfortable participants are sharing their experiences. Putting participants at ease during an individual or group interview is a skill in itself that takes practice, patience, and experience. A colleagues of ours is one of the most accomplished interviewers we have met. She has a way of making anyone feel comfortable; we believe it is partly because interviewees and focus group participants can tell she truly cares about what they are saying. It is also because she is a fantastic human being. The information she elicits during interviews and the depth of conversation she facilitates is a model to aspire to. We will also add, though, analyzing her interviews is no fun. It is her small talk and willingness to allow participants to veer off course from time to time that builds a rapport that, in turn, yields rich data once she steers participants back to the protocol's focus. So, there is a definitely a trade-off between richness of data and efficiency of data collection (and analysis).

Third, consider the number of people or groups of people from whom you would like to gather feedback. If this number is large, it might be wise to consider focus groups over interviews as a data collection method. If you do decide to conduct focus groups, the composition of a focus group should be carefully determined. A focus group within which there is a power imbalance (e.g., employees and managers, teachers and administrators, patients and doctors) is unlikely to foster the kind of rich discussion that is unique to a focus group. In choosing members for a focus group, keep in mind the roles, experience level, and even personality, should you know it, in order to compose a group of individuals who will be comfortable sharing their opinions and experiences. That being said, you should avoid choosing participants that are likely to all have the same view, as it is the variation in viewpoints that spurs a deeper conversation often revealing topics or issues that may not have otherwise been uncovered. In fact, there may be times when you purposely choose to include participants who are likely to challenge others in the group to think more deeply.

Finally, consider the kind of information you need to collect. If the questions you need answered can be asked in a closed-ended item, there is no need to conduct interviews or focus groups. Survey instruments are typically the best method for collecting responses to closed-ended questions. The strength of interviews and focus groups lies in the opportunity of the interviewer or facilitator to probe for a deeper understanding on a topic or issue that is not fully understood or to document experiences and best practices with detailed and insightful illustration.

Two resources that you might find helpful as you learn more about interviews and focus groups are *Designing and Conducting Your First Interview* (Friesen, 2010) and *Focus Groups: A Practical Guide for Applied Research* (Krueger & Casey, 2009).

9.3.3 Observations and Program Documentation

Observations are "first-hand, eyewitness experiences of places, activities and events" (Mathison, 2005, p. 285). That is, an **observation** is information learned by seeing or watching something. Observations in evaluations are either formal, using a protocol or

Observation: information learned by seeing or watching something.

checklist, or informal, which yields a more free-flowing description. Participant observations involve the researcher taking an active role in the setting while also collecting data. Nonparticipant observations are characterized by the researcher not intruding in the setting, taking a "fly on the wall" approach. The data collected are running field notes, protocols, or a blend of the two. It is best if data collected are more descriptive than evaluative (Mathison, 2005).

Program documentation consists of resources that can be used for the purposes of determining the rationale of a program, learning a program's history, understanding facts about why a program is the way it is, confirming stakeholders who are involved, and strategizing around what data still needs to be collected (Hurworth, 2005). Documents collected could be existing records, meeting minutes, annual reports, handbooks, diagrams, or strategic plans. Further, an evaluator might request newly created documents. For example, an evaluator may need participation data for their evaluation of a program that holds community meetings. The evaluator might ask that the program coordinator document the attendance at meetings and supply these data to the evaluation team. While many documents are text based, program documentation can go beyond written material. They can also be photographs, video, audio, and portfolios.

Hurworth (2005) lists several advantages of using documents, from the reliability of information to time and cost savings:

- Information from documents might be more reliable than people, given that individuals might forget dates or specific information that can be found in documents.

- Documents can save a project time and money because they can give you information that might otherwise have to be collected in more time-consuming ways.

- Documents might be more accessible than people as they are sometimes posted on websites or in public spaces.

Research literature about similar programs might also be useful documentation for an evaluation. An evaluator might use library or internet research to find information about theories and programs similar to their current evaluation project. Research literature would be useful for an understanding of theory that undergirds the program (see Chapter 5).

Program documentation: resources such as meeting minutes, annual reports, strategic plans, handbooks, diagrams, videos, audio recordings, and portfolios.

Evaluators might also explore previously conducted evaluations or studies that are similar to the current study. These would provide an evaluator with standards and previous findings to measure what their evaluation is up against.

Whatever method(s) you choose, data collection should be as unobtrusive as possible, minimizing the time and resources required of participants. To avoid burdening subjects, try to keep interviews and surveys to under an hour. Remember, participants are volunteers. They are willfully giving you their time and attention to help your evaluation; be respectful by limiting your intrusions. When the time and effort asked of participants is considerable, you might recognize that by providing gift cards or another form of compensation for their time.

Finally, it is important to consider how you will manage the data you collect. All collected data should be stored in a secure site and should only be accessible by the evaluation team, unless consent forms or memos of understanding (MOUs) stipulate that additional persons may access the data. Electronic data should be placed into secured, password-protected folders. Any recorded interviews or focus groups should be removed from recording devices once the data are stored electronically. Paper surveys, documents, and any hard copy data should be placed in folders within secure locked filing cabinets. In the next section, we will discuss organizing data in more detail.

After data collection, organizing your data is paramount. Data organization will facilitate analysis, interpretation of results, and report writing. Throughout data organization, keep considerations around the completeness of the data at the forefront of your thinking. Meyers, Gamst, and Guarino (2006) pose several questions to help us do that:

- Do the data accurately reflect the responses made by evaluation participants?

- Are some data missing?

- Is there a pattern to the missing data?

While these are general questions to consider when organizing data, there are some data organization considerations that are specific to quantitative and qualitative data collection methods.

9.4 ORGANIZING QUANTITATIVE DATA

Whether survey data are collected electronically or using paper, the data still need to be organized in a way that facilitates analysis. As such, collected data are organized into **variables**. Variables are data elements that can be measured and have different values.

9.4.1 Codebooks

Each data element collected is a different variable, and each variable has different values. For instance, if data are collected regarding a person's attendance at counseling sessions, the variable might be the number of days they attended counseling over a set period of time. The values of that variable would range from 0 to the total number of counseling sessions attended. For each data element you collect, you will have an associated variable name and a set of possible values. In some cases, the values of the variable may be different from what actually appears on the survey. For instance, it is customary to code "yes" as 1 and "no" as 0.

Variables: data elements that can be measured and have different values.

FIGURE 9.4 ● Codebook Example		
Variable	**Item**	**Coded Values**
Q1	What is your position at the clinic?	1 = RD/Nutritionist 2 = Coordinator 3 = Supervisor 4 = Manager 5 = Other
Q2	Do you currently make referrals for children with possible developmental delays at your clinic?	0 = No 1 = Yes 2 = Not Sure
Q3	What is your current level of confidence with regard to discussing developmental concerns with families?	1 = Not at all confident 2 = Slightly confident 3 = Moderately confident 4 = Very confident
Q4	How would you rate your level of knowledge regarding developmental disabilities?	1 = No knowledge 2 = Slightly knowledgeable 3 = Moderately knowledgeable 4 = Very knowledgeable

Codebook: a file that records the variable name for each data element collected, the item or question that was used to collect the data, and how the data were coded when prepared for analysis.

Delimited file: a data file that uses a predetermined character, such as a tab or comma, to indicate new data items or columns.

Creating a codebook to organize your data aids in later interpretation of data and also provides valuable documentation should someone who is not familiar with the survey need to work with the data file. See Figure 9.4 for an example of a codebook.

Once the codebook is set up, you can begin working with the data. If the data are not already in the statistical analysis package you will be using, you will need to take steps to transfer the data in preparation for analysis.

9.4.2 Working With Quantitative Data Files

For electronic surveys, such as those conducted using Qualtrics or SurveyMonkey, data items can be downloaded into a delimited file or spreadsheet software such as Microsoft Excel. A delimited file uses a predetermined character to indicate a new variable in the file; common delimited file types include comma-separated values (CSV) files or tab-separated values (TSV) files. Space-delimited values are sometimes used as well. However, if it is possible your data could have spaces within fields or responses, it is best to avoid delimiting with spaces. Another format used for organizing data is fixed-width files in which, regardless of the data stored within a field, a fixed number of characters is allocated in the file. Electronically downloaded files can then be imported into a software package, such as SPSS, SAS, R, or Stata, for data analysis.

If data are not collected electronically, for example, by phone surveys or observation, they might be recorded directly into a spreadsheet or data analysis software. If you are using paper surveys, a member of the research team would need to either scan the surveys or enter the data by hand. For data that are entered by hand, it is important to have procedures to check data quality. For instance, you might consider having two researchers double-enter the data to ensure accuracy or spot check data that has been entered to detect systematic data input errors. Downloading files is not always smooth and entering data by hand raises the risk of error; thus, procedures for checking data quality should be instituted.

9.4.3 Data Checking

For quantitative data, the evaluation team must practice **coding clean**. This means checking data to see if they are accurate (Meyers et al., 2006). One must make certain that every single variable has valid values or codes. For instance, if "yes" is to be coded 1 and "no" as 0, it is important to check that the data for that item are either 0 or 1.

If you found a value that was not valid, then you have some choices. Let's take an example of a study involving the profile ratings for 500 schools. The scale for profile ratings ranges from 1 to 100. Your knowledge of these profiles tells you that the most frequent rating is 75 and that most ratings are in the range of 60 to 90. After you collect scores, you note a value of 30, prompting your focused attention. After examining the scores, you might determine that 30 is correct, meaning that one school has a relatively low rating. Your choice at that moment could be to leave it be, and in the future potentially drop that case if it is the only outlier and not representative of the sample.

However, you might discover that the number was recorded erroneously. You could find out that the score should actually be 60. If that is the case, then you would input the correct value into your data file. Another scenario is that the value is wrong but you are unable to determine the correct one. You could then treat it as a missing value. Regardless of the method used to handle outliers or missing data, it is important to document how any exceptions were handled. Such documentation can be critical if another researcher attempts to replicate your analyses or if a stakeholder questions how data were analyzed in order to reach the results found in the evaluation. See Radhakrishna, Tobin, Brennan, and Thomson (2012) for further information about data checking.

Coding clean: procedures used to verify that data have been recorded correctly.

QUICK CHECK

1. What methods can be used to collect new data for an evaluation? What types of existing information might be helpful for an evaluator?
2. What is a codebook? How does a codebook help organize your data?

9.4.4 Storing Quantitative Data Files

To ensure that data can be retrieved easily, be sure to put files into clearly labeled electronic folders. These folders could have names such as "raw data" or "cleaned data." The file names within those folders should incorporate the type of data and the date it was last used. An example could be "19.03.12_SY2019-20 School Profiles Data_ clean." From this, we know that on March 12, 2019, someone saved cleaned School Profiles Data from the 2019–2020 school year. Whichever format you choose, ensure that you are consistent and that all team members are aware of the format. If you have de-identified student data, you should keep files with any names matched with ID numbers in a separate password-protected file, so that nonteam members do not have access.

9.5 ORGANIZING QUALITATIVE DATA

Before collecting your qualitative data, it is good idea to develop a file naming scheme. The naming of data files should not include identifying information for individuals. We cringe when we see a participant's name as part of the file name (e.g., giancolainterview .doc or katrinanotes.txt), but it is more common than you might think. Neither the raw data file, whether that be an audio recording or observational notes, nor any file associated with the raw data, such as a transcription file, should include the interviewee's name. Developing a file naming structure can prevent this from occurring. Having a procedure in place for naming files is important in any evaluation, but is especially important if a consent form was signed assuring confidentiality and safeguarding of data. Figure 9.5 shows a file naming scheme for an evaluation that consisted of over 40 interviews.

If your evaluation team has multiple people conducting interviews, as was the case with the evaluation that the file naming scheme was based on, it is important that everyone on the team be trained in using the appropriate naming of files. It is also important that the team be briefed on the appropriate procedures for storing data, as well as for tracking interviews, focus groups, or observations. Creating procedures for tracking data collection and aligning interviews with their corresponding file name will be discussed in the next section.

FIGURE 9.5 ● File Naming Structure Example

Project Name: Community Advisory Council (CAC) Evaluation

File Naming Format: CAC<MMDD>_<county label><interview label>#

<u>Project and Date</u>

CAC: Community Advisory Council

MM: Month of Recording (e.g., 06 for June)

DD: Day of Recording (e.g., 02 for the 2nd day of the month)

<u>County Labels</u>

N: New Castle County

K: Kent County

S: Sussex County

<u>Interview Labels</u>

CM#: Community Member (# should be sequential in order of interviews)

CO#: Community Organization Leader (# should be sequential in order of interviews)

LG#: Local Government Representative (# should be sequential in order of interviews)

UR#: University Representative (# should be sequential in order of interviews)

OM#: Other Member (# should be sequential in order of interviews)

Example 1: For the first community member interview conducted in Kent County on 5/9

CAC0509_KCM1

Example 2: For the ninth local government representative interview conducted in New Castle County on 7/24

CAC0724_NLG9

9.5.1 Working With Qualitative Data Files

Much like with quantitative data, with qualitative data it is important to first make sure you have collected the data you need. Some questions you could ask yourself include "Are field notes complete?" and "Did interviews get transcribed?" and "Are file names consistent with the file naming structure?" During data collection, when interviews, focus groups, or observations are being conducted and files created, another important procedure to determine is how to track what data are collected and when. For instance, if the evaluation includes interviews and focus groups, the

TABLE 9.2 ◆ Data Tracking Document Example						
Interviewee	Date/Time/ Location of Interview	Interviewer	File Name	Date Sent to Transcription	Date Received From Transcription	Notes (dates contacted, mode of contact, special considerations)

evaluation team can record dates and times of interviews on a secure, shared file. In addition, this file could include the name of the data file from the interview, when the data file was sent for transcription, and when it was received back. Processes such as this are critical for large projects involving multiple evaluators. However, even for small projects, keep your data organized so you can easily reference what data have been collected and where they are stored. Table 9.2 shows an example of an interview tracking document.

It is also important that data be quality checked. Compared to quantitative data checking, qualitative data quality checking occurs on a more continual basis. You might data check as data are being collected, immediately after data collection, and/or after analysis. Below, we list examples of quality checks for qualitative data. These data quality reviews could happen at any stage once data collection takes place:

- Reviewing transcripts midway through the project to see if all questions were answered adequately

- Two observers discussing their observations of the same site to ensure that they captured a setting accurately

- After analysis is complete, conducting member checks, where an evaluator asks a study participant to review early findings for accuracy

9.5.2 Storing Qualitative Data Files

As with organizing quantitative data, clearly labeled electronic folders in which to store data should be created for qualitative data. These folders might be named *interview protocols, interview tracking, raw data files, transcriptions,* or *data analysis.* The file naming structure and data/interview tracking documents might be stored in the *interview tracking folder,* while the actual data files are stored in *raw data files.* Finally, audio-recorded qualitative data that are transcribed into a text file might be stored in the *transcriptions* folder. These text files can be easily imported into common qualitative analysis software packages, such as Dedoose or nVivo. Organizing and quality checking data is an important step in preparation for analysis. Chapter 10 will provide an overview of methods for qualitative data analysis.

9.6 CHAPTER SUMMARY

Informed consent is an individual's agreement to participate in an evaluation with full knowledge of potential benefits or risks. A **consent form** is a document used to obtain informed consent from a potential evaluation participant of legal age, while an **assent form** is used for persons under the age of 18 or another individual who is not able to give legal consent. Note that informed consent from a parent or guardian, in addition to **assent** from a youth under age 18, must be granted prior to a youth's participation in an evaluation. Consent can be **active consent** or **passive consent**.

There are many methods available for evaluators for data collection. **Survey instruments** are questionnaires that give your participants a standard set of questions and response categories. **Existing data** are data collected on an ongoing basis by a particular institution or agency. **Interviews** are verbal exchanges guided by questions that focus on a particular topic, while group interviews, or focus groups, are used for the same purpose but include a small group of individuals. **Observations** are used to collect information by seeing or watching something. **Program documentation** includes resources such as meeting minutes, annual reports, strategic plans, handbooks, diagrams, video, audio recordings, and portfolios.

Collected data are stored in data files as variables. **Variables** are measurable data that can have different values. **Codebooks** are used to aide in recording and interpreting data; a codebook is a file that records the variable name for each data element collected, the item or question that was used to collect the data, and how the data were coded when prepared for analysis. **Coding clean** includes procedures to verify that data have been recorded correctly.

Reflection and Application

1. List three components of an exemplary consent letter.

2. With a partner, draft a consent letter for a project.

3. If you designed an evaluation of a curriculum to involve a conversation with a principal, a survey of 30 teachers, and one classroom observation, describe exactly what data collection and tools you and your team would need.

4. Using your study in number 3, summarize some actions you would take to check and organize your data.

IMPLEMENT, PART 2

Analyzing the Data

Coauthored With Katrina Morrison

In God we trust: all others bring data.

—W. Edwards Deming

Upon completion of this chapter, you should be able to

- Demonstrate steps in qualitative data analysis.

- Contrast three common quantitative data analyses.

- Discuss potential solutions to unexpected and unintended circumstances during evaluations.

10.1 CHAPTER IN CONTEXT

This chapter continues the Chapter 9 discussion on implementing the evaluation, Step 3 in the embedded evaluation framework. Its focus will be on analyzing the data you have collected and organized, as well as addressing unforeseen circumstances.

Data analysis is sense making. It is an iterative process that might start as early as data collection, as you begin to hear or see certain patterns in the data being collected. For

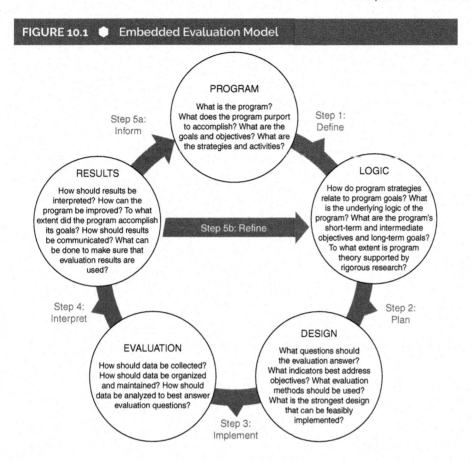

FIGURE 10.1 ● Embedded Evaluation Model

the most part, however, analysis will happen toward the end of data collection. In this section, we discuss some well-recognized steps in both qualitative and quantitative analyses.

10.2 QUANTITATIVE DATA ANALYSIS: DESCRIPTIVE STATISTICS

Once quantitative data are checked, cleaned, and organized, it is time for analysis. If you have had a research methods or statistics course, you likely learned about different techniques for analyzing data. In the next two sections, we will briefly review two approaches to analyze quantitatively measured data—descriptive and inferential statistics.

Descriptive statistics are perhaps the most commonly used approach to summarize quantitative data. Chua and Mark (2005) state that "descriptive statistics are used to describe, summarize, and represent more concisely a set of data" (p. 400). Thus, a **descriptive statistic** is a number that summarizes your data in a meaningful way. Descriptive statistics describe your data in a succinct manner. They might be as simple as the average age of the participants in a program or the number of males and females participating in an activity. Descriptive statistics are especially useful in understanding or making sense of large quantities of information. For example, if you have five quiz scores in your data set, you could easily eyeball them to get a sense of the average score and how the five scores might vary. However, if you have quiz scores for 5,000 individuals, simply eyeballing the data does not work. It is too much for our brain to digest and synthesize. So, how can we describe large amounts of information in a way that we can make some generalizations? We could use descriptive statistics such as means, standard deviations, frequency distributions, and correlations.

10.2.1 Mean and Standard Deviation

The **mean** is a statistic that indicates the average value for a variable in a data set. It is calculated by dividing the sum of values for a variable by the number of cases for that variable. **Standard deviation** is a statistic that indicates the amount of variation for a particular variable in a data set. Typically, mean and standard deviation are reported together, along with the number of cases in a data set. See Table 10.1 for an example of mean and standard deviation using the quiz score example described above.

Using data analysis software, such as SPSS or SAS, it is just as easy to calculate mean and standard deviation for 5 cases as it is for 5,000 cases. So, while calculating the mean by hand is feasible for a small number of cases, it can be calculated just as quickly (if not more quickly) using data analysis software. Once mean and standard deviation are calculated, mean is fairly easy to interpret. While interpreting standard deviation takes a little more thought, it is still very straightforward. Remember the normal curve? The standard deviation assumes a normal distribution of data and tells us that approximately 68% of the values for a variable are within one standard deviation of the mean, 95% of values are within two standard deviations of the mean, and over 99% are within three standard deviations of the mean. Some common statistics have a set mean and standard deviation that allow us to easily interpret them. For instance, intelligence quotient (IQ) scores are set on a scale that has a mean of 100 and a standard deviation of 15. This tells us that about 68% of IQ scores fall within one standard deviation of the mean, that is, between 85 and 115. A quick story from one of us: When my daughter was tested at a young age, I was told she had an IQ over 140. How might you interpret this? My interpretation was, "Wow. Are you sure she is mine?" I have not had my IQ tested, but I am certain both of my daughters are much brighter than I am. How am I certain? They remind me every day that teenagers know everything and moms don't have the capacity to understand what they are going through (yes, that is sarcasm). Standardized tests such as SATs and ACTs

Descriptive statistic: a number that summarizes a data set in a meaningful way.

Mean: a statistic that indicates the average value for a variable in a data set.

Standard deviation: a statistic that indicates the amount of variation for a particular variable in a data set.

TABLE 10.1 ● Mean and Standard Deviation

Variables in Data Set		Mean and Standard Deviation
Student	Quiz Score	
1	63	Number of cases = 5
2	96	Mean = Sum of Values/Number of Cases
3	89	= (63 + 96 + 89 + 74 + 93)/5 = 415/5
4	74	= 83
5	93	You can also calculate the standard deviation by hand, but it is simpler to input the data in a statistical software package and run descriptive statistics. Doing so shows us that the standard deviation = 14.02.

also have a set mean and standard deviation, based upon the normal curve, that allow you to easily interpret individual scores. Can you think of other common measures that have a set mean and standard deviation?

Mean is considered a measure of central tendency. That is, it is an indicator of the average of a set of data. Mean is a calculated, arithmetic average. Two other measures of central tendency are median and mode. Median and mode are positional averages, in that they refer to a location in a data set. Mode is the value or values with the highest number of occurrences. If two numbers share the highest frequency, the data set is said to be bimodal. Median is the midpoint of the data set. One half of the values in the data set fall below the median and one half fall above the median. Standard deviation is a measure of variation. It is an indicator of how widely dispersed values are in a data set. Two additional measures of variation are range and variance. Range is the difference between the highest and lowest value in a set of data. Variance is simply the standard deviation squared.

10.2.2 Frequency Distribution

Another frequently used descriptive statistic is a frequency distribution. A **frequency distribution** is a summary statistic indicating the number of cases in your data set for a certain value or range of values. It is commonly used for categorical data where mean and standard deviation are inappropriate, such as race and gender. It can also be used for numerical data for which there is a great deal of variation. For example, if your standard deviation is high, that is an indicator that your data are very dispersed around the mean and that the mean may not be a great indicator of the central tendency of your data. In such cases, frequency distributions may give a better or additional summary of your data to aid in interpretation.

Frequency distribution: a statistic indicating the number of cases in your data set for a certain value or range of values.

Frequency distributions represent your counts of groups in your data. These groups could be based on demographics, such as gender or race. Additionally, a frequency distribution can inform you of how many individuals answered a question in a particular way. For example, a frequency distribution could show you the number of people who answered no on the survey question "Do you perceive that this program enabled you to find a job you were satisfied with?" In its most basic form, a frequency distribution could give you a count for each value of a variable. However, values can also be grouped to facilitate interpretation. For instance, a variable representing an adult's age might have values ranging from 18 to over 100 years. You could create a frequency distribution that tells you the number of people in your data set who are 18, 19, 20, and so on. However, the purpose of descriptive statistics is to provide a summary of your data in a way that helps you to interpret and make sense of the information. For age, it might make more sense to create groupings and count the number or percentage of individuals within each group. For example, 20% of your cases may be younger than 25 years, 25% between 26 and 35 years, and so forth.

Table 10.2 shows an example of a frequency distribution for a survey item with values ranging from strongly agree to strongly disagree. The frequency distribution includes the number of respondents (frequency of responses for each category), percentage of respondents responding for each category, and the cumulative percentage of respondents. From the distribution, we can see that half of respondents (50.4%) strongly agreed that the program increased their understanding of how to actively listen to family members' concerns. Many respondents (81.1%) either agreed or strongly agreed that the program increased their understanding of how to actively listen to family members' concerns. Less than 20% of respondents disagreed or strongly disagreed that the program increased their understanding of how to actively listen to family members' concerns. The above three sentences are an example of how you might write these findings in narrative form.

TABLE 10.2 ● Example of Analysis Output

	Number of Respondents	Percentage of Respondents	Cumulative Percentage of Respondents
Strongly Agree	64	50.4	50.4
Agree	39	30.7	81.1
Disagree	20	15.7	96.8
Strongly Disagree	4	3.2	100.0
Total	127	100.0	

Note: Q25. As a result of participating in this program, I better understand how to actively listen to family members' concerns.

10.2.3 Correlation

Means, standard deviations, and frequency distributions are used to describe a single variable. What if you wanted to examine the relationship between two variables? A **correlation** is a statistic that describes strength and direction of a relationship between two variables. The most common correlational statistic is the Pearson r. The Pearson r demonstrates the degree to which a linear relationship exists between two quantitatively measured variables. The correlation, also called correlation coefficient or r, ranges from +1 to –1. The closer the statistic is to +1 or –1, the stronger the relationship; that is, when one variable moves, the other does as well. The direction of the relationship between variables is represented by the + or – sign. A positive correlation is one where as one variable increases, the other variable increases as well; or, when one variable decreases, the other variable decreases along with it. A negative correlation tells us that as one variable increases, the other decreases.

For example, a correlation of –0.96 is a strong negative correlation. It tells us that as one variable increases, the other decreases. On the other hand, a correlation of 0.15 is a weak positive correlation. It tells us that as one variable increases or decreases, there is a lower likelihood that the other variable will increase or decrease, respectively. A correlation of 0 tells us there is no relationship between the two variables. What do you think the correlation is between the amount of time spent studying and the grade received on a test?

10.3 QUANTITATIVE DATA ANALYSIS: INFERENTIAL STATISTICS

For the statistics gurus reading this, you may be wondering why correlation was discussed as a descriptive statistic. It is because correlations are a very useful statistic for describing the relationship between variables in a data set. However, they can also be used to draw conclusions based on your data about a larger population. In this way, correlations are also considered inferential statistics.

An **inferential statistic** is a number calculated based on one data set that is used to draw conclusions about the greater population that your data set is intended to represent. For instance, if you conduct a survey with students from across your university, your data set includes information for a sample of university students. You might use descriptive statistics to describe the data in your sample. However, you may also want to use inferential statistics to draw conclusions about how representative your findings are of all students at the university, or even the population of all university students across your state or beyond. Thus, inferential statistics can help you to draw conclusions that go beyond simply describing your data. Inferential statistics allow you to make inferences based on a sample of data to describe a potential relationship beyond the data.

Correlation: a statistic indicating the strength and direction of the relationship between the values for two variables.

Inferential statistic: a number calculated based on one data set that is used to draw conclusions about the greater population that your data set is intended to represent.

10.3.1 Null and Alternate Hypotheses

Let's use an example of a program aimed at improving the English-speaking skills of families who are learning English as a second language. As part of this program, volunteer tutors within the community work with families who are learning English. Program leadership may want to understand whether family satisfaction with the volunteer tutor is associated with the number of days the volunteer spent working with the family. In our example, we would examine the relationship between the number of days the volunteer spent working with a family and the family's response to the question "On a scale of 1 to 5, with 1 being lowest and 5 being the highest, how satisfied are you with the volunteer tutor who worked with your family?"

If we calculate the correlation between these two variables, results might show that family satisfaction scores increase as their participation (i.e., the number of days they met with their volunteer tutor) increases. The calculated correlation coefficient is descriptive of our data set. However, we can also determine the probability that any difference we detect within our sample data set is true for the greater population.

We might set what is called a **null hypothesis** (H_0), "null" meaning nothing or zero. Thus, our null hypothesis would be that there is no relationship between family satisfaction and level of participation. The opposite of the null hypothesis is the **alternate hypothesis** (H_1). The alternate hypothesis states that there is a significant difference or relationship among the variables. Remember, we are testing the null hypothesis because we hope it is wrong; what we would prefer to see is a significant difference that would allow us to accept the alternate hypothesis.

Null hypothesis (H_0): a statement to be tested and either accepted or rejected; typically states that any relationship or difference found among variables is by chance.

Alternate hypothesis (H_1): the opposite of the null hypothesis; states that any difference or relationship measured is true, real, and significant.

Significance level (α): the level of confidence we have in our findings; also referred to as alpha level.

***p*-value:** the probability that a difference detected for the sample would *not* be true for the population.

10.3.2 Significance Testing

In hypothesis testing, we are examining if there is a difference or relationship among the data. We assume there is not (thus, the null hypothesis). Then, we set a level, called a **significance level (α)** or alpha level, at which we would be willing to accept that any difference we detect is not representative of the population. That is, the significance level is our threshold for error in the findings and, further, it indicates our degree of confidence in our findings.

In conducting the actual test of significance, the results will give us a *p*-value. The *p*-value tells us the probability that any difference detected is by chance alone and thus would not be true for the population.

For example, if we set a significance level of 0.05, we are asserting that it is acceptable to us to have a 5% likelihood that we detect significance in our sample when it would not be present in the larger population. If the probability that the results are by chance is greater than our significance level, we accept the null hypothesis (that there is no relationship or difference). If the *p*-value is less than our significance level, we reject the null hypothesis and accept the alternate hypothesis. Many researchers set a significance level at .05, while those who are more conservative use .01 or even .001.

Are you having flashbacks to your statistics or research methods course? What is provided in this chapter is a brief review of terms and statistical tests; if you have not yet had an introductory statistics or research methods course, you may find you want more information. Some additional resources will be suggested at the end of this section.

Before we move on to other important statistics, there are two other terms to briefly review: type 1 and type 2 errors. In hypothesis testing, a **type 1 error** occurs when you make an error in rejecting the null hypothesis. That is, you assert that there is a difference or relationship among variables when in fact there is none. It is a false positive. The significance level we set is our threshold for making a type 1 error. Thus, type 1 errors are also denoted by alpha (α). On the other hand, a **type 2 error** occurs when we make an error in accepting the null hypothesis. That is, we conclude there is no relationship when in fact there is. It is a false negative. Type 2 errors are denoted by beta (β).

10.3.3 Power and Effect Size

Statistical **power** is the probability that we make the right decision in rejecting the null hypothesis. This is what we hope for: to find a significant difference or relationship in our data. The **effect size** is a statistic that indicates the degree of difference or relationship between variables that our research design is able to detect. Our goal would be to be able to detect even small differences or relationships among variables and recognize them as significant. If we accept the null hypothesis, then we are saying there is no effect to measure. If we reject the null, we are saying there is indeed an effect. However, is the knowledge that there is a significant effect enough? Understanding the size of the effect gives us a sense of the magnitude of the relationship between variables or the difference in group means. Effect size is one of the most important statistics to consider when designing studies and reporting results. Taking effect size into account when designing studies provides an indication of the rigor of the design; stronger designs can typically detect a smaller effect size. When reporting results, effect size gives readers a sense of not just the significance of findings, but the magnitude of the differences detected. Effect size comparing two means is calculated using Cohen's *d* (Cohen, 1988). Cohen's *d* is the standardized mean difference and is calculated by subtracting the mean of group 2 from the mean of group 1 and then dividing by the standard deviation. See Table 10.3 for Cohen's *d* effect size descriptions.

For more information on quantitative data analysis, see *Statistics for the Behavioral Sciences* (Privitera, 2015), *Research Methods in Psychology: Investigating Human Behavior* (Nestor & Schutt, 2018), and *Research Methods, Statistics, and Applications* (Adams & Lawrence, 2018).

type 1 error (α): the error made when the null hypothesis is rejected when it should have been accepted; a false positive.

type 2 error (β): the error made when the null hypothesis is accepted when it should have been rejected; a false negative.

Power: the probability that the null hypothesis is rejected when it should have been rejected.

Effect size (*d*): the size or magnitude of the difference between variables; studies aim to detect small effects.

TABLE 10.3 ● Effect Size		
Size of Effect	**Cohen's *d***	**Description**
Small	0.2	Difference in means is 0.2 standard deviation
Medium	0.5	Difference in means is half a standard deviation
Large	0.8	Difference in means is 0.8 standard deviation

10.3.4 Correlations, *t*-Tests, and Regression

The calculated correlation coefficient along with our predetermined level of significance allows us to make inferences about how likely the sample results are reflective of the greater population. If we set a significance level of 0.01, we are indicating that we need to be at least 99% confident that the coefficient calculated from the sample is representative of the population. In calculating our correlation coefficient, we might find a *p*-value of 0.00237. For these results, we would assert that the correlation coefficient is significant at the $p < .01$ level. On the other hand, if the measured *p*-value is 0.0727, we would assert that the coefficient is not significant. See Meyers, Gamst, and Guarino (2006) for more information on interpreting *p*-values and about conducting correlation analyses. One caution about correlation that we are sure you have heard repeatedly in research methods and statistics courses is that just because two variables are related through correlation, it does not mean that changes in one variable cause changes in another variable. Correlation is not causation.

Another common inferential statistic is the ***t*-test**. It is used to determine if the difference between two means is significant. For instance, for a program intending to decrease depression, you might want to examine whether the depression level of patients prior to treatment is different from that posttreatment. A *t*-test could be used to compare the mean level of depression at the start of the program to the mean level after the program; the *t*-test would analyze the differences between the two means and provide you with a *p*-value to interpret whether the difference measured is indeed significant. This is called a paired sample *t*-test, because the two means tested are from the same group. For the same program, let's say you also measured the level of depression for a group of individuals who did not receive the program. You could also use a *t*-test to compare the means of the program group versus the nonprogram group; the *t*-test would analyze the differences between the two means and provide you with a *p*-value to interpret whether the difference measured is indeed significant. This is called an independent sample *t*-test, because the data were collected from two different, unrelated groups of individuals.

Another method of inferential statistics is regression. **Regression** analysis allows you to examine the relationship between one or more variables and another variable. It can also determine how predictive one or more variables are of a certain outcome. Simple linear regression is when you use one variable to predict another variable; multiple regression

t-test: a statistical method used to determine if the difference between two means is significant.

Regression: a statistical method used to examine how predictive one or more variables are of another variable.

is when you use more than one variable to predict another variable. Logistic regression is a form of regression where the dependent variable (i.e., the variable to be predicted) is dichotomous (i.e., has only two values, such as yes or no). Regression can help us to determine how predictive a set of variables is of an outcome, as well as which of our variables are more predictive of the outcome than others.

For example, it might be important for a program to know if certain characteristics of participants help predict certain outcomes. This information could help program developers target specific supports. We might be curious if a participant's age is associated with greater satisfaction with the program. We would hypothesize that younger participants (i.e., those between the ages of 18 and 22) are more satisfied than older participants, because the program works with them to explore an occupation that will help them secure employment after college and/or later in life. Examining how age can be used to predict program satisfaction is an example of simple linear regression.

As stated above, multiple regression takes into account multiple factors that might affect a particular outcome. For example, we might want to know if age, gender, and race help predict one's satisfaction with a program. Multiple regression can be used to examine how these variables can collectively predict satisfaction, as well as which variables in particular are more predictive than others. See Table 10.4 for a summary of the more common quantitative analysis methods.

TABLE 10.4 ● Quantitative Data Analysis at a Glance				
	Descriptive Statistics		**Inferential Statistics**	
Statistical Method	**Mean and Standard Deviation**	**Frequency Distribution**	**Correlation**	**Regression**
Example Question	How did students perform on the final exam?	How many people were satisfied with the program?	To what extent is depression related to self-esteem?	Does attending more counseling sessions reduce delinquent behavior?
Data	Scores on a final exam	Survey data in which program participants rated their satisfaction with the program from Very Satisfied to Very Dissatisfied	Measures on a depression scale Measures on a self-esteem scale	Number of counseling sessions attended Number of behavior infractions before and after the program
Analysis	Calculate the average score as well as the variation of scores around the average	Count the number of responses for each category and calculate the percentage of responses based on these counts	Examine correlation between depression and self-esteem variables	Examine how predictive the number of counseling sessions attended is of changes in behavior infractions pre-/post-program

10.4 QUALITATIVE DATA ANALYSIS

In this section, we discuss analysis strategies for qualitative data. We will focus on interview and focus group data, since they are most often used to incorporate individuals' in-depth perceptions. While there are many different approaches to analyzing qualitative data, a three-step framework for qualitative data analysis will be described here: coding, synthesis, and making assertions. We end the chapter with an overview for analyzing other types of qualitative data.

10.4.1 Analysis Step 1: Coding

Coding is a part of analysis. Codes are essentially labels that assign meaning to data. Researchers apply codes to "chunks" or excerpts of data. The main function of codes is to categorize similar data so a researcher can find and cluster the segments that relate to the same question or theme. To code, you apply a notation or code that summarizes a chunk of data.

Miles, Huberman, and Saldana (2014) state that coding is a means to condense your data to the most important information for your research study. Coding thus allows you to retrieve the most meaningful materials and bring together passages of data that belong together. However, not every part of the data needs to get a code. Some data are not very useful. For instance, transcribed banter about a recent vacation between an interviewer and participant probably does not need a code. In short, parts of field notes and transcripts might contain information that is not relevant to the research question.

10.4.1.1 Developing Codes

Codes can be predetermined based on research questions and literature, developed along the way of collecting data and conducting an analysis, or based on a combination of both. Prespecified codes are referred to as **deductive codes**. A code list that is deductive, often referred to as a "start list," is derived from the conceptual framework, evaluation questions, hypotheses, or key variables (Miles et al., 2014, p. 81). Deductive codes are also called "a priori" codes. *A priori* is Latin for "from the earlier" and refers to concepts, terms, and hypotheses that a researcher develops prior to the evaluation. Table 10.5 shows an example of codes and their associated definitions from an evaluation of a training program that matches doctoral students/trainees with both faculty and family mentors. The example codes specifically relate to faculty mentor interviews about their experiences with the training program.

Another method of coding is inductive coding. **Inductive codes** are not determined in advance of data analysis but rather emerge during data collection and analysis. They come about when the researcher has uncovered an important factor or theme. A combination of deductive and inductive coding can allow the researcher to predetermine some codes, but be open to additional themes that might emerge as the data are analyzed.

Codes: labels that assign meaning to data.

Deductive codes: prespecified codes developed from evaluation questions; also called a priori codes.

Inductive codes: codes that emerge during data collection and analysis.

	Code	Definition
	TABLE 10.5 ● Predetermined Codes and Definitions for a Study of a Training Program	
1	**Background**	Any information about the number of years someone has been a mentor
2	**Faculty's expectations/ satisfaction**	Faculty's expectations of the program, the extent to which they are being met, and their overall satisfaction with being a mentor
3	**Online discussions**	Description and overall perception of online discussion activities
4	**Activities: challenges/ suggestions**	Challenges pertaining to any of the activities and suggestions for improvement
5	**Experience with mentee**	Any discussion about a mentor's experience with their mentee/trainee (positive or challenging)

In the next section, three fundamental coding approaches are discussed: descriptive, in vivo, and process. All can be used within one study to help make meaning from qualitative data.

10.4.1.2 Approaches to Coding

Descriptive codes summarize data in a word or a phrase. With descriptive coding, you would generate a list of topics used to categorize data or note patterns. The example below shows a code applied to an excerpt of interview data.

Code: INTERACTION WITH PEERS

> *Interviewer: What kinds of topics or areas of experience do you think you and your family help the trainees to understand or understand better?*
>
> *Interviewee: The interpersonal relationships, how strained they can become when my child is stressed. Also, the trainee had great interaction and watching my child interact with peers. When my child is with our family he would act one way, then when he is in a school setting with lots of chaos and lots of noise for an extended period of time, and having to focus on nonpreferred items for activity, he would act another way.*

In vivo codes use words or phrases from the participants' language. Miles et al. (2014) say that in vivo coding is especially useful for beginning qualitative researchers who are learning how to code and want to emphasize their study participant's voice. They are put into quotation marks to distinguish them from codes the researcher developed. These codes are useful because they could suggest patterns in the setting, particularly if participants repeat a phrase.

Code: "TRULY VALUING THE PARENT EXPERIENCE"

> *Interviewer: With regard to your two trainees, how did that host family experience work?*

Descriptive codes: codes that summarize data in a word or phrase.

In vivo codes: codes that use words or phrases from the participants' language.

Interviewee: For one of my trainees really, an area of growth for her was truly valuing the parent perspective and seeing it on an equal plane along with professional opinion. And I think the family experience really helped in that way in helping her to realize more the importance of valuing, authentically, truly valuing the parent experience.

Process codes label and index observable and conceptual action in the data. But they can also apply to actions that "emerge, change, occur in particular sequences, or become strategically implemented" (Miles et al., 2014, p. 75). Process coding is useful for highlighting participant actions and interactions.

Code: PREPARING RESEARCH PAPERS FOR LEADERSHIP PROJECT

Interviewer: To what extent do you feel you've been helpful or you served as a valuable resource for your trainee over the course of this year or last year?

Interviewee: I think that there's increased research and program development opportunities. By having a trainee, we were able to work on their leadership to get a research paper ready for publication, and I think that it does keep the communication open with other disciplines to be able to plan and to hold the trainings for all the trainees as a whole.

Once you've developed codes, it is important to capture the definition in a codebook or table. Providing detailed information regarding each code is critical when multiple researchers might be coding data for the same research project. Understanding and sharing codes among researchers working on the same evaluation helps ensure that the codes are applied consistently. For example, a code called "Benefits" might mean different things depending on the context. Researchers need to be able to retrieve the right excerpts for analysis, so having clearly defined codes enables accurate organization and analysis.

To arrive at final definitions for your codes that are clear and useful, two or more researchers might code the same data set and then discuss how well the codes worked or did not work. This discussion will help you arrive at a shared understanding of what codes connote and which chunks of data are rightly associated with a code. Clarifying definitions also helps with reliability. If time permits, having each coder code the same text independently allows researchers to check for consistency, so they can be confident that codes fit the data excerpts and that results from multiple coders have adequate reliability. Be open to codes changing, as conversations among researchers working on the same evaluation might lead to important revisions.

Process codes: codes that label and index observable and conceptual action in the data.

Simultaneous coding: coding in which a researcher applies two or more codes to a data chunk.

10.4.1.3 Applying Multiple Codes

Simultaneous coding is when a researcher applies two or more codes to a data chunk or when multiple, different codes overlap on a piece of data. It is appropriate to use simultaneous coding when the data suggest multiple meanings that justify more than one code. In the passage below, the person describes interactions with staff and gives suggestions. Thus, the passage was simultaneously coded STAFF INTERACTIONS and SUGGESTIONS.

Codes: STAFF INTERACTIONS; SUGGESTIONS

> *Interviewer: Is there any suggestion you would provide to the staff as you continue through the project? Anything that you feel that maybe they didn't think about or should think about or consider moving as we go forward with the work?*

> *Interviewee: I know staff had requirements, like you had to put in so many hours, and last year that trainee did not do that. You know? So, I don't know if there's a tracking system. Like maybe halfway through the program, say, "Okay, I need an update. How are things going? How many hours do you have?" That would be nice if they did that. That would help because truly, I kept reaching out to staff last year, saying, "Is she gonna call me? Like, I haven't heard from her." So, I did let them know.*

10.4.2 Analysis Step 2: Synthesis

After you've coded and you've retrieved excerpts associated with specific codes, the next step is to further synthesize the data by reading over your coded output and starting to make sense of the information. There are several approaches to synthesis that you can use for one data set. One approach is **narrative description** in which you write a passage that elaborates on a code. This is a straightforward way to communicate a finding to a reader. Below is an example of a narrative description.

Code: SUGGESTIONS

> *One faculty mentor said that the number of hours could be shortened or that trainees could be given credit for their hours they are already doing as part of their clinical program. The same interviewer thought that a different perspective could be integrated into activities. This faculty member suggested that an occupational therapist come in to lecture.*

> *Another faculty mentor thought that trainings could be differentiated according to level so that trainees could take the one that matched their level of advancement. The faculty mentor said if this change were made, the trainings would be relevant for trainees at all levels.*

Narrative description: writing a passage that elaborates on a code.

A **matrix** can be used to chart data for an "at-a-glance" view that could aid in exposing patterns in the data. The matrix in Table 10.6 illustrates various observations trainees had of their family mentor and child and provides a quick glance at the number of trainees who had different observational opportunities.

Matrix: used to chart or table data to aid in seeing patterns in the data.

TABLE 10.6 ● Matrix Example: Trainee Observations of Family Mentor and Child				
Trainee	**Doctor's Appointment**	**Outdoor Trip**	**Home Visit**	**School Visit**
1	X		X	X
2		X		
3	X			
4	X	X	X	X
5	X		X	X
6	X	X	X	

Network displays can also be used to illustrate a process. A network display is a map with lines and arrows to indicate how people, components, or actions connect and flow. Figure 10.2 provides an example. In it, we see how an analysis of a trainee's growth as a practitioner is unfolding. Among the components are the faculty mentor's support, a leadership project, exposure to family mentor, and the trainees' positive perceptions of those experiences with their family mentor. We can also visualize relationships between some of these components.

Jottings are short pieces of writing that allow you to comment on chunks of data. Often, researchers jot as they are reading raw interview data or field notes, or reviewing a particular document. It is the researcher's in-the-moment reflections and commentary on the data. Examples of what jottings entail include

- Personal reactions to what a participant says or does

- Notes to ask probing questions about a topic in the future

- Critique of protocols

- Early understanding of what a participant is saying

Jottings are useful because they could be used in later stages of analysis, can underscore deeper issues that should get attention, and might help clarify codes.

10.4.3 Analysis Step 3: Assertions

After you have coded, read your output, and synthesized data, the next stage is to begin discerning findings. A generalization about your coded output is referred to as a **theme**. Themes are important findings within your data. A **memo** is a thought or idea about your codes and themes. A memo might be a thought drawn from one theme or a thought that relates multiple themes. From your memos, which may be based on multiple codes or themes, you will develop an **assertion**. An assertion is a statement made based on the

Network displays: a map with lines and arrows to indicate how people, components, or actions connect and flow.

Jottings: short pieces of writing that allow you to comment on chunks of data.

Theme: an important finding in your data based on codes.

Memo: a thought or idea about your codes and themes.

Assertion: a statement made based on themes found within your data.

FIGURE 10.2 ● Network Display Example

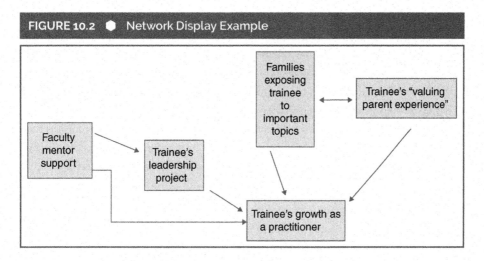

themes found within your data. It is helpful if there is one strong assertion and multiple quotes to support that assertion. Memos at this stage are not merely descriptive summaries; rather, they generate higher-level meaning from the data.

Below is an example of an analytic memo based on the code VISITS. We begin with an assertion and put it in bold print to make it easier to see. Note that there are multiple quotations. This gives you a sense of the finding's strength and some choices for quotes to include in the final product.

> **Overall, mentors believed that family visits were the most meaningful learning experiences for volunteers.** They said that the volunteer learned the accommodations families made in various parts of their lives, such as while grocery shopping. One mentor said,
>
> *That, I think, is the most valuable among the different things that they received. The fact that they get to spend time and observe the child and how a disability is impacting the family, even at dinner, the accommodations they have to make to get to a grocery store, or to any therapy location they need to be at. So, I think that that, even though it's 20 hours, it's perhaps not a lot. It still feels like they get sort of a look into the life of a child and their family, given that they have this facility.*
>
> Another mentor said: *My student had a very positive experience and would often talk about the experience afterwards when we were doing our weekly meetings. That was one of the ones that she brought up more than anything else. So, it's a good one.*
>
> And another said: *So, for one of my students, it went really well. She was able to learn—she was able to gain a lot from the experience, understand more.*

Documents, field notes, and literature are additional types of qualitative data. Qualitative data that are not interviews are generally analyzed and reviewed much like any interview transcript. However, the researcher looks for emergent themes that are relevant for the evaluation. For observations that involve protocols or rubrics, these instruments often shape the analysis, providing categories and "look fors" that influence how you read the data. As with all of the previously described approaches to analysis, it is important to write your findings from documentation, observation field notes, or literature reviews in narrative form. These "pieces" can then be integrated with other findings. In the chapters that follow, we will delve deeper into interpreting findings and formally writing them for your audience.

If you would like to learn more about qualitative data analysis, see *Qualitative Research and Evaluation Methods* (Patton, 2014) and *Qualitative Data Analysis: A Methods Sourcebook* (Miles et al., 2014).

10.5 MANAGING THE UNEXPECTED AND UNINTENDED

As much thought as you put into evaluation design and data collection, there will be events that happen that you did not plan or expect. Trying to anticipate the unexpected can help you plan in advance for contingencies. Stufflebeam (2004) provides an *Evaluation Design Checklist* that includes recommendations specific to analyzing data that can guide you in planning and conducting your data analysis. However, even with the best of planning, there might be major changes to the program you are evaluating, barriers to collecting data, and difficult partners to manage. Below we list nine circumstances that you could face when you conduct an evaluation:

- Changes to the program
- Tense relationship with the client
- Negative findings
- Null findings
- Insufficient data
- Barriers to obtaining data
- Client wants to see raw data
- Client wants revisions to the product
- Client does not agree with findings

We elaborate on these circumstances and provide some suggestions on how to manage them in the following sections. Though we cannot offer direct solutions, as unexpected situations are indeed unexpected and have unique elements, we hope that these suggestions are helpful should situations arise that are not anticipated.

10.5.1 Unanticipated Program Changes

One unexpected circumstance presents itself when the program you are evaluating changes as your evaluation takes place. Changes could include, for example, staff turnover or a reduction in funding. Such developments are largely out of an evaluator's hands; it is hard to prevent programs from changing. However, there are a few strategies that can help you stay abreast of changes and continue your research. First, it can be helpful if, as the evaluator, you "keep tabs" on events through periodic check-ins with program staff. Establishing and maintaining a strong working relationship with the staff will aid you in keeping up with any program changes. Another response to program changes could be to change your research design. If your evaluation involves examining outcomes, it might be difficult to rely on findings if the program changes drastically. You could redesign the project so that it focuses more on implementation. This way, your narrative will include the changes that took place, along with any other key information about implementation. Finally, you could be explicit about program changes in your final product and urge the reader to interpret findings with caution, given that significant events transpired that affected your research.

Some texts advise an evaluator to actively engage in program maintenance and act as a "watchdog" to ensure that programs do not implement too many changes and to be in some control of events (Weiss, 1972). Assuming the position of "watchdog," however, would compromise one's role as an external evaluator doing unbiased research. You cannot fully prevent or avoid changes to programs, but you can be ready with potential responses should they arise.

10.5.2 Strained Relationships With Clients

Another unexpected situation arises when you and the client and/or staff are not enjoying the best relationship. Perhaps they are distrustful of you. Maybe the client is very demanding toward you and questions decisions you make as the evaluator. One way to avoid this is to build rapport with the client and staff as early as possible and continue those efforts throughout the duration of the project. Establish cordial yet professional relationships by communicating periodically with phone calls, emails, or in-person meetings and by being transparent about the evaluation and its progress. If your timeline allows for it and you do not think it would be too disruptive, you could invite your client to read over protocols that you will use for the evaluation as well as an early draft of the final product. The more inclusive your evaluation is—collaborating during logic model development, design of surveys and interview protocols, and the reporting of findings—the more likely it is that the evaluation will be used by stakeholders to improve the program.

Another strategy for easing tension with clients is to incorporate theory into your research. Theories address general approaches that undergird a program's practices. Weiss (1972) suggests that focusing on theories redirects any potential critiques away from the program and toward more generalized approaches. Presumably, people will feel less defensive if critiques target higher-level approaches rather than their specific activities. Integrating theory, Weiss suggests, is helpful not only for strengthening relationships with stakeholders, but also for the evaluation in general. Weiss argues that since they address general approaches, theories help provide insights about future programming regardless of staff in place. Again, this could facilitate an improved evaluator–client relationship because of the long-term utility of the study.

10.5.3 Negative Findings

While you are collecting data or after you have analyzed the data, you might find that certain interviewees expressed strong criticisms of the program. There are several ways to handle negative findings. First and foremost, however, data are what they are; when findings are derived directly from the data, and you can defend those findings through the data, the results stand on their own. Interpretation, on the other hand, is disputable.

Typically, we report negative findings just like we would any other finding. However, the negative quotation or finding could be so contentious that you might consider dealing with it outside of the regular evaluation report. For instance, if the negative finding might allow someone to deduce an identity or if it could harm someone in any way, raising the finding discretely and privately would be best.

You could start by saying to the client, "We wanted to tell you about some critiques that might alarm you, and that we did not want to put into the report," then follow with the finding. Another approach you could take is to report on the negative finding but in a milder tone than that used in the direct quote. You could say, "Some interviewees shared criticisms about the program," then provide a summary of the critique. Another idea is to consider submitting a confidential addendum to the evaluation report.

How to handle such situations depends largely on the audience and the purpose of the evaluation, as well as the nature of the negative finding. If the report will remain internal and the client asked to hear every critique, then it might make sense to retain the negative finding in your report. However, if you know that the product will be widely disseminated, you might consider talking to your client about the finding and leaving it out of the publicly disseminated product. In either case, careful thought, discussions with team members, and a possible conversation with the client are all key to handling this issue.

10.5.4 Null Findings

Null findings occur when your evaluation reveals that the program or policy had no effect. Evaluators and program staff may dislike null findings, because there is nothing glamorous about them. There is nothing positive for a program to be proud of, but also nothing negative that an evaluator might feel adds to the greater body of research. However, null findings are valuable. First of all, there are financial implications. Continuing a program that has no impact, positive or negative, is a waste of resources. Program staff acting upon null findings and discarding an ineffective program is responsible and can be reported as such. Second, if you have null findings, it is important to share them. Sharing null findings may prevent someone from undertaking a similar program only to find for them too it was a waste of resources.

10.5.5 Insufficient Data

After analysis, you might find that some interview questions did not get addressed or that a few more observations at a site are needed. Depending on the evaluation deadline, you could decide to go ahead and collect these data. If you have the phone numbers or email addresses of some of the interviewees, you could follow up with them to ask your questions. If you need additional observations, you could contact the site and attempt to visit again. Observations might be trickier to achieve than additional interviews because unexpected visits could disrupt previously scheduled occurrences at the site. If you find that certain data are missing, you could also choose to make the most of what you have and be clear in your product about what your findings are based on.

10.5.6 Barriers to Obtaining Data

When attempting to acquire records from another agency, you might face delays or other barriers to getting the data. For instance, if you needed student-level data on grades and test scores, you would need to consider that (1) these would not be gathered until after grades and test scores are calculated, (2) the school would still need to enter them into a system, and (3) the school would need to send those data to you. All of these factors could contribute to delays in retrieving the data. One strategy to implement prior to the study is to establish a clear understanding with the agency regarding the timeline of your research. You should also be up front with the people seeking the evaluation about the realities of retrieving the data. In some cases, evaluators will stipulate in their contract with clients that their report will be produced three months after obtaining data. This way, they are covered in case data acquisition is delayed.

You might also face barriers with collecting qualitative data. For instance, your evaluation might require you to observe and interview individuals at 12 different schools in a state. However, 4 of those schools have not responded to your requests to set up that fieldwork. In such a case, you could alert a governing body of the schools, telling them about the difficulty and asking them to contact the schools on your behalf. Or you could select another 4 schools to replace the ones that did not respond. Whatever your choice, you should be sure to notify your client and request input regarding the decision to be made.

10.5.7 Client Requests Raw Data

It does not happen often, but sometimes a client may ask to see transcripts or raw quantitative data, out of curiosity and/or for more specific insights. Should this occur, please remind the client that per your agreement with study participants, you cannot share raw data because it will reveal their identities.

10.5.8 Client Requests Report Revisions

A client might want certain changes to early drafts of your report. This could be because the product will be disseminated to a wide audience and they want the product to be readable, engaging, and framed in a particular way, especially if the audience includes potential funders. Suggested revisions might involve wording of findings or more accurate definitions of program components in introductory sections. Other noted changes might pertain to aesthetics; perhaps the client would like an infographic rather than text in one section. To prepare for this potential occurrence, it is wise to share your product with a client at least a week before the final deadline so that you can address their feedback. It is also wise to keep in mind your product's audience and the purpose of the evaluation as you develop the product.

10.5.9 Client Disagrees With Findings

On rare occasions, you might have clients disagree with the findings. In such cases, it is good practice to discuss the client's concerns to see if there is a way they might be addressed. In many cases, if your findings are truly grounded in the data and you can offer sound evidence of the findings you report (without identifying any individuals who participated), the client may, after reflection, come to accept the findings. However, if the nature of the disagreement is truly that the client feels the findings are wrong or unfair, offer the client the opportunity to write a letter that can be attached to the report, detailing their objections. The following "In the Real World" suggests several ways the evaluator might respond in a difficult situation; what would you do?

In sum, an evaluator cannot predict or prevent everything that can happen during a study. Moreover, even if an evaluator addresses an unforeseen issue, there is no guarantee that they will have the perfect solution. However, an evaluator can anticipate some circumstances and plan ahead on how to handle them. Changes could happen to the program or there might be obstacles to obtaining data. We provided some possible situations along with responses. Interestingly, a common thread across each is the benefit of the evaluator establishing a positive relationship with the client as early in the evaluation as possible. This way, the evaluator is better positioned to foresee, circumvent, and/or address challenges. Even in the absence of strong rapport, an evaluator who is communicative, relational, transparent, ethical, and who does rigorous research with integrity and professional judgment is prepared to at least manage unexpected and unintended events that may occur during an evaluation.

IN THE REAL WORLD ...

The **Sunshine After-School Company** runs 20 after-school programs at 20 different sites. Each year, Sunshine contracts an evaluator to assess its program using a rubric based on youth development principles and to produce a report based on evaluation findings. These evaluations are required for Sunshine to receive its funding, and funders use findings to make decisions on sustaining the programs. One year, Sunshine wanted the evaluator to conduct a youth focus group at each of the 20 sites as part of the evaluation. At one site, the focus group took longer than the planned 30 minutes. Why? Because during the group, four of the six students extensively described their dislike of one staff member at their site. They said that the staff member was rude to youth, did not teach or manage groups well, and did not come prepared for after-school programming. The students, however, said that they greatly appreciated all the other staff. In fact, at the 19 other sites the evaluator visited, participants had glowing comments about staff.

What do you think the evaluator should do?

a. Put the children's quotes about the one staff member in the report—the funders should know!

b. Schedule a conference call with the specific after-school program's site director to report what the children said, without revealing their identities.

c. Email Sunshine's executive director and the specific site's director as soon as possible, saying that you want to meet with them to discuss some critiques you heard and how to include them in the report, if at all.

d. Keep the children's negative perceptions about the staff person to yourself.

QUICK CHECK

1. How can a correlation be both descriptive and inferential?
2. What is the difference between a code, a theme, and an assertion?
3. How might you handle a situation in which the client is unhappy with your report?

CASE STUDY
Youth Abstinence-Plus (YAP) Program

Table 10.7 presents the evaluation matrix for the YAP program showing data collection and analysis methods for each indicator.

TABLE 10.7 ● YAP Evaluation Matrix

	Logic Model Component	Evaluation Question(s)	Indicators	Targets	Data Source	Data Collection	Data Analysis
Program Strategies/Implementation	Materials promoting sexual abstinence	What were the content and format of materials promoting abstinence? In what ways were materials promoting abstinence made available to youth?	Content and format of abstinence materials Method of delivering abstinence materials to youth	By program start, materials promoting sexual abstinence are developed and implemented with fidelity	Fidelity of implementation rubric	Rubric administered at start of program and quarterly thereafter	Rubric data analyzed for evidence of implementation fidelity
	Education regarding safe sex practices	What were the content and format of education regarding safe sex practices? In what ways was education regarding safe sex provided?	Content and format of education regarding safe sex practices Method of delivering education regarding safe sex to youth	By program start, education regarding safe sex practices is implemented with fidelity	Fidelity of implementation rubric	Rubric administered at start of program and quarterly thereafter	Rubric data analyzed for evidence of implementation fidelity
	Access to contraceptives	In what ways, from whom, and at what locations were contraceptives available to youth? What types of contraceptives were made available to youth?	Distribution method of contraceptives to youth Types of contraceptives available to youth	By program start, methods of access to contraceptives will be implemented with fidelity	Fidelity of implementation rubric	Rubric administered at start of program and quarterly thereafter	Rubric data analyzed for evidence of implementation fidelity

Early and Intermediate Objectives						
Increase the availability of materials on abstinence	To what extent did youth have access to materials on abstinence?	Availability of abstinence materials to youth	Within one week of program start, abstinence materials will be available to all youth	Program records	Program records examined monthly	Program records analyzed for evidence of availability of materials
Increase the number of youth who receive materials on abstinence	To what extent did the number of youth who received materials on abstinence increase? In what ways did youth obtain materials related to abstinence?	Number of youth receiving abstinence materials Method of receiving abstinence materials	Within three months of program start, all youth will have received materials on abstinence	Inventory of materials	Inventory data collected monthly	Inventory data analyzed for evidence of material distribution
Increase the availability of education regarding safe sex practices	To what extent was education regarding safe sex practices made available to youth?	Availability of education regarding safe sex practices	Within one week of program start, education regarding safe sex will be available to all youth	Program records Training schedule	Program records and training schedule examined monthly	Program records and training schedule analyzed for evidence of availability of education
Increase the number of youth who receive education regarding safe sex practices	To what extent did the number of youth who received education regarding safe sex practices increase? How did youth receive education regarding safe sex?	Number of youth receiving education on safe sex practices *Method of receiving education on safe sex practices*	Within three months of program start, all youth will have received education on safe sex practices	Training sign-in sheets	Sign-in sheets collected after each session and analyzed monthly	Basic descriptive statistics of sign-in sheet data

(Continued)

TABLE 10.7 ◆ (Continued)

Logic Model Component	Evaluation Question(s)	Indicators	Targets	Data Source	Data Collection	Data Analysis
Increase the number of youth who have access to contraceptives	To what extent did the number of youth with access to contraceptives increase? To what extent were youth aware of their access to contraceptives?	Number of youth who have access to contraceptives Number of youth who are aware of their access to contraceptives	Within three months, all youth will have access to contraceptives Within six months, all youth will be aware of their access to contraceptives	Program records	Program records examined monthly	Program records analyzed for evidence of access to contraceptives
Increase the number of sexually active youth who obtain contraceptives	To what extent did the number of sexually active youth who obtain contraceptives increase? Where did youth obtain contraceptives? What types of contraceptives did youth obtain?	Number of sexually active youth who obtain contraceptives *Demographics of youth who obtain contraceptives* *Method and location of receiving contraceptives* *Types of contraceptives received*	Within one year, there will be a 25% increase in sexually active youth who obtain contraceptives	Inventory of contraceptives	Inventory data collected monthly	Basic descriptive statistics of inventory data

Increase the number of youth who understand the benefits of abstinence	To what extent did the number of youth who understand the benefits of abstinence increase? What did youth learn about abstinence?	Number of youth who understand the benefits of abstinence *Nature of youth's understanding about the benefits of abstinence*	Within six months of the start of the program, all youth will be able to describe the benefits of abstinence	Youth survey	Survey administered at start of program and at end of program	Basic descriptive statistics of survey data *t*-test examining pre/post differences
Increase the number of youth who understand the benefits of practicing safe sex	To what extent did the number of youth who understand the benefits of practicing safe sex increase? What did youth learn about practicing safe sex?	Number of youth who are able to describe the benefits of practicing safe sex *Nature of youth's understanding about the benefits of practicing safe sex*	Within six months, all youth will be able to describe the benefits of practicing safe sex	Youth survey	Survey administered at start of program and at end of program	Basic descriptive statistics of survey data *t*-test examining pre/post differences
Increase the number of sexually active youth who use contraceptives	To what extent did the number of sexually active youth who use contraceptives increase? What types of contraceptives did youth choose to use? How often did youth use contraceptives in sexual situations?	Number of sexually active youth who use contraceptives *Demographics of youth who use contraceptives* *Types of contraceptives used* *Frequency with which contraception is used*	Within one year, there will be a 20% increase in the number of sexually active youth who use contraceptives	Youth survey	Survey administered at start of program and at end of program	Basic descriptive statistics of survey data *t*-test examining pre/post differences

(Continued)

TABLE 10.7 ◈ (Continued)

Logic Model Component	Evaluation Question(s)	Indicators	Targets	Data Source	Data Collection	Data Analysis
Improve safe sex practices among sexually active youth	To what extent did safe sex practices among sexually active youth improve? In what ways did safe sex practices improve?	Number of sexually active youth who practice safe sex *Demographics of youth who practice safe sex* *Nature of safe sex practices used* *Frequency with which contraception is used*	Within one year, there will be a 20% increase in sexually active youth who practice safe sex	Youth survey	Survey administered at start of program and at end of program	Basic descriptive statistics of survey data *t*-test examining pre/post differences
Increase the number of youth who choose abstinence	To what extent did the number of youth who choose abstinence increase?	Number of youth who choose abstinence *Demographics of youth who choose abstinence* *Self-reported reason for youth choosing abstinence*	Within one year of program start, there will be a 20% increase in the number of youth who choose abstinence	Youth survey	Survey administered at start of program and at end of program	Basic descriptive statistics of survey data *t*-test examining pre/post differences

20% Long-Term Goals						
Decrease the spread of STIs among youth	To what extent did the spread of STIs, including HIV, decrease?	Number of youth diagnosed with STI/HIV *Demographics of youth diagnosed with STI/HIV*	Within two years of program start, there will be a 20% decrease in the number of youth in the community diagnosed with STI/HIV	Youth survey Public health records	Survey administered at start of program and at end of program Public health records examined annually	Basic descriptive statistics of survey data *t*-test examining pre/post differences Health records analyzed using basic descriptive statistics
Decrease the youth pregnancy rate	To what extent did the youth pregnancy rate decrease?	Number of youth who become pregnant *Demographics of youth who become pregnant*	Within two years of program start, there will be a 20% decrease in the number of youth in the community who become pregnant	Youth survey Public health records	Survey administered at start of program and at end of program Public health records examined annually	Basic descriptive statistics of survey data *t*-test examining pre/post differences Health records analyzed using basic descriptive statistics

10.6 CHAPTER SUMMARY

Data analysis is important for condensing and making sense of the data. In quantitative analyses, descriptive statistics, bivariate correlations, and regression are often used for evaluations. A **descriptive statistic** is a number that summarizes a data set in a meaningful way. Descriptive statistics include means, standard deviations, and frequency distributions. An **inferential statistic** is a number calculated based on a data set that is used to draw conclusions about the greater population that your data set represents. Correlations can be both descriptive and inferential. Other inferential statistics include *t*-tests and regression analyses.

For qualitative data, analysis can be broken down in to three main steps: coding, synthesizing, and memo writing. **Codes** are labels that assign meaning to data; deductive codes are prespecified codes developed from evaluation questions; inductive codes are codes that emerge during data collection and analysis. A **theme** is an important finding in your data based on codes. **Memos** are thoughts or ideas about codes and themes. **Assertions** are statements made based on themes found within your data.

Reflection and Application

1. Did you take the SAT or ACT when you were preparing for college? Look up the mean and standard deviation for both tests. If you received a 1350 on the SAT and your friend received a 29 on the ACT, who did better?

2. What do you think the relationship is between years of education and income? Do a quick search on the internet to see if you can find any studies that measured this using a correlation coefficient. How would you interpret this correlation coefficient?

3. What are the steps to analyzing qualitative data? Illustrate the steps in a diagram.

4. How are descriptive statistics, bivariate correlations, and simple regression different from one another?

5. With a partner, role-play one of the challenges discussed in section 10.5 and your response to that challenge.

INTERPRET

Interpreting the Results

Coauthored With Akisha Osei Sarfo

The arts celebrate multiple perspectives. One of their large lessons is that there are many ways to see and interpret the world.

—Elliott Eisner

Upon completion of this chapter, you should be able to

- Explain the importance of ongoing examination of evaluation results.
- Describe how embedded evaluation facilitates the examination of results in relation to implementation.
- Identify ways in which evaluation results can be overinterpreted or misinterpreted.
- Explain how to address different stakeholder needs in the communication of evaluation results.
- Compare and contrast different methods of communicating evaluation results.
- Create an evaluation report outline.

FIGURE 11.1 ● Embedded Evaluation Model

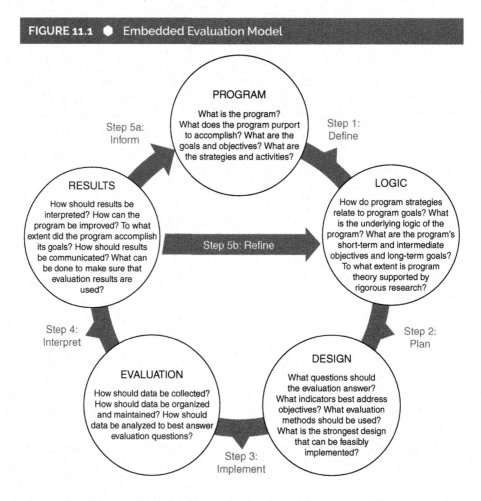

11.1 THE HOME STRETCH

The purpose of collecting and analyzing evaluation data is not the statistics you calculate or the analytical methods that you use, but rather the conclusions that you draw from the data. The process of coming to a conclusion can vary from goal to goal and objective to objective. One of the most difficult tasks is defining vague goals and objectives, such as "sufficient training" or "adequate progress." However, if the embedded evaluation process has been followed, you have gone to great lengths to understand the program and plan its evaluation, and you have already developed targets for your indicators. Because of this, your interpretation of results will likely be more straightforward and less cumbersome. Once you have designed and implemented the evaluation, you are coming down the home stretch. Yet two important steps are still to come. While I believe defining the program at the start of the evaluation is the most critical step to a useful evaluation, interpreting results and then using those results to inform program improvement are critical to the evaluation having an impact on policy, program, or practice.

11.2 EXAMINING RESULTS

It is not wise to wait until the end of an evaluation to analyze your data and interpret your results. For instance, if evaluation results from implementation reveal that program activities were not put into place, continuing with the measurement of short-term and intermediate objectives is likely a waste of resources. Similarly, if the evaluation of intermediate objectives reveals that outcomes are not as envisioned, an important question would be whether the program should be modified, scaled back, or discontinued. Do results indicate that the program is not working as expected? Or do results reveal that the program's theory is invalid and needs to be revisited? Was the program implemented as planned? Is it reasonable to think that making a change in the program could improve results? These are important questions to consider before moving on to the measurement of progress toward long-term goals.

Thus, to enhance the usefulness of evaluation findings and provide meaningful recommendations, examination of results is an ongoing process. Results should be regularly examined in relation to implementation, short- and long-term goals, and program theory. In evaluating a program's implementation, you may want to verify that all intended project activities are being conducted as planned and relevant stakeholders are involved in key processes. Likewise, examination of indicators collected related to short-term and intermediate objectives can provide information on necessary mid-course adjustments and program modifications. The advantages of continuous evaluation monitoring are twofold. First, ongoing examination of results can help determine the degree to which the project is on track toward meeting long-term goals, as well as whether the implementation timeframe should be revised. Second, continuous review of findings can help to assess whether the developed program theory is suitable for what is observed to be taking place in practice. In other words, ongoing examination of results can determine if evaluation findings support the program's theory or if the theory needs to be adjusted.

There is one caveat to this approach. If your evaluation is solely summative in nature, data analysis is often postponed until the end of the evaluation when all data are available. For instance, in an evaluation using a randomized controlled trial (RCT) that is only focusing on measuring impact for summative decision making, the evaluator would likely analyze the data once collection is complete. RCTs are sometimes completed in phases; as such, data analysis may be completed at the end of each phase. However, just because data are not analyzed until collection is complete does not mean they should not be looked at. Continually monitoring the data as they are collected will allow you to catch any potential problems with data collection early on in the process. Potential problems might be nonresponse to a survey or incomplete responses to an electronic survey. Recognizing such problems early will allow you to investigate why response rates might be low or why complete responses are not being recorded, and enable you to remediate the problems before the evaluation is adversely impacted.

Steps of embedded evaluations impact and influence each other, as information in one step can lead to changes in a previous step. As such, waiting until the end of an evaluation to examine and report significant findings can waste valuable resources. Imagine this scenario: A year into the implementation of a new science program, it is discovered that teachers have not been trained on the new curriculum. It has also been discovered that some of the equipment necessary to implement curriculum is still in its original packaging and stacked in a storage closet. How might this affect implementation progress? What are the implications for interpreting findings at the end of the school year regarding changes in science teaching practices and student learning? One might conclude the program is ineffective when it did not have the opportunity to be implemented. Likewise, if findings are positive, one might conclude that the program worked when it was never put in place. The ongoing examination and reporting of findings related to implementation, as well as short-term and intermediate objectives, enable program leadership to determine the degree of implementation, assess findings related to early program adoption, and foster the discussion of whether program modifications might be needed to improve findings. By examining evaluation results on a regular and ongoing basis, evaluators and program staff have the opportunity to investigate unanticipated findings and plan accordingly.

11.2.1 Quality Improvement

Quality improvement is similar to evaluation. In fact, I like to refer to it as evaluation within an evaluation. While evaluation examines the entire program, **quality improvement (QI)** is a systematic process through which components of a program can be examined to improve implementation and outcomes. There are many available models to incorporate QI into your evaluation, including Lean and Six Sigma (George, Rowlands, Price, & Maxey, 2004; Pyzdek & Keller, 2018), Total Quality Management (TQM; Deming, 2000; Juran, 1992), and Root Cause Analysis (RCA; Joint Commission Resources, 2017). The model I have found most useful is **Plan-Do-Study-Act (PDSA)**. The PDSA model is used for rapid quality improvement initiatives in which a process or small project is piloted (Deming, 2000; Health Resources and Services Administration, 2011). During the pilot, the evaluator in collaboration with program staff use several PDSA cycles of improvement to test and fine-tune the program change, prior to expanding its use in other settings and with other stakeholders. During the *Plan* phase, program staff plan the pilot's implementation. The *Do* phase is the implementation

Quality improvement (QI): a systematic process through which programs can be examined to improve implementation and outcomes.

Plan-Do-Study-Act (PDSA): a quality improvement process useful for piloting and testing program changes.

FIGURE 11.2 ⬡ PDSA Infographic/Data Placemat Example

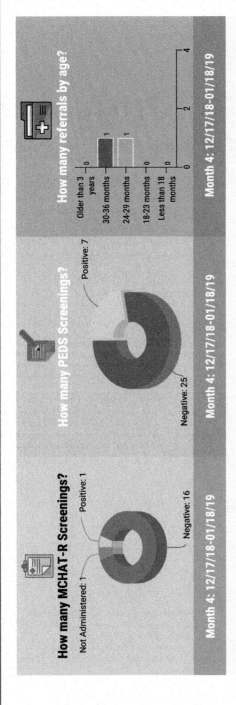

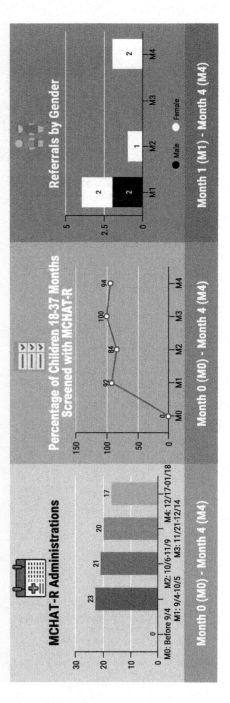

FIGURE 11.3 ● PDSA Process

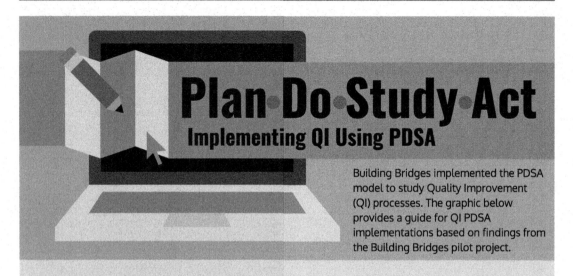

Plan·Do·Study·Act
Implementing QI Using PDSA

Building Bridges implemented the PDSA model to study Quality Improvement (QI) processes. The graphic below provides a guide for QI PDSA implementations based on findings from the Building Bridges pilot project.

ACT

What should be done based upon findings?
* Identify necessary changes.
* Determine next steps based on reflections.
* Move on to "Plan" to plan next steps.
Example:
Based on reflection from findings, program staff implemented changes, such as additional training, and processes for screening families when there were language barriers. Changes were tested in the next PDSA cycle.

PLAN

What do we want to accomplish?
* State objectives for the process improvement.
* Make a plan to implement the improvement.
* Move on to "Do" to implement the change.
Example:
Pediatric practices were identified that did not have routine screening of children for Autism Spectrum Disorder (ASD). An intervention was planned that included providing several education and trainings for office staff, nurse practitioners, and doctors.

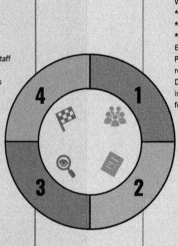

STUDY

What are the findings from the process improvement?
* Analyze the documented findings.
* Summarize what was learned from the QI project.
* Reflect on findings from the process QI project.
* Move on to "Act" to take action on findings.
Example:
Monthly data collections were reviewed; reports were provided to pilot sites. Early PDSA iterations showed problems with recording all data elements, as well as language barriers for screening families who did not speak English or Spanish.

DO

What is occurring during the process improvement?
* Implement QI project/process improvement.
* Monitor the process changes.
* Document implementation and unexpected events.
* Move on to "Study" to analyze documented findings.
Example:
The ASD screening pilot was implemented at two pediatric practices. The M-CHAT-R was used to screen patients younger than 37 months. Data from each practice were collected monthly.

stage, in which program staff implement the pilot. During this phase, evaluators collect information regarding implementation of the piloted change and results from that implementation. Concurrent with testing the program change, the *Study* phase is continually examining data and working closely with program leadership to identify areas of improvement. Finally, during the *Act* phase, modifications based upon findings during the study phase are determined. Once modifications are determined, the PDSA cycle starts anew with the modification being planned, implemented, studied, and revised. See Figure 11.2 for an example infographic from a PDSA pilot. This infographic was presented to staff monthly during the study phase of a PDSA initiative to examine where improvements could be made. The pilot used the Modified Checklist for Autism in Toddlers, Revised Version (MCHAT-R) as a tool to assess whether a child was at risk for Autism Spectrum Disorder (ASD; Robins et al., 2014). See Figure 11.3 for a summary of the PDSA process.

11.2.2 Member Checking

Another method for examining results, from the standpoint of confirming findings or determining the credibility of findings, is **member checking**. Member checking is the process of reviewing results, particularly qualitative results, in order to reduce researcher bias. The process seeks to verify, validate, or determine the credibility of the researcher's account and results (Doyle, 2007; Lub, 2015; Stake, 1995). Member checking allows research participants to provide systemic feedback after having the opportunity to review, check, confirm, or deny presented evaluation results (Lub, 2015; Stake, 1995). Practices like member checking and the involvement of participants and stakeholders in the interpretation process allow for verification of results prior to making changes based upon findings.

11.3 INTERPRETING RESULTS

Interpretation of results should be made in conjunction with the program's logic model and evaluation matrix. When interpreting results, the evaluation questions derived from your logic model and the indicators collected to address those questions should guide discussions. In addition, interpreting data collaboratively with stakeholders can facilitate understanding and use of findings. O'Sullivan (2004) provides many useful tips for involving stakeholders in collaboratively analyzing data and reviewing findings.

Interpretation should address the relationship between implementation and long-term goals. Presuming that the program was implemented and ongoing results were promising, to what extent do those results vary by the fidelity or type of implementation of program activities? This is especially important for programs that are implemented by different people and/or at different sites.

Member checking: the process of reviewing qualitative results to reduce researcher bias, as well as to verify, validate, or determine the credibility of the researcher's account and results.

For instance, the Responsive Classroom (www.responsiveclassroom.org) intervention has multiple components. Responsive Classroom is an approach to improve social-emotional learning and create educational environments conducive to learning. Responsive Classroom components include Morning Meetings, Interactive Modeling, Teacher Language, Logical Consequences, and Interactive Learning Structures. An evaluation of the impact of Responsive Classroom on school climate might not only focus on overall changes in climate across schools implementing the program, but also relate *how* the program was implemented at different schools to outcomes. For instance, do all components of Responsive Classroom need to be implemented with fidelity to have optimal impact on school climate? Also, how is climate different at schools that implement the entire program versus schools that implement only the Teacher Language and Morning Meetings components? During interpretation, consider how the program worked for different groups of participants and under different conditions.

Results should also be examined in relation to the proposed program's theory. Do evaluation findings support the program's theory? Were the assumptions underlying the program's theory validated? If not, how did the program work differently from the proposed theory? How can the theory and the logic model representing this theory be changed to reflect how the program worked? The logic model can be used as a tool to present evaluation findings, as well as to explain the relationships among components of the program. Updating the logic model to include results can be a useful reporting and dissemination tool.

11.3.1 Evaluation Standards of Accuracy

The Joint Committee on Standards for Educational Evaluation (1994) includes 12 standards related to accuracy of reported evaluation results. One such standard (A11) pertains to Justified Conclusions and states evaluation conclusions should be justified explicitly in evaluation reporting, so stakeholders can make determinations about the accuracy of the interpretation. Some of the other accuracy standards pertain to keeping accurate program documentation, considering the context of the program when interpreting findings, collecting reliable and valid information, using appropriate analytical techniques, and ensuring impartial reporting of findings. Stufflebeam and Coryn (2014) report on the Joint Committee's standards regarding merit and worth and extend them to include the dimensions of probity, feasibility, safety, significance, and equity. Their dimensions of value provide a useful framework for synthesizing evaluative information according to accuracy standards. Four of these dimensions—merit, worth, significance, and probity—are addressed here:

1. Merit: Evaluations that take into account and explicitly address accepted standards of quality in the field; evaluations that have intrinsic value.

2. Worth: Evaluations that are valuable to a group of people or in an area of need; evaluations that have extrinsic value.

3. Significance: Evaluations that take into consideration the implication of findings, including their importance and potential influence beyond the program itself.

4. Probity: Evaluations that are conducted with integrity, using ethical practices and honest interpretation of data.

These dimensions guide evaluators such that evaluations are mindful of providing reliable and valid evidence justification for interpretation of findings.

11.3.2 Cautions During Interpretation

Two common errors during results interpretation are overinterpretation and misinterpretation of results. Unless the evaluation design was a randomized, controlled experiment, results interpretation cannot reliably claim causal relationships. Indeed, there may be relationships between the program's activities and its outcomes (and hopefully there will be!), but unless all rival explanations for findings can be ruled out, causal associations cannot be claimed. Doing so would be an **overinterpretation** of your results.

Additionally, when interpreting results, it is important to consider possible alternative theories for your results. Considering and recognizing other explanations for or contributors to the findings from an evaluation does not diminish the significance of the findings, but rather shows an understanding of the environment within which the program was implemented.

Overinterpretation leads to **misinterpretation**. Misinterpreting a finding means that you have interpreted it incorrectly. It might be due to overinterpretations, asserting causality when the evaluation design does not support such claims, or wrongly concluding what the results actually mean. For example, students completing an end-of-semester course evaluation may rate the professor highly if their grade was high and they liked the friendliness of the instructor. On the other hand, students who are failing the course because they did not turn in assignments might rate the course as low quality and the professor as ineffective. Measures intending to measure quality, but that are based on or highly influenced by satisfaction, are often misinterpreted.

Another example is using report card grades in elementary school as a measure of achievement. Often in elementary schools, grades include factors unrelated to actual learning, such as attendance, effort, and participation. My daughter had a teacher who would give extra credit points if students brought in canned foods for the local food bank. Interpreting her grade as a pure measure of academic achievement would be a misinterpretation.

Overinterpretation: to claim that findings are a direct result of a program's activities or strategies in the absence of a research design that would warrant causal conclusions.

Misinterpretation: to claim that findings are something different than they are, that is, interpreting findings incorrectly.

QUICK CHECK

1. When should evaluation results be examined? Why is it important to review evaluation results on an ongoing basis?

2. How can quality improvement models be used as part of the ongoing process of examining results?

3. How can member checking be used during results examination to improve the credibility of results?

4. How might evaluation results be interpreted incorrectly?

Over time, it is a combination of factors, some unrelated to the program itself, that interact to create results. Documenting the program's environment can guard against misinterpretation of results and instead provide a thoughtful description of the circumstances under which the results were obtained.

11.4 COMMUNICATING EVALUATION RESULTS

As discussed in the previous section, programs have the best chance of success if evaluation findings are communicated to program staff on an ongoing and regular basis. These formative findings are critical to program improvement. Setting a schedule for regular meetings between program staff and the evaluation team, as well as building these communications into the evaluation timeline, will ensure that evaluation findings can truly help the program during its operation. Evaluators can provide quick feedback at any stage of the program to help improve its implementation. For instance, if an evaluator notices from observing professional development sessions that teachers are leaving the training early to attend another faculty meeting, the evaluator might give quick feedback to program staff that the timing of sessions may not be convenient (and for this reason, teachers are not receiving the full benefit of the training).

Quick feedback: a method of providing ongoing and timely informal feedback to program staff to improve operations.

Suppose the evaluator finds during the early stages of the program (through interviews or classroom observations) that teachers are struggling with the technology needed to use the program in their classroom. The evaluator can give quick feedback at a monthly meeting or through an email that technology support and technical assistance are needed in the classroom. Remember, however, an evaluator should not report on individual teachers or classrooms unless consent to do so has been obtained. Doing so could violate the ethical obligation to participants in the evaluation and undermine future data collection efforts. Even quick feedback should maintain confidentiality.

11.4.1 Determining the Audience

In addition to relaying evaluation findings on an ongoing basis for formative purposes, it is also important to communicate summative evaluation findings regarding the extent of the program's success. The first step to communicating results is to determine the audience. If there are multiple audiences, (e.g., program staff and policymakers), you may want to consider multiple methods of reporting findings, including reports, presentations, discussions, and short briefs. It might be useful to make a list of (1) all people and organizations that should receive communication regarding results and (2) any other stakeholders who would like to know about the evaluation findings. For each audience, ask yourself these questions:

- What background do they have regarding the program?

- What will they want to know?

- How much time and interest will they have?

- What do you want the audience to know?

Thinking through these questions will help you tailor your communication. Here are some tips to keep in mind:

- If the audience already has background information on the program, try to focus on providing only specific findings from your evaluation. If the audience is not familiar with the program, you can use the program theory and logic model to introduce the program and provide a description of how the program is intended to work.

- Address the goals and objectives that you believe the audience would most want to know about.

- If the audience wants information immediately, write a short summary of major findings and follow up with a longer, more detailed report.

- Do not be afraid to include recommendations or identify possible areas for change. Recommendations are a critical piece to making sure evaluation findings are used appropriately. If evaluation findings indicate change is needed, you are going to have to talk about it sooner or later, and having it in the report is a good way to start the conversation.

Effective communication and reporting of evaluation results promotes the development of successful programs, informs program improvement, and can help to end failed program efforts. Evaluation findings, if carefully derived, qualified, and presented, provide participants and stakeholders with an evidence-based foundation upon which to make informed decisions.

11.4.2 Determining the Methods of Reporting

The key to communicating evaluation outcomes is to make complex ideas, procedures, and results understandable to those with limited backgrounds in the subject. While evaluation results can be reported in both formal and informal ways, they should be presented in formats that are most comprehensible to intended audiences. This includes consideration of things such as reporting method, presentation language and tone, as well as the depth of detail.

A formal evaluation report is not the only way to communicate results. It is one way and perhaps the most traditional way, but there are many other methods available that may be more accessible and useful to the intended audience. Other reporting methods include

- Memo or letter;
- Infographic or data placemat;
- Evaluation or policy brief;
- Newsletter;
- Conference call or individual phone call;
- Presentation before a board or committee, or at a conference;
- Publication in a journal, newspaper, or magazine;
- Storytelling;
- Workshop; or
- Web page or blog.

Evaluation reports typically have a common format. First is an executive summary or overview that notes key findings. In fact, some audiences will only read the executive summary, so it is important that it includes the most important information and perhaps enough information to convince the reader to keep reading. Other sections might include

- Introduction (including program background and theory);
- Evaluation design (including logic model, evaluation questions, and evaluation methods);
- Results (including all findings from the evaluation, organized by evaluation question);

- Conclusions (including your interpretation of the results);

- Recommendations (including how the program should proceed based on your findings); or

- Limitations (including limitations based on evaluation design, analysis of data, and interpretation of findings).

Whether your communication takes the form of a formal evaluation report, a brief, or an infographic, it is important to include some, if not all, of the above sections. For example, a full evaluation report would have all sections, while a brief might include introduction, results, and conclusions. An infographic, on the other hand, may have a small bit of information on the program itself but would likely primarily focus on the results and conclusions. Reporting structure will be discussed in more detail below.

11.4.3 Formal Reports, Briefs, Infographics, and Presentations

The breadth and depth of an evaluation report will likely depend on the evaluation questions asked and the size and scope of the program evaluated. In some cases, there are the several types of reports developed for one evaluation, with separate versions for different audiences (Weiss, 1998). These report types are discussed below. Evaluators should discuss the reporting expectations with program staff at the start of the project to ensure the reports are responsive, useful, and informative. Six primary types of reporting are described below: formal reports, quick reports, briefs, infographics, presentations, and storytelling.

Formal Reports. Most commonly, a written comprehensive report is developed for key stakeholders and sponsors. This report, typically given at the end of the evaluation, details the purpose of the evaluation, evaluation design, results, conclusions, and discussion. Its purpose is to respond directly to the evaluation objectives and questions. While this type of report may be useful for some stakeholders, it may be quite burdensome for those looking for a brief summary. In such cases, it is more suitable to develop a shorter version of the evaluation and its findings, such as a brief or infographic (discussed below). Large, comprehensive reports are the most likely to be tossed aside by audiences that find little value in the details of the study. However, they provide important documentation for the evaluation and critical information to program leadership. In addition, for many evaluations that are federally funded, a formal report is required at least annually. When creating formal reports, I typically refer to them as research reports or technical reports.

Quick Reports. In many evaluations, equivalent value is found in both formal reporting and informal reporting. Waiting until year-end to provide evaluation findings wastes many opportunities for the evaluation to positively impact the program. Providing frequent and ongoing information to program staff enables them to monitor and improve implementation. I typically refer to this as quick or supplemental reporting. For instance, several programs I evaluate have regular training sessions for parents, community members, and service providers. One of the early objectives of this program is to increase participation in training and another is to increase participant knowledge. At the end of each session, we collect participation logs and administer a survey to examine participant knowledge, as well as to gather participant feedback. My policy is to turn around the evaluation results from these sessions within one week. We analyze data and provide program staff with a quick report that I refer to as a supplemental report. These reports have enabled program staff to respond to issues with training in a timely manner and to the benefit of the program. At the end of the year, we also aggregate findings across sessions and create a more formal evaluation report of the training program.

Briefs. Another useful way to communicate evaluation findings is through research briefs. A brief is a shortened form of the full evaluation report. It is similar to an executive summary and is often created to accompany the formal report. In fact, sometimes I use the brief as the executive summary in the full report. That way, in addition to being part of the formal report, it can also be used as a stand-alone document. Briefs usually take the form of a one- to four-page document highlighting program implementation progress in addition to both intermediate or final evaluation results. They are typically geared toward an audience that might find the results useful, but does not need to read or would not be interested in reading the full report. Thus, evaluation briefs are more likely than longer reports to be read due to their shortened length and concentrated information.

Infographics. Infographics are increasingly being used in evaluations to provide quick, graphically enhanced one-page documentation of results. Infographics allow you to present or communicate a snapshot of results that is both easily accessible and understandable for clients. The inclusion of graphics gives readers a unique presentation of results that can be shared with many stakeholders. The infographic in Figure 11.4 was used to highlight specific findings related to chronic absenteeism in the 2015–2016 school year, in preparation for an evaluation to understand more about chronic absenteeism. Similar to an infographic is a data placemat. Data placemats are infographics in landscape mode that can be used to facilitate conversation among program staff or program participants around evaluation results (see Figure 11.2). I have used them in QI projects as a way for participants and staff to come to their own conclusions about findings and propose changes based on those findings. We use them over lunch data talks as the placemat, so staff have them in front of them while they eat and can jot down notes directly on the placemat. As you can see from the data placemat in Figure 11.2 and the infographic in Figure 11.4, these one-page reviews of data use both graphics and text to emphasize key points and findings.

There are many web-based tools to aid you in making infographics, some of them free to students. The infographic software I use (venngage.com) allows our evaluation

FIGURE 11.4 ● Infographic Example: Chronic Absenteeism

TRENDS AND ISSUES RELATED TO
CHRONIC ABSENTEEISM

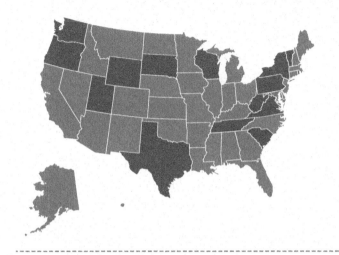

7 million students
were reported chronically absent during the 2015–2016 school year.

Chronic absenteeism has been defined as missing 15 days of school or more.

Research shows that chronic absenteeism ...

...negatively affects student **achievement.**

...negatively affects students starting as early as **kindergarten.**

...increases the chances a student will **drop out** of school.

...negatively impacts students' **peers** as well.

...increases feelings of **alienation** and social disengagement.

...has more harmful effects on **at-risk students** including minority students, low-income students, English learners, and students with disabilities.

team to share and collaborate on the same infographics. I also use this infographic software in one of my courses. My students are always shocked at how easily they can create professional-looking infographics in a very short period of time. I do believe that providing evaluation data using infographics has the potential to increase use and facilitate a greater impact from evaluation findings. I have found many stakeholders no longer want traditional evaluation reports, because they do not have the time or patience to read them. Providing infographics streamlines the process of sharing findings and allows stakeholders to easily share evaluation results with others. However, we do still create traditional evaluation reports to support our infographics, as a one-page report does not have space for background information, description of the evaluation design, how the data were collected and analyzed, and a presentation of all findings. If an infographic is well done, it even may prompt someone to read the entire evaluation report.

Oral Reports/Presentations. Oral reporting or presentations of evaluation findings usually accompany a written report. Presenting evaluation findings orally allows for increased engagement from stakeholders and communities. For example, I have found that many in attendance at an oral presentation may have read the evaluation brief or seen the infographic, yet are present to engage in a question-and-answer session about the evaluation and its findings to increase their understanding.

The evaluation field has recently pressed the need for reporting in more culturally sensitive or responsive ways, citing that oral reports can be more effective at communicating evaluation findings than written reports in certain contexts as they increase receptivity due to historical oral traditions of many communities (Hood & Rosenstein, 2005). All reporting methods should be culturally sensitive and socially responsible in their format and content.

Storytelling. Storytelling is an approach to sharing evaluation findings through the voices of the participants and using multiple modes of delivery (California Endowment, 2007). It is authentic, providing genuine and accurate context to findings (Smith-Halstead, 2011). Storytelling might involve video excerpts and narrative accounts in the participants' own words, as well as theater, poetry, music, and art. Note that storytelling is an approach that should be planned for from the start of an evaluation. Personal stories and narratives are collected and their mode of collection may be relevant to the storytelling.

Finally, with so many reporting methods, it is easy to lose track of what reports are created for each evaluation. Yet it is critically important to know what information has been released and in what form. "In the Real World" shares a system that is used by the Center for Research in Education and Social Policy to track dissemination efforts.

IN THE REAL WORLD . . .

The Center for Research in Education and Social Policy (CRESP) at the University of Delaware distributes over 50 reports each year in multiple formats. To keep track of what reports were released and the version numbers of various reports, CRESP created a cataloging, report numbering, and tracking system. The system includes six types of evaluation reports: Technical Reports, Supplemental Reports, Research Briefs, Policy Briefs, Infographics, and Research Reports. Each report is used for different purposes; however, the number system to track released reports is the same. The beginning letter(s) of each report number indicates the type of report, followed by the year of release. At the end of each report number is the sequential number of the report and the version number. For example, S19-049.2 would indicate the report is the second version of the 49th report produced in the 2019 supplemental report series. RB19-002.1 would indicate the report is the first version of the second report produced in the 2019 research brief series.

Report Type	Report Series	Description
Technical Report	T series	Comprehensive and/or annual evaluation reports detailing methods and findings across multiple components of an evaluation. Technical reports include an executive summary and recommendations. These reports are provided to program staff to understand program effectiveness and inform summative decision making, as well as to program funders to satisfy reporting requirements.
Supplemental Report	S series	Small, quick evaluation reports presenting results with little interpretation. Supplemental reports do not have an executive summary or recommendations. These reports are provided to program staff to understand program progress and inform program improvement.
Policy Brief	P series	Reports that are research syntheses, summarizing recent research on a topical area. Policy briefs are intended to assist with evidence-based program or evaluation design as well as to inform policy making. These reports are typically disseminated widely and posted on the CRESP website.
Infographic	I series	One-page graphical representations of program findings. These reports are provided to program staff who often distribute them to program participants and other stakeholders.
Research Report	R series	Reports that detail research design and findings, similar to technical reports but are intended for a research audience. Research reports are disseminated widely and posted on the CRESP website.
Research Brief	RB series	Two- to four-page reports that summarize research or evaluation findings. Research briefs are similar to executive summaries but may incorporate elements of infographics. They are typically disseminated widely and posted on the CRESP website.

11.4.4 Writing the Report

Beyond providing a comprehensive albeit concise report for stakeholders, a strong evaluation report must leave the reader convinced of the substance of the report and with a clear understanding of what to do next. The content of the report, while often technical, should be concise and its message clear. Those not directly familiar with the program or the evaluation, or even the technical know-how for conducting an evaluation, should also be able to appreciate the report and, after a brief review, walk away knowing what worked, what did not work, and what needs to be done next.

While there are many methods of reporting, as discussed above, the formal evaluation report (referred to as technical report or research report above) is the primary or "base" report from which briefs, infographics, and presentations might be developed. A technical report or research report is more often than not a fairly standardized document that includes the following core components: cover page, executive summary, introduction, program description, evaluation design and methods, evaluation findings, conclusions, recommendations, references, and appendices. Some may also want to include acknowledgments, a table of contents, and a list of tables or figures. The following provides an overview of a standard set of elements for an evaluation report.

Cover page: the first page of an evaluation report; includes the title of the report, authors, and date of report.

Cover Page. While it may go without saying that a **cover page** is needed, there are several recommended details, which, if omitted, can result in challenges later on. Each evaluation report cover page should include the title of the report, recipient names, authors, the date of the report, and a preferred citation. While a cover page is more technical than informative, it does provide the opportunity to present your report professionally.

Executive summary: a synopsis of the program, evaluation, and key findings; designing the executive summary as a stand-alone brief gives flexibility with dissemination of findings.

Executive Summary. An **executive summary** is often included to provide an overview of what can be found in the full report. An executive summary is a synopsis of the program, the evaluation, and key findings. Stakeholders can use and share executive summaries to highlight the progress of their programs without having to share the details of the full report. Designing the executive summary such that it is also a stand-alone brief gives you the flexibility to disseminate either document depending upon the audience.

Table of contents: an optional section that is usually included for larger reports to guide the reader through the document.

Table of Contents (optional). A **table of contents** is usually included for larger reports to guide the reader through the document. It includes the headers of each section along with their starting page number. It also allows the reader to know, in detail, what to expect in the report and on what page to find particular information.

Introduction: a report section that includes an overview of the program and the evaluation; typically provides background information on the program and details the structure of the report, including a description of each section and the contents they cover.

Introduction. The **introduction** typically begins with an overview of the program and the evaluation. It may also give background information on the program, as well as describe the structure of the report including a description of each section and the contents they cover. The introduction is a good place to highlight the goals of the report as well as how and for whom it is intended to be used.

Program Description. Because evaluations are specific to the programs that they intend to examine, a relatively detailed **program description** is needed early on in the report. The description should include the history of the program, such as the length of time it has been in place, where it has been implemented, and in what ways it was implemented, noting changes as appropriate. A description of the funding for the program and recognition of any partners or organizations responsible for program operations are also commonly integrated into this section. A detailed description of program goals and objectives should be provided with an eye toward helping the reader understand the problem that the program is intended to address and the benefits that the program is designed to achieve. Along with the program's goals, listing the program's strategies can assist the reader in understanding how the program intends to reach its goals. Finally, the program's logic model representing the theory behind the program should be included in this section.

Evaluation Design and Methods. The **evaluation design and methods** section is the first part of the report to provide the reader with specific details of the evaluation. This section of the report has two subsections: evaluation design and evaluation methods.

Evaluation design includes three components: evaluation purpose, evaluation questions, and overall design. First, this section includes a description of the purpose of the evaluation, outlining how the evaluation intends to inform the program. If specific measures were taken to tailor the evaluation to the local context or culture, a description of efforts should be embedded in this section. If the evaluation builds on prior work, this section can be used to describe what has been done in the past with a particular emphasis on the similarities or differences in methods, as well as any key takeaways or results upon which this report may build. Any limitations and constraints of the evaluation should also be addressed. Nearly every evaluation is limited by time or funding, which typically drive what can and cannot be evaluated. The section can incorporate what was not evaluated alongside the limitations or constraints inherent in the evaluation design.

Second, the evaluation questions used to focus the evaluation are included in the evaluation design section. While the primary evaluation questions should be clearly delineated in the text, it is helpful to include the evaluation matrix in the report to detail the evaluation questions associated with each program objective.

Next, the evaluation design includes the overall design of the evaluation. This section will include a general description of the program participants, as well as how participants were identified for inclusion in the evaluation. For example, if the evaluation

Program description: a report section that provides a detailed description of the program; includes the history of the program, a recognition of any program funders, an accounting of program goals and objectives, a list of the program's strategies, and a copy of the program's logic model.

Evaluation design and methods: a report section that details both the evaluation design and evaluation methods; evaluation design includes a description of the evaluation purpose, evaluation questions, and overall research design; evaluation methods includes a description of indicators, targets, data sources, data collection methods, and data analysis procedures; the evaluation matrix should be included in this section.

included a sample of participants, this section would explain how the sample was selected, the sample size, and a description of the sample. If the program was implemented at multiple sites, the sites should be described along with how they were chosen. Similarly, if the program was implemented with more than one group, each group will be described along with how they came to participate in the evaluation. Most important, this section will identify whether the evaluation design was nonexperimental, quasi-experimental, or a randomized controlled trial. It will delineate the length of the evaluation and the number of measures used to examine impact (e.g., pre/post, post-only, etc.). Any special features of the design, for instance, whether it used time-series data, involved longitudinal data collection, or used matched pairs, should be described. A detailed description of the evaluation design is necessary so the reader can understand the rigor behind the evaluation and thus be able to interpret findings within an appropriate framework.

The second subsection is evaluation methods. Here, the methods used to collect the data necessary to address the evaluation questions are described. In addition to detailing the methods used to collect data and ascertain findings, it may also be useful to provide readers with insight as to why these particular methods and approaches were used. Similarly, if a theoretical framework was used to guide the evaluation, this might be included in the evaluation design and methods section. The evaluation matrix introduced when discussing evaluation questions can be reintroduced and used to connect evaluation questions to indicators and targets, as well as the particular data sources or measures used to examine indicators. In addition to showing how the data were collected, the matrix will explain when the data were collected and how they were analyzed. In addition, a description of instruments used for data collection would be included. If the instruments included surveys or interview protocols that are not copyrighted, consider including them in an appendix. Finally, if there are any methodological limitations that go above and beyond the limitations discussed in the design subsection, they should be noted here.

Evaluation Findings.   The **evaluation findings** section is typically organized sequentially in alignment with the evaluation questions. Following each question, data informing the question are presented, often including tables, in addition to the analytical findings. Sample size parameters, response rates, and similar information such as the proportion of omitted responses will help the reader understand and interpret the representativeness of the data. At the close of this section, a brief summary of each finding by evaluation question should be provided with as much clarity as possible.

Conclusions.   The **conclusions** section should be used to summarize any evaluation findings in a shortened but comprehensive manner. Conclusions should draw upon and make connections to overarching evaluation goals. A conclusion should provide a broad

---

Evaluation findings: a report section where results are organized sequentially in alignment with the evaluation questions; data informing each question are presented with details regarding statistics or themes, as well as sample sizes.

Conclusions: a report section where evaluation findings are summarized in a shortened, comprehensive manner; conclusions should consider the implications of findings on the program.

perspective and consider the implications of evaluation findings on the program. Often, conclusions will mirror the content included in the executive summary.

Recommendations. The intention of the **recommendations** section is to bring to light the value of the evaluation. It should clearly convey an actionable message to the reader. Whereas findings often describe impacts or shortcomings, the recommendations offer solutions. Here, the evaluator is able to translate findings into actionable strategies intended to improve the program or its processes, or expand positive effects. Recommendations also seek to alleviate the causes of negative effects and to improve the outcomes of problematic practices. They can elevate promising or positive practices and outcomes. A practice that has proven helpful is drafting a list of recommendations early in the report development process to share with program staff, in order to garner feedback on their feasibility and solicit input on specific wording. Allowing the potentially impacted groups to think about and shape recommendations before the evaluation report is issued can be fundamentally critical to future implementation. The insight and finesse needed to directly and clearly state what changes are needed is not easy, and is often best developed in concert with evaluation team members in an iterative approach. Recommendations are ideally written succinctly with little ambiguity, though the inclusion of suggestions or programming options can more gently address needs. Above all, recommendations should be practical, should consider costs (affordability), and should seek to maximize implementation feasibility all while being backed by the data that inform them.

References. As is the case with any report, a list of **references** in a standardized style, for instance, APA (American Psychological Association), MLA (Modern Language Association), or CMS (Chicago Manual of Style) format, should be included.

Appendices. Appendices can be used to provide supplementary material to the report. For instance, **appendices** might include copies of data collection instruments such as surveys or focus group discussion guides and may also incorporate larger data tables.

11.5 ENHANCING REPORTING AND COMMUNICATION

Whether you present evaluation findings using a written report or through an oral presentation, an important way to enhance the communication of findings is by summarizing them in either a tabular or graphical format. The following "In the Real World" includes a few hints on how reporting and communication of evaluation findings might be enhanced.

Recommendations: the last major section of the report; used to translate findings into actionable strategies intended to improve the program or its processes.

References: a list of resources cited in the evaluation report.

Appendices: supplementary material located at the end of the report.

IN THE REAL WORLD . . .

In their series of interviews with expert evaluators, Fitzpatrick, Christie, and Mark (2009) talked with Debra Rog about her experiences evaluating the Homeless Families Program (HFP), a housing program for homeless families. She shares how and when she communicated results from the evaluation. Her comprehensive reporting was intended to inform multiple audiences, including the Robert Wood Johnson Foundation (RWJ) and the U.S. Department of Housing and Urban Development (HUD). She hoped to influence future policy development. Her work demonstrates the breadth of reporting that can occur throughout an evaluation:

We communicated results in a variety of different ways. We presented results at the annual program meetings to key stakeholders from RWJ, HUD, and the sites throughout the process. We also tried to communicate information to the sites every three months. In the fourth year of the evaluation, we actually made a formal presentation in each of the five sites on their own site-specific interim results using a community forum.

Regarding the community forum, Rog shared,

The forums were generally designed for the purposes of information sharing, with some sites strategically inviting some more political guests in the hope of sparking interest for continued funding. In most sites, having descriptive data, even if not definitive on outcomes, was a step above what officials usually have on service programs.

Rog further explained other methods of communicating results:

We also made a couple of presentations at HUD and at a number of academic, professional, service provider, and homelessness meetings. The Foundation also arranged a Capitol Hill briefing after HFP ended, in which we presented the evaluation findings, the national office described its role, and a few sites described their projects. The meeting was a chance to bring the results to federal policymakers, folks in other interested national associations and agencies, and other providers. (Fitzpatrick et al., 2009, p. 149)

11.5.1 Clarity

Write or communicate your evaluation report in language and tone appropriate for targeted audiences. Avoid unnecessary evaluation or statistical terminology. Most important, use language that is culturally appropriate and respectful of cultural values and protocols (Hood, Hopson, & Kirkhart, 2015). Addressing clarity and the cultural appropriateness of language used in your report will likely increase the credibility and utility of evaluation results.

11.5.2 Timeliness

When evaluation findings and reports are presented at appropriate times, they are found to be most utilized by program stakeholders. While your evaluation plan should document reporting times, you must be aware of other opportune times to present evaluation findings—particularly when they can significantly enhance or hinder implementation efforts. Providing formal and informal reports of findings is likely to improve implementation, as well as build trust and enhance collaboration between evaluators and program staff.

11.5.3 Limitations

While we all aim to implement our evaluations perfectly, we often face limitations. It is ethically sound to acknowledge where your evaluation falls short, and it is therefore recommended to explicitly include these limitations in your report (Weiss, 1998). Stakeholders are more likely to trust evaluative findings knowing that they are transparent about any evaluation limitations. Did your response rates fall short? Did you have a representative sample of respondents? Acknowledging shortcomings of an evaluation can add value and credibility to the report and to your role as an evaluator.

11.5.4 Graphics

An effective way to enhance the use of evaluation results is to embed graphics into the report. While the report will likely include descriptive text summarizing evaluation results, too much text can make it difficult to interpret or synthesize findings. Organizing results visually can increase readers' understanding of what happened during the evaluation and what conclusions to draw. There are several approaches to graphically displaying data to make them more digestible to various audiences. Using tools such as charts or tables enhances the readers' ability to comprehend results and make connections to the conclusions. Your report may have several different types or structures of data that you would like to highlight. You may have both qualitative and quantitative data, but you may also have single data points, comparative data, or trends in data that need to be displayed. Determining the best way to organize and display data in your report is key to having readers interpret evaluation findings properly.

Opportunities to graphically display evaluation findings are endless, regardless of the type of data you want to display (e.g., quantitative or qualitative) or the scope of detail desired. Displaying data graphically, or data visualization, uses images that are representative of data to enhance readability and comprehension. In addition, graphics assist viewers with the exploration, examination, and communication of data (Azzam, Evergreen, Germuth, & Kistler, 2013). Products resulting from this process include, but are not limited to, tables, bar charts, pie charts, line charts, timelines, and heat maps. Table 11.1 shows some commonly used graphics.

TABLE 11.1 ● Commonly Used Graphic Formats

Graphic	Quantitative Data	Qualitative Data	When to Use
Pie Chart	X		Compares parts of a whole
Bar/Column Chart	X		Displays/compares size or amounts

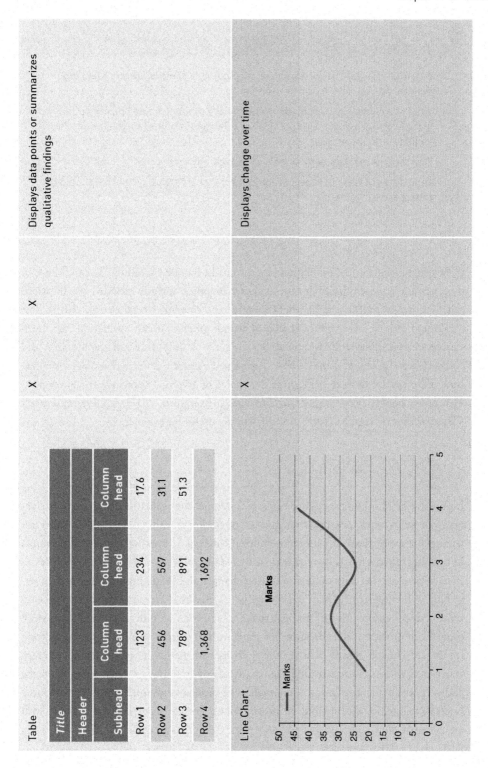

Table

Title			
Header			
Subhead	Column head	Column head	Column head
Row 1	123	234	17.6
Row 2	456	567	31.1
Row 3	789	891	51.3
Row 4	1,368	1,692	

X   X   Displays data points or summarizes qualitative findings

Line Chart

Marks

— Marks

X   Displays change over time

QUICK CHECK

1. Why is it important to consider the audience when communicating evaluation results?

2. What stakeholder groups might prefer to have evaluation findings presented using a formal evaluation report? What stakeholder groups might prefer to see findings in an infographic?

3. What are the primary components of an evaluation report?

4. What type of data is best represented in a bar chart? What type of data could be represented in a table?

Data visualizations in the evaluation report must be handled carefully. Be careful not to over- or underrepresent findings in your chosen graphics, and any included visualizations must accurately reflect and highlight targeted information (Azzam et al., 2013). The most important factors in your decision to include graphics in any evaluation communications are readability and interpretability. Be sure that font, text and graphic sizes, and colors clearly display data and results. Stephanie Evergreen, an expert in data visualization, offers several tools to help guide the choice of graphics to include in your report. Two of her books, *Presenting Data Effectively* (Evergreen, 2017) and *Effective Data Visualization* (Evergreen, 2016), are particularly useful for evaluators.

11.6 CHAPTER SUMMARY

Interpretation of findings does not begin at the end of the evaluation. Rather, for evaluation to have an impact, examination and interpretation of findings are ongoing processes throughout every phase of a program's implementation. In that way, evaluation is much like quality improvement. Frameworks such as **Plan-Do-Study-Act (PDSA)** and processes such as **member checking** can aid in testing changes and validating findings. Still, interpreting evaluation results may not always be as easy as it appears. The challenge is to create a clear interpretation of findings that does not over- or undersell results but instead provides information and direction for program improvement. When communicating findings, evaluators should consider the audience, the method of reporting, how to represent data within the report, and the timing of communication. Depending upon the audience, evaluation communication might take various forms, including formal reports, briefs, infographics, storytelling, or presentations. Formal reports typically begin with an **executive summary** and include an **introduction, program description, evaluation design and methods** section, **evaluation findings, conclusions,** and **recommendations.**

Limitations can be incorporated into the design and findings sections, or presented in a separate section. Some reports may also include a table of contents, references, and appendices. Considering culture and context throughout the interpretations communication process is vital to ensuring the utility and credibility of the evaluation such that findings are used to inform programs and policy.

Reflection and Application

1. How is evaluation like the quality improvement process? How might the PDSA framework be incorporated into evaluations as a method of examining results of small programmatic changes?

2. Why is it important to consider accuracy standards, including merit, worth, significance, and probity, when examining and interpreting data?

3. For an evaluation based on a nonexperimental design, how might you present findings that show a relationship between a program's therapy intervention and decreased incidences of anxiety? How might you present these findings differently if the evaluation was based on an RCT design?

4. How might you report findings from the above evaluation of a program to decrease anxiety to the funder? How might you report the same findings to a policymaker?

5. Go to the Evergreen Data website (www.stephanieevergreen.com) and explore some of the example data visualizations. What visualizations do you find the most intuitive and informative? How might you incorporate these visualizations in your evaluations?

6. Venngage is a web-based infographics software platform. Go to the Venngage website (www .venngage.com) and create a trial account. Try creating your own infographic.

INFORM AND REFINE

Using Evaluation Results

Coauthored With Allison Karpyn

Evaluations should always be conducted in ways that increase the likelihood that the findings will be used for learning, decision making, and taking action.

—Hallie Preskill and Nathalie Jones (2009)

Upon completion of this chapter, you should be able to

- Explain the role of historical context in evaluation use.
- Develop a comprehensive list of stakeholders and their interests.
- Describe how evaluation results can be used for program improvement and accountability.
- Explain how evaluation results can be used to examine cost-benefit and cost-effectiveness.
- Discuss how people influence the use of evaluation results.
- Identify critical factors that drive the use of evaluation findings.
- Discuss effective techniques for presenting evaluation findings.
- Describe the change process in the context of evaluation use and impact.

FIGURE 12.1 ⬡ Embedded Evaluation Model

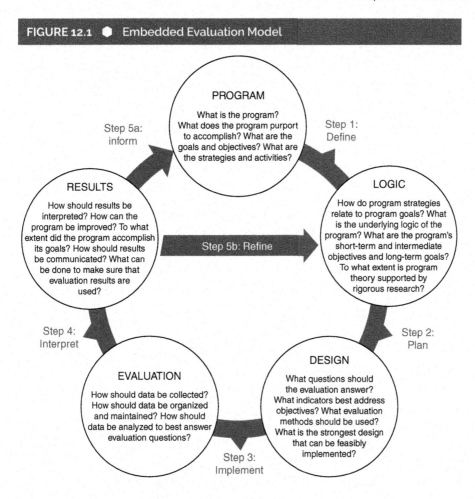

12.1 PURPOSE OF EVALUATION

The primary purpose of evaluation is to produce actionable findings that can be used for decision making. As discussed in Chapter 1, this decision making may be focused on improving the program or on drawing conclusions about effectiveness and impact. Thus, a critical component of the embedded evaluation process, informing and refining the program, is dependent upon the use of evaluation results. As evaluators, we are responsible for not only reporting findings, but also facilitating their use by different stakeholders.

At first glance, the question "How do I make sure the evaluation results are used?" may seem unnecessary. After all, isn't the purpose of evaluation to use the findings? Moreover, if a funder or project partner requests data, why is it that we, as evaluators, should even worry about how those results are used? As it turns out, the practice of evaluation is not as simple as conducting the evaluation and handing over the results. Instead, time and strategic attention are given to working with program partners and policy leaders to ensure meaningful and actionable results are achieved in a way that supports program growth and ultimately improves outcomes for individuals.

Earlier chapters have focused on the ways that funders and critical program partners are integrated into the evaluation design such that findings are tailored toward needs, and processes are enabled to ensure ongoing bidirectional input. Further, we have discussed how reports can be structured to provide thorough yet accessible data, and how to generate synthesized recommendations relevant to the end user.

The focus of this chapter is the fifth and last stage in the embedded evaluation process—using evaluation results. Its emphasis is on how we as evaluators can facilitate the use of the evaluation results in terms of both outcomes and process findings. Our goal is to support program improvements and accountability as well as to help advance conclusions so that the field of interest can grow.

This chapter is organized in several sections addressing first how you can promote the utilization of findings in a pre-evaluation phase and then, once the evaluation begins, ways in which utilization efforts can be supported. We conclude with a discussion of how data dissemination can be undertaken, with an emphasis on the role of people and personalities, and approaches during the post-evaluation phase to support program improvement and continually refine a program's theory of action. We move beyond the nuts and bolts of the content of an evaluation, past its design or even its alignment with the key stakeholders' objectives. Our emphasis shifts toward the importance of heightened awareness of the politics of evaluation and the role that personality and communication styles play. Indeed, the change process that evaluation is intended to inform requires careful integration and understanding, diligence in presenting data that at times may be difficult to hear, and a sensitivity to the importance of staffing and staff quality.

12.2 PRE-EVALUATION: EFFORTS TO PROMOTE UTILIZATION

Throughout this text, we refer to the importance of designing an actionable evaluation, one in which the funder, program leadership, and policymakers can understand and use results. The embedded evaluation approach we have followed adopts this viewpoint from Patton's utilization-focused evaluation. As introduced in Chapter 4, utilization-focused evaluation (UFE) is a collaborative approach to evaluation that is focused on how evaluation results will be used by stakeholders (Patton, 2008, 2013). Considerations of use should begin during the earliest stages of evaluation. Indeed, an actionable evaluation starts with a clear understanding of the program, study questions based on the program's theory, and a foundation of mutual understanding of the purpose behind the evaluation. As such, the first stage in accomplishing evaluation utilization comes well before the reporting phase; it begins in the development of clear communication channels and the establishment of crucial and trusted relationships with funders, key stakeholders, program leadership, and staff. Further, developing a process that requires from the start of the partnership that the evaluation team and the program leadership team define the program, design the evaluation, examine data, and determine reporting mechanisms together creates a foundation for collaboration, mutual ownership of results, and, ultimately, utilization.

12.2.1 Knowing Your Stakeholders

Knowing your stakeholders and thinking through their likely interests and needs when it comes to the evaluation is essential. Reviewing the range of possible stakeholder groups, including specific facets of government, names of legislators and their staffers, school leadership, corporations, parents, the media, and lobbyists, who may be interested in results, negative or positive, is prudent. Of course, too, there is also a considerable benefit to understanding the funding agency and the names of critical stakeholders within that agency. The perspectives of the funder, including historical interests, the rationale for the investment, and the larger portfolios of work that the funder is currently investing in should also be identified. Establishing a common understanding of who the most critical stakeholders are early on helps to shape the context for evaluation use and the format of evaluation products or reports.

Once stakeholders have been identified and listed, a **stakeholder matrix** might be created. A stakeholder matrix is simply a spreadsheet or table that includes each stakeholder group and the specific interests they may have in the evaluation results. For example, a policymaker interested in economic development may be most interested in the economic impacts of the program in terms of job creation, changes in neighborhood housing prices, and related indicators. Because social programs often reach across sectors, it is often valuable to sit down with program leadership to discuss the variety of process and outcome indicators and their potential meaning to specific stakeholders. Ask questions such as these:

1. To what extent should evaluation reporting emphasize some issues more than others?

2. How will stakeholders use evaluation findings?

3. Which stakeholders are likely to be critical in order for findings to impact the program or policy?

Stakeholder matrix: a spreadsheet or table that includes each stakeholder group and the specific interests they may have in the evaluation results.

4. What are some outcomes that may be new for the field, or of interest to a stakeholder group that is just coming to know this work?

5. To what extent is broadening the appeal of the evaluation findings to those outside of the typical or identified stakeholder groups relevant or valuable?

Such conversations may have economic, educational, health, and criminal justice implications. Further, during conversations, it may also be prudent to discuss methods of presenting information to stakeholders who are likely to accept evaluation findings, as well as those who may be inclined to disagree with the impact or relevance of the findings. For example, determining what contrary-minded stakeholders believe and potentially would be persuaded by is an essential context for reporting.

12.2.2 Understanding Prior Evaluation Efforts

Historical context matters. An organization's likelihood to use evaluation results is, not unlike many systems, predicated on a historical context of prior research and attempts at change. Historical foundations of understanding may include attempts (successful or not) at changing a system to improve accountability, as well as efforts to implement penalties or rewards. Understanding attempted policy change efforts that failed or resulted in compromise is important to planning how evaluation results might be shared to increase the likelihood of use.

For example, some educators who have taught for decades have seen many "reforms" come and go. These reforms might be a new curriculum, a new method of teaching mathematics or reading, improved standards of learning, or overhauled assessment practices. It is not uncommon to hear educators who have lived through many reform efforts be skeptical that the latest and greatest way of helping their students learn is just another fad that will eventually fade away with time (and be replaced with a new reform). Consciously or subconsciously, individuals weigh the amount of time that is required to complete a survey or interview with the likelihood that their voice will be heard and acted upon. If the historical context includes instances where opinion was sought but not used, future evaluations may bear the brunt and those consulted may view data collection as a waste of their time. Asking a question on a survey or in an interview implies that someone wants to hear the response such that aggregated findings across respondents can influence change. If there is no intention of trying to effect change, or if history indicates there is little likelihood of change, the lack of use of evaluation findings not only reflects on the program and policy leadership, but also on the evaluation team. As such, if as an evaluator you are concerned that an evaluation is a **compliance-only evaluation**, being conducted as a formality or to placate a stakeholder, and that there is no intention to do more than check off that it is complete, you may want to move on to another evaluation. As evaluators, we have an obligation to report accurate findings, but we also have

Compliance-only evaluation: an evaluation that is conducted as a formality to satisfy a regulation or stakeholder, with no intention by program leadership to use the evaluation findings.

a responsibility to those participating in our evaluation to respect their time and not knowingly waste it.

Examining the prior or ongoing work of other like-minded organizations or programs is also a valuable way to understand at this early stage the possibility that evaluation findings may conflict with or support prior reports. The context helps set the stage for appreciating how the assessment results from the present study may create unique types of attention in the media, elevate tensions, or create synergies between organizations. Further, uncovering early on how seemingly similar evaluations differ can help to explain how an evaluation may fill gaps left by prior research, and how methods may vary or align with the work of other groups. Together, these details can begin to shape a draft report deck that incorporates a shell of the evaluation results even before data are analyzed.

12.2.3 Beginning the Conversation Regarding Use

Knowing your stakeholders and prior evaluation efforts are important to understand the context within which the evaluation will be conducted. Yet neither is sufficient to ensure ongoing use of evaluation results through program implementation. To do this, it is important to work closely with those who have the authority and ability to make programmatic decisions. Thus, perhaps the most important stakeholder is the leadership of a program responsible for continual changes to a program to foster program improvement. To increase the likelihood that evaluation results are useful to and used by program leadership, it is important that the evaluation process be participatory from start to finish. Before the evaluation begins, including program leadership in program theory and logic model development, as well as discussions around defining indicators and prioritizing data collection, helps to create the opportunity for evaluation to have an impact on ongoing programmatic decision making. This process may even include exploring with program leadership anticipated reactions to different findings, as such discussions may lay the groundwork for utilization.

QUICK CHECK

1. How can preliminary findings be used to stimulate discussion about evaluation needs and purposes?

2. What are the ways in which the early phases of evaluation can be structured to support the use of findings?

3. When should the history of the program be examined and why?

4. As evaluators, we have responsibility to program leadership to report accurate findings. Who else do we have responsibility to and what implications does this responsibility have for compliance-only evaluations?

5. Who should be included in pre-evaluation efforts to promote utilization?

12.3 DURING EVALUATION: ONGOING UTILIZATION EFFORTS

While planning efforts are effective at setting the stage for evaluation use, there is often no substitute for real data. If your program design and evaluation were inclusive processes that involved stakeholders and participants from the start, it is more likely that your evaluation findings will be used for program improvement and accountability. Involving others in your program's evaluation encourages a shared sense of responsibility for the program as well as a shared investment in the program's success. Hearing about a program at its very start and not again until an evaluation report is provided does not foster the ownership among staff, stakeholders, and participants that is needed for a successful program. So, how do you make sure your evaluation report, along with all of your hard work and informative results, is not put on a shelf to gather dust? Make evaluation a participatory process from understanding and defining the program in Step 1 to informing the program and stakeholders through findings in Step 5.

12.3.1 Using Evaluation for Program Improvement

One of the most important uses of evaluation findings is for **program improvement**. Program improvement is the process of utilizing evaluation findings for formative decision making, to shape and inform the program in an effort to improve program operations and results.

In fact, for many audiences, evaluation communication should focus on improvement. To do this, evaluation communication and reporting should include not only positive findings, but also findings that may not be flattering to the program. These not-so-positive findings are the basis for program improvement.

Program improvement: using evaluation findings for formative decision making, to shape and inform the program in an effort to improve program operations and results.

When discussing evaluation results with program leadership, ask whether the findings are what they expected. Has the program accomplished what was intended? If yes, ask if they see areas where it can be made even better. If findings were not as positive as expected, ask the program leadership why they think the program was not as successful as anticipated. Did the program not have enough time to be successful? Was the implementation delayed or flawed? Whether evaluation findings are better or worse than hoped for, using evaluation results on a regular and ongoing basis is vital to program improvement.

12.3.2 Using Evaluation for Accountability

Accountability: using evaluation findings for summative decision making, to make determinations about the future of the program.

Another important use of evaluation findings is for **accountability** purposes. Accountability is the process of utilizing evaluation findings for summative decision making, that is, to make determinations about the future of the program. Using evaluation findings to hold the program accountable for its effectiveness and impact includes making the difficult decisions about whether to continue a program, scale it back, expand its reach, replicate it elsewhere, or discontinue operations. Designing and implementing programs takes valuable resources; evaluation findings can help program leadership determine whether the expenditure is worth the results.

Accountability pertains to basic questions, such as whether the program was indeed implemented and whether program funding was faithfully spent on the program, and to more involved questions, such as whether the program is a sound investment. Because accountability has multiple facets, it is important for your evaluation reporting to include all findings, good and bad, so that informed decisions can be made regarding the program's future. While evaluation reporting can be used for program marketing or for encouraging new funding, evaluation findings should include sufficient information for decisions regarding accountability. A caution, however, is that decisions regarding accountability should be made carefully and be based on evidence from multiple sources derived from a rigorous evaluation.

12.3.3 Examining Cost-Benefit and Cost-Effectiveness

The impact of a program on outcomes such as improved eating behaviors, increased student learning, decreased drug use, or reduced recidivism are often used to make accountability decisions. However, without clear negative findings, it is sometimes difficult to determine if an outcome is positive *enough* to continue a program. In such cases, program funders look to indicators of the efficiency of a program, or the **return on investment (ROI)**. ROI is the program's contribution in terms of outcomes or dollars saved in relation to the cost of the program.

Funders, as well as program leadership, often want to know the value-added of a program, in terms of either dollars saved or benefits to participants or society. As introduced in Chapter 1, cost-effectiveness analysis (CEA) and cost-benefit analysis (CBA) are summative evaluation techniques that focus on estimating the efficiency of a program in terms of outcomes observed (cost-effectiveness) or dollar costs saved (cost-benefit). CBA is typically represented by **net economic benefits (NEB)** or a **benefit cost ratio (BCR)**. NEB is calculated by subtracting the total program costs from the dollar value of total program benefits. Similarly, BCR is calculated by dividing the dollar value of total program benefits by total program costs. Programs that have a higher NEB or a BCR greater than one are typically determined to have economic benefit.

The amount saved from a program's implementation is often dependent upon the time frame within which the analysis is conducted. Some savings might be measurable in the short term, though many times the true cost savings of a program are not realized until years or decades later, such as long-term impacts of early childhood programs. In such cases, examining cost-effectiveness by relating program costs to early or intermediate outcomes may provide enough evidence until a comprehensive cost-benefit analysis can be completed.

Return on investment (ROI): the degree to which a program or intervention is considered efficient; the program's contribution in terms of outcomes or dollars saved in relation to the cost of the program.

Net economic benefits (NEB): a cost-benefit statistic calculated by subtracting the total program costs from the dollar value of total program benefits.

Benefit cost ratio (BCR): a cost-benefit statistic calculated by dividing the dollar value of total program benefits by total program costs.

In their CEA and CBA of drug treatments, Belenko, Patapis, and French (2005) examined the cost associated per unit outcome and economic benefit, respectively, of various interventions. CEA analysis of costs per outcome revealed that the cost per each individual who abstained from drugs was lower in outpatient settings ($6,300 per abstinent case) than in residential ($14,900 per abstinent case) or inpatient settings ($15,600 per abstinent case). They also calculated the cost-effectiveness for reduced drug use by individual in each of the three settings, as well as cost-effectiveness of methadone maintenance versus methadone detoxification in terms of each life year gained. Belenko et al. also conducted a CBA analysis of program costs in relation to economic benefits. In their examination of the substance abuse treatment, they found that the economic benefit, as measured through reduced incarceration and lower costs associated with victims of substance abuser crime, outweighed the program costs. BCRs ranged from 1.33 to 39.0, across the interventions and sites studied. For instance, in calculating CBA for drug courts in Kentucky, BCR was 2.71, meaning that for every dollar spent on drug courts, $2.71 were saved. For more on the efficacy of drug courts, see "In the Real World" below.

Henrichson and Rinaldi (2014) provide a comprehensive guide on cost-benefit analysis. Their guide uses justice policy as a case example, though the processes described are useful for any evaluation. They outline six steps from identifying the potential impacts of the program to reporting the results. The U.S. Department of Health and Human Services' Calculating the Costs of Child Welfare Services Workgroup (2013) also has

IN THE REAL WORLD . . .

Drug courts have been studied by many researchers. A drug court provides an alternative to a criminal trial. In drug courts, multiple treatments, sanctions, and services are used to decrease drug use and criminal activity, as well as reduce recidivism for drug-related offenses. Findings indicate that drug courts are effective at reducing drug use and subsequent crime (Aos, Miller, & Drake, 2006; Latimer, Morton-Bourgon, & Chretien, 2006; Lowenkamp, Holsinger, & Latessa, 2005; Marlowe, 2010; Shaffer, 2006; Wilson, Mitchell, & MacKenzie, 2006).

Bhati, Roman, and Chalfin (2008) examined the extent to which drug courts, in addition to reducing crime, were cost-effective. Results indicated that drug courts have substantial net economic benefits to the criminal justice system. They found

that for every dollar invested in the drug court program, net benefits averaged $2.21. In other words, their analysis showed that drug courts have a 221% return on investment. They also found that more targeted drug courts, focusing on the most serious offenders, had a 336% return on investment.

In a research update from the National Association of Drug Court Professionals (2018), the group delineates the 10 components of effective drug courts, that is, drug courts associated with the kind of benefits found in the Bhati et al. (2008) study. The association concludes that policy efforts should focus on replicating and expanding the use of drug courts, paying particular attention to fidelity of program implementation according to the 10-component drug court best practices model.

a useful guide, advocating an eight-step process to cost analysis. The eight-step process includes documenting the resources necessary for program implementation, including direct and indirect costs, estimating the costs per participant, and examining how costs vary across implementation.

12.3.4 Refining the Program's Theory

Evaluation findings can be used to refine the program's theory. As mentioned earlier, the logic model is a living model and its underlying assumptions of the program's theory should be dynamic, changing as new information is learned. If the culture in which the program is implemented is a learning culture, using findings to improve the logic model is a natural process. However, in other environments, it may not be as easy to apply evaluation findings to logic model improvement. Regardless, if a program is to continue, it is good practice to keep the program logic model up-to-date so that it is an accurate reflection of the mechanisms through which the program's strategies are related to the program's goals.

An up-to-date logic model can facilitate future evaluation and serve as the cornerstone of a program. A program's theory and logic model should be part of the core documentation of the program and can be used to train new program participants, as well as to explain the program to participants, administrative staff, potential funders, and other stakeholders.

12.3.5 People Drive Action

Formal processes are essential, yet sometimes they are not enough. People drive action and our ability as evaluators to generate findings that stimulate action should be a measure of our success.

Distributing ongoing evaluation findings through a variety of mechanisms, including reports, evaluation briefs, infographics, and presentations, as well as through project meetings and conversations, is critical for fostering use. And, while ultimately it is the program leadership's decision whether to make changes based on findings or to implement evaluation recommendations, evaluators can increase the likelihood of findings being used by fostering relationships with staff and stakeholders through participatory methods and by making evaluation recommendations relevant and actionable for decision makers.

Finally, yet first and foremost, it is people who make decisions regarding a program's operation. People drive the action, and sometimes this action is based on data and sometimes it is not. Sometimes decisions are logical and rational, and sometimes they are not. Influencing change through evaluation may not always be through the more formal means mentioned above, but rather influence might also occur through informal conversations and indirect methods. One such indirect method is identifying change agents and capitalizing upon their **legitimate power** or **referent power** to influence

Legitimate power: power gained through formal means, such as the position a person holds in an organization.

Referent power: power derived from someone's personality or their connections with others.

QUICK CHECK

1. How can you use evaluation results for program improvement?
2. Why is using evaluation results for accountability important?
3. What formal methods can you use to influence use of evaluation findings?
4. What can evaluators do to increase the likelihood that evaluation findings will be used?

change. Legitimate power is power and authority gained through formal means, such as the position a person holds in an organization. Referent power is derived from personal attributes, such as charisma, and connections with others who hold authority. As an evaluator, you have **informational power**, in that you understand evaluation and can interpret findings. Evaluators can use this informational power to work with those who have legitimate or referent power to influence change. Please note, there are other types of power, and depending on the resource or management text, you may find varying names for sources of power. These three types of power are especially relevant for evaluators in influencing change. For more information on power, a quick search on the web will give you many and varying definitions and types of power!

12.4 POST-EVALUATION AND DATA DISSEMINATION

Sometimes we learn best from our mistakes. I was once asked to help a school district evaluate its procedures for implementing wellness committees and related tasks. They were interested in input into the school meals program as well as other policies related to ensuring staff and students had healthy meals, strong physical activity programs, and a comprehensive approach to well-being. The district had initially developed a robust committee in response to federal changes to school and district wellness policy requirements, but more recently realized that what was once a very productive effort had lost momentum. As a result, I was brought in to evaluate procedures and report findings to the district superintendent. I soon realized, however, that because of the hierarchy of the system, personnel had begun to feel insulted that I neglected to provide feedback to them directly. In this case, the committee was comprised of principals, longtime volunteers, and school board members, who for the most part were very open to shifting their approach. However, by circumventing the committee, the superintendent and I were creating a dynamic that was only inhibiting progress. While indeed the superintendent needed to be aware of the findings and the recommended program modifications,

Informational power: power gained by having access to information that may not be readily known or understood.

he too simply wanted to fix the problem. After realizing that my efforts had alienated an important group critical to the change process, with the superintendent's support I was able to shift the approach such that I worked collaboratively with the committee. By working with the established wellness committee, I was able to achieve action, staff were reinvigorated, and the superintendent was pleased with the renewed progress in the district. Indeed, because the committee was so responsive, the findings presented in the report to the superintendent became more of a summary of the operational findings alongside the progress that had been made in response to improving the functionality of the committee. Had I continued to report results only, directly, and formally to the superintendent, the committee would likely have interpreted findings in a more punitive way, which could have stifled their passion and momentum for change. Reporting the right data to the right level of the organization at the right time and in the right format is of critical importance when it comes to managing personalities and influencing change.

The experience above and the information on power in the previous section serve as examples of how evaluators need to listen and pay attention to those around them to make sure that findings have an impact. Several critical questions can help support an evaluator's ability to think through navigating the people side of the evaluation as it pertains to a process of change:

- What are the possible and probable impacts of the evaluation recommendations on specific people or groups of people, including program staff, mid-level management, and leadership?

- What constraints (human, logistic, funding, etc.) are there on leadership that may challenge their ability to make recommended changes? Can I anticipate these constraints and help strategize an approach that could still motivate change?

- What will program staff likely react to when I present evaluation results?

- What will program leaders or funders most likely react to when I present these findings and recommendations?

- Are there ways to word negative findings and potentially controversial recommendations that are less inflammatory and more likely to garner support?

- What is the right level of hierarchy and timing for reporting these findings? Should they go directly to a program manager, or are they better suited for a higher-level director? What are the implications for each?

- What is the right format for my data and results? Is this the kind of information that is best suited for a phone call? A report? Moreover, if it is a report, do recommendations belong at the beginning of the report, the end of the report, or somewhere in between?

There are no right or wrong answers to these questions. Yet they are important considerations for evaluators so that when we report results, we maximize the likelihood that the findings will be used. The "In the Real World" example shares another experience in which people were the key to effective program implementation and evaluation.

12.4.1 Meta-Evaluation

In addition to listening to stakeholders, evaluators should strive to have their own evaluations evaluated. The evaluation of an evaluation is called a meta-evaluation (Scriven,

---

IN THE REAL WORLD . . .

Several years ago, I was in a meeting serving as an evaluator when it hit me that often some of the most fundamental differences in program implementation and design are not the curriculum, or the timing of the program, or even the level of fidelity between the program design, theory, and implementation. Sometimes it is just people. It struck me because in this particular meeting, the staff person who was in charge of data collection was magnificent. She had unique charisma, excellent rapport with the community as well as teachers and residents, and a personality that made people want to help her. She was enormously efficient and, in comparison to other staff who were also quite competent, she was far more productive. I thought to myself, "Without her, where would this program be?" Yes, this scenario can play out in many other ways. Many of us have probably encountered a staff member who is the opposite—slow to act, somehow always rubs people the wrong way, perhaps inadequately skilled for the job, and generally seems to drag down operations.

I raise these issues because, in all truth, people are one of the most critical factors driving our ability to facilitate the use or impact of evaluation results. Even after the tenets of an evaluation are decided, including stakeholder needs, and we have ensured the nuts and bolts are covered and evaluation questions are closely aligned with the goals of the project, there remains an underlying context that is defined by

people: the individuals in leadership positions; change agents, or people who have influence or power to facilitate change; and those responsible for program implementation for whom the evaluation findings will likely have a substantial impact. These are impacts that go beyond the surface of program changes and deeper into the way that organizations are structured or should be structured; they relate to the actual capacity that a program may have to change its operations or double down on specific facets of program delivery that need more attention.

Much of the ability of an evaluator to be successful in his or her role hinges on the capacity to understand the likely influences of evaluation findings on people and tailor the delivery of such information, perhaps even over time, in such a way that it enables change and does not unintentionally shut down lines of communication.

1969, 2009; Stufflebeam, 1978). Meta-evaluations can be conducted using the Joint Committee's Program Evaluation Standards (see Chapter 1) or other standards in the field. Further, meta-evaluations can be used to improve an evaluation in progress, as well as to provide feedback on an evaluation already conducted. Unfortunately, meta-evaluation has not yet become routine in the field of evaluation; however, evaluations that could potentially influence and impact major policies and practices are often critiqued by other evaluators. These critiques focus on evaluation design, methods of data collection, biases in the evaluation, conflict of interest of evaluators, misinterpretation and overinterpretation of results, and any other area that might threaten the validity of the findings.

12.4.2 Understanding the Change Process

Take a moment to think about the last time a significant change in your life or workplace was announced. What questions did you ask or want to ask? It is true that even the most open-minded of us often react somewhat negatively to announcements of change. From policymakers to parents, change is often met with concerns about stress, the anticipation of problems, and many reasons why it would be easier to maintain the status quo. Change is all around us and sits at the foundation of the purpose of evaluation. Change and change processes are well studied across organizations and by human behavior experts, and as a result, there exist many models, explanations, and strategies to help organizations understand and plan for change. Leadership creates the momentum and tactical approaches necessary to navigate change.

12.4.3 CBAM: Concerns-Based Adoption Model

One frequently used model to assess the change process in order to facilitate improvement is the concerns-based adoption model (CBAM; Hall & Hord, 1987). CBAM includes three frameworks for assessing the change process: stages of concern, levels of use, and innovation configurations.

According to CBAM, we can identify a stage of change by examining the kinds of questions that individuals ask. Table 12.1 includes the seven stages of concern and a description of each. Concerns at the start of the change process, such as "What does this mean for me?" are often articulated at the purely "self" level. As change progresses, concerns shift to asking about the task and then ultimately inquiring about the impact of the change on an intended audience, such as students or community members. For example, if someone asked to change the timing of an after-school program to accommodate a new curriculum, you may initially ask, "How much later will I have to work?" After a while, your questions may shift to wondering more about implementation processes, such as "What kinds of content will I need to teach to adjust for the additional time?" And finally, you may ask questions that focus on the intended outcome and the benefit

CBAM: concerns-based adoption model; a model of change that includes three frameworks for assessing the change process: stages of concern, levels of use, and innovation configurations.

Stage of Concern	Description	How Program Staff Might Respond
TABLE 12.1 ● Stages of Concern		
0	Unconcerned	Not interested or too busy to be concerned with the program.
1	Informational	Interested in learning more about the program.
2	Personal	Concerns about how the program will affect personal routines and responsibilities.
3	Management	Concerns about how much time it will take to implement the program.
4	Consequence	Concerns about how the program might affect other people who are involved with the program.
5	Collaboration	Interested in sharing what has been learned about the program or ideas regarding the program with other individuals implementing the program.
6	Refocusing	Based on experience with the program, ideas about how the program might be modified or improved.

Source: Hall and Hord (1987).

to the individuals for whom the change is intended to help, such as "How will this new curriculum affect children?"

These questions lead to a model that articulates seven stages of concern (SoC) that an individual might go through and can be helpful in determining where a particular program is in the change process. Knowing where individuals are in the change process and how concerns may vary across program staff or participants can inform program training and adjustments. CBAM also provides tools to examine the levels of use (LoU) of the innovation, or levels of adoption of the change, as well as the various configurations with which program components might be implemented. The third tool, innovation configurations (IC), can be especially helpful when examining fidelity of implementation.

SoC can be measured through a 35-item questionnaire, interview, or open-ended survey. IC involves creating an IC map that describes how change may be viewed along a continuum, from the ideal implementation model to a model that is not at all what program developers intended. LoU focuses on five levels of use and three levels of nonuse and can be assessed using a structured interview. More information on CBAM, the Stages of Concern Questionnaire (SoCQ), or other components of the concerns-based adoption model can be found at the American Institutes for Research website (https://www.air.org/resource/cbam-concerns-based-adoption-model).

While the CBAM model is detailed in its approach, what is most important for the evaluator to understand is that evaluation has two components, an emotional component and a capability component. Each of us experiences a change differently. For evaluators, that means it will be essential to recognize the potential impact of recommendations both in terms of logistical next steps and in terms of more personal considerations. Someone who is in an early stage and is considering how the change affects them personally will need to have information provided that directly addresses their concerns before advancing to talk about logistics and procedures.

In addition to monitoring the types of questions that are being asked, it is also useful to remain attentive to the ways that people behave in reaction to the announcement of a change. While one person may take absolutely no interest and, for all intents and purposes, ignore the suggestion or new recommendation, another could articulate a plan to begin implementation in the future. The latter person might begin promptly adapting to the change with a deliberate intention to integrate that change with other facets of their work and coordinate with others as the innovation emerges. Change is a process, and individuals will advance new ideas and procedures based on their position along a continuum.

12.4.4 Evaluation Influence

Beyond the direct use of an evaluation is the broader impact that the evaluation may have. This broader impact is called evaluation influence. Henry and Mark (2003) define evaluation influence as "evaluation consequences that could plausibly lead toward or away from social betterment" (p. 295). That is, evaluation influence is when the evaluation itself affects the lives of people. This influence could come from formative evaluation data, where early or intermediate evaluation findings are used by the program and this use has an impact. The influence could also be beyond an individual program; evaluation findings might influence a policy change that impacts multiple communities (Alkin & King, 2017).

12.4.5 Change Takes Time

Change takes time. It is a process that will occur differently for different individuals. Factors like emotions, skills, and capabilities all come into play when an individual hears a change is likely to occur, understands the details of the change, and begins to recognize and adopt a new approach. While leaders may be experiencing their own set of thoughts and feelings about a change, they must remain aware of the importance of people in the process and, to the extent possible, address concerns with those to whom they provide oversight in a way that is sensitive. Also, as we know from our own lives, concerns are not static but are likely to shift and evolve as people grow and learn. The embedded evaluation framework allows us to show incremental findings as a program strives to achieve

QUICK CHECK

1. What are some important considerations for evaluators when navigating the people side of evaluation use?
2. Why is it important for evaluators to understand the change process?

long-term goals, and can help to set realistic expectations among stakeholders regarding the time it takes to observe change related to indicators.

While we may want to see the impact of evaluation recommendations right away, in most cases, change does not happen quickly. People need to process the evaluation findings, determine for themselves how the findings impact policy and practice, decide how to proceed based on evaluation evidence, and then go through the appropriate process and get the proper approvals before any policy changes will occur. As mentioned earlier, including key stakeholders throughout evaluation design and implementation can facilitate the change process. However, even with a participatory evaluation and positive findings, policy change will occur on its own timeline.

12.5 CHAPTER SUMMARY

The intent of evaluation is to produce actionable findings. Critical to the use of these findings is understanding stakeholders and their interests and planning throughout the evaluation to increase the likelihood that evaluation results will be used. Before the evaluation, evaluators can review stakeholder interests, document prior evaluation efforts, and begin conversations with project leadership such that they are involved throughout the evaluation process. During the evaluation, evaluators can work to facilitate the use of evaluation findings for **program improvement** and for **accountability**. In addition, ongoing evaluation findings can be used to update and improve the program's theory. While stakeholders should be engaged throughout the evaluation, during the evaluation it is important to examine who has the power and authority to make programmatic changes. Post-evaluation use and dissemination rely heavily on people and, as such, it is important for evaluators to understand the change process. The concerns-based adoption model (**CBAM**) is a useful tool for understanding and assessing the concerns of program staff throughout the change process. Finally, it is important to remember that even when stakeholders are involved in the evaluation, change agents are targeted, and the context of previous change efforts is examined, change occurs in stages and change takes time.

Reflection and Application

1. In what ways can evaluation findings be reported that recognize that change is a process?

2. How can stakeholder interests be addressed in formal and informal reporting?

3. What are the constraints that may limit the use of evaluation results? How might these constraints be overcome?

4. Think about a time in your life when a change or new approach was introduced (for example, moving to a new town, changes to accommodate new safety regulations being put into place, or new workplace procedures requiring a modification in your schedule). How did you initially react? Why do you think you reacted that way? How did your concerns change over time? Why do you think that is? Reflecting back, what would you have done differently?

5. How might cost-effectiveness or cost-benefit analyses be used to facilitate use of the evaluation results? Do you think different stakeholder groups may respond differently to CBA versus CEA? In what ways?

CASE STUDY APPLICATIONS

Evaluation's most important purpose is not to prove, but to improve.

—Daniel L. Stufflebeam (2003)

Upon completion of this chapter, you should be able to

- Describe how the embedded evaluation approach can be applied to a new program.
- Describe how the embedded evaluation approach can be integrated into an existing program.

Two real-world examples are provided in this chapter to illustrate the embedded evaluation approach. The first case study uses an embedded approach to design the evaluation for a new program. The Leadership Education for Neurodevelopmental and Related Disabilities (LEND) program intends to improve the quality of life for children with neurodevelopmental disabilities and their families by increasing the number of highly trained professionals. The second case study uses an embedded approach within an existing program. The Accelerating Clinical and Translational Research (ACCEL) program intends to improve health by improving the quality of clinical and translational research. Finally, the Youth Abstinence-Plus (YAP) case study introduced in earlier chapters is included in its entirety.

13.1 LEND EVALUATION

In July 2016, the Maternal and Child Bureau of the Health Resources and Services Administration of the U.S. Department of Health and Human Services awarded the University of Delaware's Center for Disabilities Studies a five-year grant to operate a Leadership Education for Neurodevelopmental and Related Disabilities (LEND) program in the state of Delaware. The Delaware LEND program is one of 52 such programs across the country. The purpose of these programs is to train future leaders in a variety of health-related disciplines in order to improve the health of children who have, or are at risk of developing, neurodevelopmental disabilities or other similar conditions, such as autism spectrum disorder and developmental disabilities (ASD/DD).

The long-term goals of the Delaware LEND program are to

- Increase the number of highly trained professionals, especially from underrepresented groups, serving children and youth with ASD/DD and their families;

- Improve health and well-being for children and youth with ASD/DD; and

- Improve quality of life for children and youth with ASD/DD and their families.

To accomplish this, the program employs seven primary strategies:

1. Long-term trainee recruitment and training

2. Undergraduate career support

3. Continuing community-based education

4. Competency-based trainee curriculum

5. Community-based partnerships

6. Community-based technical assistance

7. Dissemination of resources

13.1.1 LEND Evaluation Design

The LEND evaluation uses a longitudinal cohort design. During evaluation design, the evaluation team and program staff met one or two times per month to define the program's theory and create the logic model. Currently, the evaluation team meets monthly with program staff to discuss implementation, review findings, and plan evaluation activities. At each meeting, we discuss the logic model and make any necessary adjustments.

Five cohorts of trainees will participate in the program over five years. At the start of the program, each trainee completes a leadership skills assessment. The first year involves active participation, in which the trainees attend two to three didactic sessions each month and are assigned both a faculty and family mentor. Data collection methods include didactic surveys, trainee interviews, faculty mentor interviews, family mentor interviews, and program staff interviews. Further, at the end of the active training year, participants complete a post-leadership skills assessment; thereafter, a follow-up leadership skills assessment and survey is administered annually after training completion. In years 1 and 2 of the program, the evaluation focused on three program components: long-term trainee recruitment and training, competency-based training curriculum, and dissemination of resources.

Didactic surveys are completed by trainees in Qualtrics, an electronic survey platform, at the end of each didactic session. It is a short survey designed to gauge the trainees' satisfaction with each of the sessions and the extent to which trainees believe they improved their knowledge or understanding of the focal content of each workshop. The survey also provides trainees an opportunity to raise any questions for program staff. Participants complete the survey on their phone or other handheld device. Sessions are on Fridays, and we have a report of findings to program staff within five working days. This enables program staff to respond to any questions raised by trainees and to incorporate any feedback into future sessions.

Interviews are conducted annually and are typically completed face-to-face. However, if interviewees prefer, we will also conduct interviews over the phone or using video conferencing software. Interview protocols were developed to gather data about the components of the LEND program from the perspective of trainees, faculty mentors, and family mentors. The trainee and faculty mentor interview protocols include questions pertaining to components of the project such as mentoring, the didactic sessions, the leadership project, and clinical and community observations, as well as overall satisfaction with the program and general suggestions for improvement. The family mentor interview protocol focuses specifically on the "A Day in the Life" family mentoring component of the LEND program, as well as satisfaction with the program and perceptions of impact.

In year 3 of the program, in addition to evaluation of the long-term trainee component, the evaluation team is working with the program on a needs assessment focused in two areas: (1) training, support, and services needs for families and (2) training and support needs for providers. Years four and five of the evaluation will expand the evaluation to include additional strategies implemented by the program, as the implementation of program activities has been staged across years.

In addition to informal evaluation feedback as needed and at monthly meetings, supplemental evaluation reports for program activities (e.g., didactic sessions) and an annual evaluation report are provided to program staff.

13.1.2 LEND IRB Review

The Institutional Review Board (IRB) determined that the LEND evaluation could not be categorized as exempt, and instead required an expedited IRB review (see Chapter 3 for information on IRB protocols and reviews). The LEND evaluation IRB was expedited and received approval under review category number 7 (research on individual or group characteristics). LEND trainees complete a consent form at the start of the program, indicating their understanding of the evaluation and its intended use. Because of its nonexempt status, the LEND evaluation is required to submit to IRB for continuing review annually.

13.1.3 LEND Logic Model

See Figure 13.1.

13.1.4 LEND Evaluation Matrix

See Table 13.1.

The LEND evaluation is conducted in partnership with the Delaware LEND project. Part of a national network of LEND programs, the Delaware LEND is led by the University of Delaware's Center for Disabilities Studies and represents a collaboration between multiple University of Delaware departments, Nemours/Alfred I. duPont Hospital for Children, and several other community partners. LEND is funded through the Health Resources and Services Administration under the Autism CARES Act, grant number T73MC30116 (Principal Investigators: Mineo/Freedman).

13.2 ACCEL EVALUATION

In an effort to improve and encourage the growth of clinical and translational research (CTR) within Delaware, five partner institutions joined with the National Institutes of Health (NIH) to build research capacity in the state. The Delaware Clinical and Translational Research program (DE-CTR), also known as ACCEL (Accelerating Clinical and Translational Research), has supported multiple basic, clinical, and translational research projects through mentoring, education, faculty development, and infrastructure improvements.

I was invited to evaluate the ACCEL program while it was in its sixth year. My first goal was to understand the program. I have to say, the ACCEL program was one of the most complex programs I have evaluated. It is more of a systems change initiative than a well-defined program. There are many moving parts, including programs within programs, multiple grant opportunities, collaborative ventures, and partnerships. The acronyms for this project alone spanned five pages! Nonetheless, after immersing myself in the program and countless discussions with program leadership, staff, and partners,

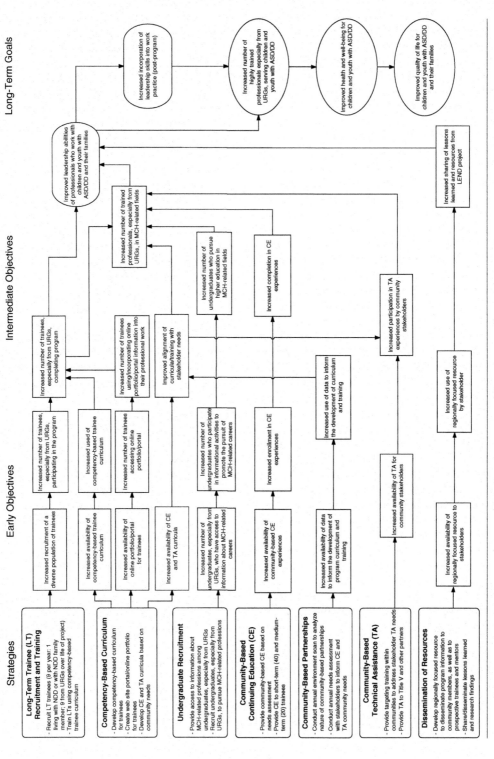

FIGURE 13.1 ● LEND Logic Model

Note: MCH = maternal child health; NDD = neurodevelopmental disorder; URGs = underrepresented groups.

TABLE 13.1 ● LEND Evaluation Matrix (partial)

	Logic Model Component	Evaluation Question(s)	Indicators	Targets	Data Source	Data Collection	Data Analysis
Strategies/Activities	Long-term trainee (LT) recruitment and training	In what ways and to what extent were LTs recruited and trained?	Implementation of LT recruitment and training	By program start, recruitment and training are implemented with fidelity	Fidelity of implementation rubric	Rubric administered at start of program and quarterly thereafter	Rubric data analyzed for evidence of implementation fidelity
	Competency-based curriculum	In what ways and to what extent was a competency-based trainee curriculum developed and implemented?	Creation of competency-based trainee curriculum	By trainee start, curriculum materials are developed and implemented with fidelity	Fidelity of implementation rubric	Rubric administered at start of program and quarterly thereafter	Rubric data analyzed for evidence of implementation fidelity
	Dissemination of resources	In what ways were resources made available to stakeholders? To what extent and in what ways were lessons learned from project shared?	Implementation of dissemination plan	By year 2, dissemination plan will be implemented with fidelity	Fidelity of implementation rubric	Rubric administered at start of year 2 and annually thereafter	Rubric data analyzed for evidence of implementation fidelity

(Continued)

TABLE 13.1 ◆ (Continued)

	Logic Model Component	Evaluation Question(s)	Indicators	Targets	Data Source	Data Collection	Data Analysis
Early/Intermediate Objectives	Increased recruitment of a diverse population of trainees	To what extent did the recruitment of trainees, especially from URGs, increase?	Number of recruitment contacts/ activities, particularly focused on URGs	At least 20% of recruitment contacts will be focused on URGs	Program records	Program records examined quarterly	Basic descriptive statistics of recruitment contact data, overall and by URGs
	Increased number of trainees, especially from URGs, participating in program	To what extent did the number of trainees, especially from URGs, participating in the program increase?	Number of trainees participating in program (overall and by URG)	At least 10 new trainees each year; At least 20% of new trainees are from URGs	Program records	Program records examined quarterly	Basic descriptive statistics of recruitment data, overall and by URGs
	Increased use of competency-based trainee curriculum	To what extent did use of the competency-based trainee curriculum increase?	Number of trainees attending didactic sessions using the competency-based curriculum	At least 10 competency-based didactic sessions will be held each semester; 100% of trainees will attend each didactic session	Training schedule; Didactic session attendance records	Training schedules examined twice a year; Attendance records examined twice a year	Basic descriptive statistics of training schedule data; Basic descriptive statistics of attendance records
	Increased number of trainees, especially from URGs, completing program	To what extent did the number of trainees completing the program increase?	Number of trainees completing the program (overall and by URG)	100% of trainees will complete the program	Program records	Completion records examined annually	Basic descriptive statistics of completion records

Long-Term Goals						
Improved leadership abilities of professionals who work with children and youth ASD/DD and their families	To what extent did the leadership abilities of professionals who work with children and youth with ASD/DD and their families improve?	Scores on leadership skills assessment Number of trainees/professionals exhibiting improved leaderships skills	During the training program, 100% of trainees will increase their leadership skills scores by at least 20% At least 50% of trainees/professionals will exhibit improved leadership skills within one year of completing the program	Leadership skills assessment Provider interviews	Leadership skills assessment administered at start of program and annually thereafter Provider interviews conducted one year after trainee completion of program	Repeated measures t-test examining pre/post scores on leadership skills assessment Interviews coded and analyzed for themes; data examined for evidence of improved leadership abilities
Increased number of highly trained professionals, especially from URGs, serving children and youth with ASD/DD	To what extent did the number of highly trained professionals overall and from URGs increase?	Number of highly trained professionals overall and by URG serving children and youth with ASD/DD	At least 75% of trainees will remain in the field serving children and youth with ASD/DD	Trainee follow-up survey	Survey administered to trainees at start of program and annually thereafter	Basic descriptive statistics of survey data
Improved quality of life for children and youth with ASD/DD and their families	To what extent did the quality of life for children and youth with ASD/DD and their families improve?	Number of families reporting improved quality of life for themselves and their children	10% increase annually in the number of families reporting improved quality of life	Family survey (parents/caregivers of children with ASD/DD)	Survey administered to families statewide every two years	Basic descriptive statistics of survey data Independent samples t-test to measure change across administrations

Note: URGs = underrepresented groups.

I was able to draft a logic model depicting theory relating the many program components to the kind of systems change the program leadership envisioned.

The long-term goal of ACCEL is to improve health through three strategic aims:

- Increasing the capacity of researchers (investigators) to conduct impactful clinical and translational research

- Increasing opportunities that facilitate impactful clinical and translational research

- Improving community engagement and outreach research programs

To accomplish these goals, ACCEL has multiple strategies organized around six cores:

1. Administration (ADMIN)

2. Pilot projects

3. Professional development (PD)

4. Biostatistics, epidemiology, and research design (BERD)

5. Community engagement and outreach (CEO)

6. Tracking and evaluation

As an example, I will expand upon the PD Core, a key component of the CTR program intended to provide the necessary resources, networking opportunities, research support, and mentoring assistance for new or early-stage researchers and clinicians who want to be part of research efforts and/or accelerate their careers. The PD Core is responsible for providing training, mentoring, networking, and collaboration opportunities to these junior investigators (JIs). The PD Core has four specific aims:

1. Enhance collaboration and team building among junior investigators.

2. Increase the extramural funding rate for junior investigators.

3. Bridge the translational divide between the early development of materials, devices, and medicines and successful preclinical testing.

4. Improve the ability of junior investigators to communicate effectively with members of their research teams and the community.

These aims are accomplished through focused programs directed by a team of accomplished researchers and educators. One of these programs is the Junior Investigators Network (JIN). JIN is a peer networking and mentoring group of over 150 JIs, including those who have received Institutional Development Award (IDeA) program funding, those who have unsuccessfully applied for IDeA funding, and those who are interested in applying for such funds. JIN members are included in ACCEL programs and in quarterly group networking and mentoring events. ACCEL intends to leverage the JIN to help build clinical and translational research teams; provide mentoring and mentor training; and build clinical and translational research expertise. I think by now you are getting my comment about a lot of acronyms!!

13.2.1 ACCEL Evaluation Design

The ACCEL evaluation uses a repeated-measures, nonexperimental design. Due to the complexity of the program and the multiple evaluation needs across all six cores as well as for the overall program, I found that the evaluation needed to be more structured than a typical evaluation. I will explain this structure in the next few paragraphs.

The three strategic aims of ACCEL are listed in the previous section. In addition to these overarching aims, each ACCEL core has its own specific aims. The four specific aims of the PD Core were mentioned previously. The Tracking and Evaluation Core also has four specific aims (SAs):

1. Define metrics to guide data collection, analysis, and reporting (SA1).

2. Monitor and report progress for core-specific aims and overall strategic aims (SA2).

3. Monitor processes and design process improvement to improve quality (SA3).

4. Develop and share best practices in tracking and evaluation (SA4).

Over the past nine months, as I have learned more about the program and its expected evaluation (from ongoing conversations with program leadership), it became clear that the Tracking and Evaluation Core needed more structure than the specific aims allowed. Thus, I have organized our evaluation activities around three functional areas:

1. Key performance indicator (KPI) tracking (includes SA1 and SA2)

2. Core-based evaluation support (includes SA3 and SA4)

3. Targeted studies (includes SA4 and a new area examining impact)

KPI tracking includes refining existing and developing new metrics to monitor and report progress for the program as a whole, as well as for each core. This functional area also includes creating six-month indicator reports for ACCEL and each core. These reports will be used to facilitate a reliance upon data and to enable each core to make decisions based upon data. Because some of the data infrastructure is not in place to collect all metrics identified as important to monitoring progress, we are also developing procedures to support the necessary data collection.

Core-based evaluation support includes diagnostic evaluation support for each core. The evaluation team works with each core to determine evaluation needs in order to understand data, examine processes, and assess activities. For example, we are working with the PD Core to evaluate workshops and examine support and training needs of the junior investigators. We are conducting a community engagement study with the CEO Core to examine the influence and effectiveness of its community advisory model and to provide feedback on how the community advisory committee might be best structured to meet community needs. For the Pilot Projects Core, we plan to retrospectively study successful and unsuccessful projects funded by the core to determine the factors that might facilitate or be a barrier to success. For the Administration Core, we examine cross-core communication on an ongoing basis. And for the BERD Core, we are planning a needs assessment to inform future programming. Because of the many support needs in this functional area, we are prioritizing evaluation work based on resource availability.

Targeted studies intend to illustrate the impact of ACCEL on the health of Delawareans. These studies will be based on purposefully select cases where an ACCEL-funded investigator or a researcher who receives ACCEL support has had an impact with their work. For the most part, they will be retrospective, mixed-method case studies that show how ACCEL support has contributed to positive outcomes for Delawareans.

The ACCEL evaluation team has regular meetings with program leadership and each core. Leadership meetings are monthly and evaluation meetings with each core are quarterly. Informal discussions are held frequently and as needed to facilitate evaluation efforts. In addition, the evaluation team meets quarterly with evaluators of the other NIH-funded CTR centers to share best practices, discuss challenges, and build collaborations across CTR centers.

13.2.2 ACCEL IRB Review

Prior to my evaluating the ACCEL program, it was considered exempt under exemption category number 2 (surveys, interviews, observations of public behavior). This required a continuing review every three years. However, upon redesigning the evaluation using the embedded approach and resubmitting through IRB (under the Revised Common Rule), the evaluation was determined to not meet the definition of human subject research (HSR) according to federal regulations. While the evaluation is not currently considered HSR, we still submit any revisions to the evaluation or new instrumentation through the IRB, should the evaluation revision require a change in IRB status. Further, as with any evaluation, we abide by the AEA Guiding Principles for Evaluators and the Program Evaluation Standards (see Chapter 1).

13.2.3 ACCEL Logic Model

See Figures 13.2–13.5 for the ACCEL logic model and Table 13.2 for the ACCEL evaluation matrix.

FIGURE 13.2 ● ACCEL Logic Model: Strategies Expanded (partial)

Long-Term Trainee (LT) Recruitment and Training
- Recruit LT trainees (9 per year: 1 living with NDD or with NDD family member; 9 from URGs over life of project)
- Train LTs using competency-based trainee curriculum

Competency-Based Curriculum
- Develop competency-based curriculum for trainees
- Create website portal/online portfolio for trainees
- Develop CE and TA curricula based on community needs

Undergraduate Recruitment
- Provide access to information about MCH-related professions among undergraduates, especially from URGs
- Recruit undergraduates, especially from URGs, to pursue MCH-related professions

Note: MCH = maternal child health; NDD = neurodevelopmental disorders; URGs = underrepresented groups.

FIGURE 13.3 ● ACCEL Logic Model: Early Objectives Expanded (partial)

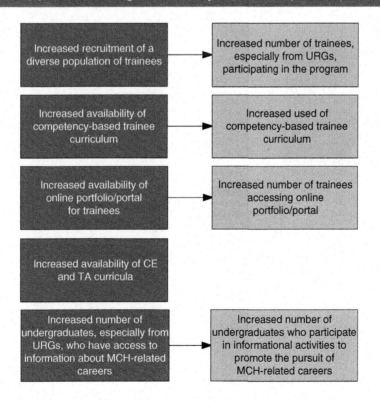

Increased recruitment of a diverse population of trainees → Increased number of trainees, especially from URGs, participating in the program

Increased availability of competency-based trainee curriculum → Increased used of competency-based trainee curriculum

Increased availability of online portfolio/portal for trainees → Increased number of trainees accessing online portfolio/portal

Increased availability of CE and TA curricula

Increased number of undergraduates, especially from URGs, who have access to information about MCH-related careers → Increased number of undergraduates who participate in informational activities to promote the pursuit of MCH-related careers

13.2.4 ACCEL Evaluation Matrix

See Table 13.2 in page 300.

The ACCEL evaluation is conducted in partnership with the DE-CTR ACCEL project. The DE-CTR is supported by an Institutional Development Award from the National Institute of General Medical Sciences of the National Institutes of Health under grant number U54-GM104941 (Principal Investigator: Binder/Macleod).

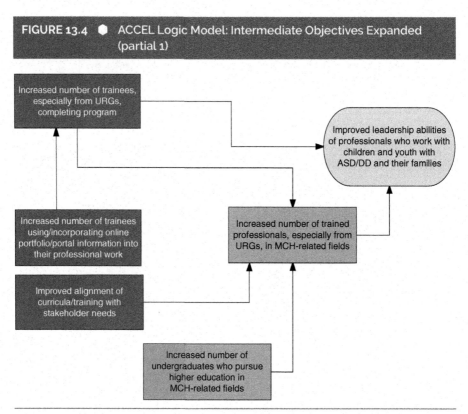

FIGURE 13.4 ● ACCEL Logic Model: Intermediate Objectives Expanded (partial 1)

Note: MCH = maternal child health; URGs = underrepresented groups.

FIGURE 13.5 ● ACCEL Logic Model: Long-Term Goals Expanded (partial)

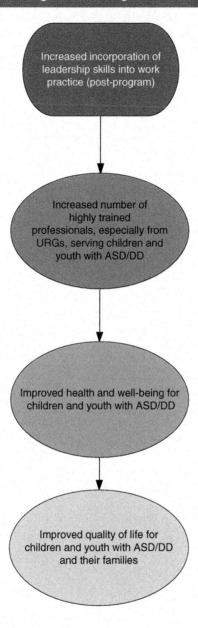

TABLE 13.2 ● ACCEL Evaluation Matrix—Partial

	Logic Model Component	Evaluation Question	Indicators	Targets	Data Source	Data Collection	Data Analysis
Strategies	Administration	In what ways were ADMIN Core activities implemented?	Implementation of ADMIN Core activities	Ongoing fidelity of implementation	Program documents (e.g., meeting minutes)	Program documents reviewed quarterly	Documents analyzed for evidence of ADMIN activities implementation
	Pilot projects	In what ways were PILOT grant opportunities and activities implemented?	Implementation of PILOT projects activities	Ongoing fidelity of implementation	Program documents (e.g., meeting minutes, grant opportunities, training schedules)	Program documents reviewed quarterly	Documents analyzed for evidence of PILOT grant opportunities and activities implementation
Early And Intermediate Objectives	Increased availability of pilot grant opportunities within ACCEL	To what extent did availability of pilot grant opportunities within ACCEL increase?	Availability of pilot grants to ACCEL members	Each year, at least two calls for pilot grants will be released to ACCEL members	Program records	Program records reviewed twice a year	Program records reviewed for availability of pilot grants
	Increased access to research retreats	To what extent did access to research retreats increase?	Availability of research retreats	At least one research retreat will be held each year	Program records	Program records reviewed twice a year	Program records reviewed for access to research retreats

Logic Model Component	Evaluation Question	Indicators	Targets	Data Source	Data Collection	Data Analysis
Increased participation in research retreats	To what extent did participation in research retreats increase?	Attendance at research retreats, by institution, model of attending (in person, virtual), and researcher level	At least 20 junior investigators will attend a research retreat each year	Attendance records	Attendance records reviewed after each retreat	Basic descriptive statistics of attendance record data
Increased number of grant applications from research retreat attendees (JumpStart)	To what extent did the number of grant applications from research retreat attendees increase?	Number of grant applications from research retreat attendees	At least 75% of research retreat attendees will submit a JumpStart grant application	Grant submission records	Grant submission records reviewed twice a year	Basic descriptive statistics of grant submission records, in conjunction with research retreat attendance records
Increased applications to participate in ACCEL pilot grant opportunities	To what extent did applications to participate in ACCEL pilot grant opportunities increase?	Number of applications to participate in ACCEL pilot grant opportunities	Each grant cycle, at least 25 applications for each pilot grant opportunity; Each grant cycle, at least 2 applications from each institution	Grant submission records	Grant submission records reviewed twice a year	Basic descriptive statistics of grant submission records, by topic and institution

(Continued)

TABLE 13.2 ● (Continued)

Increased number of high-quality pilot projects funded within DE-CTR	To what extent did the number of high-quality pilot projects funded within DE-CTR increase?	Scores of pilot grant applicants Number of pilot projects funded	At least 50% of scores on grant applications will show evidence of high quality Each grant cycle, at least six grants funded for each pilot grant opportunity Each grant cycle, at least one project funded from each institution	Grant funding records	Grant funding records reviewed twice a year	Basic descriptive statistics of grant scores Basic descriptive statistics of grant submission records, by topic and institution
Increased production of high-quality research (indicators include publications)	To what extent did the production of high-quality research increase?	Number of pilot grants leading to funded proposals Number of publications submitted to peer-reviewed journals Number of publications accepted to peer-reviewed journals	Each year, funded proposals will increase by 10% Each year, publications and submissions will increase by 10%	Investigator profiles	Investigator profiles examined quarterly	Basic descriptive statistics of investigator profile data

	Logic Model Component	Evaluation Question	Indicators	Targets	Data Source	Data Collection	Data Analysis
Long-Term Goals	Improved funding of ACCEL researchers	To what extent did the funding of ACCEL researchers improve?	Number of successful funding applications from researchers affiliated with ACCEL	Each year, funding of ACCEL researchers will increase by 10%	Investigator profiles	Investigator profiles examined quarterly	Basic descriptive statistics of investigator profile funding data
	Improved clinical and translational research in areas of need	To what extent did clinical and translational research in areas of need improve?	Number of funded proposals by investigators conducting clinical and translational research in areas of need / Quality of clinical and translational research in areas of need	Each year, funding of research proposals in areas of need will increase by 10% / Each year, at least four cases will be identified for case studies of quality research in areas of need	Investigator profiles / Case study/interviews focusing on clinical and translational research in areas of need	Investigator profiles examined quarterly / Two to four case studies conducted annually	Basic descriptive statistics of investigator profile research area data / Case study data coded and examined for themes and evidence of improved CTR research
	Improved health of the citizens of Delaware and the nation	To what extent did the health of the citizens of Delaware and the nation improve?	Impact of research by ACCEL investigators, as determined through investigator profiles, grant funding, publications, and progress reports	Each year, at least two cases will be identified for targeted case studies	Targeted case studies focusing on ACCEL's impact on health	One to two targeted case studies conducted annually	Case study data examined for evidence of impact on health on Delawareans

(Continued)

13.3 YAP EVALUATION

For decades, researchers and practitioners have debated abstinence-only programs versus sexual education programs as a means to decrease the incidence of unintended pregnancy and the spread of sexually transmitted infections (STIs) among youth. Even with the growing evidence that abstinence-only programs are not effective at delaying sexual activity or reducing STIs, these programs became very popular during the early 2000s. In fact, some researchers found that abstinence-only programs had negative unintended consequences related to denying youth access to information about safe sex and protection from disease. On the other hand, sexual education programs have been criticized as promoting sexual activity, though little evidence supports this claim.

An alternative that combines these two approaches is an abstinence-plus program that combines safe sex education with a strong message that promotes abstinence. The Youth Abstinence-Plus (YAP) program includes a focus on abstinence, education regarding safe sex for those youth who find themselves in sexual situations, and access to contraceptives for youth who plan to engage in sexual activity. YAP is a fictitious program, used as a case study throughout the text, and presented in this section in its entirety.

The YAP program long-term goals are to

- Decrease the pregnancy rate among youth;

- Decrease the spread of STIs among youth; and

- Increase the number of youth who choose sexual abstinence.

The YAP program strategies are to provide

1. Materials on the benefits of abstinence;

2. Education regarding safe sex; and

3. Access to contraception.

Ideally, the program staff, key stakeholders, and evaluation staff would hold a series of meetings to discuss why the program's strategies will result in the goals that were specified. The following is the expanded logic that might evolve from such meetings.

Providing materials on promoting sexual abstinence and a message about the benefits of sexual abstinence among youth will increase access to materials on abstinence, leading to an increased number of youth who receive the message about the benefits of abstinence, leading to an increased number of youth who understand the benefits of abstinence. An increase in the number of youth who understand the benefits of abstinence will lead to an increase in the number of youth who choose sexual abstinence, which will lead to a decrease in the pregnancy rate among youth and a decrease in the spread of STIs.

Providing youth with education regarding safe sex practices will increase access to education regarding safe sex practices, leading to an increase in the number of youth who receive education regarding safe sex practices, which will lead to an increase in the number of youth who understand the benefits of safe sex practices. An increase in the number of youth who understand the benefits of safe sex practices will lead to improved safe sex practices among youth who are sexually active. Improved safe sex practices among sexually active youth will decrease the pregnancy rate among youth and decrease the spread of STIs among youth.

Providing youth access to contraceptives will increase the number of youth who have access to contraceptives, which will increase the number of sexually active youth who obtain contraceptives. An increase in the number of sexually active youth who obtain contraceptives will increase the use of contraceptives among sexually active youth, leading to improved safe sex practices among sexually active youth. Improved safe sex practices among sexually active youth will decrease the pregnancy rate among youth and decrease the spread of STIs among youth.

13.3.1 YAP Logic Model

See Figure 13.6 on the next page.

13.3.2 YAP Evaluation Matrix

After (1) learning about the YAP program, (2) identifying the program's strategies and goals, (3) brainstorming the theory underlying the program, and (4) developing the program's logic model, the YAP evaluation design process now turns to creating evaluation questions.

Creating a table with a separate row for each component in the logic model is recommended. Categorizing and labeling the components by strategy, early and intermediate objectives, and long-term goals will help to easily align components and questions in the table with the logic model. Questions are created directly from the YAP logic model. Remember, questions should be open-ended. However, they should also be very straightforward and address the logic model component clearly. There is no need to be especially creative with evaluation questions or to worry about the repetitive nature of the question prompt. The important part is making sure your questions cover the relevant aspects of the logic model component so that program staff can make effective decisions regarding the program's implementation, operation, and impact. Once questions are developed, indicators and targets are derived from the questions. Finally, data sources are identified, and data collection procedures and data analysis techniques determined.

The YAP evaluation matrix is shown in Table 13.3.

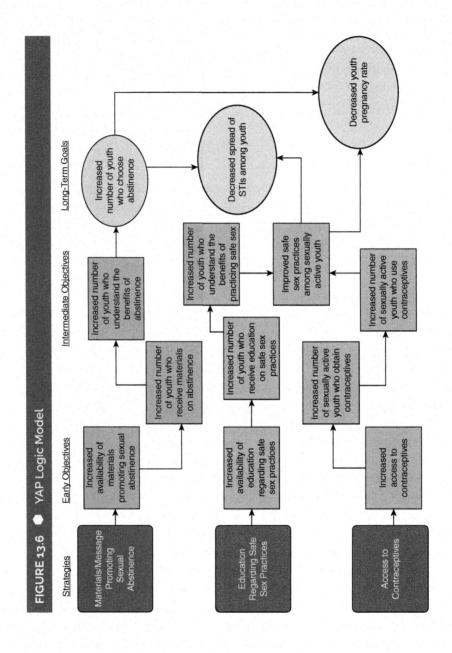

FIGURE 13.6 ● YAP Logic Model

TABLE 13.3 ● YAP Evaluation Matrix

	Logic Model Component	Evaluation Question(s)	Indicators	Targets	Data Source	Data Collection	Data Analysis
Program Strategies/Implementation	Materials promoting sexual abstinence	What were the content and format of materials promoting abstinence? In what ways were materials promoting abstinence made available to youth?	Content and format of abstinence materials *Method of delivering abstinence materials to youth*	By program start, materials promoting sexual abstinence are developed and implemented with fidelity	Fidelity of implementation rubric	Rubric administered at start of program and quarterly thereafter	Rubric data analyzed for evidence of implementation fidelity
	Education regarding safe sex practices	What were the content and format of education regarding sex practices? In what ways was education regarding safe sex provided?	Content and format of education regarding safe sex practices *Method of delivering education regarding safe sex to youth*	By program start, education regarding safe sex practices is implemented with fidelity	Fidelity of implementation rubric	Rubric administered at start of program and quarterly thereafter	Rubric data analyzed for evidence of implementation fidelity
	Access to contraceptives	In what ways, from whom, and at what locations were contraceptives available to youth? What types of contraceptives were made available to youth?	Distribution method of contraceptives to youth *Types of contraceptives available to youth*	By program start, methods of access to contraceptives will be implemented with fidelity	Fidelity of implementation rubric	Rubric administered at start of program and quarterly thereafter	Rubric data analyzed for evidence of implementation fidelity

(Continued)

TABLE 13.3 ● (Continued)

	Logic Model Component	Evaluation Question(s)	Indicators	Targets	Data Source	Data Collection	Data Analysis
Early and Intermediate Objectives	Increase the availability of materials on abstinence	To what extent did youth have access to materials on abstinence?	Availability of abstinence materials to youth	Within one week of program start, abstinence materials will be available to all youth	Program records	Program records examined monthly	Program records analyzed for evidence of availability of materials
	Increase the number of youth who receive materials on abstinence	To what extent did the number of youth who received materials on abstinence increase? In what ways did youth obtain materials related to abstinence?	Number of youth receiving abstinence materials *Method of receiving abstinence materials*	Within three months of program start, all youth will have received materials on abstinence	Inventory of materials	Inventory data collected monthly	Inventory data analyzed for evidence of material distribution
	Increase the availability of education regarding safe sex practices	To what extent was education regarding safe sex practices made available to youth?	Availability of education regarding safe sex practices	Within one week of program start, education regarding safe sex will be available to all youth	Program records Training schedule	Program records and training schedule examined monthly	Program records and training schedule analyzed for evidence of availability of education

Increase the number of youth who receive education regarding safe sex practices	To what extent did the number of youth who received education regarding safe sex practices increase? How did youth receive education regarding safe sex?	Number of youth receiving education on safe sex practices *Method of receiving education on safe sex practices*	Within three months of program start, all youth will have received education on safe sex practices	Training sign-in sheets	Sign-in sheets collected after each session and analyzed monthly	Basic descriptive statistics of sign-in sheet data
Increase the number of youth who have access to contraceptives	To what extent did the number of youth with access to contraceptives increase? To what extent were youth aware of their access to contraceptives?	Number of youth who have access to contraceptives *Number of youth who are aware of their access to contraceptives*	Within three months of program start, all youth will have access to contraceptives Within six months, all youth will be aware of their access to contraceptives	Program records	Program records examined monthly	Program records analyzed for evidence of access to contraceptives

(Continued)

TABLE 13.3 ● (Continued)

Logic Model Component	Evaluation Question(s)	Indicators	Targets	Data Source	Data Collection	Data Analysis
Increase the number of sexually active youth who obtain contraceptives	To what extent did the number of sexually active youth who obtain contraceptives increase? Where did youth obtain contraceptives? What types of contraceptives did youth obtain?	Number of sexually active youth who obtain contraceptives *Demographics of youth who obtain contraceptives* *Method and location of receiving contraceptives* *Types of contraceptives received*	Within one year of program start, there will be a 25% increase in sexually active youth who obtain contraceptives	Inventory of contraceptives	Inventory data collected monthly	Basic descriptive statistics of inventory data
Increase the number of youth who understand the benefits of abstinence	To what extent did the number of youth who understand the benefits of abstinence increase? What did youth learn about abstinence?	Number of youth who understand the benefits of abstinence *Nature of youth's understanding about the benefits of abstinence*	Within six months of the start of the program, all youth will be able to describe the benefits of abstinence	Youth survey	Survey administered at start of program and at end of program	Basic descriptive statistics of survey data *t*-test examining pre/post differences

| Increase the number of youth who understand the benefits of practicing safe sex | To what extent did the number of youth who understand the benefits of practicing safe sex increase? What did youth learn about practicing safe sex? | Number of youth who are able to describe the benefits of practicing safe sex *Nature of youth's understanding about the benefits of practicing safe sex* | Within six months of program start, all youth will be able to describe the benefits of practicing safe sex | Youth survey | Survey administered at start of program and at end of program | Basic descriptive statistics of survey data t-test examining pre/post differences |
| Increase the number of sexually active youth who use contraceptives | To what extent did the number of sexually active youth who use contraceptives increase? What types of contraceptives did youth choose to use? How often did youth use contraceptives in sexual situations? | Number of sexually active youth who use contraceptives *Demographics of youth who use contraceptives* *Types of contraceptives used* *Frequency with which contraception is used* | Within one year of program start, there will be a 20% increase in the number of sexually active youth who use contraceptives | Youth survey | Survey administered at start of program and at end of program | Basic descriptive statistics of survey data t-test examining pre/post differences |

(Continued)

TABLE 13.3 ● (Continued)

	Logic Model Component	Evaluation Question(s)	Indicators	Targets	Data Source	Data Collection	Data Analysis
Long-Term Goals	Improve safe sex practices among sexually active youth	To what extent did safe sex practices among sexually active youth improve? In what ways did safe sex practices improve?	Number of sexually active youth who practice safe sex *Demographics of youth who practice safe sex* *Nature of safe sex practices used* *Frequency with which contraception is used*	Within one year of program start, there will be a 20% increase in sexually active youth who practice safe sex	Youth survey	Survey administered at start of program and at end of program	Basic descriptive statistics of survey data *t*-test examining pre/post differences
	Increase the number of youth who choose abstinence	To what extent did the number of youth who choose abstinence increase?	Number of youth who choose abstinence *Demographics of youth who choose abstinence* *Self-reported reason for youth choosing abstinence*	Within one year of program start, there will be a 20% increase in the number of youth who choose abstinence	Youth survey	Survey administered at start of program and at end of program	Basic descriptive statistics of survey data *t*-test examining pre/post differences

Decrease the spread of STIs among youth	To what extent did the spread of STIs, including HIV, decrease?	Number of youth diagnosed with STI/HIV *Demographics of youth diagnosed with STI/HIV*	Within two years of program start, there will be a 20% decrease in the number of diagnosed STI/HIV cases among youth in the community	Youth survey Public health records	Survey administered at start of program and at end of program Public health records examined annually	Basic descriptive statistics of survey data *t*-test examining pre/post differences Health records analyzed using basic descriptive statistics
Decrease the youth pregnancy rate	To what extent did the youth pregnancy rate decrease?	Number of youth who become pregnant *Demographics of youth who become pregnant*	Within two years of program start, there will be a 20% decrease in the number of youth in the community who become pregnant	Youth survey Public health records	Survey administered at start of program and at end of program Public health records examined annually	Basic descriptive statistics of survey data *t*-test examining pre/post differences Health records analyzed using basic descriptive statistics

APPENDICES

SPECIAL TOPICS

Tell me and I forget. Teach me and I remember. Involve me and I learn.

—Benjamin Franklin

APPENDIX A: NEEDS ASSESSMENT

Escobedo, P., Gonzalez, K. D., Kuhlberg, J., Calanche, M. L., Baezconde-Garbanati, L., Contreras, R., & Bluthenthal, R. (2019). Community needs assessment among Latino families in an urban public housing development. *Hispanic Journal of Behavioral Sciences, 41*(3), 344–362.

APPENDIX B: POLITICS AND POLICY

Diem, S., Young, M. D., & Sampson, C. (2019). Where critical policy meets the politics of education: An introduction. *Educational Policy, 33*(1), 3–15.

APPENDIX C: DEVELOPMENTAL EVALUATION

Patton, M. Q. (2016). What is essential in developmental evaluation? On integrity, fidelity, adultery, abstinence, impotence, long-term commitment, integrity, and sensitivity in implementing evaluation models. *American Journal of Evaluation, 37*(2), 250–265.

APPENDIX D: TRANSLATIONAL RESEARCH EVALUATION

Grazier, K. L., Trochim, W. M., Dilts, D. M., & Kirk, R. (2013). Estimating return on investment in translational research: Methods and protocols. *Education & the Health Professions, 36*(4), 478–491.

Visit **edge.sagepub.com/giancola1e** to download the articles and accompanying critical thinking questions.

NEEDS ASSESSMENT

Community Needs Assessment Among Latino Families in an Urban Public Housing Development

Patricia Escobedo,[1] Karina Dominguez Gonzalez,[1] Jill Kuhlberg,[2]
Maria "Lou" Calanche,[3] Lourdes Baezconde-Garbanati,[1] Robert Contreras,[4]
and Ricky Bluthenthal[1]

Abstract

Studies examining the health of public housing residents are limited. In response, community-based participatory research principles were used to develop an intervention aimed at improving health outcomes related to multifactorial risk behaviors among Latino families living in a low-income neighborhood. A two-part needs assessment was completed to guide the intervention: interviews with parents ($n = 10$) and a group model building (GMB) workshop with youth and parents ($n = 40$) to explore the parent-youth dynamic. Interviews indicated that poverty, youth disobedience, and inadequate communication between parents and youth led to parental

[1]University of Southern California, Los Angeles, CA, USA
[2]The University of North Carolina, Chapel Hill, USA
[3]Legacy LA, Los Angeles, CA, USA
[4]Bienestar Human Services, Inc., Los Angeles, CA, USA

Corresponding Author

Patricia Escobedo, Department of Preventive Medicine, Keck School of Medicine, University of Southern California, 2001 N. Soto Street, 3rd Floor Mail, Los Angeles, CA 90032, USA. Email: pescobed@usc.edu

stress. During the workshop, balancing and reinforcing feedback loops involving Communication, Trust, and Respect between youth and parents were identified. Based on these findings and collaboration with a community advisory board, a bilingual, mindfulness-based meditation intervention was designed to address community needs: positive parent-child interaction emphasizing trust and communication, stress reduction, and family well-being.

In the United States, Latinos constitute 18% of the total population, yet represent nearly 20% of the nation's poor (Semega, Fontenot, & Kollar, 2017). Among children living in poverty in the United States, more than a quarter are Latino (Semega et al., 2017), signifying a critical health disparity as child poverty is associated with lower educational attainment, higher prevalence of emotional and behavioral problems, chronic diseases, adulthood morbidity, and reduced life expectancy (Blane, Bartley, & Smith, 1997; Kozyrskyj, Kendall, Jacoby, Sly, & Zubrick, 2010; Singh & Ghandour, 2012; Singh, Siahpush, & Kogan, 2010).

Living in poverty may also exacerbate existing disparities in health outcomes among Latinos. Compared with Whites, Latino adults suffer disproportionately higher rates of mortality related to obesity, diabetes, and cirrhosis (Centers for Disease Control and Prevention [CDC], 2015). Many Latinos face linguistic and cultural barriers when accessing health care, which can result in less satisfaction with quality of medical care and reduced health seeking (Garcia & Duckett, 2009). Latino adolescents may be especially vulnerable. Compared with their White peers, Latino adolescents have a higher prevalence of depression, which is concerning as depression is associated with substance use, lower academic attainment, and eating disorders (Chaiton, Cohen, O'Loughlin, & Rehm, 2009; Lee & Liechty, 2015; Liechty & Lee, 2013). Family structure and family functioning may also influence health outcomes. Parent-child conflict among Latino families was associated with higher levels of depressive symptoms and conduct problems (Gonzales, Deardorff, Formoso, Barr, & Barrera, 2006; Smokowski et al., 2014). In addition, Latino adolescents in single parent families reported high levels of economic adversity, depression, and family stress (Zeiders, Roosa, & Tein, 2011). Overall, these disparities indicate a need for culturally tailored interventions that address multiple risk factors among Latino families. Tailored interventions are especially needed in communities of concentrated poverty such as low-income and public housing developments.

Nearly 1.2 million U.S. households live in government-subsidized public housing developments (U.S. Department of Housing and Urban Development, 2017); however, studies examining the health of public housing residents are limited. Earlier research found that when compared with the general population, public housing residents reported a higher prevalence of chronic health conditions, tobacco use, physical inactivity, and are more likely to rate their health as fair or poor (Digenis-Bury, Brooks, Chen,

Ostrem, & Horsburgh, 2008; Manjarrez, Popkin, & Guernsey, 2007). Given that many Latino public housing residents are foreign-born and Spanish speaking (Chambers & Rosenbaum, 2014; Harley et al., 2014; Quintiliani et al., 2014), more research on Latino families in public housing is needed.

To address this gap, a community-campus partnership, known as the Partners for Strong Healthy Families (PSHF), was established with the goal of improving the health and well-being of Latino families living within and around the Ramona Gardens public housing community in Los Angeles through the development of a family-based health intervention. The PSHF is founded on a partnership between the following three organizations: (1) the University of Southern California (USC); (2) Bienestar, a Latino AIDS service organization; and (3) Legacy LA, a community-based nonprofit organization focused on youth development in the Ramona Gardens community. Engaging public housing residents in the identification of community health needs is a fundamental step toward the implementation of culturally tailored community-based interventions (Bowen et al., 2013). Several studies have successfully used community-based participatory research (CBPR) approaches to identify health needs within underserved Latino communities (Bopp et al., 2012; Corona, Gonzalez, Cohen, Edwards, & Edmonds, 2009; Dulin, Tapp, Smith, De Hernandez, & Furuseth, 2011; Valenzuela, McDowell, Cencula, Hoyt, & Mitchell, 2013). Using collaborative partnerships and shared decision-making between partners to develop research questions of importance to all stakeholders allows researchers to move beyond basic or applied research approaches in order to design a tailored research strategy that is culturally competent and accordant with the specific life experiences, cultural traditions, and languages of the participants in the study (Baker, White, & Lichtveld, 2001; McQuiston, Parrado, Martínez, & Uribe, 2005). The specific health issues and outcomes assessed by the PSHF pilot intervention were determined using the results of a community needs assessment, which integrated two community participatory processes: the first, a group model building (GMB) workshop using a community-based system dynamics (CBSD) approach, and the other, key informant interviews developed using CBPR principles. Both processes involved the engagement of adolescents and parents living within the Ramona Gardens public housing development and surrounding communities.

This article described the development of the PSHF intervention by providing an overview of the GMB workshop designed to understand and improve the relationships between parents and youth living in the Ramona Gardens community and the findings from the key informant interviews. We provide a description of the planning process and structure of the GMB workshop and report the results and insights generated from the workshop and key informant interviews.

METHOD

Participants

Participants were recruited from the Ramona Gardens public housing development and surrounding community. Ramona Gardens houses an estimated 2,000 residents who are almost exclusively Latino (City of Los Angeles, 2015). The development is located 3 miles east of downtown Los Angeles within the neighborhood of Boyle Heights, where nearly all residents are Latino (90.9%), speak Spanish at home (85%), and nearly half are foreign-born (47%) (U.S. Census Bureau, 2016). The needs assessment integrated two community-based participatory processes: the first, key informant interviews, which were followed by a GMB workshop using a CBSD approach.

Key Informant Interviews

Sampling and recruitment. Parents were eligible to participate in key informant interviews if they lived in the Ramona Gardens community (inclusive of both the public housing complex and the surrounding neighborhood) and had a child of middle school or high school age. Parents receiving services from Legacy LA who were eligible for the study were contacted over the phone or in person by bilingual Legacy LA staff members and *promotoras*. To recruit eligible parents in the community not receiving Legacy LA services, Legacy LA staff members and promotoras conducted door-to-door recruitment visits in the housing project, where eligible parents were invited to participate. All participants were offered transportation to the Legacy LA office. Recruitment of eligible fathers proved to be challenging, as the majority of families contacted were single-mother households; however, four fathers were recruited using community outreach and referral sampling. Each parent received US$10 in cash after the completion of the interview.

Procedures

A semi-structured interview guide was developed in collaboration with USC faculty, and community partners Bienestar Human Services and Legacy LA. Participants had the option to complete the interview in English or Spanish. Prior to each interview, interviewers obtained verbal consent, and a written copy of the consent form was provided to parents in their preferred language.

During the interview, parents were asked to share information about (1) their personal history in the community, (2) knowledge about helping agencies or individuals in the community (e.g., recreational leagues, religious organizations, city and county services, and other formal and informal groups or individuals interested in the well-being of families in the community), (3) family communication, (4) sources of stress, and (5) community health issues and health resources. Lastly, parents were asked about community perception of research and health interventions and what kind of intervention topics, design, and incentives would increase participation and retention among Ramona Gardens families.

Six mothers and four fathers were recruited for a total of 10 parent interviews. Average duration of interviews was 40 minutes. All interviews were digitally recorded and transcribed. Eight parents requested an interview in English, and audio-recordings of English interviews were completed by a professional transcription service. Two parents requested interviews in Spanish, and audio-recordings were translated and transcribed by a bilingual member of the university research team.

Data Analysis

Thematic content analysis was conducted using software package Atlas.ti7. A thematic data analysis approach was taken to understand the following domains: community strengths, risks to youth and families, sources of parent and youth conflict, sources of stress, community health, and community perception of research and health interventions.

Community-Based System Dynamics

CBSD is a participatory approach, which involves communities in the process of understanding the dynamics of an identified problem from a feedback perspective (Hovmand, 2014). CBSD is appropriate when the goal of a project is to build a community's capacity to interpret problems with a holistic perspective and arrive at a shared understanding of a problem (Munar, Hovmand, Fleming, & Darmstadt, 2015). Using the CBSD approach, collaborators can gain insight into the issues surrounding parent-youth (PY) relationships in Ramona Gardens to design more effective interventions for its residents and to empower parents and youth to address the problems in their relationships. CBSD draws on GMB practices, including the use of structured activities carried out by trained facilitators from the community with system dynamics modelers in supportive roles. These activities use models to initiate deeper insights and conversations about problems and systems that are changing over time, using the formal diagramming conventions of system dynamics, including causal loop diagrams (CLDs) (Hovmand, 2014; Hovmand et al., 2012; Richardson & Andersen, 1995; Vennix, 1996).

Procedures

The approximately 3-hour workshop with parents and youth included several scripted activities designed and adapted to involve and build capacity of the Ramona Gardens community members in generating a deeper understanding of the dynamics of PY relationships. Group facilitators consisted of Legacy LA and Bienestar staff members, and bilingual research team members trained in CBSD methodology. Parent activities were conducted in Spanish, while youth activities were conducted in English. Discussions with parents and youth were conducted in English and Spanish.

Graphs over time. To begin, parents and youth were divided into separate groups, with parents working on one end of the room and youth on the other. Participants were asked to draw graphs showing how variables that affect or are affected by the PY relationship have changed over time. Variables could include feelings (e.g., respect), behaviors (e.g., communication), activities/responsibilities (e.g., school), people (e.g., friends), and items (e.g., Internet). Parents shared their graphs with other parents, while youth shared their graphs with other youth participants. All participants then reconvened for a large group discussion to summarize key findings. Next, to understand which variables parents and youth felt were key to understanding the dynamics of the PY relationship, participants were asked to mark the five to six graphs they felt were most important. Facilitators tallied votes and listed the most popular PY variables.

CLDs. Following a meal break, parents and youth again divided into separate groups, where facilitators introduced the design and function of CLDs. Using examples relevant to parents and youth, facilitators described the concepts required to draw CLDs, which included causal arrows, polarity, and reinforcing and balancing feedback loops. In small groups, participants were asked to draw CLDs showing how different variables and experiences, identified during the graphs over time activity, are interrelated. Groups could choose variables from the list of most popular PY variables, as well as other variables they felt influenced the PY relationship. Facilitators actively coached participants, helping groups understand CLD concepts as well as identify and characterize feedback loops. After 30 minutes, participants presented CLDs to their respective groups by explaining how the feedback loops they found influence the PY relationship. Lastly, parents and youth reconvened to discuss and evaluate their workshop experience with facilitators. Trained note takers transcribed all group discussions during the workshop. All graphs and CLDs were labeled and collected by research team members to assist with data analysis.

Data Analysis

All parent and youth CLDs were reconstructed by Jill Kuhlberg using Venism DSS modeling software. Using the transcribed notes, individual diagrams were updated as needed (arrowhead direction and/or polarity changed) to ensure they reflected the story told by participants. Once all diagrams were updated, they were examined to identify the most commonly occurring variables across parent and youth CLDs. Transcribed notes were also reviewed at this time to determine how terms used in the diagrams could serve as links between the CLDs created by different groups. Finally, one synthesized CLD combining both parent and youth stories in English and Spanish was created using this iterative process.

RESULTS

Key Informant Interview Results

A total of six mothers and four fathers were interviewed. Nine parents currently lived in the Ramona Gardens housing development, with length of residency ranging from 1.5 to 30 years (M = 13.85 years). Three of the parents were married, two were living with a partner, and five were single parents. The number of children living in each household ranged from 2 to 7 (M = 4.2), with ages of children ranging from 2 to 22 years (M = 11.2 years).

Community change. A common theme was the noticeable decrease in violence, crime, drug deals, and gang activity within the Ramona Gardens community over the past decade. Parents felt this was due to increased police presence, a decrease in gang activity, and a proliferation of programs for youth in the Ramona Gardens and Boyle Heights community. Increased police presence in the community, including police patrols, installation of security cameras, and community outreach efforts, was also attributed to the increase in neighborhood safety. Most parents appreciated the efforts made by law enforcement to control and discourage gang activity; however, two fathers who themselves were raised in the Ramona Gardens community felt that police and law enforcement stereotyped young men in the neighborhood as gang members and arrested groups of young men without provocation, causing tension between police and families. One father described how his nephews are stopped by police "all the time and for no reason, they're just out there just, you know, with friends and they [the police] go there . . . they already think, these guys are doing something, even though you're not."

Longer term residents felt that previous generations of Ramona Gardens residents became involved in gang activity due to a lack of youth development programs in the Boyle Heights area. Parents felt that youth now had access to numerous youth programs, and "if they're always busy they won't have time to be out in the streets, looking for something to do." Although all parents agreed that neighborhood safety had increased significantly over the past years, a lingering fear of gang violence and crime discouraged some families from enrolling their children in sports and youth programs in Ramona Gardens and the Boyle Heights community.

Risks to youth and parenting. In the Ramona Gardens community, dropping out of school, along with gang involvement, violence, and substance use, was perceived as the greatest risk to youth. Longer term residents felt it was difficult to discourage their children's interest in gang activity and substance use as both are pervasive within the community:

> There are many youth in our community who want to get involved in the wrong things, go down the wrong path and we as parents need to help them. We as parents should motivate them, speak with them, we should be communicating with them. If their self-esteem is low, we should raise it up. Tell them that if they want something, they need to earn it. To keep moving forward. (Grandmother)

Conflicts between parent and children and overall family stress were perceived as risk factors for gang involvement. Disrespectful behavior by children and ineffective communication between parent and child were identified as major sources of stress within families. Children often ignored instructions or directives, refused to follow directives given by parents, argued with parents, used inappropriate language with parents, or did not return home by a given curfew:

> I think a lot of conflict is the disrespecting. You know, that's one of the biggest ones, disrespect, a lot of kids nowadays don't find it something that we need to continue to have. The disrespecting happens at a young age, and I'm talking about 5-6 years old. You know, we got 5-year-olds and 6-year-olds disrespecting their mom and, and saying no. As soon as they say no, that's a problem, because they shouldn't be allowed to tell you no. I think they need to learn that the respect you give, you shall receive, and a lot of times it's confusing, they think they got to get the respect from the homies instead of the family, and it's like, no, it's, you got it backwards. Family needs to be involved more to stop all of that. (Mother)

Being a single parent was associated with greater parent-child conflict and family stress, as single parents, especially working mothers, found it difficult to cope with and respond to disrespectful behavior from children. Several single mothers felt that agencies providing counseling services, nutrition, and health resources, and youth mentorship were at times difficult to locate in the surrounding community but were used regularly to help overwhelmed parents with their child's academic progress, health needs, and behavioral challenges. Mothers felt that free parenting classes were needed to help parents improve positive interaction with children and to demonstrate effective disciplinary strategies.

Stress and coping. Financial difficulties and poverty were the greatest source of stress among families. Even among households with two working parents, parents described difficulties paying monthly rent, utilities, and providing the basics for their family. One mother felt that she could not provide her children the material possessions they wanted; she could only afford what was needed, which caused conflict between parents and children. Parents also felt stressed about unemployment and job security. Other sources of stress were related to household and community violence, child misbehavior, and financial stress. Several mothers described family therapy and counseling services as beneficial and integral to stress reduction, increasing self-esteem, and overall family functioning and well-being.

Community health needs. The most concerning health issues within the community were related to diet, physical activity, and mental health. Parents mentioned psychological stress, diabetes, hypertension, obesity, and unhealthy diet. Many negative health outcomes were attributed to a high-fat diet and lack of access to fresh produce. Vendors sold foods like "churros, chips, nachos and tamales" in the housing development, making it easy to eat inexpensive and high-fat foods. The nearest market is a liquor store with limited produce options and "inflated" prices. All parents agreed that in order to access a larger and more affordable selection of fresh produce, families were required to travel outside the community as there were no grocery stores within walking distance. The estimated distance to these larger grocery stores varied depending on whether the parent used public transportation or their own vehicle. The parents describing grocery stores as easily accessible all owned a personal vehicle. Parents who used public transportation described the journey to and from the grocery store as tiresome and time-consuming and estimated the nearest grocery store as being several miles away. However, parents who owned vehicles estimated the nearest grocery store as being half a mile to a mile away from Ramona Gardens. Parents who were unhappy with the produce price and selection at the local liquor store wanted access to a farmer's market, "a healthy supermarket," or more frequent trips from a local produce truck. However, one parent expressed some hesitation about the affordability of organic or natural markets in his community: "How are you going to have that here, you're going to have a poor community, those are expensive stores, you know, like it's just hard when the community's poor and you're trying to live rich, eat like the rich."

Nearly all parents felt that the Ramona Gardens Recreation Center was an important health resource because it offered numerous sports programs for youth at reduced prices. The surrounding parks were also mentioned as important areas for recreation and exercise, especially for youth. Those who mentioned the parks described them as a place for physical activities like skateboarding, basketball, and running; however, several mothers expressed concern about personal safety when playing outdoors. Concern over personal safety was perceived as a barrier to physical activity for both parents and youth, and though most parents felt that residents were willing to venture outside their home and walk freely around the housing development, some parents did not feel comfortable leaving their home later in the evening.

> Two years ago we donated 27 bikes to the school, we're trying to get kids on bikes, to you know, to lose the weight and kids get their bikes stolen all the time. Keeping them active is a little bit harder. We try to give out skates, give out things that they could use to physically help them, but people walk into the projects and just intend to steal stuff, so. They can only do so much with that. (Mother)

Several parents recommended that group exercise classes for adults also be offered at the Ramona Gardens Recreation Center to encourage adults and parents to exercise. Some parents felt that the installation of outdoor exercise equipment in the nearby parks would increase physical activity among parents because parents could exercise while also supervising their children. Parents also felt it was important to involve the entire family in group or family-based classes to increase positive interaction among family members.

Increasing community participation. Most parents felt that families would commit to 1 to 6 hours per week, while others specified once or twice a week, with a duration of 3 months at most. Overall participation and time invested in a program would depend on the goals and outcomes, child care availability, and transportation. Parents expressed a preference for family-based activities that focus on exercise, nutrition, and parenting classes. Parents felt that incentives such as gift cards, free groceries, and child care would be attractive incentives and increase participation. All parents felt that a university-sponsored program focusing on health and well-being would be welcomed into the community. Parents also felt it was imperative for researchers to communicate directly with the community and meet with community members at Ramona Gardens before the start of the intervention program to explain how the intervention would benefit the participants and the community. It was recommended that researchers partner with community leaders such as the Ramona Gardens Advisory Council to discuss community needs and resources. While many parents were aware of the university's affiliation with the local county hospital, some felt that the university could improve its relationship with the community by offering health and counseling services to Ramona Gardens residents and providing referrals to local social and health services.

GMB Results

Graphs over time. Several themes surfaced during the graphs over time exercise. Both parents and youth indicated that the PY relationship is affected by an increase in the time youth spend with friends, increased hours worked by parents, increased use of technology (e.g., computers, cell phones, video games), increasing fear of deportation, and a decrease in trust and communication over time. Several youth graphs described increasing household responsibilities and police presence in the community, while parents described declining respect between parents and youth and the declining number of parents and youth who communicate in the same language.

CLDs. CLDs allow participants to see how variables related to the PY relationship are interrelated. Both parents and youth identified several reinforcing processes (labeled R1, R2, and R3 in Figure 1) linking *Confianza*/Trust, *Respeto*/Respect, and *Communicación*/Communication with both virtuous and vicious cycles. Other reinforcing loops that emerged included involvement in sports (R4 in Figure 1). Youth felt that when parents had less trust in them, this led to less involvement in sports and other school activities, which reduced overall school involvement, lowering grades, and further weakening parental trust. Both parents and youth identified the youth's friends as influential factors, especially friends who parents felt were negative influences on their children. Spending more time with friends also reduced time spent on at-home responsibilities (R5 in Figure 1), which was undesirable for the youth.

The use of technology and electronics was mentioned by all small groups. The more parents and youth use technology and electronics, the less they communicate, and the less they communicate, the more likely they are to use technology (R6). Parents and youth also identified several balancing processes (B1-B5 in Figure 1). Parents and youth reported several benefits associated with technology use (B1), which included stress reduction, assistance with schoolwork, and daily communication between parents and youth. Interestingly, youth identified an interesting balancing process (B2) related to sports, such that higher involvement in sports created time management issues, which took a toll on youth health over time. When health declined, youth were less likely to participate in sports. Two other important balancing processes involved trust between parents and youth. When parental trust is higher, youth are allowed to use more electronic devices, but spending an excessive amount on these devices negatively affects youth academic outcomes, reducing parental trust (B3). Trust in youth also allows parents to feel comfortable working outside the home, but more time spent at work decreases communication with the youth, which reduces trust (B4). Lastly, the dual influence of police in the community is represented as a reinforcing process, where police encourage students to do well in school (R6), yet police arrests decrease school attendance, and decreased attendance leads to more problems with the police.

Intervention Development

Feedback from the community, in both forms, directly impacted intervention development. The funded grant had originally proposed to focus on substance use and

FIGURE 1 ⬡ Casual Loop Diagram Combining Both Parent and Youth Stories

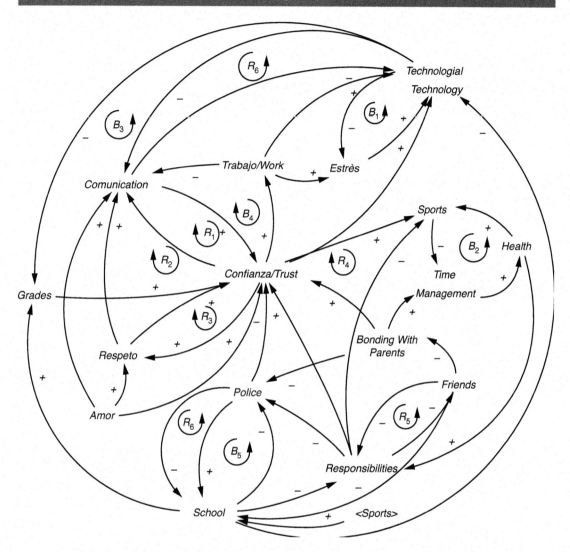

sexual risk behaviors (U.S. Department of Health and Human Services, National Institutes of Health, 2018). However, neither issue was identified as an important concern for youth or parents using either method. Interpretation of these results in collaboration with our community partners led the team to focus on an intervention that would improve trust and communication between youth and parents, while assisting both with skills that would improve stress management in the home, school, and workplace.

DISCUSSION AND IMPLICATIONS FOR PRACTICE

We presented findings from a community needs assessment consisting of two community participatory processes: a GMB workshop with parents and adolescents living in Ramona Gardens community and key informant interviews with parents of adolescents living in and around the Ramona Gardens community. Meaningful engagement of community members is an essential step in the successful implementation of culturally tailored community-based interventions (Bowen et al., 2013). The insights gained from this needs assessment process are important given that studies using CBPR principles to identify health needs among Latino public housing residents are scarce.

Findings from the GMB workshop and key informant interviews suggest several potential next steps to address the issues related to PY relationships and health needs in the Ramona Gardens community.

By having Ramona Gardens community members visualize the PY relationship system and identify balancing and reinforcing feedback loops that lead to conflict within their own families, stakeholders can collaborate to design a family-based intervention that balances or controls specific virtuous or vicious cycles in the system. The proposed PSHF intervention should focus on strengthening the reinforcing processes that increase levels of *Confianza*/Trust, *Respeto*/Respect, and *Communicación*/Communication among parents and youth. These processes are particularly important given that communication and respect emerged as common themes throughout the interview process, serving as both risk and protective factors.

Interviewed parents felt that positive encouragement increased positive PY interaction and was protective against gang involvement and substance use. In addition, disrespectful behavior by youth and ineffective communication between parents and youth were major sources of stress within families, especially within single parent households. GMB workshop findings also indicated that spending time with friends decreased bonding with parents; therefore, the intervention should develop a family-based intervention that includes educational components for both parents and children, an intervention format supported by interviewed parents.

During the GMB workshop, police interaction was characterized with both reinforcing and balancing processes, as police would encourage youth to achieve higher academic success, yet increased police presence led to more arrests. Arrests decreased school attendance, leading to more problems with the police. Interaction with police was also a concern among the interviewed parents. Interviews indicated that negative interaction with the police was a greater concern among fathers and men in the community; therefore, a separate parent intervention program could be provided to fathers, which includes sessions addressing the impact of policing tactics on the health and well-being of men in the Ramona Gardens community.

Although there was moderate overlap between themes and experiences discussed during the GMB workshop and the parent interviews, each approach offered unique findings to inform the development of the intervention. The GMB workshop revealed reinforcing and balancing feedback loops related to the use of technology. Although technology use was associated with stress reduction, it was also associated with less PY communication, and lower academic achievement and involvement. Given this, the proposed intervention should be implemented without the use of electronic devices.

Parent interviews revealed that although all parents felt that community safety had improved, a lingering fear of gang activity and violence discourages some families from enrolling children in local sports programs. Parents were also concerned with safety and transportation; thus, the intervention and any informational sessions and activities should be held in a nearby location recognized by community members as a safe space for youth and families. Parents were receptive to USC's involvement in a community-based health intervention program; however, before the pilot intervention begins, it is imperative for the academic research team to discuss intervention goals and outcomes directly with community members. The academic research team must also explain how the intervention will benefit the participants and community involved, not just the university partners.

Limitations

These preliminary findings are based on a small sample of Ramona Gardens community members. Additional GMB workshops and key informant interviews should be conducted with a larger sample of mothers and fathers to determine whether key differences in opinions and perspectives exist between mothers and fathers in the Ramona Gardens community.

CONCLUSION

Based on GMB workshops and interview findings and collaboration with a community advisory board, a bilingual, family-based meditation intervention will be designed to specifically address community needs: positive parent-child interaction that emphasized trust and communication, stress reduction, and family well-being. It is worth noting should the intervention be effective, we would expect to see improvements in substance use and sex risk behaviors, which were the original goals of the study. The use of CBPR, GMB, and key informant interviews provided important insights on how to achieve public health outcomes for low-income, racial/ethnic minority parents and youth in a manner that builds on family and community strengths and concerns.

Declaration of Conflicting Interests

The author(s) declared no potential conflicts of interest with respect to the research, authorship, and/or publication of this article.

Funding

The author(s) disclosed receipt of the following financial support for the research, authorship, and/or publication of this article: This paper was supported by grant R24MD007978 from the NIH National Institute on Minority Health and Health Disparities (NIMHD). The NIH had no role in study design, collection, analysis, and interpretation of data, or writing of report. The content is solely the responsibility of the authors.

AUTHOR BIOGRAPHIES

Patricia Escobedo received her BA from the University of California, Berkeley, and her MA from California State University, Northridge. She is currently a doctoral student in the Health Behavior Research Program in the Department of Preventive Medicine at the University of Southern California (USC). Her research interests include health disparities among ethnic minorities and vulnerable populations, community-based participatory research, tobacco control, and multiple substance use.

Karina Dominguez Gonzalez earned her BA from California State University, Dominguez Hills, and her MPH from USC. She is a research specialist in the Department of Preventive Medicine at the Keck School of Medicine of USC. Her work and research focus on a wide range of health issues, including utilization of preventive care, HIV and hepatitis C prevention, education and testing, cancer care, at-risk youth education, behavior modification, and substance abuse prevention and treatment.

Jill Kuhlberg earned her BA from the University of California, San Diego, and her MSW and PhD from Washington University. She is a postdoctoral research associate in Health Policy and Management at University of North Carolina (UNC) Gillings School of Global Public Health. Research interests include understanding and addressing social and public health–related issues at the local and international level using community-based system dynamics. Areas of expertise include community-based system dynamics, systems science, and community participation.

Maria "Lou" Calanche earned her BA from Loyola Marymount University and master's of public administration from USC. She is the founder and executive director of Legacy LA, a youth development program serving at-risk Latino youth living in the Ramona Gardens neighborhood and surrounding communities. Legacy LA provides youth with academic support, leadership development, mentoring, and arts programming.

Lourdes Baezconde-Garbanati is a tenured professor in Preventive Medicine, associate dean for Community Initiatives at the Keck School of Medicine, and associate director for Community Outreach and Engagement at the Norris Comprehensive Cancer Center at USC. She conducts research on health disparities among vulnerable population groups and is a widely recognized national and international community-engaged scholar in the areas of culture and community health, with an emphasis on Hispanic/Latino health.

Robert Contreras received his BS from California State University, Los Angeles, and MBA from Loyola Marymount University. He is deputy executive director at Bienestar Human Services. Bienestar is a community-based social services organization based in the Greater Los Angeles area that identifies and addresses emerging health issues faced by Latino and Lesbian, Gay, Bisexual, Transgender, and Queer (LGBTQ) populations. Bienestar's education and support programs include HIV/AIDS treatment and prevention, sexually transmitted infections (STIs), mental health services, substance use, and harm reduction.

Ricky Bluthenthal is a professor in the Department of Preventive Medicine and is associate dean for Social Justice at the Keck School of Medicine at USC. His research has established the effectiveness of syringe exchange programs, tested novel interventions and strategies to reduce HIV risk and improve HIV testing among injection drug users and men who have sex with men, and examined health policy implementation and how community conditions contribute to health disparities.

APPENDIX B

POLITICS AND POLICY

Where Critical Policy Meets the Politics of Education: An Introduction

Sarah Diem,[1] Michelle D. Young,[2] and Carrie Sampson[3]

Abstract

The study of educational politics and policy through a critical frame allows for a more nuanced, holistic understanding of the complexities associated with education policy, from creation through implementation to evaluation. The contributions to this special issue of *Educational Policy* illustrate the work of critical education policy scholars engaged in research focused at the federal, state, and local levels. In this introductory article, we introduce basic elements of critical policy analysis (CPA), including fundamental ontological and epistemological claims and their implications for investigating educational policy. From this foundation, we preview the articles included in this collection, highlighting their frameworks, methods, and focus.

Keywords

critical policy analysis, educational policy, politics of education

Traditional positivist approaches to educational policy analysis have long dominated the field (Cibulka, 1995; Levinson, Sutton, & Winstead, 2009; Nagel, 1984; Young, 1999; Young & Diem,

[1] University of Missouri, Columbia, MO, USA
[2] University of Virginia, Charlottesville, VA, USA
[3] Arizona State University, Tempe, AZ, USA

Corresponding Author

Sarah Diem, University of Missouri, 202 Hill Hall, Columbia, MO 65211, USA. Email: diems@missouri.edu

2014). In these approaches, policy making is generally considered a deliberate, linear process where an identifiable set of actors apply reason and research strategies to ensure the best policy outcomes (Monkman & Hoffman, 2013; Rist, 1994). Traditional policy analysis (TPA) approaches in education tend to include the following four tenets:

1. TPA focuses considerable energy on planning, adopting, implementing, examining, and/or evaluating policy-related educational changes or reforms. Change or reform is typically viewed as a deliberate process that can be planned and managed.

2. TPA frames research behavior as goal-driven, where rational individuals weigh the costs, benefits, and subsequent outcomes of a given action or strategy.

3. TPA takes for granted that researchers are capable of obtaining, accumulating, and understanding the knowledge necessary for identifying and deciding between policy solutions as well as planning for implementation and evaluation.

4. TPA assumes that researchers can evaluate policies, policy alternatives, and practices and express their evaluations to stakeholders in manners that can be used to identify and ameliorate problems (Diem, Young, Welton, Mansfield, & Lee, 2014; Young & Diem, 2017).

Although traditional approaches to educational policy analysis can vary in design and application, they reinforce the perspective that "empirical research can access the information needed to understand, design, plan, problem solve, and implement effective educational policies and practices" (Diem et al., 2014, p. 1071).

Dissatisfied with theoretically narrow and rationally driven approaches to policy analysis, a number of researchers have questioned the nature of policy, how it is created, its impact, and traditional approaches to policy analysis. These scholars use critical frameworks to question traditional approaches to analysis (McDonnell, 2009; Young & Diem, 2017). Influential critical policy scholars like Ball (1991, 1993, 1994), Apple (1982), and Popkewitz (1997, 2000) comprised the first generation of critical education policy researchers (Levinson et al., 2009), problematizing the rational approach of traditional educational policy research and emphasizing the role of power and ideology in the policy process. Others, including legal scholars, such as Bell (1976, 1980), Harris (1993), and Guinier (2004), and critical education scholars, such as Ladson-Billings and Tate (1995), Solórzano and Ornelas (2002), and Young (1999), also played a fundamental role in offering significant critiques to educational policies influencing minoritized communities (e.g., school desegregation, advanced placement, curriculum, and parental engagement).

The use of critical frameworks accelerated as the accountability movement took shape across the globe (Diem et al., 2014; Young & Diem, 2017). Young and Diem (2017) put it this way: "As power and control in education became increasingly consolidated and as the movement toward accountability and consolidation marched across the globe, a growing number of educational policy scholars, dissatisfied with traditional frameworks, began using critical frameworks in their analyses" (p. 3). For example, Carpenter (2017) used critical policy analysis (CPA) to examine how dominant federal education policy discourses are constructed through the deliberative performance of politics. Gill, Cain Nesbitt, and Parker (2017) used counternarratives of African American leaders to explore a shift in policy discourse from a focus on desegregation to an emphasis on color- and context-blind testing and accountability. Marshall and Young (2013) and Young and Marshall (2013) applied feminist CPA to examine the power and patriarchy prevalent in the culture and context of accountability policy that repress and silence women in educational leadership, and Whiteman, Maxcy, Fernández, and Paredes Scribner (2017) used CPA to explore marginalizing professional logics of school administration.

In recent politics of education scholarship, we have seen many examples of education policy and politics research emphasizing a turn to critical analysis. For example, the articles included in the 2016 special issue of *Educational Policy*, "Educational Policy and the Cultural Politics of Race," provide critical perspectives on the importance of race in frameworks devised "to understand the cultural politics of race in educational policy formation, implementation, and analysis" (Dumas, Dixson, & Mayorga, 2016, p. 7), disrupting traditional approaches to the role of race in the policy process. Similarly, the articles included in the 2017 special issue of the *Peabody Journal of Education*, "Neoliberal Policy Network Governance and Counter-Networks of Resistance: Actions and Reactions From Across Policy Arenas," provide critical perspectives on the use of neoliberal networks to influence education policy.

The contributions to this special issue of *Educational Policy* illustrate the work of critical education policy scholars engaged in policy research focused at the federal, state, and local levels. The contents of this issue are particularly timely given the extreme neoliberal education agenda of the Trump administration that threatens public education. This scholarship brings to bear critical theoretical perspectives on educational policy issues as influenced by a variety of actors. As Mitchell (1990) observed nearly three decades ago, "both the content and the form of schools is determined through the conflicts and coalitions found at the core of local, state and national political systems" (p. 166). The study of educational politics and policy through a critical frame strikes at the core of such issues. "Critical policy researchers engage in critique, interrogate the policy process, and the epistemological roots of policy work, examine the players involved in the policy process, and reveal policy constructions" (Diem & Young, 2015, p. 841).

CRITICAL APPROACHES TO EDUCATIONAL POLICY

Our research on CPA revealed that scholars who engage in CPA believe critique is important in a democratic society (Diem et al., 2014). Critical policy scholars seek to push back at timeworn, traditional policy approaches to educational policy, offering a number of different perspectives and developments that aim to critique and offer alternative strategies and perspectives for examining educational policy issues (see, for example, Atwood & López, 2014; Ball & Junemann, 2012; López, 2001; Lugg & Murphy, 2014; Mansfield, Welton, & Grogan, 2014; Sampson, 2016; Sampson & Horsford, 2017; Winton & Brewer, 2014; Young & Reynolds, 2017). In our research on CPA, we found scholars who employ this approach in their work tend to focus on five concerns. These include the following:

1. Concern regarding the difference between policy rhetoric and practiced reality

2. Concern regarding the policy, its roots, and its development (e.g., how it emerged, what problems it was intended to solve, how it changed and developed over time, and its role in reinforcing the dominant culture)

3. Concern with the distribution of power, resources, and knowledge as well as the creation of policy "winners" and "losers"

4. Concern regarding social stratification and the broader effect a given policy has on relationships of inequality and privilege

5. Concern regarding the nature of resistance to or engagement in policy by members of nondominant groups (Young & Diem, 2017, p. 4)

To illustrate, Young (1999) and Fernández and López (2017) utilized CPA to analyze and question the power dynamics of Latin parental engagement in education, Ball and Junemann (2012) used CPA to explore new philanthropies and policy networks in educational policy making, and Welton, Harris, Altamirano, and Williams (2017) applied CPA to examine the politics of student voice as it related to power and school policy within a high school class focused on social justice education.

CPA scholars also pay attention to the many complexities of contexts and systems in which policy is designed and implemented (Weaver-Hightower, 2008). They emphasize policy contexts, "reflecting the complexity of the policies, people, schools, and communities they impact and tended to take time to provide the historical and or cultural context of the policy issue under examination" (Diem & Young, 2015, p. 844). Thus, CPA offers opportunities to identify underlying problems and alternative solutions that address these contextual and systemic complexities in ways that TPA might overlook.

One of the key distinguishing features of CPA is the relationship between theory and method. In CPA, methodology and theoretical perspectives work hand in glove (Diem et al., 2014; Young, 1999; Young & Diem, 2017).

According to Young (1999), the research frame one uses dictates, to a large extent, the way one identifies and describes policy problems, the way one researches these problems, the policy options one considers, the approach one takes to policy implementation, and the approach taken for policy evaluation (p. 681).

CPA scholars have drawn on a variety of critical perspectives and methods in their exploration of policies, policy contexts, policy processes, policy communities, and policy impact. As such, CPA is an interdisciplinary approach that cuts across the humanities and social sciences (Young & Diem, 2017). The ability to analyze educational policies through multitheoretical and interdisciplinary approaches results in policy analyses that have more depth and breadth (Diem et al., 2014), and as Ulmer (2016) stressed, "Understanding policy differently might ultimately lead to better policy" (p. 1392). Although CPA scholars often employ qualitative methods in their research (Diem & Young, 2015), as this special issue demonstrates, CPA scholars' use of quantitative methods also offers unique insight on the policy process, particularly from a macroperspective.

The politics of education as a field has undergone a significant transformation since its early years, both in terms of focal areas and theoretical frameworks. The purpose of this special issue of *Educational Policy* is to demonstrate how different critical theoretical frameworks are being used in educational policy and politics scholarship to explore the politics of education at local, state, and federal levels. "The profound shifts taking place in contemporary social life require a shift in our research traditions" (Young, 1999, p. 705). CPA represents such a shift and offers the promise of broader, deeper, and potentially more complex understandings of educational policy issues. Although critical approaches to the analysis of educational policy and politics were introduced several decades ago, CPA scholars are still working to establish a firm foothold. To further advance CPA and the opportunity to understand policy differently, the articles included in this issue provide insight into theoretical and methodological approaches used by contemporary critical policy researchers in the United States and Canada.

OVERVIEW OF THE SPECIAL ISSUE

Along with this introduction, the special issue includes 11 articles and an afterword by Michael Apple that reflects on the contents of the issue and its implications for critical policy scholarship on the politics of education. The articles are organized into three sections. The first section, *Thinking Critically About Local Level Policy and Politics*, includes pieces that critically analyze the interplay between educational politics, policy making, interpretation, and implementation, paying particular attention to the role traditional and nontraditional educators play in policy making as well as the politics of race and disability. The second section, *Critiquing the State's Role in Educational Policy and Politics*, features articles that apply CPA in the analysis of the state's role in making and/or shaping educational policy. The third section, *Questioning Federal Education Policy, Politics, and Bureaucracy*, contains articles that critically examine the federal role in education policy.

Thinking Critically About Local Level Policy and Politics

This first section includes five pieces. The first article, by Diem, Holme, Edwards, Haynes, and Epstein, uses the lenses of interest convergence and zone of mediation to examine how gentrification affects school districts' pursuit of integration. Gentrification is proliferating across U.S. cities and restructuring the urban core, changing the demographic makeup and opportunities for those who have long called these spaces their homes. Diem et al. analyzed how five U.S. school districts located in gentrifying metropolitan areas are responding to demographic change. Importantly, their examination focuses on school districts that are pursuing strategies that seek to racially and economically integrate their school settings in the midst of fairly rapid gentrification.

Two of the articles in this section focus on parent engagement: one on engagement in fundraising and the other on engagement in their children's education. Grounded in institutional ethnography, Winton's research focuses on district-level policy concerning the coordination of school fundraising in Toronto, Ontario, Canada. She illustrates the problematic nature of school fundraising and how middle-class parents use education policy to benefit their own children. Oliva and Alémans' article focuses on Latinx mothers' efforts to create and implement school policy based on their conceptualizations of teacher quality as well as the standards they use to assess the effectiveness of teachers in their children's schools. They utilize a muxerista politics of education approach in their CPA to counter the dominant discourse around parent engagement and center the voices of Latinx mothers as leaders and political actors in the policy process.

Duarte and Brewer's article similarly focuses on the need to pushback and resist dominant education policy by examining the ways writing teachers articulate how they resist curricular policy. Duarte and Brewer use Certeau's (1984) theory of consumption, which argues for a resistance to the everydayness and an understanding of how this resistance is then reappropriated toward liberation. Through CPA, they illuminate the everyday experiences of teachers working in a neoliberal system and how teachers subvert pressures to fall in line with the standardized writing curriculum.

In this section's final article, Parekh and Brown employ quantitative methods to examine policy decisions around special education in the Toronto District School Board. Their CPA applies a critical disability studies lens founded in historical materialism to look at the academic outcomes of students placed in a half-time special education program. Their findings push policy makers, educators, and advocates of special education students to be more nuanced in how they respond to and construct disability, which, if not appropriate, can further limit students' access to postsecondary education.

Critiquing the State's Role in Educational Policy and Politics

The second section features four articles that explore a variety of actors at the state level, such as state legislatures and State Boards of Education (SBOEs), as well as how interactions among policy actors and their networks shape and reshape problem framing and policy making. The articles in this section demonstrate how state-level politics and policy activities affect educational equity and opportunity at the local level as well as how policy intentions and actions are understood and enacted at the state and local level.

Koyama and Chang's article examines how a variety of stakeholders—principals, teachers, parents, and community-based organization staff—make sense of and negotiate federal immigration policy and state education policies. Their application of CPA to data collected through a 3-year ethnography of refugee networks in Arizona utilizes critical discourse analysis and select pieces of actor network theory to examine "the ways in which language works within, and because of, power relations," and how policy discourses fail to benefit the actual needs of refugee youth, which only further isolates and weakens their academic learning experiences.

Similarly, and also focused on Arizona as one of three case sites, Sampson explores the impact of state-level policy on school districts' capacity to provide adequate educational opportunities for English learners (ELs). Using a multiple case study approach, she examines state-level policies in three large and diverse school districts located in Arizona, Nevada, and Utah. From district-level perspectives, she frames her analysis using CPA and illustrates how state-level policies were symbolic, restrictive, or exclusionary toward ELs. Although these findings reflect district-level efforts to engage, resist, and navigate state-level policies and politics on behalf of ELs, the results demonstrate how state-level policies compromised school districts' ability to provide ELs with adequate educational opportunities.

Using quantitative methods, Tabron and Ramlackhan's CPA focuses on a particular state-level policy, the Texas Top 10% Policy (TTPP), and the opportunities the policy provides for African American students with disabilities to access selective public higher education institutions in Texas. They utilize DisCrit, an intersectional critical lens of race and ability, in their quantitative analysis to "explore and critique the meritocratic guise of college access for African American students with disabilities." Their findings challenge the assumptions of policies like the TTPP, which were enacted to provide more geographic and racial diversity in Texas higher education public institutions but instead maintain disparities.

Young, VanGronigen, and Reynolds round off the section on the state's role in educational policy with a critical examination of some of the most powerful policy makers in states: SBOEs. These authors frame SBOEs as networked policy actors focusing on their power, authority, and policy-making functions as well as their networks and the discourses constructed through the performance of their policy work. By examining the work of the SBOE, the interests of its members, and its member networks, Young et al. are able to provide insight into the growing influence of nonelected network members on state education policy.

Questioning Federal Education Policy, Politics, and Bureaucracy

This third and final section includes two articles that critically examine the federal role in education policy. Contributions in this section examine how current school reform initiatives are informed by historically related elements at the federal level.

Carpenter uses Hajer's (1995) notion of policy storylines as an analytical device to critically examine how policy actors over the past four decades have constructed and then acted on economic and educational problems, many of which were framed as crises. Carpenter reveals how these policy storylines helped to provoke reforms focused on efficiency, accountability, and rationality. His analysis assists practitioners and scholars in illustrating how the dominant discourses associated with these reforms can influence policy responses and what practitioners and policy makers deem as appropriate policy solutions.

Horsford uses select tenets of critical race theory to frame her CPA of school integration in the New Jim Crow and to examine its paradoxes and shortcomings. She argues that to reclaim school desegregation's original intent of ensuring that Black children are shielded from racial discrimination and have access to well-resourced public schools, the research on school desegregation needs to be desegregated. She argues that anti-Black racism and White self-interest must be at the forefront if desegregation is to be achieved and if equitable educational opportunity is to exist.

FINAL REMARKS

Collectively, the articles included in this special issue of *Educational Policy* offer alternative methodological and theoretical strategies for examining a variety of educational policy issues:

> [T]he undoubted value of these analyses lies in their attempt to problematize policy through several of its "levels" or "dimensions" or "moments" of activity and effect; and in their insistence on continuing to ask basic sociological questions about the relationship between educational practices and social inequalities. (Ball, 1994, p. 2)

The articles in this special issue provide novel insight and new perspectives on conventional policy issues and problems of leadership practice. We hope these alternative strategies and new perspectives provide readers the opportunity to consider various approaches to policy research and potential policy solutions to existing educational inequities.

Declaration of Conflicting Interests

The author(s) declared no potential conflicts of interest with respect to the research, authorship, and/or publication of this article.

Funding

The author(s) received no financial support for the research, authorship, and/or publication of this article.

ORCID iD

Carrie Sampson: https://orcid.org/0000-0002-6927-104X

AUTHOR BIOGRAPHIES

Sarah Diem, PhD, is an Associate Professor of Educational Policy and Leadership in the Department of Educational Leadership & Policy Analysis at the University of Missouri. Her research focuses on the sociopolitical and geographic contexts of education, paying particular attention to how politics, leadership, and implementation of educational policies affect outcomes related to equity, opportunity, and racial diversity within public schools.

Michelle D. Young, PhD, is a Professor of Leadership at the University of Virginia. Young works with universities, practitioners, and state and national leaders to improve the preparation and practice of educational leaders and to develop a dynamic base of knowledge on excellence in educational leadership. Her work is published in the

Educational Researcher, the *American Educational Research Journal,* the *Educational Administration Quarterly,* and the *Journal of Educational Administration,* among other journals. She is the Editor of the *Handbook of Research on the Education of School Leaders.* Her work has significantly increased the focus of education research on leadership preparation, and brought that research to bear on the work of policy makers. Young is currently chairing the revision of national educational leadership preparation standards.

Carrie Sampson, PhD, is an Assistant Professor in the Division of Educational Leadership and Innovation at Mary Lou Fulton Teachers College, Arizona State University. Her research focuses on educational leadership, policy, and equity from three interrelated perspectives—democracy, community advocacy, and politics.

DEVELOPMENTAL EVALUATION

What Is Essential in Developmental Evaluation? On Integrity, Fidelity, Adultery, Abstinence, Impotence, Long-Term Commitment, Integrity, and Sensitivity in Implementing Evaluation Models

Michael Quinn Patton[1]

Abstract

Fidelity concerns the extent to which a specific evaluation sufficiently incorporates the core characteristics of the overall approach to justify labeling that evaluation by its designated name. Fidelity has traditionally meant implementing a model in exactly the same way each time following the prescribed steps and procedures. The essential principles of developmental evaluation (DE), in contrast, provide high-inference sensitizing guidance that must be interpreted and applied contextually. In lieu of operationalizing DE fidelity criteria, I suggest addressing the *degree of manifest sensitivity* to essential principles. Principles as sensitizing concepts replace operational rules. This means that sensitivity to essential DE principles should be explicitly and contextually manifest in both processes and outcomes, in both design and use of findings. Eight essential principles of DE are identified and explained. Finally, 10 threats to evaluation model fidelity and/or degree of manifest sensitivity are identified with ways to mitigate those threats.

[1]Utilization-Focused Evaluation, St. Paul, MN, USA

Corresponding Author

Michael Quinn Patton, Utilization-Focused Evaluation, 740 Mississippi River Blvd. South, Suite 21E, St. Paul, MN 55116, USA. Email: mqpatton@prodigy.net

Keywords

developmental evaluation, fidelity, principles, sensitizing concepts

Bob Williams was awarded the 2014 AEA Lazarsfeld Theory Award for his cumulative contributions bringing systems approaches into evaluation. In accepting at the Awards Luncheon in Denver, attended by more than 400 evaluators, Bob explained the origin of the word system.

> The word "system" comes from the Greek word *synhistonai* (a verb incidentally, not a noun) meaning "to stand together." So I'd like to invite all that can do so to stand for a moment.
>
> I'm now going to ask some of you to sit down. I'd like to remain standing anyone who to some extent feels that you have applied systems and complexity ideas—of whatever shape or form and to a greater or lesser extent—in your evaluation practice.

Almost no one sat down. One person among the distinguished guests at the head table on stage sat, noticed that all others remained standing, and quickly stood back up.

Bob was visibly flabbergasted and said, "Well, that's not what I expected."

In the Systems in Evaluation Topical Interest Group session that followed the luncheon, some questions arose: What understandings and perceptions of applying systems approaches in evaluation had kept that diverse group of people on their feet? Do these people share common understandings and perceptions? Has systems thinking really permeated so deeply into evaluators' practice? Do their practices actually incorporate the core characteristics of the overall approach? Thus, did the fidelity problem arise for those who view systems thinking as central to their practice?

The questions about application of systems thinking in evaluation could be applied to almost any approach. This article will lay out the scope of the *fidelity challenge* in implementing distinct evaluation approaches, illustrate the challenge with specific examples, and use developmental evaluation (DE) to introduce a new way of thinking about and dealing with fidelity. I'll also examine some of the threats to fidelity and ways of handling those threats.

The Fidelity Challenge in Implementing Distinct Evaluation Approaches

An experienced DE practitioner recently told me, "More often than not, I find, people say they are doing Developmental Evaluation, but they are not."

The fidelity challenge concerns the extent to which a specific evaluation sufficiently incorporates the core characteristics of the overall approach to justify labeling that evaluation by its designated name. Just as fidelity is a central issue in efforts to replicate effective programs to new localities (are the replications faithful to the original model on which they are based?), evaluation fidelity concerns whether an evaluator following a particular model is faithful in implementing all the core steps, principles, and processes of that model.

- What must be included in a "theory-driven evaluation" to justify its designation as *theory-driven* (Coryn, Noakes, Westine, & Schröter, 2011)?

- What is the core of appreciative inquiry evaluation (MacCoy, 2014; Preskill & Catsambas, 2006)?

- What are the essential elements of Aboriginal Program evaluations (Jacob & Desautels, 2014) or indigenous methods generally (Chilisa, 2012)?

- What must occur in a participatory evaluation to deem it *genuinely* participatory (Cousins, Whitmore, & Shulha, 2014; Daigneault & Jacob, 2009)? Cousins and Chouinard (2012) reviewed 121 pieces of empirical research on participatory evaluation published from 1997 through 2011 and found great variation in approaches conducted under the "participatory" umbrella.

- What is essential to utilization-focused evaluation (Patton, 2008, 2012)? I've seen a great many evaluations labeled *utilization-focused* that provided no evidence that primary intended users had been identified and engaged to focus the evaluation on those users' priorities.

- And what, you may wonder, are the core systems ideas that Bob Williams was referring to in the incident above? He coedited the first expert anthology on *Systems Concepts in Evaluation* (Williams & Iman, 2007). He estimates that as many as a thousand separate frameworks and methods fall under the systems banner because there is no single agreed-upon definition of a system. Nor is there ever likely to be. But having analyzed the great variety of systems frameworks, he asserts that there are three core ideas that characterize systems thinking: attention to the inevitable arbitrariness of boundaries, taking into account a variety of perspectives, and dynamic, entangled inter-relationships. This means that a systems approach to evaluation must specify how boundaries of the evaluation were determined and the implications of those boundaries; whose perspectives are included (and whose omitted), again with what implications; and that inter-relationships must be documented and analyzed (Williams, 2005, 2008, 2014; Williams & Hummelbrunner, 2011; Williams & Iman, 2007; Williams & van 't Hof, 2014).

Fidelity to the Formative–Summative Distinction

To illustrate the challenge of fidelity, consider our oldest, most basic, and most sacrosanct distinctions: formative and summative. The formative–summative distinction was first conceptualized for school curriculum evaluation by philosopher and *evaluator extraordinaire* Michael Scriven (1967). He called evaluating a curriculum to determine whether it should be approved and disseminated for widespread adoption a *summative evaluation*, evoking a summit-like decision or a summing-up of effectiveness. Summative evaluation began as a purpose designation, the purpose being to inform a major decision about the merit, worth, and significance of a curriculum, program, product, or other intervention to determine its future (kill it, cut it back, continue as is, enlarge it, and take it to scale). But the term summative evaluation quickly expanded to designate any evaluation conducted at the end of a program or project. A distinct and important purpose morphed into a timing designation: end of a program. Which is ironic—and distorting—since most summative decisions must be made months before the actual end of a program, long before evaluation final summative reports are submitted. I review scores of reports labeled "summative" every year, virtually none of which are written or timed in such a way as to inform an actual summative decision by identifiable summative decision-makers. Fidelity to the original meaning of summative has been largely lost from my perspective.

And what of formative evaluation? Scriven argued wisely that before a curriculum was summatively evaluated, it should go through a period of revision and improvement, working out bugs and problems, filling in gaps, and getting student reactions, to ensure that the curriculum was ready for rigorous summative testing. The purpose of formative evaluation was to form, shape, standardize, and finalize a model so that it was ready for summative evaluation. But, as happened with summative evaluation, the idea of formative evaluation morphed from its original purpose as the label came to be applied to any evaluation that improves a program. Though formative and summative designations were conceptualized hand in glove, the purpose of formative being to get ready for summative, that expectation often goes unfulfilled. Just as summative morphed from a clear purpose to a matter of timing (end of program), I now see a great many midterm evaluations designated as "formative" simply because the evaluation takes place in the middle of a funding cycle. These supposedly "formative" evaluations are often midterm accountability exercises determining whether the program is adhering to implementation specifications and meeting milestone performance measures. From my perspective, fidelity to the original meaning of formative has been largely lost. For example, in teaching evaluation workshops, I regularly find participants equating formative evaluation with process evaluation and summative evaluation with outcomes evaluation. Not so.

Let me reiterate. Scriven originated the formative–summative distinction under the assumption that the purpose of evaluation is *to test and judge a model*. Formative evaluations were meant to improve the model. Summative evaluations were meant to test the model and judge its merit, worth, and significance based on whether it produces the desired outcomes and those outcomes can be attributed to the program. The terms formative and summative have become dominant both within evaluation and among those who fund and use it. But evaluation practitioners have become sloppy about what actually constitutes a formative or summative evaluation and the connection between the two. The relationship has evolved from one with a clear division of labor centered around well-specified commitments, expectations, and criteria of excellence to an open noncommittal relationship: sometimes living together, sometimes not, sometimes connected, sometimes not, and sometimes true to original ideals about what the relationship was supposed to be, but more often not.

Emergence of DE

DE emerged from my commitment to respect the fidelity of formative and summative evaluation. I had a 5-year contract to evaluate a philanthropic foundation leadership program, and 2.5 years were to be formative, to stabilize and standardize the model, followed by 2.5 years to test and judge the model's effectiveness. During the formative period, the senior program staff and foundation leadership came to realize that they didn't want to create a standardized model. Instead, they realized that they would need to be continuously adapting the leadership program as the world changed. To keep a leadership development program relevant and meaningful, they concluded, they would need, over time, to continuously update and adapt what they did; who and how they recruited people into the program; use of new technologies; and being attentive to and incorporating developments in public policy, economic changes, demographic transitions, and social–cultural shifts. They came to understand that they didn't want to improve a model or test a model or promulgate a model. Instead, they wanted to keep developing and adapting the program. They wanted an approach that would support ongoing adaptation and timely decisions about what to change, expand, close out, or further develop. This was different from formative evaluation. And they concluded that they would never commission a summative evaluation because they wouldn't have a standardized model that could be summatively evaluated. Our discussions about what they wanted and needed kept coalescing around ongoing adaptation and development so we called the approach DE. (For more details about this designation and how the DE terminology emerged, see Patton, 2011, pp. 2–4.)

Let me say a bit more about the distinct purpose and niche of DE as it has developed, which will set the stage for the emergent fidelity problem in the practice of DE, and the solution I offer, for the first time, in this article.

The Niche and Purpose of DE

DE provides evaluative information and feedback to social innovators to inform adaptive *development* in complex dynamic environments. DE brings to innovation and adaptation the processes of asking evaluative questions, applying evaluation logic, and gathering and reporting evaluative data to support project, program, initiative, product, and/or organizational development with timely feedback.

The DE niche focuses on evaluating innovations in complex dynamic environments because that's the arena in which *social innovators* are working. These are people who want to change the way things are in major ways. Innovation as used here is a broad framing that includes creating new approaches to intractable problems, ongoing program adaptation to changed conditions, adapting effective principles to new contexts (scaling), systems change, and rapid response adaptation under crisis conditions. *Social innovation* is shorthand for any kind of emergent/creative/adaptive interventions for complex problems.

Traditional evaluation approaches advocate clear, specific, and measureable outcomes that are to be achieved through processes detailed in a linear logic model. Such traditional evaluation demand for up-front, preordinate specificity doesn't work under conditions of high innovation, exploration, uncertainty, turbulence, rapid change, and emergence. Indeed, premature specificity can do harm by constraining exploration, limiting adaptation, reducing experimental options, and forcing premature adoption of a rigid model, not because such a model is appropriate, but because evaluators demand it in order to do what they understand to be good evaluation. DE emerged as a response to the need for an alternative way to engage in evaluation of social innovations and adaptive developmental processes in complex dynamic environments.

The book on DE was published in 2011. In the relatively short time since, DE has become recognized and established as a distinct and useful evaluation approach (Dickson & Saunders, 2014; FSG, 2014; Lam & Shulha, 2014; Preskill & Beer, 2012). The attention garnered has also raised a major question: *What are the essential principles of DE?*

Treating Essential Principles as Sensitizing Concepts

Before listing the essential principles of DE, let me describe the developmental approach used to identify them. A core group of DE practitioners shared ideas and reactions in an interactive, clarifying, and developmental process.[1] We wanted to avoid a recipe-like or checklist approach to DE based on operationalizing key concepts and dimensions. Instead, we view these essential principles as *sensitizing concepts* that must be explicitly addressed in DE, but how and the extent to which they are addressed depends on situation and context. This is a critical departure from the usual approach to "fidelity," which has traditionally meant to implement an approach operationally in exactly the same way each time. Fidelity has meant adherence to a recipe or highly prescriptive set of steps and procedures. The essential principles of DE, in contrast, provide guidance that must be interpreted and applied contextually—but *must* be applied in some way and to some extent if the evaluation is to be considered genuinely and fully developmental.

In lieu of operationalizing DE fidelity criteria, I am designating this approach: *assessing the degree of manifest sensitivity*. In lieu of fidelity, I prefer to examine the *integrity* of an approach. For a DE to have integrity, the essential DE principles should be explicitly and contextually manifest in both processes and outcomes, in both design and use of findings. Thus, when I read a DE report, talk with those involved in a DE, or listen to a DE presentation at a conference, I should be able to see/detect/understand how these essential principles of DE informed what was done and what resulted. Let me elaborate just a bit. The notion of judging the integrity of an approach by assessing the degree of manifest sensitivity to essential principles flows from the notion of fieldwork guided by sensitizing concepts (Patton, 2015a). A sensitizing concept raises consciousness about something, alerts us to watch out for its relevance, and reminds us to engage with the concept throughout our fieldwork within a specific context. Essential principles of DE sensitize us to what to include in DE practice.

Consider the concept *innovation*. DE is innovation-focused, one of the essential principles I'll elaborate in a moment. Here is what the concept of innovation does in a DE process. It focuses our attention on social innovators, that is, people who are trying to bring about major change. We are alerted by their definition of what they are doing ("innovation") to find out what they mean. We pay attention to and document what they are doing and how they talk about what they are doing. We interact with them about what is going on and the implications of their efforts and documented results. We gather data about what is unfolding and emerging. We observe and provide feedback about how what is actually happening matches expectations and hopes. We work with those involved to interpret what is happening and judge what is working and not working and thereby adapt, learn, and move forward. In so doing, we are engaging with them around the notion of "innovation" and deepening both their and our understanding of what is meant by innovation in that context. The definition and meaning of innovation is likely to evolve, deepen, and even morph as part of the DE inquiry.

In this process, DE becomes part of the change process itself, part of the intervention. It happens like this: In inquiring into the meaning of innovation within a context and particular change-focused initiative, and providing feedback about what is learned as well as further questions generated, DE affects and alters the innovation process and outcomes.

Now then, in hearing about such an inquiry, I can make a judgment about the degree of manifest sensitivity to innovation in that particular DE and judge the integrity of the overall DE by making a similar assessment of each DE principle. Table 1 presents the eight essential DE principles (Patton, 2016).

TABLE 1 ● Eight Essential Developmental Evaluation (DE) Principles		
Essential DE principles	**What to look for to assess the *degree of manifest sensitivity* and sensibility in DE practice, from design to use of findings**	**Examples of contextual evidence of the essential DE element being incorporated in practice**
1. **Developmental principle:** Illuminate, inform, and support what is being developed, by identifying the nature and patterns of development (innovation, adaptation, and systems change) and the implications and consequences of those patterns	Something (the innovation) is being *developed*. The evaluation tracks what is being developed and the implications of what emerges. The evaluation itself is developed (emergent design) as the innovation develops	The evaluation's purpose, supporting *development* and adaptation of the innovation, is explicit and that focus is maintained throughout. The evaluation design's emergence and adaptations are documented and their implications discussed
2. **Evaluation rigor principle:** Ask probing evaluation questions; think and engage evaluatively; question assumptions; apply evaluation logic; use appropriate methods; and stay empirically grounded—that is, rigorously gather, interpret, and report data	DE is *empirically driven*, and *evaluative thinking* undergirds all aspects of the engagement	Data are gathered, reported, and interpreted about the implications of what is being developed; DE findings and feedback inform next steps in the adaptive process
3. **Utilization-focused principle:** Focus on intended use by intended users from beginning to end, facilitating the evaluation process to ensure utility and actual use	Intended use by intended users focuses the evaluation	Social innovators and their supporters are the primary intended users of DE and clearly identified as such. The explicit purpose of the evaluation is to support the development and adaptation of the innovation (vs. improvement, accountability, or summative judgment)
4. **Innovation niche principle:** Elucidate how the change processes and results being evaluated involve innovation and adaptation, the niche of developmental evaluation	A commitment to innovate is explicit and authentic: a fresh and effective response to an intractable social challenge or problem or to an emergent one	DE has helped the social innovation develop and adapt within the context where the innovation is occurring
5. **Complexity perspective principle:** Understand and interpret development through the lens of complexity and conduct the evaluation accordingly. This means using complexity premises and dynamics to make sense of the problems being addressed; to guide	The characteristics of the *complex dynamic system* in which innovation and evaluation are occurring are described. The complexity characteristics of the innovation being developed and evaluated are also	The nature and degree of uncertainty, turbulence, nonlinear interactions, and dynamical patterns are highlighted. DE is explicitly aligned with the complexity of the innovation. Sensitivity to and implications of emergence,

(Continued)

TABLE 1 ⬤ (Continued)

innovation, adaptation, and systems change strategies; to interpret what is developed; to adapt the evaluation design as needed; and to analyze emergent findings	described. The DE design, process, and outcomes reflect these complexity characteristics	adaptation, and context are manifest
6. **Systems thinking principle:** Think systemically throughout, being attentive to interrelationships, perspectives, boundaries, and other key aspects of the social system and context within which the innovation is being developed and the evaluation is being conducted	Attention to interrelationships, perspectives, and boundaries undergirds and informs both the innovation processes and the developmental evaluation	The design, data collected, findings presented, and use of findings demonstrate systems understandings and systems thinking. Contextual sensitivity is explicit and evident throughout the evaluation
7. **Cocreation principle:** Develop the innovation and evaluation together—interwoven, interdependent, iterative, and cocreated—such that the developmental evaluation becomes part of the change process	The developmental evaluator is close enough to the action to build a mutually trusting relationship with the social innovators. The collaborative process is active, reactive, interactive, and adaptive	In the process of collaboration, adaptations and developments are *cocreated*. DE becomes part of the intervention (cocreation). How this occurs and with what implications and consequences are discussed
8. **Timely feedback principle:** Time feedback to inform ongoing adaptation as needs, findings, and insights emerge, rather than only at predetermined times (e.g., quarterly or at midterm and the end of project)	Feedback of findings is timely and ongoing (not just delivered at predetermined times, like quarterly, or midterm and the end of project)	Evidence is reported about how the DE feedback was engaged, useful, and used in close conjunction with real-time decision-making and adaptations

Note: Adapted from Patton (2016).

DE as an Integrated Approach

For an evaluation to merit the label "DE," all of the principles in Table 1 should be addressed to some extent and in some way. As noted in Table 1, this is not a pick-and-choose list. All are essential. This means that there is evidence in the DE process and results that these essential principles have been addressed in some meaningful way or, for specific contextual reasons, not incorporated explicitly. For example, let's imagine working with a social innovator and/or funder who hates the word "complexity," thinks it is overused jargon, so the DE process avoids explicitly using the term *complexity* but does explicitly address emergence, adaptation, and nonlinearity. Such negotiations are part of contextual sensitivity and adaptability and part of the essential DE learning process and should be reported.

Moreover, the essential principles are interrelated and mutually reinforcing. Being utilization-focused (#1) requires staying attuned to the priority purpose of the evaluation, namely developmental (#8) support of innovation and adaptation (#2). DE occurs in a complex dynamic system (#3) that requires understanding and applying complexity concepts and systems thinking (#4) with timely feedback (#6). Utilization-focused engagement is collaborative (#5) and evaluative (#7), making the DE part of the intervention.

EMPOWERMENT EVALUATION (EE) AS A CONTRARY EXAMPLE, OR NOT

What must be included in an EE to justify the label *empowerment*? Miller and Campbell (2006) systematically examined 47 evaluations labeled "empowerment evaluation" published from 1994 through June 2005. They found wide variation among practitioners in adherence to EE principles and weak emphasis on the attainment of empowered outcomes for program beneficiaries. Brad Cousins (2005) wrote a "critical friend" review of EE entitled, "Will the Real Empowerment Evaluation Please Stand Up?" Cousins reviewed a number of EE case examples and concluded that any particular EE approach will depend on "which combination of principles are most important, given the needs of the local context and the impetus for the empowerment evaluation in the first place" (p. 201). The 10 empowerment principles are as follows: (1) improvement, (2) community ownership, (3) inclusion, (4) democratic participation, (5) social justice, (6) community knowledge, (7) evidence-based strategies, (8) capacity building, (9) organizational learning, and (10) accountability.

In 2009, Stewart Donaldson as the director of the Claremont University Summer Evaluation Institute organized and moderated a debate about the value of EE between David M. Fetterman, Michael Scriven, and me (Donaldson, Patton, Fetterman, & Scriven, 2010). In the debate, I asked David Fetterman, which of the 10 EE principles he had identified were actually essential. Fetterman responded to my question by explaining that there are "high, medium and low levels of each of these principles. . . . You don't always have to do the highest. It depends on your circumstances and situations, but [the principles] give you a gauge and a guide of how to do these things." He continued, "I'm not a purist, not by a long shot. I get along here. You do what you need to do. If you have an idea, theory, a voice, match it up with every day's activities" (Donaldson, Patton, Fetterman, & Scriven, 2010, p. 49). At the time, I didn't consider that a very clear or satisfactory answer. The latest book on EE (Fetterman, Kaftarian, & Wandersman, 2014) clarifies that there are also *zero levels* of adherence to, implementation of, or attention to the principles. *Zero.* In essence, there are no critical, essential, or core EE principles. It's a pick-and-choose menu. Which ones and how many you engage to merit calling the effort an EE is unspecified on purpose. Part of the EE process is to decide which EE principles to engage and at what level to engage with whatever principles are selected for engagement. In reviewing the new book, I cited as evidence of the pick-and-chose approach Laura Leviton's chapter entitled, "Foundation Strategy Drives the Choice of Empowerment Evaluation Principles." Leviton is a former president of the American Evaluation Association and also a Thought Leader in evaluation generally and philanthropic evaluation in particular. In essence, she portrays a foundation-EE relationship that can involve some *hooking-up* now and then around certain mutually attractive principles but ongoing and full commitment is not on the table. Dating, not marriage. Not even co-habiting. Occasional mutual companionship. Always good to have the boundaries of relationships clarified (Patton, 2015b, p. 16).

Other case examples in the book include some, but not all, of the principles, while several do attend to all, but with varying degrees of emphasis. In responding to this observation, Fetterman, Wandersman, and Kaftarian (2015) explained,

> The essence of EE is a systematic way of thinking, not a single principle, concept, or method. Empowerment evaluation, first and foremost, helps people evaluate their own programs and initiatives. It is the use of evaluation concepts, techniques, and findings to foster improvement and self-determination. It is an evaluation approach that aims to increase the likelihood that programs will achieve results by increasing the capacity of program stakeholders, to plan, implement, and evaluate their own programs.

> We presented the theories, concepts, principles, and steps guiding EE. However, his (Patton's) focus was almost exclusively on the principles.

> It is the gestalt or whole package that makes it work. Empowerment evaluation theory, concepts, principles, and steps are used to guide practice. Patton's critique is off-target because it focuses on individual parts or principles, failing to recognize that empowerment evaluation is more than the sum of its parts (including "essential" parts). (pp. 10–11)

Ah, but that last parenthetical clarification gets to the heart of the matter. *Essential parts. Essential:* "a thing that is absolutely necessary" (Online dictionary, 2015). What is *essential* is never stated. Quite the contrary, a menu of options is offered. Pick-and-choose. The supposed "gestalt or whole package that makes it work" is ultimately ephemeral because the essence is absent. My sense is that in an effort to be inclusive, responsive, and flexible, EE theorists and advocates have created a metaphorical fruit salad of many possible ingredients, none of which is essential, but as long as some of the ingredients are fruit, it can be called a fruit salad. That said, Fetterman (2005) has stated that incorporation of more empowerment principles is better than fewer.

> As a general rule, the quality [of an empowerment evaluation] increases as the number of principles are applied, because they are synergistic. Ideally each of the principles should be enforced at some level. However, specific principles will be more dominant than others in each empowerment evaluation. The principles that dominate will be related to the local context and purpose of evaluation. Not all principles will be adopted equally at any given time or for any given project. (p. 9)

It sounds to me like assessing the degree of manifest sensitivity to principles would work for EE too.

ELABORATION OF A SENSITIZING CONCEPT APPROACH TO THE CHALLENGE OF EVALUATING DE INTEGRITY

Operationalizing a concept involves translating it into concrete measures. This constitutes a well-established, scholarly approach to empirical inquiry. However, concepts like innovation, complexity, emergence, and adaptation are best treated as sensitizing concepts in the tradition of qualitative inquiry, not as operational concepts in the tradition of quantitative research (Patton, 2015a). Since the distinction between sensitizing versus operational concepts is critical to the issue of fidelity and integrity in evaluation approaches, it may be useful to explicate this distinction and its implications for dealing with the essential principles of DE. (This reprises my previous discussion of process use as a sensitizing concept; Patton, 2007.)

Three problems plague operationalization. First, "underdetermination" is the problem of determining "if testable propositions fully operationalize a theory" (Williams, 2004, p. 769). Examples include concepts such as homelessness, self-sufficiency, resilience, and alienation that have variable meanings according to the social context. For example, what "homeless" means varies historically and sociologically. A second problem is that objective scholarly definitions may not capture the subjective definition of those who experience something. Poverty offers an example: What one person considers poverty, another may view as a pretty decent life. The Northwest Area Foundation, which has as its mission "poverty alleviation," has struggled trying to operationalize poverty for outcomes evaluation; moreover, they found that many quite poor people in states such as Iowa and Montana, who fit every official definition of being in poverty, do not even see themselves as poor, much less "in poverty." Third is the problem of disagreement among social scientists about how to define and operationalize key concepts. Sustainability, for example, can be defined as continuation of a healthy system or the capacity of a system to adapt (Gunderson & Holling, 2002, pp. 27–29; Patton, 2011, p. 199). The second and third problems are related in that one researcher may use a local and context-specific definition to solve the second problem, but this context-specific definition is likely to be different from and conflict with the definition used by other researchers inquiring in other contexts. One way to address problems of operationalization is to treat complexity and innovation as sensitizing concepts and abandon the search for a standardized and universal operational definition. This means that any specific DE would generate a definition that fits the specific context for and purpose of the evaluation.

Sociologist Herbert Blumer (1954) is credited with originating the idea of "sensitizing concept" to orient fieldwork. Sensitizing concepts include notions like victim, stress, stigma, and learning organization that can provide some initial direction to a study as one inquires into how the concept is given meaning in a particular place or set of circumstances (Schwandt, 2001). The observer moves between the sensitizing concept and the real world of social experience, giving shape and substance to the concept and elaborating the conceptual framework with varied manifestations of the concept. Such an approach recognizes that although the specific manifestations of social phenomena vary by time, space, and circumstance, the sensitizing concept is a container for capturing, holding, and examining these manifestations to better understand patterns and implications.

Evaluators commonly use sensitizing concepts to inform their understanding of a situation. Consider the notion of context. Any particular evaluation is designed within some context, and we are admonished to take context into account, be sensitive to context, and watch out for changes in context. But what is context? Systems thinkers posit that system boundaries are inherently arbitrary, so defining what is within the immediate scope of an evaluation versus what is within its surrounding context is inevitably arbitrary, but the distinction is still useful. Indeed, being intentional about deciding what is in the immediate realm of action of an evaluation and what is in the enveloping context can be an illuminating exercise—and stakeholders might well differ in their perspectives. In that sense, the idea of *context* is a sensitizing concept.

High-Inference Versus Low-Inference Variables and Concepts

Another way to think about and understand principles as sensitizing concepts is to treat them as "high-inference concepts." The distinction between high-inference and low-inference variables originated in studies of teacher effectiveness research in higher education (Rosenshine & Furst, 1971).[2]

High-inference teacher characteristics are global, abstract, such as "explains clearly" or has good rapport, while low-inference characteristics are specific, concrete teaching behaviors, such as "signals the transition from one topic to the next," and "addresses individual students by name," that can be recorded with very little inference or judgment on the part of a classroom observer (Murray, 2007, pp. 146–147).

The thrust of the research on teacher effectiveness has been to emphasize low-inference variables that require minimum interpretation as opposed to high-inference variables that require considerable judgment on the part of the observer (Cruickshank & Kennedy, 1986). In contrast, principles-focused practice is necessarily high inference. Addressing degree of manifest sensitivity is a high-inference approach to assessing fidelity and integrity when assessing claims that a particular evaluation approach is being followed.

Rigid and Nonrigid Designators

Philosophers of language have devoted considerable attention to different uses of language for different purposes. One critical distinction is between rigid and nonrigid designators. A rigid designator is highly specific and context free, the equivalent of an operational definition or rule. A nonrigid designator depends upon context for meaning such that the interpretation of a term must take into account the situation and the purpose intended by the person speaking. Nonrigid designators apply to the "messy social-psychological world of pragmatics, analyzing the wealth of meaning that must be gleaned not from the words alone but from the context in which the words are produced, including, importantly, the speaker's intentions in uttering them, which furthermore take the speaker outside of his own mind and into the mind of his audience" (Goldstein, 2015, p. 50). Rigid versus nonrigid designators and absolute versus pragmatic (contextual) definitions and meanings take us into the territory of strict constitutional constructionism (focusing on original intent) versus contextual adaptation of interpretation to changing times and situations. A major division on the Supreme Court of the United States concerns different interpretations of what *fidelity to the constitution* means. But I digress. Principles as sensitizing concepts are essentially nonrigid designators in the philosophy of language.

Threats to Fidelity, Integrity, and Manifest Sensitivity

Pondering fidelity to evaluation approaches and reflecting on what constitutes integrity in calling an evaluation "developmental" have led me to consider what threats to fidelity and integrity may emerge. I have identified 10 threats: adultery, abstinence, virginity, impotence, *complexus interruptus*, divorce, evaluation transmitted disease, poor performance, poor boundary management, and mania. Table 2 presents the threats and identifies common symptoms. These are serious threats, potentially hiding around every corner. Be afraid. Be very afraid. But also be ready. Table 2 provides strategies for countering the threats.

TABLE 2 ⬢ Ten Threats to Evaluation Approach Fidelity and/or Manifest Sensitivity			
Threat	**Nature of the threat**	**Symptoms and problems**	**Response options**
1. Adultery (aka *free love*)	Dabbling with multiple approach partners: start with DE, throw in some theory-driven, a dash of empowerment evaluation, add formative and summative to offer familiarity, heavy infusion of accountability ...	• Incoherence • Conflicting directions • Surface implementation of each • Confusion • Dissipating resources • Attention deficit, unfocused	✓ Honor the holistic integrity of whatever evaluation approach is chosen ✓ Make an informed, judicious commitment ✓ When using and integrating multiple approaches, which can be appropriate, do so thoughtfully with careful documentation and explicit justification
2. Abstinence	Refusing to even consider using an overall evaluation approach or model	• Focus only on methods • Ethical, utilization, and political issues reduced to technical options and concerns	✓ Ground methods decisions in the larger context of the evaluation's purpose, context, and intended uses
3. Lack of experience (virginity)	Lack the confidence and knowledge to try a new approach for the first time	• Fear • Performance anxiety • Analysis paralysis (can't decide what to do)	✓ Team with a trusted and trustworthy more experienced practitioner ✓ Find a mentor ✓ Start small with a very manageable assignment
4. Impotence	Lack the power, influence, and/or position to advocate for and implement a new approach to evaluation	• Frustration • Boredom (same old, same old all the time) • Rigidity: Forcing new evaluation opportunities and situations into old, comfortable, well-trodden approaches • Stress	✓ Understand the source of the problem. Look for windows of opportunity to demonstrate the value of an alternative approach ✓ Offer exposure to the vast panorama of options and approaches available in evaluation ✓ Don't rush the preparatory work for beginning an evaluation. Take time to understand a particular context and respond sensitively to the needs of stakeholders in that context

5. Complexus interruptus	Funder of DE or those who commissioned the evaluation want to change course half-way through the evaluation from being complexity- and innovation-driven to being bottom line accountability oriented; or the evaluator is told to stop DE and start doing summative in mid-stream	• Surprised: Didn't see this coming • Anger: Changing the rules in the middle of the game • Concern: How do you recreate the baseline needed for the shift in purpose?	✓ Be vigilant and repetitive about explaining and reaffirming the niche, purpose, and appropriateness of DE to funders and other key stakeholders ✓ Be especially alert to changes in personnel that will require immediate relationship-building to stay the course
6. Divorce	The evaluation approach isn't working. Advocates and adversaries want to go their separate ways. DE becomes a lightning rod for other issues	• Conflict • Blaming • Scapegoating • Disassociation	✓ Divorce may be better than continuing a bad, conflict-laden, unproductive relationship ✓ Extract lessons and move on
7. Evaluation transmitted disease	Skepticism, even cynicism: "The evaluation approach doesn't matter. In the end it's all pretense and going through the motions. Nobody cares. Just comply with what's required."	• Low energy • Evaluation feels like drudgery—because it is • Lack of cooperation	✓ Begin by acknowledging you have a problem. The problem isn't the way of the world. The problem is you ✓ Get selective. Find an evaluation you can believe in
8. Poor performance	Lack knowledge, competence, commitment, and sensibility to do a good job in appropriately implementing DE	• DE chosen because it has cache, makes you look cutting edge, generates some buzz • What is done doesn't match core principles of the approach	✓ Commit to a job well done, an approach well-implemented ✓ Identify resources to up your game ✓ Be professional. Take responsibility for adhering to the evaluation standards and principles
9. Poor boundary management	Letting the evaluation expand to include much more than available resources can support. Role confusion around relationships: What are appropriate roles and boundaries for a developmental evaluator?	• Stress • Conflict • Feeling overworked and underappreciated	✓ Realize that this is a common issue, not just about you ✓ Negotiate boundaries ✓ Better to do a good job on a smaller number of things than a poor job on a lot of things

(Continued)

TABLE 2 ● (Continued)			
10. Mania	Overselling the approach; overzealous; overapplication. Applying the approach beyond its niche and focused purpose	• People turn away when they see you coming so they don't have to listen to your inane exhortations about the wonders of this new approach	✓ Better to undersell and overdeliver than to oversell and underperform ✓ Form relationships with some skeptics and cynics (see Threat 7)—always in large supply in evaluation ✓ Chill

Note. DE = Developmental Evaluation.

CONCLUSION

> A rose is a rose is a rose is a rose.
>
> —Gertrude Stein, *Sacred Emily* (1913, p. 3)

And a DE is a DE is a DE. Would that it were so. But, actually, it depends. It depends on the extent to which all eight of the essential DE principles have been explicitly and effectively addressed. That's the point of this article. Labeling an evaluation "developmental" or "utilization-focused" doesn't make it so. An assessment of manifest sensitivity to a model's essential principles is necessary to judge the integrity of the approach. In closing, let me illustrate why this matters using colonoscopies as an example and cautionary tale.

A colonoscopy is a colonoscopy is a colonoscopy. Or is it? Are there variations? Does it matter how the process is done? A colonoscopy is an examination of the colon with a flexible scope, called an endoscope, to find and cut out any polyps that might cause colon cancer. A study of 12 highly experienced board-certified gastroenterologists in private practice found that some were 10 times better than others at finding adenomas, the polyps that can turn into cancer. One factor distinguishing the more effective from less effective colonoscopies was the amount of time the physician spent examining the colon (which involves an effort evaluation). Those who slowed down and took more time found more polyps. Some completed the procedure in less than 5 min, and others spent 20 min or more. Insurers pay doctors the same no matter how much time they spend. But the stakes are high for patients. More than four million Americans a year have colonoscopies, hoping to protect themselves from colon cancer. The cancer, which kills about 55,000 Americans a year, is the second-leading cause of cancer death in the United States (Kolata, 2006a, 2006b).

So is it true that a colonoscopy is a colonoscopy is a colonoscopy? No more so than that a DE is a DE is a DE. Fidelity matters, whether to prescribed medical practices or evaluation sensitizing concepts. *Caveat emptor.*

Declaration of Conflicting Interests

The author declared no potential conflicts of interest with respect to the research, authorship, and/or publication of this article.

Funding

The author received no financial support for the research, authorship, and/or publication of this article.

Notes

1. Evaluation practitioners involved in developing and/or reviewing the essential DE elements: Mark Cabaj, Nathaniel Foote, Jamie Gamble, Mathias Kjaer, Chi Yan Lam, Kate McKegg, Nora Murphy, Donna Podems, Hallie Preskill, James Radner, Ricardo Ramirez, Rolf Sartorius, Lyn Shulha, Nan Wehipeihana, and Ricardo Wilson-Grau. Different views naturally emerged so the final list of essential elements presented here is my own perspective informed by their feedback.

2. I am indebted to Mel Mark who introduced me to this literature.

APPENDIX D

TRANSLATIONAL RESEARCH EVALUATION

Estimating Return on Investment in Translational Research: Methods and Protocols

Kyle L. Grazier,[1] William M. Trochim,[2] David M. Dilts,[3] and Rosalind Kirk[4]

Abstract

Assessing the value of clinical and translational research funding on accelerating the translation of scientific knowledge is a fundamental issue faced by the National Institutes of Health (NIH) and its Clinical and Translational Science Awards (CTSAs). To address this issue, the authors propose a model for measuring the return on investment (ROI) of one key CTSA program, the clinical research unit (CRU). By estimating the economic and social inputs and outputs of this program, this model produces multiple levels of ROI: investigator, program, and institutional estimates. A methodology, or evaluation protocol, is proposed to assess the value of this CTSA function, with specific objectives, methods, descriptions of the data to be collected, and how data are to be filtered, analyzed, and evaluated. This article provides an approach CTSAs could use to assess the economic and social returns on NIH and institutional investments in these critical activities.

[1] Michigan Institute for Clinical and Health Research, School of Public Health, School of Medicine, University of Michigan, Ann Arbor, MI, USA
[2] Weill Cornell Medical College Clinical and Translational Science Center (CTSC), New York, NY, and Cornell University, Ithaca, NY, USA
[3] Oregon Clinical and Translational Research Institute (OCTRI), Oregon Health and Science University, Portland, OR, USA
[4] Michigan Institute for Clinical and Health Research, University of Michigan, Ann Arbor, MI, USA

Corresponding Author

Kyle L. Grazier, School of Public Health, Michigan Institute for Clinical and Health Research (CTSA), University of Michigan, 1420 Washington Heights, Ann Arbor, MI 48109, USA. Email: kgrazier@umich.edu

Keywords

ROI, return on research investment, evaluation

INTRODUCTION

With support of the National Institutes of Health (NIH), the *Clinical and Translational Science Award* (*CTSA*) program was launched in 2006 and expanded to other academic medical institutions across the country. By 2012, there were approximately 60 CTSA-supported institutions, known as *CTSAs*, with the goal of the CTSA program to provide a nationwide collaborative of integrated infrastructures to support, educate, and accelerate clinical and translational health research. The CTSA program is now under the umbrella of a relatively new NIH unit that was established in 2011, the National Center for Advancing Translational Sciences (NCATS; Clinical and Translational Science Award [CTSA], 2013).

In an era of increasingly scarce resources, important decisions with respect to which resources should be maintained by a CTSA, and which should not be renewed, become crucial for the future of all CTSAs (CTSA, 2013). Effective evaluation has been subject to much discussion within NIH, the CTSA program, and individual CTSAs in recognition that it takes on average 17 years for only 14% of scientific innovations and discovery to reach clinical practice (Balas & Boren, 2000) and the consequent importance of engaging with communities and practice-based networks to accelerate translation (Westfall, Mold, & Fagnan, 2007). The aims of this article are 4-fold: (1) to examine the concept of return on investment (ROI) as it could be applied to CTSA program resources as used at individual institutions; (2) to propose a model for applying ROI formulae using data currently collected from CTSA program required financial and operating data; (3) to propose a methodology for decision making with respect to ROI in one component of a CTSA, namely a clinical research unit (CRU); and to suggest how the methodology, an evaluation protocol, can be applied to other units within, and across, the various CTSAs supported by the CTSA program (Trochim et al., 2012).

Limited ability and experience assessing the value of CTSA research funding on accelerating the translation of scientific knowledge is a fundamental issue faced by both individual CTSAs and by the NIH CTSA program (Rubio, Sufian, & Trochim, 2012). To address this issue, we propose investigating the ROI of one key program that is common to all CTSAs, namely the CRU (McCammon et al., 2013). By carefully examining the economic and social inputs and outputs of these units, it may be possible to produce multilevel ROI computations, at the investigator, program, institutional, and national levels. The developed methodology, or evaluation protocol, will focus on achieving specific objectives, methods, descriptions of the data to be collected, how data are to be filtered and analyzed, and how the results can be used in evaluating various units. This model, while being created using one component of an individual CTSA, is developed in such a way that it is generalizable to other CTSA program aspects at an individual institution, such as pilot projects or investigator training programs.

BACKGROUND AND SIGNIFICANCE

As Botchkarev and Andru (2011) note, "ROI was conceived as a financial term and defined as a concept based on a rigorous and quantifiable analysis of financial returns and costs. At present, ROI has been widely recognized and accepted in business and financial management in the private and public sectors." Authors recognize differences in economic concepts, based on the field of the research, namely, finance or economics. In ROI, the method allows a decision maker to evaluate the timing and magnitude of expected gains to the timing and magnitude of investment costs (National Information Center on Health Services Research and Health Care Technology, 2013). The simplest ROI divides the incremental economic gain from an action by its investment costs. When controlled for similar circumstances, the higher the ROI, the greater the financial return for the given investment and, presumably, the better use of the resources. Direct costs, such as salaries and wages, can be attributed directly to the investment, or project. The same is true for the direct returns, such as increased sales revenue. Proximal measures of cost and gains, or returns, are also included, insofar as they can be identified with the specific investment, and tracked for a sufficient length of time. The analysis grows in complexity with the recognition of several important dimensions of the economic value implied by the ratio, the most important being the timing of the respective cost outlays and revenue inflows (The Cochrane Collaboration, 2013).

While ROI is fairly straightforward if costs and revenues can be directly identified to a project, difficulties arise in the use of ROI when it attempts to include indirect costs or returns, those associated with the decision, but not necessarily caused by it; for example, there are general expenses related to operating a CTSA at an institution, but it is difficult to attribute many of those expenses directly to one aspect of the CTSA, be they a project or unit. It is also difficult to quantify on the return side of the equation, the value supplied by the CTSA in generating a journal article or patent when there are multiple sources of funds available to an investigator, including grants and other outside funding. Additionally, the timing of the investment by a CTSA and the returns provided by the investment frequently differ. For example, initial clinical funding might be invested in Year 1, but the return as measured by additional grant awards may not occur until years later. These early cost/later gains scenarios require discounting future net cash flows to recognize the risk related to the uncertainty inherent in estimating those future values

(Phillips & Phillips, 2008; Zhang, Wu, & Zhang, 2008). In this article, the method does not restrict ROI to a simple ratio, but rather one that accounts for the proximal and distal costs and benefits of investments in CRUs. It should also be noted that in those CRUs that offer services for industry-sponsored trials, the calculations can often be simplified by imposing a fixed timeline on the returns.

In addition to the economic ROI, which focuses on financial value, some formulae include social costs and value, which is commonly referred to as *social return on investment* (SROI; Harvard Business School, 2000). SROI is a framework for measuring and accounting for a broader concept of "value," one that incorporates social and environmental, as well as economic costs and benefits (Gardner, 2007; International Organization for Standardization, 2013; NEF, 2013; Staiger, Richardson, & Barbara, 2005). The academic and policy-making literature have provided evidence for the importance of calculating SROI, including justification, protocols, and mechanisms for organizing and conducting a rigorous SROI in settings similar to that found in CTSAs (DeVol & Bedroussian, 2006; Pienta, Alter, & Lyle, 2010). SROI has been assessed in different fields: banking, corporate research and development, energy policy, and education policy (Blaug, 1997; Jones & Williams, 1998; Kronenberg, Kuckshinrichs, & Hansen, 2010; Nelson, Cooper, Wright, & Murphy, 2009; Raymer, 2009; Richardson, 2006; Tulchin, Gertel-Rosenberg, & Olsen, 2009). As with ROI, SROI analysis can be conducted both retrospectively, based on actual realized costs and outcomes; or prospectively, predicting how much social value will be created, for a given cost, if the activities meet their intended outcomes (Lingane & Olsen, 2004; Scottish Government, 2009).

The variation in the meaning and use of ROI, how it is calculated, and at what level, are described well in several publications. Those authors accept for their evaluation purposes an individual measure of ROI, as a metric and ratio. Other authors consider ROI "as a method of persuasive communication to senior management, a process of getting everybody's attention to the financial aspects of the decisions and stimulating a rigid financial analysis." In this case, actually calculated ROI numbers are of less importance compared to the processes of gathering/analyzing cost and benefit data (Botchkarev & Andru, 2011).

APPROACH

The approach uses quantitative and qualitative methods to determine how to extend operational protocols to assist individual CTSAs in understanding and using data representing returns on investments in research funds in CRUs. Using a discrete program within all CTSAs, the CRU, this approach encompasses unique and similar features of administrative, clinical, and research-tracking systems (Meltzer & Smith, 2011).

Basic principles drive the approach and methods: involve stakeholders; understand what changes over time; value the things that matter; only include what is relevant; be conservative; be transparent; and verify results. The proposed evaluation protocol shows that the concept of ROI models can be adapted to better understand and manage the activities of an individual CTSA with respect to investment decisions.

Measurement

Measures of the value of research awards often include "productivity." Productivity is commonly defined as a ratio between the output volume and the volume of inputs (Nordhaus, 2001). It measures how much inputs such as labor and capital are used in an economy to produce a given level of output (Linna, Pekkola, Ukko, & Melkas, 2010; Velentgas, Dreyer, Nourjah, Smith, & Torchia, 2013). Research productivity is often represented by the publications of research discoveries and how often the work is cited by others (Meltzer & Smith, 2011; National Institute of Mental Health, 2013). Rooted in the idea of a data life cycle, the scientific community has moved to recognize "that research data may have an enduring value on scientific progress as scientists use and reuse research data to draw new analysis and conclusions" (Jacobs & Humphrey, 2004; Levan & Stephan, 1991; Pienta et al., 2010). Some of these data sharing opportunities are encouraged by journals with the intent to replicate results (Anderson, Greene, McCullough, & Vinod, 2005; Glenditsch, Metelits, & Strand, 2003). NIH issued its final ruling in 2003 on the requirements to share data funded by the National Institutes (Carnegie Foundation for the Advancement of Teaching, 2010; National Institute of Health, 2003). Such data sharing, in ROI terms, can be considered secondary returns.

Data sources and collection techniques include literature review; in-person and telephone interviews; extraction of data from administrative and research data systems; surveys of a sample of investigators using and not using the CRU; online databases of independent scientist and career development (K) awards; and subsequent publications and employment. Because of interviews with the data managers at the CRU, and CTSA-specific data scans, the evaluation protocol guides the evaluator through standardized processes for collecting and aggregating data, validating for errors, and transmitting the data sets to the analyst.

CRUs are likely to report economic data more consistent with standard financial records for fixed assets such as property, plant, and equipment; and variable costs, such as those associated with personnel staffing the units. However, it is very likely that the institutions will provide different patterns of service (e.g., different eligibility rules or different terms of service) and account for these units in significantly different ways. Additional challenges include valuing different components of the CRUs, such as inpatient, outpatient, and mobile services. A key focus of interviews is on developing consistent and comprehensive definitions of terms and outcomes.

Analysis

The value or return will be a function of a number of characteristics: the awards through the CTSA and from other sources; the institutions at the time of the award and before and after; the investigator; the number of collaborations in the award, length and extent of "exposure" to the CRU of the research programs; all dependent on the scope and boundary discussions with stakeholders and on the synthesized model constructed.

There are several sets of potential models for each outcome; for instance, a model may include categorized data sharing status measures, wherein others may include principal investigator (PI), institution, and other award characteristics. Depending on the type of outcomes being measured and the context of the ROI calculation, regression models or Data Envelopment Analyses can be used. For instance, if the outcome were publication counts, Poisson regression models might be of use; whereas in the case of longitudinal publication outcomes, negative binomial regression models may be in order. A hierarchical set of models may help understand the extent to which differences in the outcome of interest may be attributable to characteristics of the unit, the stage of career, PI collaborations, or size and timing of the award. With such data, it will also be possible to compare relative effectiveness of investments across project times and across institutions.

Typically, ROI estimation is approached very simply. Total "returns" (e.g., monetized benefits) are divided by total "investments" (e.g., costs) to get the ratio of returns for each dollar invested. However, these simplistic analyses do not enable looking at distributions and variability or allow for statistical tests of differences. Using data that have not yet been aggregated into gross categories enables use of statistical methods rather than just reporting aggregate ROI.

Model development follows an iterative process, which follows a spiral development path (Ambler, 2002). That is, the model will begin as simple as possible, uncovering the basic issues involved in model development. Once these issues are resolved and tested using the data provided in the data collection phase discussed above, the model is enhanced and detailed at the next level of complexity and performance. Using such a process allows for both the development of a rapid, more local, decision tool and for the continuing development of a more complex and generalizable decision tool.

As stated before, while the basics of ROI are simple, other issues can make the use of ROI more challenging. This is particularly true when a return can only be realized years or decades after the investment (National Center for Advancing Translational Sciences, 2012). Discounted ROI is well known for being highly biased toward rapid investment returns. This is a major issue for CTSAs as, for example, investing "time" in new researchers today by allowing them to use a CRU should provide "return" in terms of new discoveries in the future; but how exactly should each be quantified? As one of the four transformative aims of the CTSA program is to provide a foundation of shared resources that could reduce costs, delays, and difficulties experienced in clinical research, including trials, this timing is particularly crucial (http://www.ncats.nih.gov/research/cts/ctsa/about/about.html).

Additionally, nonfinancial characteristics of both investment and return can be difficult to identify in commensurate terms. For example, time is the most inelastic and finite of all resources but it must be expended in teaching new investigators in hopes that they do better and more meaningful research in their subsequent careers. While it is possible to achieve significant "return" with completely one-on-one responsiveness to the researcher's demands in the CRU, the investment in time usually is prohibitive with respect to the relative investment. But, only offering group instruction or supervision (a lower investment alternative) may not provide the necessary quality (i.e., return) required. One major emphasis of the proposed modeling approach is identifying comparable metrics within a function.

Methodology Development: Evaluation Protocol

The proposed evaluation protocol addresses both standard ROI and SROI estimation methodologies but focuses on the economic ROI. Work with key stakeholders helps establish the scope and boundaries of the analysis for each program. This is not a trivial issue in ROI analysis. For example, there are a number of direct and indirect potential outcomes of given clinical trial projects: subsequent research publications; patent applications and patents received; subsequent grants received; and even the economic effects of spending the funds such as their stimulus to the local economy. There is no effective way to monetize all of these outcomes and the decision regarding which to include in ROI analysis is to some extent a matter of judgment. After meeting with stakeholders and determining their within-center approach to boundary conditions, data elements can be selected.

RESULTS: PROCESS AND STRUCTURE FOR ROI ANALYSIS

A multistep process for structuring the ROI analysis is summarized as follows:

1. Create alternative conceptual frameworks to estimate the impacts and value.

2. Survey CTSA on available sources and formats of economic and social impact data; determine costs of collecting and analyzing data.

3. Collect selected financial, service utilization, and community encounter and impact data from collaborating sites.

4. Test usability of each framework and efficacy of resulting metrics.

5. Create evaluation protocol for use by CTSA in pilot and final testing.

FIGURE 1 ● Estimating the ROI: Process Steps. ROI = return on investment.

1. Establish scope of the analysis

   Identify key stakeholders

   Map outcomes that show the relationships between inputs, outputs, and outcomes

2. Collect the data

   Recognize organizational policies & objectives that may affect materiality or significance of data and its accessibility

   Identify appropriate outcomes

   Identify & collect data

3. Analyze the data

   Calculate the ROI

   Test the sensitivity of measures

   Share findings with stakeholders and users of the analysis

   Subject the analysis to suggested changes resulting from feedback

In planning the project, it is important to identify a conceptual model that is acceptable to the CTSA; this can be determined through interviews with staff and investigators within the CTSA and the CRU itself.

The process for collecting and analyzing the data to calculate the ROI is detailed in Figure 1. Here, evaluators define relevant data, examine the quality of existing data, and standardize methods for collecting and analyzing data; these steps result in selected mechanisms for further testing and adoption. The analysis uses accounting, financial, economic, and SROI principles to identify outcomes and value impact.

Types of costs and gains, or benefits, are listed in Figure 2a and 2b. Limiting the initial work to direct and indirect costs, and not including incidental costs, is less complex and may allow the CTSA to move forward more quickly with these types of analyses.

The standard model of ROI estimates:

$$\frac{\text{Timing and magnitude of expected gains}}{\text{Timing and magnitude of expected costs}}:$$

Considering the timing and magnitude of cash flows recognizes the impact of early versus later gains and costs. This recognition is captured in the discount rate, the percentage used to discount future net cash flows to recognize the risk or uncertainty of estimating net gains into the future. Discounting cash flows requires selecting a percentage rate based on an estimate of how "risky" the investment is relative to other projects in which the funder invests. In standard businesses, the discount rate is the average of the interest rate

FIGURE 2 ● (a) ROI Financial Flows. (b) Categories of Financial Flows. ROI = return on investment.

a. Cost Categories

DIRECT	Actual cash transfers between parties that are directly attributable to X (X being the project or product)
INDIRECT	Accrue as a result of an affiliation, but less easy to monetize because they are not cash transfers
INCIDENTAL	Accrue as a result of an affiliation, but less easy to monetize because they are not cash transfers

b. Financial Flows

Financial Flows: Costs	Financial Flows: Gains
DIRECT attributable salaries & wages, equipment for X	DIRECT income from grants and fees
INDIRECT general operating and management activities of CTSA, space costs	INDIRECT extra income for CTSA overhead
INCIDENTAL increased staff turnover; lack of visibility; marginalized community	INCIDENTAL decreased staff turnover; increased visibility in community; improved community health

on their debt and the return shareholders expect on their investments in the company. This is an average weighted by the portion of the company that is financed by debt and financed by equity. In the CRU methodology, the discount rate can be selected using a sensitivity analysis varying from the interest rate on medium term interest rates in the commercial loan market to inflation rate plus 1–3%. This level of riskiness of the federal investment in the CTSA is conservative, but realistic.

SUMMARY AND CONCLUSION

This article proposes using several approaches to study quantitatively the availability, accessibility, and quality of data used to define ROI; and qualitatively seek additional process input into the financial and social models as they are developed and tested. The protocol includes identifying types of costs, impacts, and values (external, internal, financial, social); creating alternative conceptual frameworks to estimate the impacts and value of translational research on individual researchers, the research enterprise, consumers of research and clinical care, and the public; surveying CTSAs on available sources and formats of economic and social impact data; determining costs of collecting and analyzing financial data; testing usability of each framework and efficacy of resulting metrics; and creating protocols for use by CTSAs.

Creating and sustaining the next generation of clinical and translational research, researchers, and practitioners within a culture of innovation and excellence requires thoughtful and fair allocation of resources. While not the only criteria for investment, the outputs in productivity, creativity, efficiency, and better health status warrant measurement. As in business in general, CTSAs would benefit from the ability to use standardized methods and tools to measure ROI. Realizing this need, some CTSAs are embarking on efforts to identify the investment, benefits, and ROI for their CRUs. Through this testing of the proposed model, the NIH can assure that this method of accountability and resource allocation can become one of the several tested criteria to help make difficult but crucial decisions on the future of science and public health.

Authors' Note

The content is solely the responsibility of the authors and does not necessarily represent the official views of the NIH.

Declaration of Conflicting Interests

The author(s) declared no potential conflicts of interest with respect to the research, authorship, and/or publication of this article.

Funding

The author(s) disclosed receipt of the following financial support for the research, authorship, and/or publication of this article: This work was supported by awards to the University of Michigan CTSA (Grant number 2UL1TR000433); Weill Cornell Medical College CTSC (Grant number UL1RR024996); and Oregon Clinical and Translational Research Institute (OCTRI) (Grant number UL1TR000128) from the National Institutes of Health (NIH) National Center for Advancing Translational Sciences (NCATS).

GLOSSARY

Term	Definition	Location
Accountability	using evaluation findings for summative decision making, to make determinations about the future of the program	Ch. 12
Active consent	consent that is documented through the signing of a consent form	Ch. 9
AEA Statement on Cultural Competence in Evaluation	a set of four essential practices to guide evaluators in being culturally competent: • Acknowledge the complexity of cultural identity • Recognize the dynamics of power • Recognize and eliminate bias in language • Employ culturally appropriate methods	Ch. 3
AEA Evaluator Competencies	a set of competencies across five domains that define the expectations of a competent evaluator; domains are • professional practice, • methodology, • context, • planning and management, and • interpersonal skills	Ch. 3
AEA Guiding Principles for Evaluators	a set of five principles intended to guide the ethical behavior of evaluators; the guiding principles are • systematic inquiry, • competence, • integrity, • respect for people, and • common good and equity	Chs. 1, 3
Alternate hypothesis (H_1)	the opposite of the null hypothesis; states that any difference or relationship measured is true, real, and significant	Ch. 10
Amendment	a document that details proposed changes to your current research protocol; the amendment should include any accompanying documents, just like the initial protocol	Ch. 3

American Evaluation Association (AEA)	an international professional association of evaluators focused on sharing knowledge of evaluation approaches and methods	Ch. 2
Appendices	supplementary material located at the end of the report	Ch. 11
Appropriate fit	the extent to which the evaluation questions are consistent with the program's theory	Ch. 7
Assent	for persons under the age of 18 or another individual who is not able to give legal consent, an agreement to participate in an evaluation with full knowledge of potential benefits or risks. Note that informed consent from a parent or guardian, in addition to assent from a youth under age 18, must be granted prior to a youth's participation in an evaluation.	Ch. 9
Assent form	a document used to obtain assent from a potential evaluation participant	Ch. 9
Assertion	a statement made based on themes found within your data	Ch. 10
Attribution	the action of crediting measured outcomes to a program	Ch. 8
Benefit cost ratio (BCR)	a cost-benefit statistic calculated by dividing the dollar value of total program benefits by total program costs	Ch. 12
Calibrator	a continuum upon which we can consider where our beliefs fall and through which we can apply those beliefs in a particular context	Ch. 4
Case study	an in-depth examination of a person, group of people, or context	Ch. 8
Causal inference	the ability of an evaluator to claim that the program they are evaluating is responsible for the outcomes they measured; causality can be claimed with experimental designs	Ch. 4
Causation	the attribution of a program (the cause) to the measured outcomes (the effect)	Ch. 8
CBAM	concerns-based adoption model; a model of change that includes three frameworks for assessing the change process: stages of concern, levels of use, and innovation configurations	Ch. 12
CIPP evaluation	an approach to evaluation that incorporates four types of evaluation: context evaluation, input evaluation, process evaluation, and product evaluation. The CIPP model is used to improve programs and aid decision making	Ch. 4
Codebook	a file that records the variable name for each data element collected, the item or question that was used to collect the data, and how the data were coded when prepared for analysis	Ch. 9
Codes	labels that assign meaning to data	Ch. 10
Coding clean	procedures used to verify that data have been recording correctly	Ch. 9

(*Continued*)

(Continued)

Term	Definition	Location
Comparison-group design	an evaluation design that includes the examination of program effects in two or more groups, at least one of which receives the program and at least one of which does not. Strong comparison-group designs are also referred to as *quasi-experimental designs*	Ch. 8
Compliance-only evaluation	an evaluation that is conducted as a formality to satisfy a regulation or stakeholder, with no intention by program leadership to use the evaluation findings	Ch. 12
Conclusions	a report section where evaluation findings are summarized in a shortened, comprehensive manner; conclusions should consider the implications of findings on the program	Ch. 11
Confidentiality	refers to how private information provided by participants is safeguarded; evaluators should take precautions to protect the identity of participants	Ch. 3
Consent form	a document used to obtain informed consent from a potential evaluation participant	Ch. 9
Contextual conditions	resources, infrastructure, facilities, services, or any other conditions that are necessary for the program to be successful, but are not part of the program itself	Chs. 5, 6
Contextual influences	factors in the environment that may affect the program's operations and success; context can be examined using a PEST analysis examining political, economic, social, and technological influences	Ch. 5
Correlation	a statistic indicating the strength and direction of the relationship between the values for two variables	Ch. 10
Cost-benefit/ cost-effectiveness analysis	summative evaluation that focuses on estimating the efficiency of a program in terms of dollar costs saved (cost-benefit) or outcomes measured (cost-effectiveness)	Ch. 1
Cover page	the first page of an evaluation report; includes the title of the report, authors, and date of report	Ch. 11
Credibility	in evaluation, the degree of trust someone has that findings are reported accurately and should be believed	Ch. 1
Data-sharing agreement	an agreement between an evaluator and an organization that stipulates how data necessary to the evaluation will be shared, protected, and used	Ch. 9
Deductive codes	prespecified codes developed from evaluation questions; also called a priori codes	Ch. 10
Deductive disclosure	occurs when a person's identity can be determined through responses or a combination of responses	Ch. 3

Delimited file	a data file that uses a predetermined character, such as a tab or comma, to indicate new data items or columns	Ch. 9
Descriptive codes	codes that summarize data in a word or phrase	Ch. 10
Descriptive statistic	a number that summarizes a data set in a meaningful way	Ch. 10
Design rigor	the extent to which an evaluation design merits attribution of strategies to measured outcomes	Ch. 8
Early objectives	short-term outcomes associated with the program	Ch. 6
Effect size (d)	the size or magnitude of the difference between variables; studies aim to detect small effects	Ch. 10
Embedded evaluation (EMB-E)	an evaluation approach based on continuous improvement, in which program processes and practices are examined and refined to improve outcomes; a comprehensive continuous-improvement-centered, theory-based, utilization-focused approach; a framework to build evaluation into a program's design and operations, making information and data the basis upon which the program operates and thus fostering continuous improvement	Chs. 1,4,5
Empowerment evaluation	an approach to evaluation that is focused on self-determination as a way to empower stakeholders to use evaluation findings and conduct their own evaluations	Ch. 4
Epistemology	the need to understand the value we place on knowledge in making judgments about worth; epistemology relates to the "valuing" branch of evaluation	Ch. 4
Ethics	moral obligations guiding the determination of behavior as right or wrong	Ch. 3
Evaluability assessment	formative evaluation used to determine if an evaluation is feasible and the role stakeholders might take in shaping the evaluation design	Ch. 1
Evaluation	a method used to determine the value of something	Ch. 1
Evaluation design and methods	a report section that details both the evaluation design and evaluation methods; evaluation design includes a description of the evaluation purpose, evaluation questions, and overall research design; evaluation methods includes a description of indicators, targets, data sources, data collection methods, and data analysis procedures; the evaluation matrix should be included in this section	Ch. 11
Evaluation enrichments	added supports to your evaluation design that can increase the usefulness of results and credibility of findings. Some enrichments include using repeated measures, longitudinal data, and sampling, as well as logic modeling and case studies	Ch. 8
Evaluation findings	a report section where results are organized sequentially in alignment with the evaluation questions; data informing each question are presented with details regarding statistics or themes, as well as sample sizes	Ch. 11

(Continued)

(Continued)

Term	Definition	Location
Evaluation matrix	a tabular representation of the • evaluation questions, • indicators, • targets, • data sources, • data collection techniques, and • data analysis methods embedded within and associated with each component of a program's logic model.	Ch. 7
Executive summary	a synopsis of the program, evaluation, and key findings; designing the executive summary as a stand-alone brief gives flexibility with dissemination of findings	Ch. 11
Exempt	human subjects research that falls under one of eight exempt categories and is determined to pose no more than minimal risk; exempt from IRB review	Ch. 3
Existing data	data collected on an ongoing basis by a particular institution or agency	Ch. 9
Expedited review	human subjects research that is reviewed by a member of the IRB and determined to fall under one of nine categories	Ch. 3
Experimental design	an evaluation design in which participants are randomly assigned to receive the program or to a nonprogram control group. Experimental designs are also called *randomized controlled trials* (RCTs)	Ch. 8
External evaluator	an evaluator who is employed outside of the organization in which the program operates	Ch. 1
Facilitator	the interviewer in a focus group, who is responsible for not only following the protocol, but also moderating the discussion in a productive and constructive way	Ch. 9
Feasibility	the extent to which there are adequate resources available to answer the evaluation questions	Ch. 7
Federalwide Assurance (FWA)	an agreement between the government and an organization stating that it will comply with the Common Rule; includes designation of an Institutional Review Board (IRB) to review all research to ensure adequate protection for human subjects	Ch. 3
Focus group	a small group of individuals, typically six to eight, brought together to answer questions regarding a specific topic	Ch. 9
Formative evaluation	evaluation aimed at providing information to improve a program while it is in operation; evaluation used to shape the program; program staff can use interim evaluation findings to plan, shape, and improve the program prior to the evaluation of final outcomes	Chs. 1, 7

Frequency distribution	a statistic indicating the number of cases in your data set for a certain value or range of values	Ch. 10
Full review	human subjects research that does not fall under one of the eight exempt or nine expedited categories and thus is reviewed by the full IRB	Ch. 3
Goal-free evaluation	an approach to evaluation where the evaluation is not constrained by program goals, but rather focuses on the measurement of outcomes, whether intended or unintended; developed by Michael Scriven	Ch. 4
Goal trap	Focusing exclusively on the goals of the program such that unintended consequences, either positive or negative, are missed	Ch. 7
Human subject	a living individual who participates in a research study; this participation may be directly through intervention or interaction, or by the researcher having access to private data that would allow identification of the individual	Ch. 3
Ideology	a system of beliefs that we use to explain and develop solutions; a philosophy or a way of thinking about a certain topic or issue	Ch. 4
Impact evaluation	summative evaluation that measures both the intended and unintended outcomes of a program	Ch. 1
Implementation assessment	formative evaluation that examines the degree to which a program is implemented with fidelity (according to plan)	Ch. 1
Implementation failure	occurs when the program is not implemented as planned	Ch. 7
Implementation theory	a theory of action that describes the activities that precipitate change	Ch. 5
Improving programs and policies	the purpose of evaluation; to create more effective and efficient programs and policies	Ch. 1
Indicator	a statement that can be used to gauge progress toward program goals and objectives; can be derived from evaluation questions and used to measure progress toward program goals and objectives. An evaluation question may have one or more indicators. An indicator is SMA: Specific Measurable Agreed upon	Ch. 7
Inductive codes	codes that emerge during data collection and analysis	Ch. 10
Inferential statistic	a number calculated based on one data set that is used to draw conclusions about the greater population that your data set is intended to represent	Ch. 10

(Continued)

(Continued)

Term	Definition	Location
Informational power	power gained by having access to information that may not be readily known or understood	Ch. 12
Informed consent	an individual's voluntary agreement to participate in a study after being provided with and understanding information about the study, including the research purpose and research risks; an individual's agreement to participate in an evaluation with full knowledge of potential benefits or risks	Chs. 3, 9
Institutional Review Board (IRB)	a committee that is charged with protecting human subjects in research. IRBs review all research prior to the research being conducted to ensure adequate protections and safeguards are in place	Ch. 3
Intermediate objectives	mid-term outcomes associated with the program	Ch. 6
Internal evaluator	an evaluator employed by the organization that operates a program (but preferably not responsible for the program itself)	Ch. 1
Interview protocol	a predetermined set of questions to ask the interviewee during the interview	Ch. 9
Interviews	verbal exchanges guided by questions that focus on a particular topic	Ch. 9
Introduction	a report section that includes an overview of the program and the evaluation; typically provides background information on the program and details the structure of the report, including a description of each section and the contents they cover	Ch. 11
In vivo codes	codes that use words or phrases from the participants' language	Ch. 10
IRB protocol	a document that details the purpose and design of your research study; the protocol is submitted to the IRB along with any consent forms, communication with participants, and data collection instruments	Ch. 3
Joint Committee's Program Evaluation Standards	a set of 30 standards intended to guide evaluators in the areas of utility, feasibility, propriety, accuracy, and evaluation accountability	Ch. 1
Jottings	short pieces of writing that allow you to comment on chunks of data	Ch. 10
Legitimate power	power gained through formal means, such as the position a person holds in an organization	Ch. 12
Logic model	a graphical representation of a program's theory	Ch. 6
Logic modeling	the process of determining indicators for program objectives and goals based on program theory	Ch. 8
Longitudinal data	data collected over an extended period of time	Ch. 8
Long-term goals	the intended results of the program	Ch. 6

Matrix	used to chart or table data to aid in seeing patterns in the data	Ch. 10
Mean	a statistic that indicates the average value for a variable in a data set	Ch. 10
Member checking	the process of reviewing qualitative results to reduce researcher bias, as well as to verify, validate, or determine the credibility of the researcher's account and results	Ch. 11
Memo	a thought or idea about your codes and themes	Ch. 10
Meta-analysis	summative evaluation that integrates the findings of multiple studies to estimate the overall effect of a type of program	Ch. 1
Meta-evaluation	an evaluation of an evaluation	Ch. 1
Minimal risk	a criterion for human subjects research that involves the determination as to whether the research involves more risk to an individual than would be encountered in everyday life	Ch. 3
Misinterpretation	to claim that findings are something different than they are, that is, interpreting findings incorrectly	Ch. 11
Mixed methods	evaluation methods that rely on both quantitative and qualitative data	Ch. 8
Narrative description	writing a passage that elaborates on a code	Ch. 10
Needs assessment	formative evaluation that focuses on what services are needed and who needs them	Ch. 1
Net economic benefits (NEB)	a cost-benefit statistic calculated by subtracting the total program costs from the dollar value of total program benefits	Ch. 12
Network displays	a map with lines and arrows to indicate how people, components, or actions connect and flow	Ch. 10
Null hypothesis (H_0)	a statement to be tested and either accepted or rejected; typically states that any relationship or difference found among variables is by chance	Ch. 10
Objectives-oriented evaluation	an approach to evaluation where the focus of the evaluation is on how well the program met a set of predetermined objectives	Ch. 4
Objectivity	in evaluation, the degree to which an evaluator can put aside any bias and impartially interpret and report findings	Ch. 1
Observation	information learned by seeing or watching something	Ch. 9
Operations	processes involved with implementing the activities of a program	Ch. 1
Outcome evaluation	summative evaluation aimed at measuring how well a program met its stated goals	Ch. 1
Outcomes	results that occur during and after implementing a program	Ch. 1

(Continued)

(Continued)

Term	Definition	Location
Outcome statement	a statement of what the program intends to accomplish that begins with an outcome word. While goals are worded many different ways, embedded evaluation is based on goals being worded as outcome statements	Ch. 5
Overinterpretation	to claim that findings are a direct result of a program's activities or strategies in the absence of a research design that would warrant causal conclusions	Ch. 11
Participatory evaluation	an approach to evaluation that relies on a partnership between stakeholders and evaluators	Ch. 4
Passive consent	consent that is assumed due to an individual's voluntary participation after being informed about the evaluation	Ch. 9
Plan-Do-Study-Act (PDSA)	a quality improvement process useful for piloting and testing program changes	Ch. 11
Power	the probability that the null hypothesis is rejected when it should have been rejected	Ch. 10
Principles-focused evaluation (PFE)	an approach to evaluation that focuses on evaluating the implementation and outcomes of principles	Ch. 4
Privacy	refers to a participant's right to control who has access to their personal information	Ch. 3
Probe	a follow-up question used to explore responses in more detail	Ch. 9
Process codes	codes that label and index observable and conceptual action in the data	Ch. 10
Process evaluation	formative evaluation aimed at understanding the operations of a program and assessing the fidelity with which program strategies were implemented	Chs. 1, 7
Program	defined broadly in this text to include a group of activities ranging from a small intervention to a national or international policy	Ch. 1
Program description	a report section that provides a detailed description of the program; includes the history of the program, a recognition of any program funders, an accounting of program goals and objectives, a list of the program's strategies, and a copy of the program's logic model	Ch. 11
Program documentation	resources such as meeting minutes, annual reports, strategic plans, handbooks, diagrams, videos, audio recordings, and portfolios	Ch. 9
Program evaluation	evaluation used to determine the merit or worth of a program	Ch. 1
Program goal	a general statement of what a program intends to accomplish or its desired results	Ch. 5

Program improvement	using evaluation findings for formative decision making, to shape and inform the program in an effort to improve program operations and results	Ch. 12
Program stakeholder	anyone who has an interest or stake in the success of a program. Key stakeholders include program staff, community members, program participants, and policymakers	Ch. 6
Program strategies	activities the program puts into place to accomplish its goals. Strategies might include services, materials, training, resources, or a cluster of activities	Ch. 5
Program theory	the theory as to why the program should work. It is a set of underlying assumptions that explain the linkages between program strategies and program goals	Ch. 5
***p*-value**	the probability that a difference detected for the sample would *not* be true for the population	Ch. 10
Qualitative methods	evaluation methods that rely on noncategorical data and free response, observational, or narrative descriptions	Ch. 8
Quality improvement (QI)	a systematic process through which programs can be examined to improve implementation and outcomes	Ch. 11
Quantitative methods	evaluation methods that rely on categorical or numerical data	Ch. 8
Quick feedback	a method of providing ongoing and timely informal feedback to program staff to improve operations	Ch. 11
Recommendations	the last major section of the report; used to translate findings into actionable strategies intended to improve the program or its processes	Ch. 11
References	a list of resources cited in the evaluation report	Ch. 11
Referent power	power derived from someone's personality or their connections with others	Ch. 12
Regression	a statistical method used to examine how predictive one or more variables are of another variable	Ch. 10
Relevance	the extent to which answers to the evaluation questions will be useful to stakeholders	Ch. 7
Reliability	the consistency with which an instrument measures something	Ch. 8
Repeated measures	collecting the same data elements at multiple time points	Ch. 8
Request for proposal (RFP)	a solicitation for organizations to submit a proposal indicating how they would complete a specified project	Ch. 1
Research	a systematic investigation in a field of study; evaluation is a type of research	Ch. 1

(Continued)

(Continued)

Term	Definition	Location
Response rate	the percentage of people who complete your survey as a function of the number of surveys distributed. Response rate = number of surveys completed / number of surveys distributed	Ch. 9
Responsive evaluation	an approach to evaluation that focuses on program activities, responds to stakeholder needs, and values the perspectives of all those involved in the program	Ch. 4
Return on investment (ROI)	the degree to which a program or intervention is considered efficient; the program's contribution in terms of outcomes or dollars saved in relation to the cost of the program	Ch. 12
Rubric	a guideline that can be used objectively to examine subjective data	Ch. 8
Sampling	choosing a smaller group to participate in the evaluation from the larger population of program participants	Ch. 8
Semi-structured interview	an interview that includes some predetermined questions, but also retains the flexibility to include probes or follow-up questions as topics emerge	Ch. 9
Significance level (α)	the level of confidence we have in our findings; also referred to as alpha level	Ch. 10
Simultaneous coding	coding in which a researcher applies two or more codes to a data chunk	Ch. 10
Single-group design	an evaluation design focused on examining the effects of a program on one group of participants; an evaluation design without a comparison group. Single-group designs are also referred to as *nonexperimental designs*	Ch. 8
Social accountability	the need to investigate the effectiveness of social programs in order to hold program leadership accountable; social accountability relates to the development of the "use" branch of evaluation	Ch. 4
Social inquiry	the need to develop methodologies to evaluate the effectiveness of social programs; social inquiry relates to the development of the "methods" branch of evaluation	Ch. 4
Stakeholder	anyone who has an interest in or is involved with the operation or success of a program. Key stakeholder groups often include program staff, program participants, community members, and policymakers	Ch. 1
Stakeholder engagement	the extent to which stakeholders are committed to answering the evaluation questions	Ch. 7
Stakeholder matrix	a spreadsheet or table that includes each stakeholder group and the specific interests they may have in the evaluation results	Ch. 12
Standard	target that we use, implicitly or explicitly, to judge the merit or worth of a program	Ch. 1

Standard deviation	a statistic that indicates the amount of variation for a particular variable in a data set	Ch. 10
Strategies	activities put into place to accomplish program goals	Ch. 6
Structured interview	a predetermined set of questions to ask the interviewee during the interview	Ch. 9
Summative evaluation	evaluation aimed at providing information regarding effectiveness in order to make decisions about whether to continue or discontinue a program; evaluation focused on a program's impact; summative evaluation findings are used to make decisions about program funding and continuance	Chs. 1, 7
Survey instruments	questionnaires that give your participants a standard set of questions and response categories	Ch. 9
Systematic	logical and organized; undertaken according to a plan	Ch. 1
Table of contents	an optional section that is usually included for larger reports to guide the reader through the document	Ch. 11
Target	a clarification of an indicator, specifying how much progress should be made and by when in order to determine to what extent goals and objectives have been met; targets should provide a realistic timeline and yardstick for indicators. A target is RT: Realistic Time bound	Ch. 7
Theme	an important finding in your data based on codes	Ch. 10
Theory	a system of assumptions or beliefs intended to explain how something works	Ch. 5
Theory-based evaluation (TBE)	an approach to evaluation that explicitly relates what a program does to its intended outcomes, based on the underlying logic of why and how a program works. TBE involves identifying the early and intermediate objectives through which program strategies function to achieve program goals	Ch. 4
Theory of action (ToA)	a theory that describes how a program is delivered; implementation theory is a theory of action	Ch. 5
Theory of change (ToC)	a theory that describes how a change occurs; program theory is a theory of change	Ch. 5
t-test	a statistical method used to determine if the difference between two means is significant	Ch. 10
type 1 error (α)	the error made when the null hypothesis is rejected when it should have been accepted; a false positive	Ch. 10

(*Continued*)

(Continued)

Term	Definition	Location
type 2 error (β)	the error made when the null hypothesis is accepted when it should have been rejected; a false negative	Ch. 10
Unstructured interview	an interview during which questions and probes are added following up on questions that emerge during the interview	Ch. 9
Utilization-focused evaluation (UFE)	a collaborative approach to evaluation in which the evaluator prioritizes the perspectives and values of the individuals who will be most affected by evaluation findings	Ch. 4
Validity	the accuracy with which an instrument measures a construct	Ch. 8
Value	a principle or quality used to estimate importance; an estimate of importance	Ch. 1
Variables	data elements that can be measured and have different values	Ch. 9

REFERENCES

Chapter 1

American Evaluation Association. (2018). *American Evaluation Association guiding principles for evaluators*. Washington, DC: Author. Retrieved from https://www.eval.org/p/cm/ld/fid=51

Aos, S., Phillips, P., Barnoski, R., & Lieb, R. (2001). *The comparative costs and benefits of programs to reduce crime*. Olympia: Washington State Institute of Public Policy.

Beisser, S. R. (2008). *Unintended consequences of No Child Left Behind mandates on gifted students*. Baton Rouge, LA: Forum on Public Policy.

Cawthon, S. W. (2007). Hidden benefits and unintended consequences of No Child Left Behind policies for students who are deaf or hard of hearing. *American Educational Research Journal, 44*(3), 460–492. https://doi.org/10.3102/0002831207306760

Cellini, S. R., & Kee, J. E. (2015). Cost-effectiveness and cost-benefit analysis. In K. E. Newcomer, H. P. Hatry, & J. S. Wholey (Eds.), *Handbook of practical program evaluation* (4th ed., pp. 636–672). Hoboken, NJ: Wiley.

Center on Education Policy. (2006, March). *From the capital to the classroom: Year 4 of the No Child Left Behind Act*. Washington, DC: Author.

Collier, L. (2014, October). Incarceration nation. *Monitor on Psychology, 45*(9), 56. Retrieved from http://www.apa.org/monitor/2014/10/incarceration.aspx

Giliberti, M. (2015, May). *Treatment, not jail: It's time to step up*. Arlington, VA: National Alliance on Mental Illness. Retrieved from https://www.nami.org/Blogs/From-the-Executive-Director/May-2015/Treatment,-Not-Jail-It%E2%80%99s-Time-to-Step-Up

Head Start. (2019). Office of Head Start [Website]. Washington, DC: U.S. Department of Health and Human Services. Retrieved from https://www.acf.hhs.gov/ohs

Health Resources and Services Administration. (2011). *Quality improvement*. Washington, DC: U.S. Department of Health and Human Services. Retrieved from https://www.hrsa.gov/sites/default/files/quality/toolbox/508pdfs/qualityimprovement.pdf

House, E., & Howe, K. R. (1999). *Values in evaluation and social research*. Thousand Oaks, CA: Sage.

LaVelle, J. (2010, February 26). John LaVelle on describing evaluation [Blog post]. Retrieved from https://aea365.org/blog/john-lavelle-on-describing-evaluation/

Li, D. (2010). Unintended consequences: No Child Left Behind and the allocation of school leaders. Retrieved from https://papers.ssrn.com/sol3/papers.cfm?abstract_id=1584345

Lilienfeld, S. O. (2005). Scientifically unsupported and supported interventions for childhood psychopathology: A summary. *Pediatrics, 115*, 761–764.

Lincoln, Y. S., & Guba, E. G. (1980). The distinction between merit and worth in evaluation. *Educational Evaluation and Policy Analysis, 2*(4), 61–71.

McVay, D., Schiraldi, V., & Ziedenberg, J. (2004, January). *Treatment or incarceration?* Washington, DC: Justice Policy Institute. Retrieved from http://www.justicepolicy.org/uploads/justicepolicy/documents/04-01_rep_mdtreatmentorincarceration_ac-dp.pdf

Newcomer, K. E., Hatry, H. P., & Wholey, J. S. (2015). *Handbook of practical program evaluation* (4th ed.). Hoboken, NJ: Wiley.

Olweus, D., & Limber, S. P. (2007). *The Olweus Bullying Prevention Program teacher guide*. Center City, MN: Hazelden Foundation.

Petrosino, A., Turpin-Petrosino, C., Hollis-Peel, M. E., & Lavenberg, J. G. (2012). Scared Straight and other juvenile awareness programs for preventing juvenile delinquency: A systematic review. *Campbell Systematic Reviews, 2013*(5). Retrieved from http://www.campbell collaboration.org/media/k2/attachments/Petrosino_Scared_Straight_Update.pdf

Russ-Eft, D., & Preskill, H. (2009). *Evaluation in organizations: A systematic approach to enhancing learning, performance, and change* (2nd ed.). New York, NY: Basic Books.

Scriven, M. (1969). An introduction to meta-evaluation. *Educational Products Report, 2*, 36–38.

Scriven, M. (1979). Product evaluation. *Research and Evaluation Program Paper and Report Series No. 29.* Portland, OR: Northwest Regional Educational Laboratory.

Scriven, M. (2009, January). Meta-evaluation revisited. *Journal of MultiDisciplinary Evaluation, 6*(11), iii–viii.

Stufflebeam, D. L. (1978). Meta evaluation: An overview. *Evaluation & the Health Professions, 1*(1), 17–43. https://doi.org/10.1177/016327877800100102

Stufflebeam, D. L. (2001). *Evaluation values and criteria checklist.* Kalamazoo: Evaluation Center at Western Michigan University. Retrieved from https://wmich.edu/sites/default/files/attachments/u350/2014/values_criteria.pdf

Trevisan, M. S. (2007). Evaluability assessment from 1986 to 2006. *American Journal of Evaluation, 28*(3), 290–303. https://doi.org/10.1177/1098214007304589

Trevisan, M. S., & Walser, T. M. (2014). *Evaluability assessment: Improving evaluation quality and use.* Thousand Oaks, CA: Sage.

Trochim, W. M. K. (2001). *The research methods knowledge base.* Cincinnati, OH: Atomic Dog.

Washington State Institute for Public Policy. (2007). *Evidence-based juvenile offender programs: Program description, quality assurance, and cost.* Olympia, WA: Author. Retrieved from https://www.wsipp.wa.gov/ReportFile/986/Wsipp_Evidence-Based-Juvenile-Offender-Programs-Program-Description-Quality-Assurance-and-Cost_Full-Report.pdf

Washington State Institute for Public Policy. (2018). *Scared Straight benefit-cost results.* Olympia, WA: Author. Retrieved from http://www.wsipp.wa.gov/BenefitCost/ProgramPdf/114/Scared-Straight

Weiss, C. H. (1998). *Evaluation* (2nd ed.). Upper Saddle River, NJ: Prentice Hall.

What Works Clearinghouse. (2006a, September). *WWC intervention report: Too good for drugs.* Washington, DC: Institute of Education Sciences.

What Works Clearinghouse. (2006b, December). *WWC intervention report: First year experience courses.* Washington, DC: Institute of Education Sciences.

What Works Clearinghouse. (2016, July). *WWC intervention report: Financial incentives for teen parents to stay in school.* Washington, DC: Institute of Education Sciences.

Wholey, J. S. (1979). *Evaluation: Promise and performance.* Washington, DC: Urban Institute.

Wholey, J. S. (2002). *Evaluability assessment: Improving evaluation, management, and performance.* Washington, DC: General Accounting Office of the United States and University of Southern California.

Yarbrough, D. B., Shulha, L. M., Hopson, R. K., & Caruthers, F. A. (2011). *The program evaluation standards: A guide for evaluators and evaluation users* (3rd ed.). Thousand Oaks, CA: Sage.

Chapter 2

Alkin, M. C., & King, J. A. (2016). The historical development of evaluation use. *American Journal of Evaluation, 37*(4), 568–579. https://doi.org/10.1177/1098214016665164

British Broadcasting Corporation. (2014). *Victorian Britain.* London, England: Author. Retrieved from http://www.bbc.co.uk/history/british/timeline/victorianbritain_timeline_noflash.shtml

Budiansky, S., & Goode, E. E. (1994). The Cold War experiments. *U.S. News & World Report, 116*(3), 32.

Cabot, P. S. deQ. (1940). A long-term study of children: The Cambridge-Somerville Youth Study. *Child Development, 11*(2), 143–151. https://doi.org/10.2307/1125845

Carnahan, T., & McFarland, S. (2007). Revisiting the Stanford Prison experiment: Could participant self-selection have led to the cruelty? *Personality and Social Psychology Bulletin, 33*(5), 603–614.

Central Intelligence Agency. (1993). Soviet use of assassination and kidnapping [Unclassified document]. Washington, DC: Author. Retrieved from https://www.cia.gov/library/center-for-the-study-of-intelligence/kent-csi/vol19no3/html/v19i3a01p_0001.htm

Cremin, L. A. (2018). Horace Mann. *Encyclopedia Britannica*. Retrieved from https://www.britannica.com/biography/Horace-Mann

Cullen, M. J. (1975). *The statistical movement in early Victorian Britain: The foundations of empirical social research*. New York, NY: Harper & Row.

Faden, R. (1996). The Advisory Committee on Human Radiation Experiments: Reflections of a presidential commission. *The Hastings Center Report, 26*(5), 5–10.

Friendly, M. (2007). *The life and works of André-Michel Guerry (1802–1866)*. Toronto, Canada: York University. Retrieved from http://www.datavis.ca/papers/GuerryLife.pdf

Gale Group. (2002). Horace Mann (1796–1859). In *Encyclopedia of education*. Farmington Hills, MI: Cengage. Retrieved from https://www.encyclopedia.com/people/social-sciences-and-law/education-biographies/horace-mann

Garber, S. (2007). *Sputnik and the dawn of the Space Age*. Washington, DC: National Aeronautics and Space Administration. Retrieved from https://history.nasa.gov/sputnik/

Hartmann, T. (2000). A short history of grading. In *Complete guide to ADHD*. Nevada City, CA: Underwood Books. Retrieved from http://joe-bower.blogspot.com/2012/09/a-short-history-of-grading.html

Hogan, R. L. (2007, Fall). The historical development of program evaluation: Exploring the past and present. *Online Journal of Workforce Education and Development, 2*(4). Retrieved from https://pdfs.semanticscholar.org/ee2f/dbbe116a30ab7a79b19e1033a7cab434feec.pdf

Hornblum, A. M. (1998). *Acres of skin: Human experiments at Holmesburg Prison: A True Story of Abuse and Exploitation in the Name of Medical Science*. New York, NY: Routledge.

Humphreys, L. (1975). *Tearoom trade: Impersonal sex in public places*. New York, NY: Aldine.

Kaplan, R. M. (2004, December 16). Treatment of homosexuality during apartheid. *BMJ, 329*(7480), 1415–1416. https://doi.org/10.1136/bmj.329.7480.1415

Knight-Ridder News Service. (1994, June 28). Another 48 experiments used radiation on people. *Baltimore Sun*. Retrieved from https://www.baltimoresun.com/news/bs-xpm-1994-06-28-1994179077-story.html

Kristoff, N. D. (1995, March 17). Unmasking horror—A special report: Japan confronting gruesome war atrocity. *New York Times*. Retrieved from https://www.nytimes.com/1995/03/17/world/unmasking-horror-a-special-report-japan-confronting-gruesome-war-atrocity.html

Locke, E. A. (1982). The ideas of Frederick W. Taylor: An evaluation. *Academy of Management Review, 7*(1), 14–24.

Marx, J. D. (2011). American social policy in the 1960's and 1970's. *Social Welfare History Project*. Retrieved from http://socialwelfare.library.vcu.edu/war-on-poverty/american-social-policy-in-the-60s-and-70s/

McCord, J. (1978). A thirty-year follow-up of treatment effects. *American Psychologist, 33*(3), 284–289. https://doi.org/10.1037/0003-066X.33.3.284

McCord, J. (2002). Counterproductive juvenile justice. *Australian and New Zealand Journal of Criminology, 35*(2), 230–237.

McCord, J. (2003). Cures that harm: Unanticipated outcomes of crime prevention programs. *Annals of the American Academy of Political and Social Science, 587*(1), 16–30. https://doi.org/10.1177/0002716202250781

McCord, J., & McCord, W. (1959). A follow-up report on the Cambridge-Somerville Youth Study. *Annals of the American Academy of Political and Social Science, 322*(1), 89–96. https://doi.org/10.1177/000271625932200112

Miller, A. G., Collins, B. E., & Brief, D. E. (1995). Perspectives on obedience to authority: The legacy of the Milgram experiments. *Journal of Social Issues, 51*(3), 1–19.

Mukhongo, A. N. (2019). *Ralph W. Tyler—1976*. Indianapolis, IN: Kappa Delta Pi. Retrieved from https://www.kdp.org/aboutkdp/laureates/tylerralph.php

Nardi, P. M. (1995, March). "The breastplate of righteousness": Twenty-five years after Laud Humphreys' Tearoom Trade: Impersonal sex in public places. *Journal of Homosexuality, 30*(2), 1–10.

National Center for Education Statistics. (2019). *National Assessment of Educational Progress: History and innovation*. Washington DC: U.S. Department of Education, Institute of Education Sciences. Retrieved from https://nces.ed.gov/nationsreportcard/about/timeline.aspx

National Institutes of Health. (2015, April). *Statement on NIH funding of research using gene-editing technologies in human embryos*. Bethesda, MD: Author. Retrieved from https://www.nih.gov/about-nih/who-we-are/nih-director/statements/statement-nih-funding-research-using-gene-editing-technologies-human-embryos

National Institutes of Health. (2018, November). *Statement on claim of first gene-edited babies by Chinese researcher*. Bethesda, MD: Author. Retrieved from https://www.nih.gov/about-nih/who-we-are/nih-director/statements/statement-claim-first-gene-edited-babies-chinese-researcher

National Institutes of Health. (2019, March). *NIH supports international moratorium on clinical application of germline editing*. Bethesda, MD: Author. Retrieved from https://www.nih.gov/about-nih/who-we-are/nih-director/statements/nih-supports-international-moratorium-clinical-application-germline-editing

Nofil, B. (2019). *The CIA's appalling human experiments with mind control*. New York, NY: History Channel. Retrieved from https://www.history.com/mkultra-operation-midnight-climax-cia-lsd-experiments

Physicians Committee for Responsible Medicine. (2019). Human experimentation: An introduction to ethical issues. Washington, DC: Author. Retrieved from https://www.pcrm.org/ethical-science/human-experimentation-an-introduction-to-the-ethical-issues

Pinar, W. F. (2010) The Eight-Year Study. *Curriculum Inquiry, 40*(2), 295–316. https://doi.org/10.1111/j.1467-873X.2010.00483.x

Public Broadcasting Service. (2009). *What is evo-devo?* Arlington, VA: Author. Retrieved from https://www.pbs.org/wgbh/nova/article/what-evo-devo/

Resnick, D. B. (2019). *Research ethics timeline (1932–present)*. Research Triangle Park, NC: National Institute of Environmental Health Sciences. Retrieved from https://www.niehs.nih.gov/research/resources/bioethics/timeline/index.cfm

Schinske, J., & Tanner, K. (2014). Teaching more by grading less (or differently). *CBE-Life Sciences Education, 13*, 159–166.

Shadish, W. R. (2006). The common threads in program evaluation. *Preventing Chronic Disease, 3*(1). Retrieved from www.cdc.gov/pcd/issues/2006/jan/05_0166.htm

Shadish, W. R., Cook, T. D., & Leviton, L. C. (1990). *Foundations of program evaluation*. Thousand Oaks, CA: Sage.

Silverman, F. H. (1998). The "monster" study. *Journal of Fluency Disorders, 13*, 225–231.

Soh, K. C. (2011). Grade point average: What's wrong and what's the alternative? *Journal of Higher Education Policy and Management, 33*(1), 27–36.

Toulemonde, J., & Rochaix, L. (1994). Rational decision-making through project appraisal: A presentation of French attempts. *International Review of Administrative Sciences, 60*(1), 37–53. https://doi.org/10.1177/002085239406000103

Tyson, P. (2000). The experiments. In *Holocaust on Trial*. Arlington, VA: NOVA Online. Retrieved from https://www.pbs.org/wgbh/nova/holocaust/experiside.html

U.S. Department of Energy, Office of Human Radiation Experiments. (1995, July). *Human radiation experiments associated with the U.S. Department of Energy and its predecessors* (DOE/EH-0491). Washington, DC: Author.

U.S. House of Representatives, Committee on Energy and Commerce, Subcommittee on Energy Conservation and Power. (1986, November). *American nuclear guinea pigs: Three decades of radiation experiments on U.S. citizens* (ACHRE No. Con-050594-A-1). Washington, DC: Author.

Vinovskis, M. A. (1998). *Overseeing the nation's report card: The creation and evolution of the National Assessment Governing Board (NAGB)*. Ann Arbor: University of Michigan, Institute for Social Research. https://doi.org/10.1111/j.1939-0025.1980.tb03267.x

Vosburgh, W. S., & Alexander, L. B. (1980). Long-term follow-up as program evaluation: Lessons from McCord's 30-year follow-up of the Cambridge-Somerville Youth Study. *American Journal of Orthopsychiatry, 50*(1), 109–124.

Wainer, H. (1987). *The first four millennia of mental testing: From Ancient China to the computer age* (RR-87-34). Princeton, NJ: Educational Testing Service.

Weiss, C. H. (1998). *Evaluation* (2nd ed.). Upper Saddle River, NJ: Prentice Hall.

Welsh, B. C., Zane, S. N., & Rocque, M. (2017). Delinquency prevention for individual change: Richard Clarke Cabot and the making of the Cambridge-Somerville Youth Study. *Journal of Criminal Justice, 52*(C), 79–89. https://doi.org/10.1016/j.jcrimjus.2017.08.006

Chapter 3

American Evaluation Association. (2011). *American Evaluation Association statement on cultural competence in evaluation*. Fairhaven, MA: Author. Retrieved from https://www.eval.org/d/do/154

American Evaluation Association. (2018a). *American Evaluation Association evaluator competencies*. Washington, DC: Author. Retrieved from https://www.eval.org/d/do/4382

American Evaluation Association. (2018b). *American Evaluation Association guiding principles for evaluators*. Washington, DC: Author. Retrieved from https://www.eval.org/p/cm/ld/fid=51

Carlson, R. V., Boyd, K. M., & Webb, D. J. (2004). The revision of the Declaration of Helsinki: Past, present and future. *British Journal of Clinical Pharmacology, 57*(6), 695–713. Retrieved from https://www.ncbi.nlm.nih.gov/pmc/articles/PMC1884510/

Centers for Disease Control and Prevention. (2015a). *How Tuskegee changed research practices*. Washington, DC: Author. Retrieved from https://www.cdc.gov/tuskegee/after.htm

Centers for Disease Control and Prevention. (2015b). *The Tuskegee timeline*. Washington, DC: Author. Retrieved from https://www.cdc.gov/tuskegee/timeline.htm

Fischer, B. A. (2006). A summary of important documents in the field of research ethics. *Schizophrenia Bulletin, 32*(1), 69–80.

Gaw, A. (2014). *Who wrote the Nuremberg Code?* [Blog post]. Retrieved from https://researchet.wordpress.com/2014/02/23/who-wrote-the-nuremberg-code/

Gearhart, J. (2018). *Most Common Rule "2018 requirements" will take effect in 2019*. Seattle, WA: Quorum Review.

History.com Editors. (2018). *Nuremberg trials*. New York, NY: A&E Television Networks, History. Retrieved from https://www.history.com/topics/world-war-ii/nuremberg-trials

Mandal, J., Acharya, S., & Parija, S. C. (2011). Ethics in human research. *Tropical Parasitology, 1*(1), 2–3. Retrieved from https://www.ncbi.nlm.nih.gov/pmc/articles/PMC3593469/

National Commission for the Protection of Human Subjects of Biomedical and Behavioral Research. (1979). *Ethical Principles and Guidelines for the Protection of Human Subjects of Research (Belmont Report)*. Washington, DC: U.S. Department of Health, Education, and Welfare. Retrieved from https://www.hhs.gov/ohrp/sites/default/files/the-belmont-report-508c_FINAL.pdf

National Institutes of Health. (2019). *Policy and procedures: The intramural NIH Human Research Protections Program (HRPP)*. Washington, DC: U.S. Department of Health and Human Services. Retrieved from https://ina-respond.net/2016/07/20/human-research-protection-program-hrpp/

Office of Human Research Protections. (2019a). *Federalwide Assurance instructions*. Washington, DC: U.S. Department of Health and Human Services. Retrieved from https://www.hhs.gov/ohrp/register-irbs-and-obtain-fwas/forms/fwa-instructions/index.html

Office of Human Research Protections. (2019b). *Nuremberg Code*. Washington, DC: U.S. Department of Health and Human Services. Retrieved from https://history.nih.gov/research/downloads/nuremberg.pdf

Office of Human Research Protections. (2019c). *OHRP expedited review categories*. Washington, DC: U.S. Department of Health and Human Services. Retrieved from https://www.hhs.gov/ohrp/regulations-and-policy/guidance/categories-of-research-expedited-review-procedure-1998/index.html

Office of Human Research Protections. (2019d). *Revised Common Rule*. Washington, DC: U.S. Department of Health and Human Services. Retrieved from https://www.hhs.gov/ohrp/regulations-and-policy/regulations/finalized-revisions-common-rule/index.html

Protection of Human Subjects, 45 C.F.R. § 46.101-46.505 (2018). Retrieved from https://www.ecfr.gov/cgi-bin/retrieveECFR? gp=&SID= 83cd09e1c0f5c6937cd9d7513160fc3f&pitd=20180719&n=pt45.1.46&r=PART&ty=HTML

Research and Economic Development. (2019). *History of research ethics*. Kansas City: University of Missouri-Kansas City. Retrieved from http://ors.umkc.edu/research-compliance/institutional-review-board-(irb)/history-of-research-ethics

United States Holocaust Memorial Museum. (2019). *The Nuremberg Code*. Washington, DC: Author. Retrieved from https://encyclopedia.ushmm.org/content/en/article/the-nuremberg-code

Wiesing, U. (2014). *The Declaration of Helsinki: Its history and its future*. Ferney-Voltaire, France: World Medical Association. Retrieved from https://www.wma.net/wp-content/uploads/2017/01/Wiesing-DoH-Helsinki-20141111.pdf

World Medical Association. (2013, October). *Declaration of Helsinki*. Ferney-Voltaire, France: Author. Retrieved from https://www.wma.net/policies-post/wma-declaration-of-helsinki-ethical-principles-for-medical-research-involving-human-subjects/

Chapter 4

Alkin, M. C. (Ed.). (2013). *Evaluation roots: A wider perspective of theorists' views and influences* (2nd ed.). Thousand Oaks, CA: Sage.

Alkin, M. C., Christie, C. A., & Vo, A. T. (2013). Evaluation theory: A wider roots perspective. In M. C. Alkin (Ed.), *Evaluation roots: A wider perspective of theorists' views and influences* (2nd ed., pp. 386–393). Thousand Oaks, CA: Sage.

Bamberger, J. M., Rugh, J., & Mabry, L. S. (2011). *Real-world evaluation: Working under budget, time, data, and political constraints* (2nd ed.). Thousand Oaks, CA: Sage.

Bamberger, J. M., Vaessen, J. L., & Raimondo, E. R. (Eds.). (2015). *Dealing with complexity in development evaluation: A practical approach*. Thousand Oaks, CA: Sage.

Boruch, R. (1997). *Randomized experiments for planning and evaluation*. Thousand Oaks, CA: Sage.

Boruch, R. (2013). Roots, cahoots, and counsel. In M. C. Alkin (Ed.), *Evaluation roots: A wider perspective of theorists' views and influences* (2nd ed., pp. 66–80). Thousand Oaks, CA: Sage.

Cabot, P. S. deQ. (1940). A long-term study of children: The Cambridge-Somerville Youth Study. *Child Development, 11*(2), 143–151. https://doi.org/10.2307/1125845

Campbell, D. T. (1969). Reforms as experiments. *American Psychologist, 24*(4), 409–429. Retrieved from https://psycnet-apa-org.udel.idm.oclc.org/doi/10.1037/h0027982

Campbell, D. T., & Stanley, J. C. (1963). *Experimental and quasi-experimental designs for research*. Chicago, IL: Rand McNally.

Chen, H. T. (1990). *Theory-driven evaluations*. Thousand Oaks, CA: Sage.

Chen, H. T. (2013). The roots and growth of theory-driven evaluation: An integrated perspective for assessing viability, effectuality, and transferability. In M. C. Alkin (Ed.), *Evaluation roots: A wider perspective of theorists' views and influences* (2nd ed., pp. 113–129). Thousand Oaks, CA: Sage.

Chen, H. T. (2015). *Practical program evaluation: Theory-driven evaluation and the integrated evaluation perspective* (2nd ed.). Thousand Oaks, CA: Sage.

Chen, H. T., & Rossi, P. H. (1983). Evaluating with sense: The theory-driven approach. *Evaluation Review, 7,* 283–302.

Christie, C. A., & Alkin, M. C. (2013). An evaluation theory tree. In M. C. Alkin (Ed.), *Evaluation roots: A wider perspective of theorists' views and influences* (2nd ed., pp. 11–56). Thousand Oaks, CA: Sage.

Cook, T. D., & Campbell, D. T. (1979). *Quasi-experimentation: Design and analysis issues for field settings.* Boston, MA: Houghton Mifflin.

Coryn, C. L. S., Noakes, L. A., Westine, C. D., & Schroeter, D. C. (2011). A systematic review of theory-driven evaluation practice from 1990–2009. *American Journal of Evaluation, 32*(2), 199–226.

Cousins, J. B. (2013). Privileging empiricism in our profession: Understanding use through systematic inquiry. In M. C. Alkin (Ed.), *Evaluation roots: A wider perspective of theorists' views and influences* (2nd ed., pp. 344–352). Thousand Oaks, CA: Sage.

Cousins, J. B., & Earl, L. M. (1992). The case for participatory evaluation. *Educational Evaluation and Policy Analysis, 14*(4), 397–418. https://doi.org/10.3102/01623737014004397

Cronbach, L. J. (1951). Coefficient alpha and the internal structure of tests. *Psychometrika, 16,* 297–334.

Cronbach, L. J. (1982). *Designing evaluations of educational and social programs.* San Francisco, CA: Jossey-Bass.

Cronbach, L. J., & Associates (1980). *Toward reform of program evaluation: Aims, methods, and institutional arrangements.* San Francisco, CA: Jossey-Bass.

Fetterman, D. M. (Ed.). (1993). *Speaking the language of power: Communication, collaboration and advocacy.* New York, NY: Routledge.

Fetterman, D. M. (1994). Empowerment evaluation. *Evaluation Practice, 15*(1), 1–15. https://doi.org/10.1016/0886-1633(94)90055-8

Fetterman, D. M. (2013). Empowerment evaluation: Learning to think like an evaluator. In M. C. Alkin (Ed.), *Evaluation roots: A wider perspective of theorists' views and influences* (2nd ed., pp. 304–322). Thousand Oaks, CA: Sage.

Fitzpatrick, J. L., Sanders, J. R., & Worthen, B. R. (2011). *Program evaluation: Alternative approaches and practical guidelines* (4th ed.). Upper Saddle River, NJ: Pearson Education.

Mathison, S. (Ed.). (2005). *Encyclopedia of evaluation.* Thousand Oaks, CA: Sage.

Mosteller, F., & Boruch, R. (Eds.). (2002). *Evidence matters: Randomized trials in education research.* Washington, DC: Brookings Institution Press.

Patton, M. Q. (2011). *Developmental evaluation: Applying complexity concepts to enhance innovation and use.* New York, NY: Guilford.

Patton, M. Q. (2013). The roots of utilization-focused evaluation. In M. C. Alkin (Ed.), *Evaluation roots: A wider perspective of theorists' views and influences* (2nd ed., pp. 293–303). Thousand Oaks, CA: Sage.

Patton, M. Q. (2018). *Principles-focused evaluation: The guide.* New York, NY: Guilford.

Rossi, P. H. (2013). My views of evaluation and their origins. In M. C. Alkin (Ed.), *Evaluation roots: A wider perspective of theorists' views and influences* (2nd ed., pp. 106–112). Thousand Oaks, CA: Sage.

Rossi, P. H., Lipsey, M. W., & Henry, G. T. (2018). *Evaluation: A systematic approach* (8th ed.). Thousand Oaks, CA: Sage.

Scriven, M. (1991). Pros and cons about goal-free evaluation. *Evaluation Practice, 12*(1), 55–63.

Scriven, M. (2013). Conceptual revolutions in evaluation: Past, present, and future. In M. C. Alkin (Ed.), *Evaluation roots: A wider perspective of theorists' views and influences* (2nd ed., pp. 167–179). Thousand Oaks, CA: Sage.

Shadish, W. R., & Luellen, J. K. (2013). Donald Campbell: The accidental evaluator. In M. C. Alkin (Ed.), *Evaluation roots: A wider perspective of theorists' views and influences* (2nd ed., pp. 61–65). Thousand Oaks, CA: Sage.

Shavelson, R. J., & Towne, L. (Eds.). (2002). *Scientific research in education*. Washington, DC: National Academy Press.

Stake, R. E. (2011). Program evaluation particularly responsive evaluation. *Journal of Multidisciplinary Evaluation Occasional Paper Series, 7*(15), 180–201.

Stake, R. E. (2013). Responsive evaluation IV. In M. C. Alkin (Ed.), *Evaluation roots: A wider perspective of theorists' views and influences* (2nd ed., pp. 189–197). Thousand Oaks, CA: Sage.

Stufflebeam, D. L. (2011). CIPP model (context, input, process, product). In S. Mathison (Ed.), *Encyclopedia of evaluation* (pp. 61–65). Thousand Oaks, CA: Sage.

Stufflebeam, D. L. (2013). The CIPP evaluation model: Status, origin, development, use, and theory. In M. C. Alkin (Ed.), *Evaluation roots: A wider perspective of theorists' views and influences* (2nd ed., pp. 243–260). Thousand Oaks, CA: Sage.

Weiss, C. H. (1998). *Evaluation* (2nd ed.). Upper Saddle River, NJ: Prentice Hall.

Weiss, C. H. (2013). Rooting for evaluation: Digging into beliefs. In M. C. Alkin (Ed.), *Evaluation roots: A wider perspective of theorists' views and influences* (2nd ed., pp. 130–143). Thousand Oaks, CA: Sage.

Chapter 5

Aguilar, F. J. (1967). *Scanning the business environment*. New York: NY: Macmillan.

Cousins, J. B., & Earl, L. M. (1992). The case for participatory evaluation. *Educational Evaluation and Policy Analysis, 14*(4), 397–418. https://doi.org/10.3102/01623737014004397

Deming, W. E. (2018). *The new economics: For industry, government, and education* (3rd ed.). Cambridge, MA: MIT Press.

Doran, G. T. (1981). There's a S.M.A.R.T. way to write management's goals and objectives. *Management Review, 70*(11), 35–36.

Nilson, P. (2015, April). Making sense of implementation theories, models and frameworks. *Implementation Science, 10*(53). https://doi.org/10.1186/s13012-015-0242-0

Organizational Research Services. (2004). *Theory of change: A practical tool for action, results, and learning*. Baltimore, MD: Annie E. Casey Foundation. Retrieved from https://www.aecf.org/resources/theory-of-change/

Patton, M. Q. (2013). The roots of utilization-focused evaluation. In M. C. Alkin (Ed.), *Evaluation roots: A wider perspective of theorists' views and influences* (2nd ed., pp. 293–303). Thousand Oaks, CA: Sage.

Weiss, C. H. (1998). *Evaluation* (2nd ed.). Upper Saddle River, NJ: Prentice Hall.

Chapter 6

Frechtling, J. (2007). *Logic modeling methods in program evaluation*. San Francisco, CA: Jossey-Bass.

Knowlton, L., & Phillips, C. (2009). *The logic model guidebook*. Thousand Oaks, CA: Sage.

Ladd, S., Jemigan, J., Watkins, N., Farris, R., Minta, B., & Brown, S. (2005). *Evaluation guide: Developing and using a logic model*. Atlanta, GA: Centers for Disease Control and Prevention, National Center for Chronic Disease and Health Promotion, Division for Heart Disease and Stroke Prevention. Retrieved from https://www.cdc.gov/dhdsp/docs/logic_model.pdf

Roberts, D., & Khattri, N. (2012). *Designing a framework for achieving results: A how-to guide*. Washington, DC: Independent Evaluation Group and World Bank Group.

Weiss, C. (1998). *Evaluation*. Upper Saddle River, NJ: Prentice Hall.

W.K. Kellogg Foundation. (2004). *Logic model development guide*. East Battle Creek, MI: Author. Retrieved from https://www.wkkf.org/resource-directory/resource/2006/02/wk-kellogg-foundation-logic-model-development-guide

Chapter 7

BetterEvaluation. (2013). *Rainbow framework*. Retrieved from https://www.betterevaluation.org/rainbow_framework/downloads

Bucher, A. (2016). *The unintended positive consequences of Pokémon Go*. Retrieved from http://www.amybucherphd.com/the-unintended-positive-consequences-of-pokemon-go

Centers for Disease Control and Prevention. (2013). *Good evaluation questions: A checklist to help focus your evaluation*. Washington, DC: Author. Retrieved from https://www.cdc.gov/asthma/program_eval/Assessing EvaluationQuestionChecklist.pdf

Chen, H.-T. (2015). *Practical program evaluation: Theory-driven evaluation and the integrated evaluation perspective* (2nd ed.). Thousand Oaks, CA: Sage.

Doran, G. T. (1981). There's a S.M.A.R.T. way to write management's goals and objectives. *Management Review, 70*(11), 35–36.

Gugglberger, L., Flaschberger, E., Teutsch, F. (2014, July). "Side effects" of health promotion: An example from Austrian schools. *Health Promotion International, 32*(1), 157–166.

Molund, S., & Schill, G. (2007). *Looking back, moving forward: Sida evaluation manual* (2nd rev. ed.). Stockholm, Sweden: Swedish International Development Cooperation Agency (Sida), Department for Evaluation and Internal Audit. Retrieved from https://www.betterevaluation.org/sites/default/files/SIDA 3753en_Looking_back_0.pdf

Oliver, K., Lorenc, T., & Tinkler, J. (2019). Evaluating unintended consequences: New insights into solving practical, ethical and political challenges of evaluation. *Evaluation*. https://doi.org/10.1177/1356389019 850847

Plunk, A. D., Tate, W. F., Bierut, L. J., & Grucza, R. A. (2014). Intended and unintended effects of state-mandated high school science and mathematics course graduation requirements on educational attainment. *Educational Researcher, 43*(5), 230–241.

Preskill, H., & Jones, N. (2009). *A practical guide for engaging stakeholders in developing evaluation questions* (RWJF Evaluation Series). Princeton, NJ: Robert Wood Johnson Foundation. Retrieved from https://www.rwjf.org/en/library/research/2009/12/a-practical-guide-for-engaging-stakeholders-in-developing-evalua.html

Rogers, P. (2014). Overview of impact evaluation. *Methodological briefs: Impact evaluation*. Florence, Italy: UNICEF Office of Research. Retrieved from https://www.unicef-irc.org/KM/IE/impact_1.php

Rossi, P. H., Lipsey, M. W., & Henry, G. T. (2018). *Evaluation: A systematic approach* (8th ed.). Thousand Oaks, CA: Sage.

Scriven, M. (1967). *The methodology of evaluation perspectives of curriculum evaluation* (Vol. 1, pp. 39–83). Chicago, IL: Rand McNally.

Scriven, M. (1972). Pros and cons about goal-free evaluation. *Journal of Education Evaluation, 3*(4), 1–4.

United Nations World Food Programme. (2015). *Operation evaluation: Armenia: Development of sustainable school feeding* (OEV 2014/20). Rome, Italy: Author. Retrieved from https://documents.wfp.org/stellent/groups/public/documents/reports/wfp273237.pdf?_ga=2.234228249.686246493.1561771451-1396639423.1561771451

United Nations World Food Programme. (2019). [Website]. Retrieved from http://www.wfp.org/

Weiss, C. H. (1998). *Evaluation: Methods for studying programs and policies* (2nd ed.). Upper Saddle River, NJ: Prentice Hall.

Wingate, L., & Schroeter, D. (2016). *Evaluation questions checklist for program evaluation*. Kalamazoo: Western Michigan University, The Evaluation Center. Retrieved from https://wmich.edu/evaluation/checklists

W.K. Kellogg Foundation. (2017). *A step-by-step guide to evaluation*. East Battle Creek, MI: Author. Retrieved from https://www.wkkf.org/resource-directory/resource/2010/w-k-kellogg-foundation-evaluation-handbook

Chapter 8

Bamberger, J. M., Rugh, J., & Mabry, L. S. (2011). *Real-World evaluation: Working under budget, time, data, and political constraints* (2nd ed.). Thousand Oaks, CA: Sage.

Boruch, R. (1997). *Randomized experiments for planning and evaluation*. Thousand Oaks, CA: Sage.

Campbell, D. T. (1969). Reforms as experiments. *American Psychologist*, *24*(4), 409–429. Retrieved from https://psycnet-apa-org.udel.idm.oclc.org/doi/10.1037/h0027982

Campbell, D. T., & Stanley, J. C. (1963). *Experimental and quasi-experimental designs for research*. Chicago, IL: Rand McNally.

Caruana, E. J., Roman, M., Hernández-Sánchez, J., & Solli, P. (2015). Longitudinal studies. *Journal of Thoracic Disease*, *7*(11), E537–E540. https://doi.org/10.3978/j.issn.2072-1439.2015.10.63

Cohen, D., & Crabtree, B. (2006, July). *Qualitative research guidelines project*. Princeton, NJ: Robert Wood Johnson Foundation. Retrieved from http://www.qualres.org/index.html

Cook, T. D., & Campbell, D. T. (1979). *Quasi-experimentation: Design and analysis issues for field settings*. Boston, MA: Houghton Mifflin.

Cronbach, L. J. (1982). *Designing evaluations of educational and social programs*. San Francisco, CA: Jossey-Bass.

Fowler, F. J., Jr. (2013). *Survey research methods* (5th ed.). Thousand Oaks, CA: Sage.

Frechtling, J. (2007). *Logic modeling methods in program evaluation*. San Francisco, CA: Jossey-Bass.

Herman, J. L., & Winters, L. (1994, October). Portfolio research: A slim collection. *Educational Leadership*, *52*(2), 48–55.

King, N., Horrocks, C., & Brooks, J. (2018). *Interviews in qualitative research*. Thousand Oaks, CA: Sage.

Knowlton, L., & Phillips, C. (2009). *The logic model guidebook*. Thousand Oaks, CA: Sage.

Krueger, R. A., & Casey, M. A. (2014). *Focus groups: A practical guide for applied research*. Thousand Oaks, CA: Sage.

Minitab Blog Editor. (2015, September 17). *Repeated measures designs: Benefits, challenges, and an ANOVA example*. [Blog post]. Retrieved from https://blog.minitab.com/blog/adventures-in-statistics-2/repeated-measures-designs-benefits-challenges-and-an-anova-example

Mosteller, F., & Boruch, R. (Eds.). (2002). *Evidence matters: Randomized trials in education research*. Washington, DC: Brookings Institution Press.

Rossi, P. H., Lipsey, M. W., & Henry, G. T. (2018). *Evaluation: A systematic approach* (8th ed.). Thousand Oaks, CA: Sage.

Salkind, N. J. (2010). *Encyclopedia of research design*. Thousand Oaks, CA: Sage. https://doi.org/10.4135/9781412961288

Social Programs That Work. (2019). *Perry Preschool project* [Web page]. Retrieved from http://evidence-basedprograms.org/1366-2/65-2

Weiss, C. H. (1998). *Evaluation* (2nd ed.). Upper Saddle River, NJ: Prentice Hall.

W. K. Kellogg Foundation. (2004). *Logic model development guide*. East Battle Creek, MI: Author. Retrieved from https://www.wkkf.org/resource-directory/resource/2006/02/wk-kellogg-foundation-logic-model-development-guide

Wright, R. J. (2007). *Educational assessment: Tests and measurements in the age of accountability*. Thousand Oaks, CA: Sage.

Yin, R. K. (2017). *Case study research and applications: Design and methods* (6th ed.). Thousand Oaks, CA: Sage.

Chapter 9

Bradburn, N. M., Sudman, S., & Wansink, B. (2004). *Asking questions: The definitive guide to questionnaire design—For market research, political polls, and social and health questionnaires* (2nd rev. ed.). San Francisco, CA: Wiley.

Cox, J., & Cox, K. (2008). *Your opinion, please! How to build the best questionnaires in the field of education* (2nd ed.). Thousand Oaks, CA: Corwin.

Fowler, F. J., Jr. (2008). *Survey research methods* (4th ed.). Thousand Oaks, CA: Sage.

Friesen, B. (2010). *Designing and conducting your first interview*. San Francisco, CA: Wiley.

Henry, G. T. (2005). Surveys. In S. Mathison (Ed.), *Encyclopedia of evaluation* (pp. 403–404). Thousand Oaks, CA: Sage.

Hurworth, R. (2005). Document analysis. In S. Mathison (Ed.), *Encyclopedia of evaluation* (pp. 119–120). Thousand Oaks, CA: Sage.

Krueger, R., & Casey, M. (2009). *Focus groups: A practical guide for applied research* (4th ed.). Thousand Oaks, CA: Sage.

Mathison, S. (2005). Observation. In S. Mathison (Ed.), *Encyclopedia of evaluation*. Thousand Oaks, CA: Sage.

Meyers, L., Gamst, G., & Guarino, A. (2006). *Applied multivariate research: Design and interpretation*. Thousand Oaks, CA: Sage.

Radhakrishna, R., Tobin, D., Brenna, M., & Thomson, J. (2012). Ensuring data quality in extension research and evaluation studies. *Journal of Extension, 50*(3), 3TOT1.

W.K. Kellogg Foundation. (2017). *A step-by-step guide to evaluation*. East Battle Creek, MI: Author. Retrieved from https://www.wkkf.org/resource-directory/resource/2010/w-k-kellogg-foundation-evaluation-handbook

Chapter 10

Adams, K. A., & Lawrence, E. K. (2018). *Research methods, statistics, and applications* (2nd ed.). Thousand Oaks, CA: Sage.

Chua, P., & Mark, M. (2005). Statistics. In S. Mathison (Ed.), *Encyclopedia of evaluation*. Thousand Oaks, CA: Sage.

Cohen, J. (1988). *Statistical power analysis for the behavioral sciences* (2nd ed.). Hillsdale, NJ: Lawrence Erlbaum.

Meyers, L., Gamst, G., & Guarino, A. (2006). *Applied multivariate research: Design and interpretation*. Thousand Oaks, CA: Sage.

Miles, M., Huberman, A. M., & Saldana, J. (2014). *Qualitative data analysis: A methods sourcebook*. Thousand Oaks, CA: Sage.

Nestor, P. G., & Schutt, R. K. (2018). *Research methods in psychology: Investigating human behavior*. Thousand Oaks, CA: Sage.

Patton, M. Q. (2014). *Qualitative research and evaluation methods* (4th ed). Thousand Oaks, CA: Sage.

Privitera, G. J. (2015). *Statistics for the behavioral sciences* (2nd ed.). Thousand Oaks, CA: Sage.

Stufflebeam, D. L. (2004). *Evaluation design checklist*. Kalamazoo: Western Michigan University, The Evaluation Center. Retrieved from https://wmich.edu/evaluation/checklists

Weiss, C. (1972). *Evaluation research: Methods for assessing program effectiveness*. Englewood Cliffs, NJ: Prentice Hall.

Chapter 11

Azzam, T., Evergreen, S., Germuth, A. A., & Kistler, S. J. (2013). Data visualization and evaluation. In T. Azzam & S. Evergreen (Eds.), *Data visualization, part 1. New Directions for Evaluation, 139*, 7–32.

California Endowment. (2007). *Storytelling approaches to program evaluation: An introduction*. Los Angeles, CA: Author.

Deming, W. E. (2000). *The new economics for industry, government, and education* (2nd ed.). Cambridge, MA: MIT Press.

Doyle, S. (2007). Member checking with older women: A framework for negotiating meaning. *Health Care for Women International, 28*(10), 888–908. https://doi.org/10.1080/07399330701615325

Evergreen, S. (2016). *Effective data visualization: The right chart for the right data*. Thousand Oaks, CA: Sage.

Evergreen, S. (2017). *Presenting data effectively: Communicating your findings for maximum impact*. Thousand Oaks, CA: Sage.

Fitzpatrick, J., Christie, C., & Mark, M. (2009). *Evaluation in action: Interviews with expert evaluators*. Thousand Oaks, CA: Sage.

George, M. L., Rowlands, D., Price, M., & Maxey, J. (2004). *The Lean Six Sigma pocket toolbook*. New York, NY: McGraw-Hill.

Health Resources and Services Administration. (2011). *Quality improvement*. Washington, DC: U.S. Department of Health and Human Services. Retrieved from

https://www.hrsa.gov/sites/default/files/quality/tool
box/508pdfs/qualityimprovement.pdf

Hood, S., Hopson, R., & Kirkhart, K. (2015). Culturally responsive evaluation: Theory, practice, and future implications. In K. Newcomer, H. Hatry, & J. Wholey (Eds.), *Handbook of practical program evaluation* (4th ed.). Hoboken, NJ: Jossey-Bass.

Hood, S., & Rosenstein, B. (2005). Culturally responsive evaluation. In S. Mathison (Ed.), *Encyclopedia of evaluation*. Thousand Oaks, CA: Sage.

Joint Commission Resources. (2017). *Root cause analysis in health care: Tools and techniques* (6th ed.). Oakbrook Terrace, IL: Author.

Joint Committee on Standards for Educational Evaluation. (1994). *The program evaluation standards: How to assess evaluations of educational programs*. Thousand Oaks, CA: Sage.

Juran, J. M. (1992). *Juran on quality by design: The new steps for planning quality into goods and services*. New York, NY: Free Press.

Lub, V. (2015). Validity in qualitative evaluation: Linking purposes, paradigms, and perspectives. *International Journal of Qualitative Methods*. https://doi.org/10.1177/1609406915621406

O'Sullivan, R. G. (2004). *Practicing evaluation*. Thousand Oaks, CA: Sage.

Pyzdek, T., & Keller, P. (2018). *The Six Sigma handbook* (5th ed.). New York, NY: McGraw-Hill.

Robins, D. L., Casagrande, K., Barton, M., Chen, C.-M. A., Dumont-Mathieu, T., & Fein, D. (2014). Validation of the Modified Checklist for Autism in Toddlers, revised with follow-up (M-CHAT-R/F). *Pediatrics, 133*(1), 37–45. http://dx.doi.org/10.1542/peds.2013-1813

Smith-Halstead, S. (2011, August 2). *Sharon Smith-Halstead on storytelling on evaluation* [Blog post]. Retrieved from https://aea365.org/blog/sharon-smith-halstead-on-storytelling-in-evaluation/

Stake, R. (1995). *The art of case study research*. Thousand Oaks, CA: Sage.

Stufflebeam, D. L., & Coryn, C. L. S. (2014) *Evaluation theory, models, and application* (2nd ed.). San Francisco, CA: Jossey-Bass.

Weiss, C. H. (1998). *Evaluation* (2nd ed.). Upper Saddle River, NJ: Prentice Hall.

Chapter 12

Alkin, M. C., & King, J. A. (2017). Definitions of evaluation use and misuse, evaluation influence, and factors affecting use. *American Journal of Evaluation, 38*(3), 434–450. https://doi.org/10.1177/1098214017717015

Aos, S., Miller, M., & Drake, E. (2006). *Evidence-based public policy options to reduce future prison construction, criminal justice costs, and crime rates*. Olympia: Washington State Institute for Public Policy.

Belenko, S., Patapis, N., & French, M. T. (2005). *Economic benefits of drug treatment: A critical review of the evidence for policy makers*. St. Louis: Missouri Foundation of Health.

Bhati, A. S., Roman, J. K., & Chalfin, A. (2008). *To treat or not to treat: Evidence on the prospects of expanding treatment to drug-involved offenders*. Washington, DC: Urban Institute.

Calculating the Costs of Child Welfare Services Workgroup. (2013). *Cost analysis in program evaluation: A guide for child welfare researchers and service providers*. Washington, DC: U.S. Department of Health and Human Services, Administration for Children and Families, Children's Bureau.

Hall, G. E., & Hord, S. M. (1987). *Change in schools: Facilitating the process*. Albany: State University of New York Press.

Henrichson, C., & Rinaldi, J. (2014). *Cost-benefit analysis and justice policy toolkit*. New York, NY: Vera Institute of Justice.

Henry, G. T., & Mark, M. M. (2003). Beyond use: Understanding evaluation's influence on attitudes and actions. *American Journal of Evaluation, 24*(3), 293–314. https://doi.org/10.1177/109821400302400302

Latimer, J., Morton-Bourgon, K., & Chretien, J.-A. (2006). *A meta-analytic examination of drug treatment courts: Do they reduce recidivism?* Ottawa, Ontario: Department of Justice Canada, Research and Statistics Division.

Lowenkamp, C. T., Holsinger, A. M., & Latessa, E. J. (2005). Are drug courts effective? A meta-analytic review. *Journal of Community Corrections, 15*(1), 5–11.

Marlowe, D. B. (2010). *Research update on adult drug courts.* Washington, DC: National Association of Drug Court Professionals.

National Association of Drug Court Professionals. (2018). *Adult drug court best practice standards* (Vols. 1–2). Alexandria, VA: Author. Retrieved from https://www.nadcp.org/standards/adult-drug-court-best-practice-standards/

Patton, M. Q. (2008). *Utilization-focused evaluation.* Thousand Oaks, CA: Sage.

Patton, M. Q. (2013). The roots of utilization-focused evaluation. In M. C. Alkin (Ed.), *Evaluation roots: A wider perspective of theorists' views and influences* (2nd ed., pp. 293–303). Thousand Oaks, CA: Sage.

Preskill, H., & Jones, N. (2009). *A practical guide for engaging stakeholders in developing evaluation questions.* Princeton, NJ: Robert Wood Johnson Foundation. Retrieved from http://www.rwjf.org/

Scriven, M. (1969). An introduction to meta-evaluation. *Educational Products Report, 2,* 36–38.

Scriven, M. (2009, January). Meta-evaluation revisited. *Journal of MultiDisciplinary Evaluation, 6*(11), iii–viii.

Shaffer, D. K. (2006). *Reconsidering drug court effectiveness: A meta-analytic review* (Unpublished doctoral dissertation). University of Nevada, Las Vegas.

Stufflebeam, D. L. (1978). Meta evaluation: An overview. *Evaluation & the Health Professions, 1*(1), 17–43. https://doi.org/10.1177/016327877800100102

Wilson, D. B., Mitchell, O., & MacKenzie, D. L. (2006). A systematic review of drug court effects on recidivism. *Journal of Experimental Criminology, 2,* 459–487.

Chapter 13

Stufflebeam, D. L. (2003). The CIPP model for evaluation. In T. Kellaghan, D. L. Stufflebeam, & L. A. Wingate (Eds.), *International handbook of educational evaluation* (Vol. 9, pp. 31–62). Dordrecht, Netherlands: Kluwer Academic. https://doi.org/10.1007/978-94-010-0309-4

INDEX